Ahmedabad

A Society in Transition (1818–1914)

Kunjlata Shah

Popular Prakashan
www.popularprakashan.com

Published by
Harsha Bhatkal for
POPULAR PRAKASHAN PVT. LTD.
301, Mahalaxmi Chambers
22, Bhulabhai Desai Road
Mumbai - 400 026

First Published 2016
First Reprint 2016

(4426)
ISBN: 978-81-7991-867-8

Design: Anjali Sawant
Typesetting: Satyawan Rane

PRINTED IN INDIA
by Saurabh Printers (P) Ltd.
Plot No. 67 A-68, Ecotech, Ext. I
Kasna, Greater Noida-201306 (U.P)

Contents

Emergence of Industrial Working Class

Among the several social consequences of industrialisation, the most important was the emergence of the industrial working class in Ahmedabad. Initially, this class had been small and inconspicuous, but with the expansion of the mill industry, it grew rapidly and soon became an important and prominent segment of the city's population. In [illegible], the first textile mill had only [illegible] workers, but by 1914 there were more than [illegible] industrial workers working in 51 textile mills, two iron works, two tobacco factories, four dye works, three oil mills, and 25 ginning, cleaning and pressing mills in and around the city. In 1922, the number of workers further rose to 59,041.[1] From 1914 onwards, about 20 per cent of the city's population was made up of factory workers. There was a steady increase in the number of industries and a corresponding increase in the number of workers.

The emergence of the industrial working class naturally added a new dimension to the life of the city. In the pre-British period, Ahmedabad had manufactured textile goods, but the manufacturers had been artisans who owned tools and implements and worked in their own homes. With the advent of the modern textile sector, the foundation of the old system was shattered. The workers in the machine industries did not own the means of production but sold their labour for wages.

As there is no reliable statistical data available on this aspect, one has to rely on the scanty but valuable information provided by the *Ahmedabad Gazetteer* (1879) and the reports and proceedings of the Factory Commission of 1875, 1885, 1890 and 1908 and of the Royal Commission on Indian Labour in 1929–1930, *Annual Factory Reports* 1892–1923 of the Bombay Presidency

Foreword

Ahmedabad is a 'shock-city' to some and 'frugal' to others. Scholars have described it as 'unique', 'business-like' and 'pragmatic'. Whatever the brand one prefers, Ahmedabad has certainly drawn the attention of Indian and foreign historians and social scientists. Recent surveys agree that Ahmedabad is the best city in India to live in.

Ahmedabad is a city as well as a conglomeration of villages. It changes slowly but with confidence. Its inhabitants breathe a 'traditional' as well as a 'modern' sociocultural and economic environment. This is because it has persistently continued to change while maintaining its centuries-old traditions.

Well entrenched as a commercial and industrial centre of India during the Sultanate and Moghul periods, Ahmedabad maintained its self-respect and confidence during the colonial period. It demonstrated a capacity to survive British industrial invasion while learning a great deal from western experience. Thanks to its age-old *mahajan* tradition, Ahmedabad exhibited the spirit of cooperation even with the British masters. That is the reason why middle class intellectuals and businessmen were able to earn the goodwill of local British administrators, resulting in a smooth social and educational transformation.

At the same time, Ahmedabad had earned a name as the 'Manchester of India'. MK Gandhi's choice of Ahmedabad as his *karmabhumi* in 1915 was based on rational considerations. The history of Ahmedabad shows that its most enduring character is the spirit of tolerance, a tolerance of the new, the unusual and the difficult, a capacity to absorb shocks and to reshape itself in changing conditions and a willingness to seek new solutions to new problems. That is the reason why it is often said that the "Ahmedabadi is the Gujarati of Gujaratis . . . He is in Ahmedabad and everywhere"! Many other proverbs support this contention.

Kunjlata Shah with her knowledge of Gujarati language and literature has articulated her ideas and feelings with natural ease. Synthesizing various strands of the society of Ahmedabad and using the historical, cultural and literary insights, Kunjlata has traced the history of Ahmedabad from the 1818 to the arrival of Mahatma Gandhi in Ahmedabad in 1915. She traces the process of transformation and the role played by reformers, literary persons, educationists, merchants and industrialists. She has also discussed the pioneering role of the Gujarat Vernacular Society that was founded in 1848 by Alexander K Forbes.

Historians have not paid adequate attention to the importance of public charities in the areas of social and educational change and public health. Kunjlata has cited several examples of public charities' achievements in setting up schools for boys and girls, literary and academic institutes, scholarships, libraries, colleges and hospitals.

The book is based on a large number of Gujarati and English sources. The author has extensively used archival and contemporary literary sources. Her book provides insights into the dynamics of socioeconomic and cultural changes over a period of a century in Ahmedabad.

August 2015

— **Professor Makrand Mehta**
Former Head,
Department of History,
Gujarat University

Preface

This book presents a diachronic examination of the process and dynamics of the change that occurred in the society of Ahmedabad in the wake of British rule until the year 1915. It is an attempt to study the urban history of Ahmedabad in its various social aspects in the transitional period as there is a dearth of historical research in this subject. This analysis is necessary because the response and adaptation of each local community to the modernising forces generated by British rule is varied, depending on the initial conditions of that community and its socioeconomic and cultural peculiarities.

To understand the society of Ahmedabad passing through modernisation under colonial rule, I have taken a longitudinal view of history. The book, therefore, starts with a brief history of the Sultanate, Moghul and Maratha rule in the city of Ahmedabad and ends with the arrival of Gandhi in 1915. The crucial Gandhian phase is discussed briefly in the epilogue. The present study forms the link between the Sultanate period on the one hand and the Gandhian phase on the other.

Since its foundation as a capital of Gujarat in 1411 by Ahmed Shah, a Sultan of Gujarat, Ahmedabad has been the prime urban centre of trade and manufacture in the state. In medieval times, it was essentially a mercantile city with a strong commercial and corporate ethos which was woven into its various urban institutions. When it came under British rule in 1817, the medieval city of Ahmedabad, while continuing to maintain its past traditions, underwent positive transformations, particularly from the middle of the 19th century. This study elucidates how the city responded to British colonial policy and the modernising forces unleashed by British rule. It also explains how the traditional urban centre of trade and industry was gradually transformed into a modern industrial city.

The year 1859 is a turning point in the history of Ahmedabad. It was in this year that Ranchhodlal Chhotalal, a young Nagar Brahmin, established the Ahmedabad Spinning and Weaving Company to set up the first textile mill in Ahmedabad. Thereafter, the city was gradually ushered into the industrial age. The power-driven machine industry introduced a new mode of production, which brought about far-reaching changes in the economic and social life of the city. As a result of industrialisation, the traditional institutions of the pre-industrial urban society underwent some significant changes. While studying change, the continuity of traditions as evinced in Ahmedabad is also emphasised in this book.

Chapter 1 deals with pre-British Ahmedabad and traces the history of the city from its foundation in 1411 by Ahmed Shah to its takeover by the British in November 1817. It also analyses some important traditional socioeconomic institutions of Ahmedabad, such as the *mahajan* (guild of merchants), *panch* (guild of artisans), *nagarseth* (chief merchant of the city), *gnyati panch* (caste council) and *pol* (traditional neighbourhood), against the city's religious, demographic, economic and morphological background.

A new epoch in the history of Ahmedabad commenced when the British took over the city in November 1817. The traditional society of Ahmedabad made contact with powerful western traditions that had a profound impact on it. The city experienced changes as a result of the new colonial economic policy, bureaucratic set-up, modern legal system, press and modern educational system. The establishment of the Gujarat Vernacular Society, the first major voluntary association, by Alexander K Forbes was a landmark in the history of the city. It played a pivotal role in modernising Ahmedabad. The press, western education, and Gujarat Vernacular Society were instrumental in the sociocultural regeneration of the city. Chapters 2 and 3 examine the political, economic, cultural and social changes under British rule in the pre-industrial phase (1818–1861). British rule laid the foundation of a new social ethos that was favourable for enterprise.

Chapters 4 to 9 deal with different but related socioeconomic themes during the industrial phase from 1861 to 1914. However, this chronology has not been followed rigidly and occasional forays into the period beyond 1914 are made.

The commercial city responded to the challenge of British colonial policy with machine industry and *swadeshi*. Chapter 4 traces the emergence and growth of the modern textile industry in the city against its economic background. The city's political culture, with special reference to the *swadeshi* movement, is examined.

In any study of the phenomenon of social change in the 19th century in an urban centre of India, an examination of local associations and the press is significant. These were used extensively by the newly emerged middle class to bring about specific change or reforms. Chapter 5 discusses the growth and role of voluntary associations and the press in detail and shows how the city emerged as a centre of the socioreligious reform movement in Gujarat.

Chapter 6 raises some important questions on the institution of caste in the city. How did it adapt to the modernising forces under British rule? How did it change? Was it an impediment to the modernising process in the city? This chapter discusses the changes in caste and also analyses its role in modernisation. The relation of caste with the new emerging classes is examined.

The social reform movements, the growth of female education, British colonial policy and the industrialisation of the city were some of the major factors which affected the social and economic position of women in Ahmedabad. Chapter 7 examines new developments and changes in the profile of women in the city. It discusses the emergence of various women's organisations and changes in women's economic participation in the city.

The most important social consequence of industrialisation was the emergence of the working class in Ahmedabad. Initially, this class was small but with the expansion of the mill industry, it grew rapidly. Chapter 8 discusses its composition, recruitment, working conditions, lifestyle, protests and relation to other urban classes and the institution of caste.

With the expansion of the mill industry, not only did the city's population grow, but it also expanded spatially while its prosperity increased. People's lifestyle changed. The municipality of Ahmedabad played a role in changing the city's environs. All these changes are examined in Chapter 9.

The city of Ahmedabad has drawn the attention of several historians in recent times. The renowned historian Kenneth Gillion, in his brilliant work *Ahmedabad: A Study in Urban History* (Ahmedabad, 1968), has given a comprehensive history of the city in modern times. He has raised some significant questions on economic, political and cultural aspects. However, in this broad account, some aspects of social life and institutions are not given in-depth treatment. Makrand Mehta, a noted socioeconomic historian, traces the origin and development of the textile industry from 1859 to 1916 in his erudite work, *The Ahmedabad Cotton Textile Industry: Genesis and Growth* (Ahmedabad, 1982). In this work, he examines the social roots of the cotton textile industry in the city. Several research articles by Howard Spodek, Makrand Mehta, Shirin Mehta, BG Gokhale and Dwijendranath Tripathi have given valuable insights into the historical processes of Ahmedabad in its various aspects. On the occasion of the 600th anniversary of the foundation of the city, two new important and well researched books—*Ahmedabad: Shock City of Twentieth Century India* by Howard Spodek (Bloomington, Indiana, 2011) and *Ahmedabad: From Royal City to Megacity* by Achyut Yagnik and Suchitra Sheth (New Delhi, 2011)—have further enhanced historical knowledge of the city. The present study is a humble attempt to study the society of Ahmedabad in a transitional period when the city was being industrialised under British colonial rule. It delineates the social life of Ahmedabad in the 19th and early 20th centuries in an integrated and comprehensive manner. It is based on the extensive research that I did for my Ph.D. thesis *Ahmedabad: Pre-industrial to Industrial Urban Centre (1859–1930).*

The present study is built on diverse sources. In addition to the extensive use of archival sources and the government reports, contemporary local newspapers, periodicals, and caste journals in Gujarati are utilised fruitfully. Travellers' accounts, the annual reports of several local institutions, contemporary literature in Gujarati, autobiographies and biographies are researched to collect useful information. Oral tradition, preserved in the form of *garba*, *rasada* and folk stories, reveals some important social, religious and political information and is judiciously used. Some elderly residents of the city were interviewed informally to know their experiences and impressions of the city in the past. *Khatpatras*, or legal documents pertaining to the purchase, sale and mortgage of houses, shops and land, form an important primary source to reconstruct the urban history of the city and are used to substantiate this study.

I must mention that as I am dealing with 19th century Ahmedabad, and hence have used the names Bombay and Calcutta which are now Mumbai and Kolkata.

The data was collected from the State Archives of Maharashtra (Mumbai), Central Library of Mumbai, the Asiatic Society's Library of Mumbai, Forbes Gujarati Sabha, Mumbai, the libraries of the SNDT Women's University and the University of Mumbai, the library of the Gujarat Vidhyapith, Ahmedabad, BJ Institute of Ahmedabad, the library of *Gujarat Samachar* of Ahmedabad and the National Library of Kolkata.

An attempt has been made to throw new light on the growth of Ahmedabad during the very critical period of colonial rule, thereby contributing to the historical knowledge and understanding of the society of Gujarat in general and Ahmedabad in particular.

In preparing this thesis, I was helped by various individuals and institutes. I am deeply indebted to late Dr Mani P Kamerkar for her keen interest and invaluable guidance in my research.

I have greatly benefitted from discussions with Dr Dwijendranath Tripathi, Dr Shirin M Mehta, Dr R Raval, Dr Devangana J Desai, Dr Usha Thakkar, Dr Howard Spodek, Dr PN Sapre, C Taktavala, Anjali Kothari and late Dr Usha Hemmadi. I owe a special debt of gratitude to Dr Makrand J Mehta, without whose help, this thesis would not have taken this shape.

I thank the Sarabhai Foundation and the Hutheesing Kesarising Trust for providing old photographs and permitting me to print them in this book. I thank my young friend Dr Deepani Sutaria for accompanying me to photograph various sites of Ahmedabad. My special thanks are due to Aban Lalkaka Mukherji for providing photographs of Ahmedabad and the family of the Vakils.

I would like to acknowledge my gratitude to the librarians and staff of various libraries of Mumbai and Ahmedabad for their valuable help. My thanks are due to the staff of the Maharashtra State Archives for their assistance.

I am grateful to Champaklal Shah's family for their hospitality in Ahmedabad. I am greatly indebted to my husband Narendra for rendering moral support and encouragement while I was completing my research. My two sons Saumil and Ashish also bore with great patience my involvement in this work.

— **Kunjlata Shah**

Abbreviations

AMA	Ahmedabad Millowners' Association
FA	*Annual Factory Report of the Bombay Presidency*
FC 1875	*Report of the Commissioners Appointed by the Governor of Bombay in Council to Inquire into the Condition of the Operatives in the Bombay Factories and the Necessity or Otherwise for the Passing of a Factories Act, Bombay, 1875.*
FC 1885	*Report and Proceedings of the Commission Appointed to Consider the Working of the Factories in the Bombay Presidency, Bombay 1885.*
FC 1890	*Report of the Indian Factory Commission—1890.*
FC 1908	*Report of the Indian Factory Labour Commission 1908.*
GVS	Gujarat Vernacular Society
IAPA	Indigenous Articles Protection Association
RCL	Royal Commission on Labour
RCL 1892	Royal Commission on Labour, *Foreign Reports, Vol. II, The Colonies and Indian Empire with an Appendix on the Migration of Labour, Parliamentary Papers, 1892.*
RCL 1929	Memorandum Royal Commission on Indian Labour, *Memorandum from the Government of Bombay, 1929.*
RNP	*Report on the Native Papers published in the Bombay Presidency.*
TFLC 1906	*Report of Textile Factories Labour Committee Appointed by the Government of India on the 17th of December 1906 to Enquire into the Conditions of Factory Labour in India – with Appendices.*

Credit for Illustrations

Cover painting by Harshil Patel, courtesy Saumil Shah, photograph by Marushka S Shah.

Bhatt, Diwaliben and Budha Shridevi, *Aapna Nariratno*, 37.

Davar, FC, *Sir Nowroji P Vakil: A Biographical Sketch*, 44, 45, 46, 47. With permission.

Jote, Ratnamanirao Bhimrao, *Gujaratnu Patnagar Amdavad*, 52.

Jyoti Sangh, *Jyoti Vikas Yatra*, 36. With permission.

Mehta, Sharadaben S, *Jivan Sambharna*, 31, 32.

Mukherji, Aban, 2, 3.

Parekh, Hiralal T, *Gujarat Vernacularno Itihas*, Part I—4, 8.a, 8.b, 11, 13, 14.

Part II—16, 17, 18, 19, 22, 39, 40, 41, 42, 43.

____(ed.), *Vidhyaben Manimahotava Granth*, 48.

Sutaria, Dipani N, 1, 9-1 & 2, 15, 20, 21, 23, 24, 33, 34, 35-1 & 2, 51.

Tripathi, Mansukhram, *Forbes Jivan Charitra*, 7.

Vallabhji, Sundeji Punjabhai, *Rajnagarna Ratno*, 30.

Collection of the Gandhi Smarak Sangrahalaya, 54, 55.

Courtesy

1. Hutheesing Kesarising Trust, Ahmedabad, 5, 10, 12.
2. Sarabhai Foundation, 6, 29, 38, 49, 50.
3. Girdharlal Sunita Love, 26.
4. Mukherji, Aban, 53.
5. Lashkari Patel Rupa, 28.

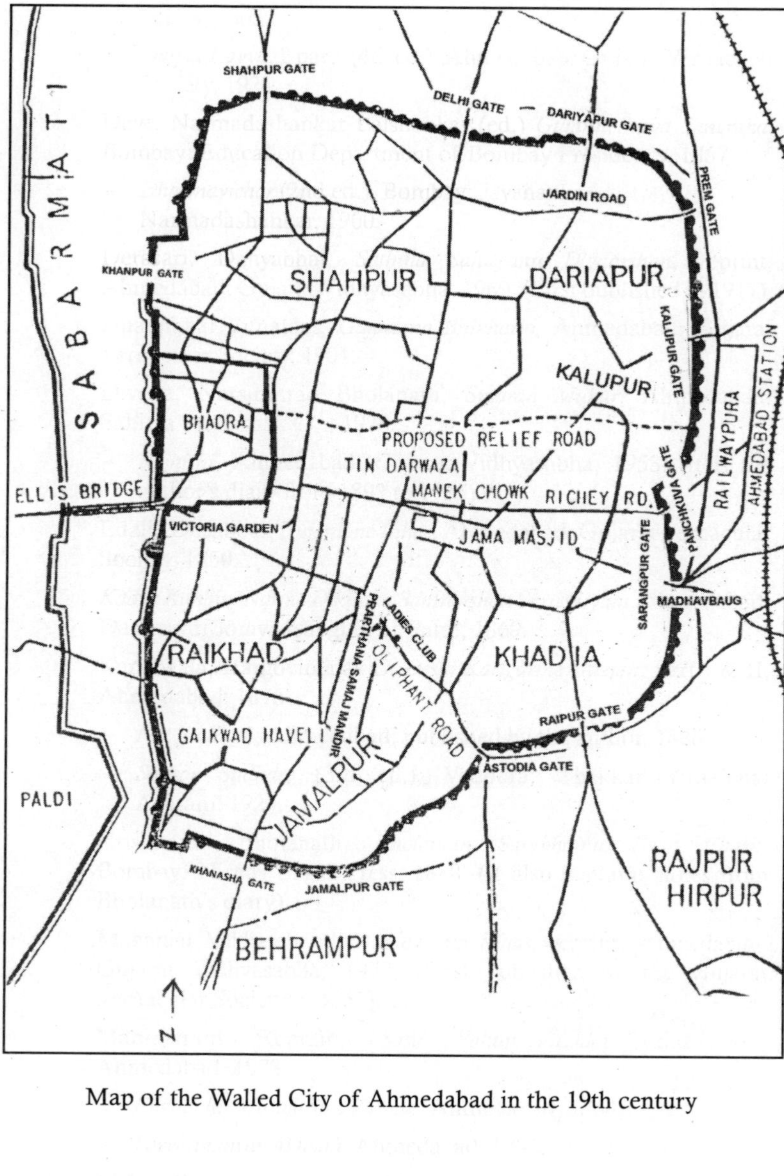

Map of the Walled City of Ahmedabad in the 19th century

There was no compensation given for accidents except payment of wages until the worker was once again fit for labour. Sickness allowance was paid for two days in a month and only when it was a result of an accident in the mill. The injured workers were not always provided for.[46] Many were maimed and had to take to begging because there was no insurance system, pension or provident scheme for the workers.

Ventilation in the mills was defective. Sometimes, steam was used instead of water for humidification in weaving sheds, which made the atmosphere humid and oppressive, especially in hot weather. Mohammad, a mill worker, in his complain to the Indian Factory Labour Commission of 1908 said: "We have to work in that great heat and are exhausted, so much so that at times men faint in that hot weather and have to be taken home in carts."[47] The air in the mills being impure and unhealthy, the operatives often contracted respiratory diseases such as tuberculosis. Long hours and confinement in a polluted atmosphere impaired the health of operatives, who aged prematurely, becoming unfit for mill work at the early age of 40 or 45. There was, therefore, an absence of older operatives in the mills, for example in 1908, in spite of the shortage of labour.[48] The worker of Ahmedabad was underweight and undersized. The children examined by the Factory Labour Commission of 1908 were found to be in poor health, thin and listless due to the overtime and overwork that they did.

The insecurity of the worker was another adverse factor. If the mill stopped in the day for some reason, the workers were sent away without compensation. They could not leave the mill while the machinery was running. In none of the mills was there any definite system of insurance against accidents or old age.[49]

Medical facilities were provided in a few of the Ahmedabad mills. Ranchhodlal's mills were better equipped than most others in welfare measures for operatives. Fines and unclaimed wages were credited to saving funds from which sick and injured workmen were given a weekly allowance. There was a small dispensary in the mill which was attended by a doctor every day. This mill also

1

Ahmedabad Before the British

Ahmed Shah, the Sultan of Gujarat, founded Ahmedabad as the new capital in 1411 on the banks of river Sabarmati. Gujarat, situated along the north-western coast of India, was composed of the peninsular region of Saurashtra and Kutch and the mainland extending from Mount Abu in the north to the river Damanganga in the south. The extraordinarily long coastline and the proximity of large parts of the province to the sea coast stimulated maritime trade. Trade and commerce were life giving sources for Gujarat.

Mercantile activities and the fertility of the soil made Gujarat a highly urbanized and commercial region. Gujarat abounded in cities in pre-British times and had developed rich urban traditions and institutions. Cities arose around the capitals, seaports and religious places. Several cities also arose on the trade routes that crisscrossed the entire province.

Its geographic position and maritime activities exposed Gujarat to outside cultural influences and opened it up to migration from Sindh, Marvad, Punjab, Malwa and other parts of India. This interaction made the people of Gujarat cosmopolitan, tolerant and adaptable. Several religious communities and ethnic groups which came from outside were absorbed into the Gujarat society.

Ahmedabad, an inland city of Gujarat, is situated 50 miles north of the Cambay Gulf. The walled city of Ahmedabad lies on the eastern bank of river Sabarmati which, until a few years ago, flowed in a thin stream in a broad bed of deep sand except in the rainy season. The Sabarmati not being a navigable river, trade to the city had to be carried on overland by bullock carts and on camels in the pre-railway period. Its strategic location at the nodal point of major inland routes and its proximity to Cambay, one of the greatest medieval ports, and other major seaports like Gogho, Broach and Surat, increased Ahmedabad's importance as a centre of commerce and trade in the medieval period. It commanded the trade routes to Delhi and Rajasthan to the north, Malwa to the east, Saurashtra and Sindh to the west and the seaports of Broach and Surat to the south. It is not surprising that Ahmedabad emerged as the prime urban centre of Gujarat soon after its foundation.

I

The early history of Ahmedabad, indeed its origin, is an interesting story. Ahmed Shah, the grandson of Muzaffer Shah and the founder of independent Muslim rule in Gujarat, wanted a new capital of his own. He planned to situate it at a strategic position from where he could keep an eye on his expanded kingdom to the south. For his new capital, he chose a site on the eastern bank of the Sabarmati, in the immediate vicinity of the ancient city of Asawal, which was a thriving trade centre situated at the meeting point of trade routes and a seat of Jain learning. The town of Asawal, with its sizeable Jain community, was absorbed into the new city of Ahmedabad. This was significant because Asawal's rich legacy of vital commercial traditions was inherited by Ahmedabad. As a result, the new capital did not remain just a political capital but emerged as a leading centre of commerce and industry in India.

Ahmed Shah built a strong fort, which was named Bhadra after the citadel of Patan, which was the previous capital of Gujarat and had the same architectural form and similar turrets. Bhadra formed the administrative headquarters around which the city grew. The political stability established by the Gujarat sultanate stimulated the growth of the new capital. The city grew in size, prosperity and wealth. The sultans and nobles continued to embellish the city with monuments, which made it one of the most picturesque cities of India. During this period, the glory and grandeur of Ahmedabad exceeded even that of Delhi and Agra.

Though the powerful Sultan Mahmud Begda later founded a new capital Champaner, he still lavished affection on Ahmedabad. Firastha, the historian, writing in 1600, says that Begda built extensive walls around the city.

Around the fort of Bhadra, residential settlements of the nobles called *puras* developed, such as Jamalpur, Raipur, Sarangpur, Kalupur, Shahapur, Khanpur and Mirzapur. The city grew in size as the population increased; about 360 to 380 *puras* arose in and around the walled city. These *puras* were like miniature cities with shops, mosque and other such features.[1] *Puras* also developed around the religious institutes and abodes of the *pirs*, or Sufi saints, living around the city. Saraspur, Rasulabad and Usmanpur were such *puras*.

Barbosa, the Portuguese traveller who visited Gujarat in the second decade of the 16th century in the year immediately following the death of Mahmud Begda, remarked that in spite of the great wealth and size of Champaner, Ahmedabad was still greater, very rich, well supplied with many orchards and gardens, and walled and embellished with good streets, squares and houses.[2]

After the Portuguese captured Div in 1538, defeating Sultan Bahadurshah, the power of the sultans of Gujarat declined and trade suffered a setback. Despite this setback, the city did not lose its glory and greatness. The Muslim historians of the period were generous in their praise for the city. In 1600, Firastha wrote, "The markets of the city are so large that 10 carts can go abreast at a time. The shops were built of baked bricks and are whitewashed." He added, "In population and other matters, there is no handsome city like Ahmedabad in Hindustan and perhaps in the world."[3]

By the end of the Sultanate period, Ahmedabad was a flourishing commercial and industrial centre manufacturing *kinkhab*, velvet, cotton textiles and other goods, which were exported not only to various parts of India but to the whole world. Its population consisted of Muslims and Hindus.

Zealously wishing to propagate the Islamic faith, the sultans of Gujarat invited many learned and pious men to settle around the city. They were given generous stipends and royal patronage.[4] Sheikh Ahmed Khattu Ganjbax, Shah Alam and Sayyid Usman were some of the eminent Sufi saints who resided in the vicinity of the city. Ahmedabad not only became the great centre of Sufism but a stronghold of the Chisti sect of Sufism since some of the Sultans were followers of the Chisti sect.

Towards the end of the 15th century, Imam Shah, a Sufi saint, founded a sect which was called the Pirana sect after its birthplace, the village Pirana ten miles south-east of Ahmedabad. Imam Shah had many Hindu and Muslim followers. He converted many Hindus of the Kanbi caste who came to be known as Momnas. The followers of this sect observed Muslim as well as Hindu customs and festivals. Imam Shah and other Sufi saints tried to bridge the gulf between Hinduism and Islam in order to create religious harmony and a spirit of tolerance in Gujarat. In a city where Hindus and Muslim shared economic activities, such religious harmony was necessary to establish commercial solidarity.

The efforts of Jain and Hindu saints reflected the same spirit and purpose. At the beginning of the 16th century, saint Dadu founded the sect Parbrahma Sampraday, generally known as the Dadu sect in Ahmedabad. He followed Kabir's teachings. His sect was open to both Hindus and Muslims.

In the 15th century, Lonka Shah, a Jain scribe of Ahmedabad who was transcribing Jain manuscripts, found that there was no sanction for idol worship in the Jain scriptures. As a protest, he founded a new sect called the 'Lonka', popularly known as 'Dhundias', which gave up the temple cult. Later in the 17th century, from this sect arose another calling itself Sthanakvasi. These sects belonged to the Swetambra Jain sect. The founder was greatly influenced by the Islamic principle which preached against idol worship. Ahmedabad became a stronghold of the Sthanakvasi sect.

These religious movements played a significant role in maintaining communal harmony in the city. The blend of religious values also brought with it a harmonious blend of cultures, which was reflected in the beautiful monuments of the city.

After Akbar's conquest of Gujarat in 1573, it became a province of the Moghul Empire. The city of Ahmedabad became the viceregal seat of the rich *suba* (a province). Gujarat remained a favourite of Moghul emperors, and Aurangzeb described it as "the beauty and ornament of India". Gujarat was placed under a *nazim* or viceroy. There was a succession of not less than 60 viceroys from 1573 to 1758. It is interesting to note that it was on one of his visits to Ahmedabad that Jehangir signed two historic documents for Sir Thomas Roe, the English ambassador sent by King James I. These documents gave the British all rights and facilities to trade and live in India.

Under the Moghuls, Gujarat enjoyed peace and order for the first 125 years of their reign. It was the most glorious period of the city. Many merchants amassed great fortunes out of their extensive mercantile activities. However, the last 50 years of Moghul rule, from 1707 to 1758 were chaotic, as Ahmedabad became a battleground of civil strife and suffered from increasing Maratha invasions.

The genesis of the institution of *nagarseth* can be traced to the Moghul rule, which played a significant role in the commercial and civil life of the city until the 19th century. The lineage of the *nagarseth* can be traced back to Shantidas Jhaveri, a great Jain merchant and court jeweller for Shahjahan. He exerted enormous influence at the imperial court and was held in great respect and honour by the merchants and *mahajans* of the city. Shantidas had built the Jain temple of Chintamani in Saraspur. Prince Aurangzeb, viceroy of Gujarat in the 1640s, in his religious intolerance, destroyed the temple and built a *masjid* on its ruins.

However, when Shantidas complained to Emperor Shahjahan, the temple was restored to him.[5] Later, when Aurangzeb became the emperor, he made amends by favouring Shantidas by granting him the *pargana* of Palitana and the sacred hill of Shatrunjay as *inam* for the benefit of the Jain community, of which Shantidas was the leader.[6]

Aurangzeb realised the economic importance of the province and encouraged trade and industry. He prohibited a very large number of imposts (*adwabs*) that had been collected in Gujarat by issuing a *farman* in 1665.[7] He also advised the *dewan* of Gujarat not to tax the Dutch and the *firanghis* in Ahmedabad. Taxes were to be collected only at Surat.[8]

Albert Mandelslo, a German traveller who visited Ahmedabad in 1638, described the city as possessing broad streets and magnificent buildings, spread over about 20 miles, its markets abounding in various commodities.[9] At this time, Ahmedabad's flourishing trade and industry were further stimulated by the political stability established by the imperial Moghuls. They also got an impetus from the economic activities of the English, Dutch and French East Indian companies, which invested large amounts of merchant capital in the Ahmedabad market. The English had opened their factory in Ahmedabad as early as 1612, the Dutch in 1630, and the French in 1669. They bought cotton and silk textiles, paper, indigo, saltpetre, sugar, dry ginger, gum, lac and myrobalan in Ahmedabad. All these products were easily available in and around the city. They all invested heavily in the market by borrowing from the local *sharafs* (bankers) as opportunities for investment were profitable.

Commodities like indigo and saltpetre were in great demand in Europe. Indigo was grown in Sarkhej, which was like a suburb of Ahmedabad. Saltpetre was got from Malpur, a place 50 miles to the north-east of the city. Another commodity in demand was paper known for its whiteness. *Mirat-i-Ahmadi* observed, "on account of its white colour, it is taken annually to different parts of India, Arabia and Turkey like gold".[10]

But the chief source of Ahmedabad's prosperity was its textile industry. Proverbially, its fortunes used to hang on three threads—silk, cotton and gold. Ahmedabad's silk was famed, especially for the bright colour of its plain silks and the durability and non-fading qualities of the brocades woven with gold and silver thread. It was a great centre for the silk-weaving industry. Raw silk was imported from Bengal, China and Central Asia, and the weavers of Ahmedabad became experts in weaving satins, taffetas and velvets of all kinds and colours. They also made carpets from a mixture of gold, cotton and silk thread. There were royal *karkhanas* (factories) which manufactured velvet and embroidered it with gold and silver. From this velvet they also made beautiful pavilions for the imperial courts. In 1635, the viceroy Sipahdar Khan sent a magnificent present of a velvet pavilion worth one lakh rupees as a *peshkash*, or gift, to Shahjahan.[11]

A great variety of cotton cloth was produced in Ahmedabad. *Bafta*, *chintz*, quilt, *dulties* and a very fine cloth called *birami* were all in great demand in Europe and in domestic markets.

Ahmedabad had become a thriving market for precious metals, stones and pearls in the 17th century. Shantidas Jhaveri, mentioned earlier, was regarded as the greatest jeweller of India and served the emperors Jehangir and Shahjahan. He lent money to the government and to the Europeans at 12 per cent.

Ahmedabad's economic importance was also due to its being a prominent food grain market for Gujarat. It was an entrepot for the transit trade, linked to Surat in the south, Sindh in the north-west, Agra in the north and Cambay in the west. Sugar, gum, lac, myrobalan and ginger were exported to West Asia.

Since Ahmedabad lay on the important trade routes, a large volume of transit trade passed through the city. Caravans consisting of 10,000 oxen bringing goods from Agra passed through Ahmedabad. The city also traded with distant centres like Mocha and Basra in West Asia and Java and Sumatra in South-East Asia. Williams Finch who visited Ahmedabad in 1651 wrote that, every 10 days, 200 carts loaded with rich merchandise from Ahmedabad left for Cambay.

Despite its strong commercial character, Ahmedabad developed equally rich religious traditions. It was a stronghold of Jainism. Rich Jain merchants, favoured by the Moghul emperors, built beautiful temples. Believing in *ahimsa* (non-violence), the Jains of Ahmedabad set up hospitals and asylums for animals, known as *panjrapol*. Such asylums also existed in Surat and Cambay.

During the Moghul regime, the city also became a vital centre of the Vaishnav sect called Pushtimarg founded by Vallabhacharya in the early 16th century. Pushtimarg appealed to Ahmedabad's mercantile community because it preached the ideal of a *grihasta bhakta*, or householder devotee, meaning one who could carry on both worldly activities and devotion. This ideal gave people the best of both the worlds.

Another influential person was Akho, a 17th century saint-poet who protested strongly against the hypocrisy of the gurus, religious rituals and caste differences. However, Akho merely exposed the evils of society and religion, offering no concrete solutions for change.

During the Moghul period, the city of Ahmedabad was the capital of the *suba* of Gujarat. Bhadra, its citadel, became the seat of Moghul administration. The city's order and peace were maintained by the *kotwal* who was the chief of the police department. His headquarters or *chabutra* was near the Bhadra Fort. In the city, at the *chaklas* (the place where four roads meet), there were *chabutras* or police stations where police patrolled day and night. Being a market town, Ahmedabad had a vast customs department which collected tax from cloth, jewel and grain markets.

The administration of the law of the city was under a *kazi*, the judicial officer, who administered criminal and civil law according to the Quran. However, a parallel informal judicial system existed in the form of *gnyati panchayats*, or caste councils, and *mahajans*, or guilds, which imparted justice by the method of conciliation and arbitration. This framework of city administration continued during Maratha rule with some modification.

The death of Emperor Aurangzeb in 1707 marked the end of a glorious epoch in the history of Ahmedabad. The period which followed, until the British took over the city in 1817, was a politically turbulent period during which the city was depopulated and shrank in size. This period was characterised by civil wars, internal dissent, oppressive Moghul viceroys, Maratha invasions and the revolts of Kolis, Bhils and Kathis. The Persian historian Ali Muhammad Khan, who was an eyewitness to the events of this period, has given a graphic and detailed account of this period in *Mirat-i-Ahmadi*. Natural calamities like famines and floods aggravated the miseries of the people of Ahmedabad. Adding to their difficulties, the port of Cambay began silting up. Consequently, the city's trade received a setback. The period was marked by chronic warfare and the decay of urban life.

Later Moghul rulers after Aurangzeb were weak and could hardly exert any influence on the distant province of Gujarat. Towards the end of the Moghul period, the Marathas appeared and did not spare the city and its neighbourhood from looting. But fortunately, this rich city was saved by the generous efforts of the *nagarseth* Khushalchand, the grandson of Shantidas Jhaveri, who with his own money bought off the invaders in 1725. To show their gratitude for this generous act, the *mahajans* and European traders agreed to pay four annas on every hundred rupees worth of goods entering or leaving the city to Khushalchand. This grant was to be in perpetuity to his family and was to be paid to his sons after his death.[12] However, Khushalchand was not to remain *nagarseth* for very long. Hamid Khan, the Nizam's deputy, sought the help of the Marathas to establish a reign of terror in Ahmedabad. He took Khushalchand into custody and released him only after a payment of Rs 6,000. Even after seeking and obtaining redress at the imperial court, Khushalchand was not reinstated immediately. All this shows that the post of *nagarseth* was not accepted as a hereditary one at that time and remained a bone of contention among the leading merchants of the city.

The common people of the city not only became victims of the inroads of the Marathas and Kolis but also of the oppression of the royal officials who imposed various kinds of fines and taxes on them. Many sold their houses and fled to other places.[13] The Brahmins of the *chorasi* or eighty-four castes protested the *vero*, or the tax, imposed on them. The deputy viceroy Anupsingh Bhandari was apprehensive of a public uprising and abolished *vero* at least for the Brahmins.[14] Thus, through collective action, the Brahmins made the government redress their grievances.

During the 50 years under the later Moghuls, the great metropolis of Gujarat was reduced to a shadow of its former glory. Its once extensive and flourishing suburbs became desolate. The city was depopulated long before the *bhagva* (saffron) banner of the Marathas was unfurled at Bhadra.

In 1758, the Marathas finally captured the city and established the duel authority of the Peshwas and the Gaikwads. Both sent their *subas* to rule the city and collect revenues. Both enjoyed equal participation in the revenues of the town and in administering justice. The charge of the eleven gates of the city was given to the Peshwas and of one gate to the Gaikwad. The Gaikwad paid the Peshwas Rs 60,000 annually for the upkeep of the gateways.

The Maratha rule in the city lasted 63 years. Misgovernment by the Marathas was greatly responsible for its further decay. Historians believe that even if Maratha rule was not the only reason for the decline of Ahmedabad, it was still an important one.[15] Though the Marathas showed tolerance and respect for social customs and traditions, they considered this rich commercial city as a mere source of revenue and tried to squeeze all they could from their new subjects. As a result, commerce and industry, the life sources of the city, suffered and dried up. The fear of illegal extraction by Maratha officials reinforced the migratory trend and the city was further depopulated.

In 1780, a British force under General Goddard, acting in alliance with Fateh Singh Gaikwad against the Peshwas, captured Ahmedabad after a fierce battle with the Peshwa *subedar*. Goddard and his battery had to make a breach in the city wall to enter the city. Goddard ordered his troops to plunder the city. Nathusha Khushalchand, the *nagarseth*, Sheikh Mohammad Sale, the *kazi*, and Mia Mirza Amin, the *padshahi dewan*—three leading members of the community of Ahmedabad—waited on him and requested him to stop the looting of the city.[16] Goddard was angry and told them that they should have surrendered before the fight. The *nagarseth* pacified him by pleading "Sir, we remained faithful to the Peshwas. Now that you and the Gaikwad have become our masters, we are faithful to you."[17] This reveals the pragmatic stance of the merchants of Ahmedabad, for they had learnt from bitter experience the art of getting along with the ruling elite. Thus, the city was saved from plunder and destruction.[18]

James Forbes, who visited the city in 1781, just after Goddard's assault, gave a graphic account of the ruinous state of the city which had long been regarded as the most splendid city of India. He wrote that the city was in a state of such decay that it seemed doomed never to recover.[19] The walls had collapsed in many places. Much of the city was bare or in ruins. The population had dwindled to a mere one lakh.[20] Except for some calico printing, brocade weaving and lacquered work in gold and silver, there were few signs of trade or manufacture.[21] James Forbes further observed that after the Marathas conquered Gujarat, the weavers of *kinkhab*, the embroiderers, jewellers, painters and inlayers of ivory, ebony and sandalwood migrated from Ahmedabad to Surat and other flourishing cities as they did not receive any encouragement in Ahmedabad.[22]

In the years 1812 and 1813, Gujarat was devastated by famine and plague so great that it was known as *Agnotoro Kal*. Plague raged through the city, killing half the population.[23] Many families lost their heirs, and the property of such families was confiscated by the Maratha officials. An incident which took place in 1812 highlights this particular problem. In this year, Fateh Singh

Gaikwad and the British resident, Carnac, received a petition protesting the Maratha government's interference in property matters. The petition showed how unfair it was that, when a man died leaving only female heirs, these heirs were denied the right of succession. The petition was accepted, resulting in an order giving inheritance rights to daughters. This order was engraved on a stone, which was placed at the city's Teen Darwaja.

For the city, the entire period of Maratha regime was one of natural calamities, famine, scarcity, riots and most of all, insecurity. The oppressive Maratha officials imposed heavy taxes. Aba Shelulkar, the *sur-subedar* of the Peshwa, not only imposed illegal extra taxes on artisans and traders but had a spacious *haveli* built for himself with forced labour and materials.[24] The local chronicler Maganlal Vakhatchand, using oral evidence, wrote in 1851 that the rich wore coarse clothes lest they be taxed by the Marathas. Only the *nagarseth* and a very few merchants were able to maintain carriages.[25] The menace of the Kathis and Kolis increased and daylight robberies became common. Citizens sought safety in the neighbourhood enclosures, or *pols*, which became more intricate and complex. Maratha rule came to an end in November 1817 when the British took over the city.

The city of Ahmedabad, in the course of its 400 years of history, emerged not only as an administrative city but also a leading centre of trade and manufacture. It had developed into a mercantile city with a strong commercial and corporate ethos.

II

In many ways, the pre-British society of Ahmedabad was an epitome of the traditional urban society of Gujarat. The city's commercial and corporate ethos was woven in its various institutions like the *mahajan*, *panch*, *nagarseth*, *gnyati panch*, or caste organisation, and *pol*. That ethos imparted a distinct character to these institutions. They played a significant role in the city's social, economic, civic and cultural life.

By the standards of medieval times, Ahmedabad was a large city. It was girdled by a wall which gave security to its inhabitants and also regulated the activities of traders and visitors who passed through its gateways. The circumference of the walled city was almost six miles, while its area was two square miles. Since the late 18th century, the walls had been in a dilapidated state.

The Bhadra was the political nucleus of the city, a fort within a fort. It was the seat of administration as well as the royal residence. Around this nucleus, the city grew. In the east, there was the Shai Maidan which led to the Jama Masjid, the dominant religious edifice that became the centre around which various markets flourished. Residential areas sprang up all around the principal market Manek Chowk. Markets also proliferated around the chief gateways of the city.

The Gaikwads had built another fort within the walled city in the south-west known as the Gaikwad Haveli, which they used as their administrative office.

The people of Ahmedabad lived in the residential areas which were known as *vasa*, *vada* or *pol*. Most people lived and worked in a collective habitat called *pol*. The *pol* can be described as an enclosed residential quarter consisting of a street with one or two gateways. The gateways were closed at night as a safeguard against thieves and invaders. There were as many as three hundred *pols* in the city.

The *pol* was an important feature of the traditional cities of Gujarat. In Ahmedabad, the *pol* was borrowed from Anhilwad Patan, the previous capital of Gujarat.[26] Thus, *pols* came into existence simultaneously with the city. Earlier, the *pol* was not so complex or intricate in form as it was in later turbulent times under late Moghul and Maratha rule. The pre-Moghul *khatpatras*, or legal documents pertaining to the sale, purchase or mortgage of houses, shops or land, refer to various *pols* of the city. *Mirat-i-Ahmadi* frequently refers to different *pols*. In the insecure period of the 18th century, *pols* developed various devices for ensuring safety and security. The housing pattern was defence oriented, and the houses in the interior were assured the best security. Houses were built in such a manner that only the walls of the houses faced the street. Doors and windows opened into the courtyard of the house. Usually, residential houses were crowded together and were multi-storeyed.

Significantly, there was no segregation of the rich and the poor in the *pol*, the rich needing even greater security, which they found here. By and large, the caste composition in the *pol* was homogeneous, and *pols* were often named after the caste residing in them, such as Kansara *pol*, Kadva *pol*, Jhaveri *pol*, Sutar *pol* and Chhipa *pol*. Occasionally, however, even homogeneous caste *pols* housed other caste members in small numbers. A few *pols* had a multicaste composition with domination by one or two castes. Sometimes, Hindus and Muslims resided together, but such *pols* were exceptions.[27] The depressed castes and the lowest castes did not stay in *pols*. They lived on the outskirts but within the walled city in their own *vadas* such as Dhed *vada*, Waghri *vada* and Kumbhar *vada*.

The *pol* had its own temple, a *parwadi*, or birdhouse, and a well. The gateway was safeguarded by a *poliya*, or a gatekeeper. Each *pol* looked after its own sanitary arrangements. The *pol* affairs were managed by a council called *panch*, which worked as a corporate institution. No resident could sell or mortgage a house to an outsider, without first offering it to the other residents of the *pol*. The house was usually sold to buyers of their own caste, but this rule was not always observed. The *khatpatras* reveal that the houses of Brahmins were sold to Vanias or even to Muslims, and those of the Vanias to the non-Vania castes.[28]

When a house was mortgaged or sold, the people of the *pol* had a right to claim an amount of 0.5 to 2 per cent of the sale proceeds. On weddings and other ceremonial occasions, the *pol* residents were given a feast by the householder. Even if not of the same caste, the members of the *pol* were expected to attend a funeral whenever there was a death in the *pol*. If the *pol* rules were slighted, the offender was fined and not allowed to light a lamp in the house or give a feast until the dues were paid, which practice was described in the local dialect as *divo devta bandh*. Money gathered from gifts, fines and the percentage on house property sales constituted a common fund, which was managed by the council or *pol panch*. It was used for repairing the *pol* gates and privies or digging a *pol* well.[29]

Thus, the *pol* was more of a social institution than a mere ecological feature of the city. It reflected the corporate spirit of the city. Nowhere else in Gujarat was the urban institution of the *pol* as strong as in Ahmedabad, and nowhere else did it have such strong corporate traditions and complexities as in Ahmedabad.

As the population of the city increased, *puras* or suburban centres arose around the walled city. They soon become an extension of the economic life of the city. In the heyday of the city, there were about 380 *puras* which resembled miniature cities.[30] At the height of Ahmedabad's glory, the circumference of the city with the *puras* was almost 30 miles.[31] During the turbulent times of the 18th century, the *puras* were deserted.

Foreign travellers who visited the city in the 17th century observed that Ahmedabad was as populous as London or Paris. But as trade and industry suffered under the tyrannical and chaotic rule of the late Moghuls and the Marathas, many migrated to safer places. When Goddard invaded the city, he estimated the city's population at one lakh.[32] Under the stable government of the Gaikwads, people came into the city once more, raising the population to two lakhs in 1811. In 1812, a devastating famine and pestilence reduced the population by half. By the time the British took over the city, it had dwindled to 80,000.[33]

The population of the city was heterogeneous in composition. It consisted of two main segments, the Hindus and the Muslims. The Jains also formed a small but vital part of this society.

Being a centre of Muslim power, Ahmedabad had a large Muslim population which at one time even exceeded the Hindu population. The city was home to the Muslim military and official elite who lived in great style with their retainers and dependents in the walled city and in the *puras*. There were also some skilled Muslim artisans who were engaged in weaving, dyeing, printing cloth and manufacturing paper. The Bohras, an important Muslim group, were traders. They traded in textiles and paper with Arabia, Persia and "Hindustan".[34] The Memons too were traders. Both these Muslim trading groups were affluent. Many Muslims left the city during the turbulent 18th century, but those who continued to live in the city fell on bad times and lived an isolated and poor life. Some lived on charity and allowances granted to them by the government, while others sold their ornaments and other valuables to survive.[35] In 1825, a survey of the city recorded the Muslim population at approximately 15,672 and the Hindus population at 57,536. Thus, at this time, only one-fifth of the population of the city was Muslim.[36]

Two important Muslim families were those of the *kazi* and the *padshahi dewan*. The *kazi's* family had held office for about 400 years, while the office of *dewan* was held by the same family for about 100 years and was granted a quarter of a rupee on merchandise worth Rs 100 brought into the city of Ahmedabad.[37] Just as the *nagarseth* was the spokesman for the Hindu and Jain communities, the *kazi* was the spokesman for the Muslim community. Though the official and military elite were generally Muslims during the Muslim rule, some Hindus, especially of Nagar and Kayastha castes, too, were employed in government services.

Ahmedabad being a mercantile city, the rich Hindu and Jain merchants formed a very vital occupational group which dominated the economic life of the city. The other significant group among the Hindus, and perhaps the largest, was the artisans who were important to this industrial city. As the textile industry was the heart of the city's economy, a large number of artisans were weavers, spinners, dyers, printers and bleachers of cloth. There were also Hindu goldsmiths, blacksmiths, carpenters, indigo manufacturers and other artisans.

As mentioned earlier, communal harmony was an absolute necessity, especially as the economic activities of the city were shared by so many different communities. This was why religious sects which emerged in the city during medieval times had placed such great stress on communal harmony and religious unity.

The institution of caste was the bedrock of traditional Gujarati society which was divided into hundreds of castes and sub-castes. The author of the *Gazetteer of the Bombay Presidency, Hindu Population*, commenting on the society of Gujarat, observed: "In no part of India, are the sub-castes so minute."[38] There were traditionally 84 sub-castes each of Brahmins and Vanias.[39] Caste dominated the social, religious and economic life of the people. An individual's role in society, status, occupation and identity were all determined by the caste into which the person was born.

One peculiar feature of the Gujarat caste structure was that the Vaishya castes or Vanias were placed higher in the hierarchy than the Kshatriyas or Rajput castes. The term *Brahmin Vania* was used to indicate that both these classes enjoyed an equally high status. The mercantile Vanias were considered higher than the martial Rajputs because in Gujarat trade and commerce were considered prestigious. Secondly, the flesh-eating, liquor-drinking Rajputs were looked down upon in a society which greatly respected the Jain doctrine of *ahimsa* (non-violence).

Theoretically, each caste has a distinctive occupation, but in Gujarat, the Brahmins, Kshatriyas, Kanbis and Kolis could pursue agriculture as their occupation, with only the Vanias abstaining from agriculture. There was more mobility in Gujarat than in other regions of India regarding the choice of occupation. Brahmins strangely enough also took to trade and arms. The Nagar Brahmins for example, followed various occupations. The *bhikshuka* Nagars performed the duties of priests, while the *grihastha* Nagars generally took up administrative posts and also took to arms. Though the Nagars as a caste group generally remained aloof from business activities, a few Nagars did enter this field. One Dayaram Mehta of Surat, for instance, was a prominent broker and merchant in the 17th century. Only the artisans' occupations were hereditary because they required hereditary skills.

The concept of ritual pollution was not so strongly developed in Gujarat as compared to other regions. The proximity of a Dhed or Bhangi was not regarded as causing pollution, though his touch was. In the city of Ahmedabad, Dheds, Chamars, Dabgars and Bhangis were regarded as the four major depressed castes.

Each caste, including its sub-castes and sub-divisions, had a governing body which was called the *gnyati panchayat*. This *panchayat* consisted of a headman and two or three leaders who held office by hereditary right. The *panchayat* formulated caste rules and regulations and also saw to it that no caste member transgressed them. The headman of the Vanias and higher castes was called *seth* and of the artisans and lower castes was called *patel.* The council regulated every aspect of an individual's life, such as clothes, food, marriage, death, ceremonies and rules regarding ritual pollution, to the extent of regulating the relationships of the caste members with other castes. In the artisan caste, the *panchayat* performed the functions of a guild and regulated even occupations.

Holding jurisdiction over all caste members, the council was authorised to punish any breach of rules, the punishments ranging from a fine to excommunication. The judicial and executive powers of the caste were backed by tradition and customs. As a general rule, the state did not interfere with caste rules. Even the Muslim rulers did not interfere with caste practices. Thus, the caste council was a powerful body which regulated the social, economic and ritual activities of its members.[40]

While their religion did not sanction caste, the Jains in Gujarat followed the caste system in the same way as did the Hindus. In Ahmedabad, Oswal Jains and Porwad Jains were predominant. The Jain and Hindu Vanias intermarried. For example, a Porwad Jain Vania could marry a Porwad Meshri Vania. In spite of religious differences, the social customs of the Jains closely resembled those of the Hindu Vanias.

The Muslim religion, though egalitarian, also followed caste divisions in India. They, too, believed in the hierarchy of caste groups. Such distinctions existed specially between the Muslims who were of foreign origin and those who were of indigenous origin or had been converted to Islam. The four groups of foreign Muslims—Sayeds, Sheikhs, Moghuls and Pathans—were considered superior to the converts. All these four categories were found in Ahmedabad, but many of them had fallen on bad days during the 18th and the 19th centuries. Among the local converts, Bohras and Memons were the well-to-do sections as they were traders and were placed higher in the hierarchy. The local converts, like Pinjaras or cotton cleaners, Ravats or horse keepers, Khatkas or butchers, occupied a lower place in the hierarchy. Endogamous rules were followed rigidly, but there were fewer restrictions on eating with members of other groups.

In this way, Ahmedabad society, the microcosm of Gujarati society, was a caste-ridden society. To meet the various needs of the city's life, various occupational castes resided in the city. Contemporary documents and publications such as the *khatpatras*, the *Mirat-i-Ahmadi*, the *Ahmedabad Gazetteer*, and the survey by the revenue department in 1824 give a good idea of the castes in the city. The various *Shravaka* (Jain) and *Meshri* (Vaishnava) Vanias formed the major commercial caste group in this mercantile city. The *nagarseth* belonged to the Oswal Jain Vania caste. Porwad and Shrimali Jain Vanias were also a high caste group. Kanbis were traders, bankers and craftsmen. Among the Brahmins, the Nagars and Audichyas were predominant. Various other occupational artisan castes were the Sonis (goldsmith), Hajams (barbers), Kumbhars (potters), Durjis (tailors), Ghanchis (oil pressers), Kansaras (coppersmiths), Kadias (brick-layers), and the Bhavsars (printers).[41]

The pre-British society of Ahmedabad probably had many features and social customs in common with traditional urban society in other parts of Gujarat. The scarcity of contemporary sources makes it difficult to reconstruct the picture of the pre-British society. However, the contemporary religious literature of Shamal

Bhatt, Akho and Vallabh Bhatt who resided in Ahmedabad and the oral traditions preserved in the form of folk songs such as *garba* and *rasada* do throw some light on the social life of Ahmedabad.

The family, Hindu as well as Muslim, was joint and patriarchal in character and was made up of members of three to four generations. The family was the economic, social and cultural unit of society. Nuclear families also existed but had many of the characteristics of a joint family. Quite often, sons separated from the family but lived close to the parental house. Surprisingly, in the survey of the city of Ahmedabad taken in 1824, there were a total of 29,050 houses for about 101,675 people, which is an average of 3.5 souls to each house.[42] This survey reveals that the size of the family in the city of Ahmedabad tended to be small and a nuclear unit rather than a joint family.

Customs regarding marriage, divorce and widow remarriage varied among castes. Endogamous rules were followed very strictly among the Hindus as well as Muslims. Child marriage was common among Hindus as elsewhere in India. The custom of dowry was prevalent among the Kanbis and the Audichya Brahmins of the city and encouraged polygamy among them. Among the Kanbis, it also led to the inhuman custom of female infanticide, known as *dudh piti ni chaal*. Dowry ranging from Rs 1 to Rs 2,000 was expected from the bride's parents. As a result, parents preferred to do away with a female child, who was a source of heavy future expenses. In 1848, the government conducted a census of the Kanbi community of Ahmedabad district under the collector Fawcett, which revealed a marked disproportion between the births and deaths of boys and girls.[43]

The customs of widow remarriage and divorce also differed among castes. The lower castes such as Bhats, Charans, the artisan castes and the Kanbis permitted divorce as well as widow remarriage, which were not permitted among higher castes such as Brahmins, Vanias and Rajputs. The poet Shamal wondered how, in the Kanbi, which was a middle caste, the custom of *natra* or divorce was permitted.[44]

The custom of *sati* was not common in Gujarat except to a small extent in the warrior class. Here it is interesting to note two cases in the family of Ranchhodlal Chhotalal, the founder of the first textile mill in Ahmedabad. Pankor, his grandmother, performed *sati* of her own free will in *Vikram samvat* 1855 (AD 1799). She was known as Satima.[45] Ranchhodlal's sister Motiben, a child widow, led the life of a celibate. District judge Norris of Ahmedabad recorded only one instance of *sati* in the district in 1819.[46] Various other evil customs existed. Heavy expenses were incurred during wedding and death ceremonies. Women sang *phatanas*, or obscene songs, on wedding days. Weeping and beating of breasts were common customs on the occasion of a death.

In a patriarchal society, the birth of a daughter was not welcomed. Every woman wanted only male children and made solemn vows in order to bear sons. Female education was almost non-existent. It was believed that if a girl were to be educated, she would become a widow.[47] In general; a woman was confined to life within her own home. A woman's life revolved around her home and family. Though the custom of *purdah* did not prevail among the Hindus, the woman's social life was limited. She rarely stepped out of her house. Further, her mobility was limited by various restrictions. She was not allowed to carry an umbrella or wear footwear, which meant she could not go out in the rain or in the hot sun. She had very sketchy social and legal rights. Strangely enough, the epigraphic and documentary evidence in Ahmedabad reveals that wives and daughters in several Hindus and Muslim communities enjoyed extensive property rights in pre-British times. The custom of *pallu*, or money given by the bridegroom or father-in-law to the bride, prevailed among certain Vania and Brahmin castes. This custom of *pallu* gave valuable property rights to women.

Almost all castes, except for the Vadnagara caste, permitted the husband to marry more than one wife. Childlessness, having only female children or inadequate dowry often led to a second marriage. Contemporary poets as well as folk songs depicted the unhappy lot of co-wives. Kanbis and Audichya Brahmins married more than once as each marriage brought them fat dowries.

III

Ahmedabad was not a holy city per se. However, being the capital of Gujarat, it became the centre of religious activities. Like many prime feudal cities, it was "at one and the same time a centre of orthodoxy and a focus of changes".[48] In Ahmedabad, while on the one hand, greater traditions of Hinduism, Jainism and Islam were patronised, enhanced and perpetuated, on the other hand, new religious sects like the Dadu sect, Sthanakvasi Jain sect, Pirana sect, Swaminarayan sect emerged, found support, and later spread to other places. New sects arose primarily as separatist movements and were reformist in character.

Some of the religious activities of the city have been mentioned earlier. The traditions of Jainism of the city of Asawal continued in later times and the city of Ahmedabad became the great centre of Jainism in Gujarat. It had also become the stronghold of Sufism under the patronage of Muslim kings. Hinduism in all its diversity flourished in the city, which abounded in Hindu temples. Ali Muhammad Khan gives a long list of temples in the city.[49] The temples of Vishnu, Shiva, Devi and Hanuman were prominent though not ornate or pretentious. The Pushtimarg sect had a large following among the mercantile community, while the Dadu, Swaminarayan and Pirana sects had a great following among artisans and the Kanbis.

The important religious personality on the eve of British rule was Sahajanand Swami, a social and religious reformer who founded the Swaminarayan sect. He made Ahmedabad his headquarters from 1804 to 1830, exerting great influence on the people of Ahmedabad and its environs. Emerging as a powerful leader of a religious and social movement, he laid great emphasis on pure devotion (*bhakti*), renunciation (*vairagya*), ethical actions (*sadachar*) and religious company (*satsang*). Sahajanand was also an active social reformer who protested against the degenerated practices of the Vallabhachari gurus. He fought against the social evils of female infanticide and *sati*. He emphasised a highly ethical life and popularised his religion by preaching it through stories and devotional songs in simple Gujarati and the Vraj languages. Being a good organiser, he institutionalised his religion by establishing *gadis*, or seats, in 1826 and building temples in Ahmedabad, Vadtal and other places. This sect became popular among the artisans and Kanbis who were a large section of the city.

Materialism did not impede the religiousness of the people. In fact, materialism and religion reinforced each other. Religion pervaded all facets of urban life. The temple or mosque became the centre of cultural, social and economic activities.

Unlike the people of Surat and Jamnagar who were nicknamed *rangilas*, or pleasure lovers, the people of Ahmedabad were practical and worldly-wise. They had developed simple habits and apparently puritan virtues. Their frugality was proverbial. These qualities made them indifferent to the finer aspects of life like dance, music and art.[50] Just as their life was more religion-oriented, their cultural activities, too, were inspired by religion. They derived recreation from *bhajans* or religious group songs, *kathas* or religious story recitations, *melas* or fairs, *garba* and *raas* or folk dances, *bhavai* or folk drama and religious festivals.

An important source of recreation was the *mela*, which was held on the occasion of religious festivals near a temple, river or lake. The Muslim counterpart of such religious fairs was the *urs*. Though there were no places of great holy significance in and around the city of Ahmedabad, 24 Hindu and Muslim fairs were held annually.[51] The largest fair or *urs* was held in honour of Shah Alam, lasted five days and was attended by thousands of people, both Muslims and Hindus. *Melas* attracted dancers, singers, *kathakars* (story tellers), actors, and acrobats. Wrestling matches, cockfights, and bullock cart races were held. Shops selling toys, cloth, vessels, trinkets and sweets were set up. People from the city and nearby villages flocked to the fair to buy these goodies and enjoy various entertainments.

The city celebrated religious festivals such as Eid, Muharram, Diwali, Holi, Janmashtami and Ram Navmi with great enthusiasm. The festival of Navratri (nine nights), was an important one for the women of Ahmedabad. In each *pol*, women gathered at night, performed *puja* in honour of the goddess Kali and played *garba* and *raas*, two popular forms of folk dance in Gujarat.

An important institution in Gujarat was the *man bhatts* or *puranis*, the traditional storytellers. They provided entertainment to the people by reciting soul-stirring stories from the epics and the Puranas, the story-telling being accompanied by music and commentary. They recited their stories usually at night, at a crossroads, in the *pol chowks* or near the temples. Many families of *puranis* and *man bhatts* resided in Ahmedabad.[52]

The only form of drama for the entertainment of the people was the popular folk drama called *bhavai* which was performed by people of the Targala or Bhavaiya castes. There were about 238 families of these castes residing in Ahmedabad in the 1820s, indicating the popularity of the *bhavai*.[53] Originally, this form of drama was dedicated to goddess Durga and stories of her exploits were enacted by the actors. It was performed in open spaces such as streets, courtyards and temples. No stage was needed. Later, popular episodes and impersonation of professionals took the place of religious episodes and were characterised by crude humour.[54]

Bhajans or religious songs sung by devotees gave great solace to the common men. Caste feasts and caste outing or *ujanis* were other occasions for enjoyment, looked forward to with enthusiasm. Such feasts were held in the *vadis* (caste lodges) or the streets.

Ahmedabad, a mercantile city, was not a seat of higher education. However, from the very beginning, it had schools that imparted elementary education as did any other city. *Vimal Prabandh*, the 15th century work by Vimal, the Jain poet of Ahmedabad, gives a vivid description of the school initiation ceremony of a child known as Nishal Garni.[55]

During Moghul rule, a few *madrasas* were established which imparted knowledge of Muslim theology. A *madrasa* was built at Khanpur during the reign of Jehangir, and two were built during the reign of Aurangzeb, one at Astodia and the other near Sujaat Khan's tomb. During the chaotic times of the 18th century, these colleges fell into decay.[56]

Indigenous elementary schools continued right up to the end of the 19th century. The descriptions of these schools recorded in the official reports and by travellers give some idea of traditional education at this time. In 1848, when Henry J Briggs visited the city, he saw several indigenous schools in the densely populated area of the city. In these elementary schools, students were taught the rudiments—reading, writing and arithmetic.[57] In Gujarat, more stress was laid on teaching numbers than on the alphabet. Great importance was given to multiplication tables (*anks*) up to forty, including fractions, and arithmetic manipulations. The children of the trading community showed great aptitude and skill in arithmetic. It is interesting to note that in contrast to Gujarat, Maharashtra taught alphabets first and then numbers.[58]

Where language was concerned, instruction was confined to the alphabet and to the formation of syllables or names, that is, joining of letters to spell proper nouns. The total absence of printed books prevented students from learning to read any book accurately.[59] The schools were small in size, and each accommodated an average of 25 boys. Classes were held in temples, mosques, the verandas of master's houses or sometimes in the open. The teacher's remuneration was generally made up of fees paid in cash or in kind. Teachers imparted knowledge orally. Subjects such as history, geography and biology were not taught at all. The quality of education was poor in content and quality by modern standards, even senior pupils not having acquired basic proficiency in reading and writing.[60]

Only the children of Brahmins and Vanias were given this education, while depressed and lower castes were not. Girls did not attend school. Some Brahmin children also acquired knowledge of Sanskrit from private teachers. The Nagar and Kayastha children studied the Persian language which was required for administrative jobs. On the whole, a very small proportion of the population acquired any education.

IV

In the courses of its 400-year history, Ahmedabad had emerged as a great, bustling manufacturing and commercial centre. The major economic activities of the city have been mentioned, more on these now.

Ahmedabad developed a sophisticated infrastructure to support its variegated economic activities. In the stable period of the Moghuls, it developed and nurtured certain business traditions and urban institutions like *mahajan*, *panch* and *nagarseth* which played an important role in the economic, social and civic life of the city. These institutions reflected the corporate ethos of the city.

The merchants of Ahmedabad were engaged in the banking, trading, jewellery and textile business. They financed the indigenous manufacturers of the city and advanced loans to the Moghul princes, the European East India companies, the Peshwas and the feudal chiefs of Kathiawar and Rajasthan. They had business branches in the major cities of India such as Calcutta, Poona, Bombay, Delhi, Malwa and Baroda. The institution of *hundi*, or bill of exchange, emerged in Gujarat in the medieval period, facilitating interstate and international trade. This customary institution was based on the security and prestige of the person who issued the *hundi*. The *hundis* issued by the merchants of Ahmedabad were honoured as far as Constantinople.[61]

Commercial and trading activities were undertaken by family or partnership firms known as *pedhis*. In Ahmedabad, as elsewhere in any pre-industrial society, economic activities were not isolated but linked with family, kin, caste and community. The family firm or *pedhi* was an important unit of economic activity. It was usually headed by the eldest male of the family. It also served as a kind of business school for the younger members of the family.[62]

The trading community had also developed its own intricate network of communication through a system of functionaries like *khapias* and *angadias* who carried news, messages and valuable commodities to different commercial centres. The merchants and *sharafs* of Gujarat adopted paper as writing material in the 16th century, a practice which must have greatly facilitated their business activities and communication.[63]

In the absence of banks and insurance companies, financial transactions were regulated by customs, usages and traditions, which ensured security and smoothness in transactions. Reliability was assured by customary guarantees provided by the institutions of *mahajans* and *nagarseths* or by the word of the *bhat* or *charan*. The *bhat* or *charan* acted as a guarantor and ensured financial, private and political agreements. His person was regarded as sacrosanct, and he could demand compliance with his demands. Otherwise, he would perform *traga* in which he would sacrifice himself or a family member and thus bring down a curse upon the defaulter. He could stage a *dharna*, which was to surround the house of an offender or keep a fast until the offender complied. This custom continued up to the advent of British rule. No deed or transaction was considered valid unless it was countersigned by a *bhat*.[64]

The mercantile community of Ahmedabad generally encouraged cordial relations with local ruling authorities. The Moghul emperors, in their turn, accorded special treatment to leading merchants. Only in the turbulent times of the 18th century were some of the local magnates like Gangadas, the silk merchant, and Khushalchand, the *nagarseth*, harassed by local authorities. At this time, the Maratha officials also extorted money from the merchants of the city.

The commercial activities of the city had a sound industrial base. The city was a leading manufacturing centre of textiles, paper, gold and silverwork. The manufacturing unit was small; it generally comprised a family of artisans and sometimes apprentices. Even the women in artisans' families were integrated into the household production system. Artisans worked in the front room of the house. In the 17th century, there were some *karkhanas*, or workshops, which fulfilled royal orders. The pavilion made in such a *karkhana* was presented to Shahjahan on the occasion of his coronation, as mentioned earlier. Many artisans who produced for internal consumption took loans from the *sharafs* to buy raw material. They sold excess stock of their goods to big export houses. Merchants guided artisans in the desired quality and design of the goods. In the manufacture of *kinkhab* (brocade) and *mashru*, high skill, specialisation and division of labour were required. The entire process of making *mashru* textiles required 36 different types of skilled workers.[65] Similarly, *kinkhab*, too, required skilled handling by different artisans. As a result, merchants had *kinkhab* manufactured by artisans under their instructions.

To regulate the various commercial and manufacturing activities, the city had developed a rich guild tradition. *Mahajans*, or guilds of merchants, and *panchs*, or guilds of artisans, were autonomous corporate institutions that contributed to the stability of commercial and industrial activities in the city. They also performed many functions of modern government and municipality. Ahmedabad was the centre of guild life in India.[66]

Guilds must have existed in a rudimentary form in Ahmedabad since the city's inception. During the stable rule of the imperial Moghuls, the corporate character of each guild was consolidated, allowing them multilateral growth. Their importance and corporate character can be attested to by the fact that a large number of *mahajans*, including Muslim *mahajans*, voluntarily agreed to pay a share from the octroi duties to *nagarseth* Khushalchand Laxmichand when he saved Ahmedabad from being ransacked by the Marathas in 1725. He had paid a huge amount of ransom to the invaders from his own pocket and turned them back. The guild system was so intensively and extensively expanded, both vertically and horizontally, that it could withstand adversity during the difficult period under the Marathas. In fact, autonomy and solidarity among these groups increased during these turbulent times.[67]

There were several kinds of merchants' *mahajans*. Cloth *mahajans* dominated the city, there being separate *mahajans* selling cotton, silk, *mashru*, *kinkhab* and handloom textiles. The *sharaf*, or banker, *mahajan* was very powerful. There were various *panchs* of skilled and unskilled artisans. Skilled artisans such as goldsmiths, cloth dyers, silk weavers, gold threaders, *mashru* cloth weavers were organised into *panchs* which occupied a higher position in the hierarchy as compared to the *panchs* of unskilled artisans such as Ghanchis (oil pressers), brick makers or potters.

The social base of the merchant's *mahajans* was broad, cutting across caste and community lines, and was thus vertical in structure. However, it was generally dominated by specific castes. For example, the *Shravak* Vanias dominated the *sharaf mahajan*. The artisan's *panch* was horizontal, usually represented homogeneous caste groups, and was coterminous with a caste. However, certain *panchs* in Ahmedabad were composed of two or three castes. There was one *panch* of carpenters with members from four different castes of carpenters. The *mashru* and silk weaver's *panchs* consisted of Kanbis as well as Vanias. Three different castes made up the guild of Kandois or confectioners.[68]

In Ahmedabad, Muslim merchants and artisans had also organised themselves into guilds.[69] The Muslim guild was known as *jamatbandhi*. It was stronger among artisans and Muslim traders like the Bohras, Memons and Khojas. Like their Hindu counterparts, Muslim guilds performed religious, occupational and social functions. Their heads were known as *patels* or *khatibs*. The organisation of *jamatbandhi* was considerably weaker in the Muslim communities of foreign origin.[70]

Mahajan and *panch* were composed of all the men of a particular trade or craft. Each guild was headed by an alderman who was known as *seth* among traders and *patel* among artisans. The alderman, with some leading men, formed a council which regulated the affairs of the guild. An entrance fee was levied on outsiders or newcomers.[71]

Both types of organisations were multifunctional in character. They regulated the profession, maintained standards, controlled prices, determined wages, fixed working hours, set holidays, fixed rates of insurance and output, controlled admissions of new members and restricted competition. Guilds also undertook the training of apprentices. They served as courts of law and possessed the right to arbitrate and conciliate in trade disputes and other matters under their jurisdiction. A breach of the guild's law was ordinarily punished by fines. However, in serious cases, the offender was ostracised. The authority of the *mahajan* over its members was absolute.[72]

The guild also collected and controlled common funds. The sources of funds included donations, fines, entrance fees, taxes and membership subscriptions. Guilds maintained routine charities from these funds and raised special funds in an emergency. *Mahajans* maintained their *vadis* or lodges from common funds. Among the *panchs*, money from common funds was spent on dinners and picnics. But the wealthier guilds of *sharafs* and merchants spent a considerable sum on charities like *sadavartas* or free kitchens, *parabs* or drinking water for travellers and *dharmashalas* or free rest houses. In Ahmedabad, *shravak* merchants regularly collected money for *panjrapols* or animal asylums while *Meshri* Vanias collected money for local temples. Muslim guilds and merchants contributed regularly to their local shrines.[73]

The *mahajans* were superior to the *panchs*. However, over time, there developed a complex hierarchy within the institutions of both *mahajans* and *panchs*. The highest position was held by the *sharafs' mahajans*, followed by the *mahajan* of cloth dealers while among the *panchs*, the highest position was occupied by the goldsmith's *panch*.[74]

Mahajans could provide stability and protection, but they were also bulwarks of conservatism. They protected guild members from outsiders and foreigners, who were not let into the commerce and economy of Ahmedabad, but they also impeded improvement and innovation in trade and craft.

In the city of Ahmedabad, there was nothing like a city *mahajan*. Earlier, there had been no spokesman for the business community to represent its opinion to the government. Gradually, the institution of the *nagarseth* emerged. The *nagarseth* became a spokesman for the entire urban populace and assumed leadership of the city. The *nagarseth* also resolved disputes among the guilds and merchants by arbitration and conciliation.

The *nagarseth* was the head of the *sharafs' mahajans*. He belonged to the Oswal Jain caste and traced his lineage to Shantidas Jhaveri, the famous jeweller and banker of the Moghul Court during the reign of Jehangir, Shahjahan and Aurangzeb. The *nagarseth* system evolved gradually and passed through three phases. The first phase was characterised by simplicity, with Shantidas Jhaveri acting as an informal mediator between the *mahajans* and the Moghul Court. The second phase, in the first half of the 18th century, was marked by conflicts among various individuals and groups for the position. The third phase was marked by the position of the *nagarseth* becoming hereditary. Shantidas Jhaveri's grandson Khushalchand Vakhatchand, aided by an imperial charter, succeeded in establishing an undisputed claim to the *nagarseth's* position not only for himself but also for his descendants. This is clear from the fact that none in the long line of subsequent *nagarseths* belonged to any other family. What started as a purely informal institution was finally formalised and legitimised with the aid of state power.[75] Later, subsequent *nagarseths* were treated with great deference by the Maratha officials and the British rulers. The *nagarseth* became the informal link between the state and the city.

During the turbulent and uncertain times of the later Moghul and Maratha rulers, institutions like the *mahajans*, *nagarseth*, *pol*, *gnyati panchayat* became stronger. The *nagarseth* became a virtual leader of the city. All these institutions acquired a new coherence, autonomy and vitality. They assumed various social, economic and civil functions and enhanced their influence in administration. Though not statutory, they had emerged out of the needs and traditions of the city.

This was the sociocultural and economic milieu of the city of Ahmedabad when the British took over in November 1817.

Notes

1. Ali Muhammad Khan, *The Supplement to the Mirat-i-Ahmadi*, translated by Syed Nawab Ali and Charles Seddon, Baroda, 1924, p.11. Henceforth cited as *The Supplement to the Mirat-i-Ahmadi.*
2. Bombay Government, *Gazetteer of the Bombay Presidency*, Vol. IV, *Ahmedabad*, Bombay 1879, p. 251. Henceforth cited as *Ahmedabad Gazetteer.*
3. Firastha, *Tawarikha Firastha*, translated in Gujarati by Atmaram Motiram Diwanji, Poona, 1917, pp. 19–20.
4. *The Supplement to the Mirat-i-Ahmadi*, p. 25.
5. Ali Muhammad Khan, *Mirat-i-Ahmadi: A Persian History of Gujarat*, translated by MF Lokhandwala, Baroda, 1965, p. 194. Henceforth cited as *Mirat-i-Ahmadi*; MS Commissariat, Studies in the History of *Gujarat*, Bombay, 1935, pp. 57–59.
6. *Ibid.*, pp. 64–68.
7. *Ibid.*, p. 231.
8. *Ibid.*, p. 235.
9. MS Commissariat, *Mandelslo's Travels in Western India*, 1638–39, London, 1931, p. 26.
10. *Mirat-i-Ahmadi*, p.12.
11. *Ibid.*, p.182.
12. MS Commissariat, *A History of Gujarat*, vol. II. pp. 420–23.
13. *Ibid.*, pp. 509–10.
14. *Ibid.*, p. 535.
15. Kenneth Gillion, *Ahmedabad: a Study in Indian Urban History*, Berkley, 1969, p. 31; Ratnmanirao Jote, *Gujaratnu Patnagar Amdavad* (in Gujarati), Ahmedabad, 1929, pp. 158–167.
16. HG Briggs, *The Cities of Gujrashtra*, London, 1849, p.212.
17. Maganlal Vakhatchand, *Amdavad no Itihas* (in Gujarati), reprint, Ahmedabad, 1977. p. 45. It was first published in 1851 in Ahmedabad.
18. Briggs, *op. cit.*, pp. 212–13; Maganlal Vakhatchand, *op. cit.*, p. 41.

19. James Forbes, *Oriental Memoirs* London, 1813 vol. III, p. 117.
20. *Ibid.*, p. 101–153.
21. *Ibid.*, p. 120.
22. James Forbes, *op. cit.*, Vol. I, pp. 257–58.
23. Maganlal Vakhatchand, *op. cit*, p. 47; *Ahmedabad Gazetteer*, p. 266.
24. Maganlal Vakhatchand, *op. cit.*, pp. 42–46; *Ahmedabad Gazetteer*, pp. 259–60; 'Shelukarno Garbo' a Gujarati folk song, manuscript preserved in the Forbes Gujarati Sabha, Bombay *Ank* 30–4, pp. 13–200.
25. Maganlal Vakhatchand,*op. cit.*, pp. 53–56.
26. Ratanmanirao Jote, *op. cit.*, pp. 320–23.
27. *Ibid.*, pp. 94–115.
28. A large number of *khatpatras* of the city are preserved in the BJ Institute of Research and Learning, Ashram Road, Ahmedabad. They are in the Persian and Gujarati languages. The *khatpatras* are given accession numbers which are cited in the present study. Accession No. 84 of 1664 and No. 30 of 1677, No. 15 of 1678 are referred here.
29. *Ahmedabad Gazetteer*, p. 295.
30. *Mirat-i-Ahmadi*, p. 95.
31. James Forbes, *op. cit.*, Vol. III., pp. 118-19.
32. *Ahmedabad Gazetteer*, p. 292.
33. *Ibid.*, p. 293; HG Briggs, *op. cit.*, p. 249.
34. *The Supplement to the Mirat-i-Ahmadi*, p. 121.
35. James Forbes, *op. cit.*, Vol. III, pp. 120–121, p. 150.
36. Maharashtra State Archives (MSA), Revenue Department, 7/117/1825, pp. 81–85.
37. Revenue Department, 196/1845, pp. 203–06.
38. Bombay Government, *Gazetteer of the Bombay Presidency* Vol. 9: Part I, *Gujarat Population: Hindus* Bombay, 1901, p. XIII.
39. *The Supplement to the Mirat-i-Ahmadi*, pp. 126–30.
40. The discussion of the main features of the castes of Gujarat is based on Dalpatram Dahayabhai's *Gnyati Nibandh, Gazetteer of the Bombay presidency*, vol. IV, pp. xii–xiv; Govinbhai Desai, *op. cit.*, pp. 153–61; Neera Desai, *Social Change in Gujarat: A study of Nineteenth Century Gujarat*, Bombay,1978,pp. 153–61; SC Mishra, *The Muslim Communities in Gujarat*; Bombay, 1964, pp. 129–38; Makrand J Mehta and Shirin M Mehta "The Caste System and the Social Reform Movement in Gujarat in Nineteenth Century", *Journal of the Gujarat Research Society*, October 1955, Vol. IXXVII, pp. 315–320.

41. *Ahmedabad Gazetteer*, pp. 292–302; Revenue Department, 7/117/1852, pp. 81–85.
42. *Ahmedabad Gazetteer*, Footnote, p. 293.
43. MSA, Political Department, Vol. 4/2181/1849, pp. 44-5.
44. *Buddhi Prakash*, December 1906, p. 375. *Buddhi Prakash* is a Gujarati monthly published by the Gujarat Vernacular Society in Ahmedabad since 1854.
45. Bhagwanlal Badshah, *The Life of Rao Bahadur Ranchorelal Chhotalal C.I.E.* Bombay, 1899, pp. 2–4.
46. Norris to Government of Bombay dated 25-9-1819, Judicial Department (CJD), 1819, p. 2895, cited in Kenneth Ballhatchet, *Social Policy and Social Change in Western India – 1817–30*, London, 1957, p. 276.
47. Neera Desai, *op. cit.*, pp. 64–65.
48. Gideon Sjoberg, *The Pre–Industrial City*, Illinois, 1960, p. 268.
49. *The Supplement to the Mirat-i-Ahmadi*, pp.146–51.
50. Ratnamanirao Jote, *op. cit.*, p.386.
51. *Ahmedabad Gazetteer*, p.302.
52. *Ibid.*
53. MR Majmudar, *Cultural History of Gujarat from Early Times to Pre-British Period*, Bombay, 1965, pp. 273–74.
54. Dayabhai Derasari, *Sathi Na Sahityanu Digdarshan* (in Gujarati), second edition, Ahmedabad, 1969, pp. 122–3.
55. Ratnamanirao Jote, *op.cit.*, pp.408–09.
56. MS Commissariat, *History of Gujarat*, Vol. II, p. 192, p. 196.
57. HG Briggs, *op. cit.*, p. 220.
58. Bombay Government, *Report of the Director of Public Instruction for the Year 1855–56*, Bombay, 1857, pp. 118–21; *ibid.*, for the year 1856–57, Bombay,1858, p. 314.
59. HG Fawcett, *Report on the Collectorate of Ahmedabad*, 1849, in *Selections from the Records of the Bombay Government, Vol. V*, New Series, Bombay, 1854, p. 71; Henceforth cited as *Fawcett's Report.*
60. Maganlal Vakhatchand, *op.cit.*, pp. 63–64.
61. MS Commissariat, *Mandelslo's Travels in Western India*, 1638–39, p. 28.
62. Howard Spodek, "Traditional Culture and Entrepreneurship", *Economic and Political Weekly, IV*, February 22, 1969, pp. M27–M31.
63. Makrand Mehta and Yatindra Dixit, "The Mahajans of Gujarat", *India Past and Present*. Vol. II, 1985, pp. 232–33.

64. Alexander Forbes, *Rasmala*, (reprint), New Delhi, 1959, pp. 558-59; Neera Desai, *op. cit.*, pp. 36–37.
65. Maganlal Vakhatchand. *op cit.*, pp. 77–78.
66. E Washburn Hopkins, *India, Old and New*, New York, 1901, p. 176.
67. *Ahmedabad Gazetteer*, p. 107.
68. Hopkins, *op. cit.*, p. 181.
69. *Ahmedabad Gazetteer*, p. 112.
70. Shirin Mehta, "Amdavad Shaherna Mahajano ane Panchoni Utpatti ane Vikas" (in Gujarati), *Arthat*, July–September, 1985, Surat, pp. 40–41.
71. *Ahmedabad Gazetteer*, pp. 107-08.
72. *Ibid.*, pp. 108–10.
73. *Ibid.*, pp. 111–12.
74. Hopkins, *op. cit.*, p. 180.
75. D Tripathi and M Mehta, "The *Nagarsheth* of Ahmedabad: The History of an Urban Institution in a Gujarat City", *Proceedings of the 39th Session of the Indian History Congress*, 1978, pp. 483–90.

2

British Rule in Ahmedabad (1818–1861) Political and Economic Changes

The unfurling of the Union Jack at Bhadra Fort in November 1817 ushered in a new epoch in the history of Ahmedabad. The city's traditional society now made vital contact with the powerful western tradition of their new rulers. The colonial policy of the British changed the pattern of the city's economy, trade, industry and commerce.

Ahmedabad came under British rule not through military conquest, but by virtue of a treaty between the British and the Gaikwads of Baroda. Prior to 1817, the city's revenues had been shared by the Peshwa and the Gaikwad. In June 1817, Peshwa Bajirao II surrendered his share of revenues and administration of Ahmedabad to the Gaikwad in perpetuity under the terms of the Treaty of Poona after the Third Maratha war. The British had by then realised the economic, strategic and political importance of Ahmedabad. Within five months of the Peshwa–Gaikwad treaty, on November 6, 1817, Captain Carnac, the Resident at Baroda, negotiated the Supplementary Treaty of Baroda with the Gaikwad, which ceded the capital city of Ahmedabad, except for the Gaikwad's *haveli*, or royal residence, situated in the south-west of city, to the British. Ahmedabad was ceded in 'payment' for an increased subsidiary force of East India Company troops and in exchange for the *Parganas* of Dabhoi, Bahadurpur and Salvi near Baroda. Later, in June 1818, against strong opposition by the Gaikwad, his *haveli* was also acquired by the British. In this manner, Ahmedabad was acquired by the British.[1]

John Andrew Dunlop, the collector of Kaira, was appointed the first British collector of Ahmedabad. On behalf of the East India Company, he took charge from the Gaikwad's officers on November 30, 1817. He found the city deserted and depopulated, its industries decayed—a mere shadow of its former glory. Dunlop's letter to the Bombay Government, dated December 17, 1817, comments: "The city also presents a melancholy picture of the same ruin as has befallen its wall; large tracts are entirely covered with the remains of houses and religious buildings... These ruins, completely deserted, form abundant retreats for disorderly persons when pursued, and increased very much the difficulties of police arrangements."[2]

The city walls were in such a dilapidated state and so broken that carts and carriages could pass through the gaps, and the walled city was as unsafe as its suburbs. Robberies and murders were common.[3] The officials at Ahmedabad kept complaining about the deteriorating state of the walls to the higher authorities in Bombay. Armed men had to accompany the women dyers of the city when they washed clothes on the banks of the river.[4] Traders were often looted just a few miles away from the city.[5]

Dunlop, not wanting to disrupt or uproot the traditions of the people, was cautious in bringing about change because he respected traditions as long as they did not interfere with British policies. Such an approach made for smooth transition from the older tradition to modernity in Ahmedabad. He wanted to revive this dying city and rejuvenate its declining industries and trade so that it would be a great source of revenue.

I

Ahmedabad city became the headquarters of the district of the same name in the northern division of the Bombay presidency. It became a part of the larger centralised uniform administrative set-up of the British. However, the peculiarities and traditions of each area lent a distinctive character to its administrative pattern. In Ahmedabad, traditional leaders and officials such as the *nagarseth*, the leader of the Hindu community, and *kazi* Mohammad Sale, the traditional officer of law, were highly respected. The British appointed the *kazi,* the law officer, in the *adalat*, or law court, and thus won the support of the traditional elite, who in their turn cooperated with the British in administering the city.

Dunlop's first task was to establish law, order and security. The situation was a trying one, especially as he had not brought with him an adequate force from Kaira. Under such difficult circumstances, he established the police department with the help of the hereditary servants of the previous government.[6] He appointed Gulam Raza, the brother of the *kazi*, as the *faujdar*, or police chief, for a salary of Rs 100.[7] Raza protected the city from the bandits who infested the surrounding countryside and established peace and order in and around the city. The broken walls rendered the city so unsafe that he had to recruit a large police force from among the turbulent tribes of the Kolis and the Rajputs, who consequently were subdued and rehabilitated.[8] They became quite prosperous and began to live in brick houses with tiled roofs.[9] These vigorous police measures enabled the British to establish order as early as 1820. By 1828, gang robberies were far rarer than they used to be, and by 1835, large and fearful raids had almost entirely ceased. By 1839, the district was surprisingly peaceful.[10]

Dunlop wanted to have the city walls repaired as they gave protection to the city and also checked smuggling, but as the repairs entailed heavy expenses, the Bombay government's permission was not forthcoming. The repairs were delayed for more than two decades until finally the expenses of the repairs fell on the people of the city. This resulted in the establishment of the embryonic city municipality.

Bhadra, the traditional administrative nucleus, became the seat of the district administration. The district being the most important unit of the British administrative set-up, the chief public offices of the district were situated within or near Bhadra. For example, Shelulkar's palace in Bhadra Fort was converted into the *adalat* and *padshahi dewankhana* became the collector's *kacheri*, or office. These old buildings, symbols of traditional power, were cleverly used by the new rulers to assert their authority over the people, which had a tremendous impact on the people.

As the collection of revenue was one of the chief functions of the colonial administration, the revenue department became the centre of the administrative machinery. This department, together with the police and judicial departments, constituted the core of the British district administration. The collector was the head of the revenue department as also the head of the district administration. He was assisted by deputy and assistant collectors.

A large judicial department was established under the district judge, who was assisted by the assistant judge, each having jurisdiction over Ahmedabad city and district from 1828 onwards. There were subordinate judges in the district stations of Ahmedabad, Dholka, Viramgam and Dhanduka. There was also a small causes court at Ahmedabad.[11] Criminal justice was administered by the magistrates.

The new administration being qualitatively different from the traditional one which had been based on hereditary offices, customs and usages, Ahmedabad experienced a major structural administrative change. Recruitment of personnel was now on merit and qualification and was non-hereditary, non-caste-based and non-religious.

The legal system in the pre-British period had allowed civil disputes to be decided by the political chief, by *panchayats*, or arbitration, or by the influence of a *bhat* security. The British rulers established a new legal system which was uniform, emphasised the principle of equality before the law, and was based on secular values. Many inhuman social customs were abolished by legislation. The customs of *sati*, slavery and female infanticide were declared illegal. These laws became instruments of social change in Gujarat. In Ahmedabad and elsewhere in Gujarat, the custom of *sati* and slavery had not been major problems, that is, had not been prevalent to a great extent. However, female infanticide was widely practiced among the communities of the Kanbis and the Rajputs of Gujarat and among the Jadejas of Kutch and Saurashtra. For Ahmedabad city and district, Act VIII of 1870 was passed for the prevention of the murder of female infants among the Kanbi castes. This Act decreased the prevailing evil to some extent.[12]

The custom of *bhat* and *charan* security for trade and property transactions regarded as sacrosanct in pre-British Gujarat soon become obsolete and fell into disuse.[13] Ahmedabad bankers, including *nargarseth* Hemabhai Vakhatchand and Hatesingh Kesarising, had to accept the dictates of the new legal administrative codes and laws in place of the dictates of the *bhats* and *charans*.[14]

The British rulers, however, did not want to change deep-rooted institutions and customs and alienate Indian communities. So arbitration by the caste *panchayats* and *mahajans* continued as an indispensable inheritance. This informal system of justice continued in parallel with the formal courts of law that dispensed justice according to western legal principles. Though a written award made by a *panchayat* could not be set aside summarily by a legal officer, a disputant was at liberty to appeal to a higher court if he had reason to believe that he had been denied justice. Reports of civil cases determined in the court of *sudder dewanee adalat* of Bombay, Surat and Ahmedabad between 1820–1848 reveal that the statute law took precedence over the Hindu law or the Muslim law whenever verdicts conflicted. However, before a decision was made, the caste customs and *shastrees* were consulted in cases involving the Hindus, while the *kazis* were consulted for Muslim civil cases. Not wanting to alienate Hindus or Muslim, the British respected their laws in matters of marriage, property and inheritance. As a result, the usage of both systems led to a certain ambivalence. The traditional system which was sometimes arbitrary and non-egalitarian undermined the British concept of equality before law and uniformity of law. The collectors and magistrates of Ahmedabad district were advised to be acquainted with Hindu and Mohammedan law.[15] In a particular case of adultery, collector Dunlop was advised by the Governor-in-council to comply with the caste rules.[16]

It is interesting to examine some actual cases decided by the *sudder dewanee adalat* which show the acceptance of indigenous law in British courts. Although not all the cases given below pertain to Ahmedabad, they show the legal and secular trends which were also developing in Ahmedabad.

In Ahmedabad, an interesting case arose in 1827, a Muslim girl named Huleema refused to marry a man named Kureem Jeewan to whom she was betrothed in childhood. Kureem Jeewan appeared in the court against Huleema, her mother and her associates. The *kazi* was consulted and a judgement given that a girl who had reached the age of puberty was at liberty to marry whom she pleased.[17]

Caste elders were often consulted by the courts before reaching decisions regarding marriage, divorce, property and other such matters. Another interesting case in Surat in the year 1842 reveals that the court upheld the decisions of the caste *panchayat*. In this case, Bai Khushalee of the Kadia (bricklayer) caste was expelled from the caste for "loss" of character; she had left her husband to live with a Muslim man. As the decision to expel her had been taken by the caste body and not motivated by malice tempered with violence, the courts refrained from interfering.[18]

In the initial stage of the establishment of the western justice system, the people of Ahmedabad preferred the indigenous judicial methods and avoided litigation. As a result, many civil and personal disputes were arbitrated by caste *panchayats* and *mahajans* in Ahmedabad.

Another remarkable blending of the old and the new is seen in the workings of the municipality of Ahmedabad. This body had originated as the Town Wall Fund Committee, formed primarily to repair the dilapidated walls of the city in April 1831. It consisted of five members—the collector, the judge of Ahmedabad, the collector of sea customs, the *nagarseth* and the *kazi*. It had been set up to repair the city walls and thereby ensure the security of Ahmedabad's citizens. In a sense, this Committee was legitimately the direct ancestor of the present-day municipality of Ahmedabad.[19]

The establishment of the municipality reveals how the traditional urban elite—businessmen and officials such as the *nagarseth* and the *kazi* who had played significant civic roles in pre-British times—were now oriented by the British to perform equally important civil tasks within the framework of the new local government. It also shows the alien ruler's respect for the elite and for the traditions of the city. Perhaps it was because of these significantly diplomatic shows of respect that the traditional leaders soon adapted themselves to their new roles.

In order to meet the expense of repairs to the town walls, the leading men of the city had agreed to the imposition of a voluntary tax in the form of town duties on certain items such as ghee, raw silk, sugar, jaggery and cotton cloth.[20] The repairs were completed by 1842. The government suggested that the enhanced duties be continued in order to provide for other improvements to the city. On this, it sought the opinion of the city leaders and the heads of the principal castes and traders, which it received in a letter signed by 43 influential men including the *nagarseth* and the *kazi*.[21] They agreed to the government's suggestion on continuing the duties and also expressed their wishes on how the funds should be expended. Thus, from 1846 onwards, the Committee undertook municipal functions such as the watering of city streets, removing filth and constructing a *dharmashala* at Vithalpura and a grain market. The Committee also maintained fire engines, illuminated some of the main streets, and built privies. In 1857, the Committee also engaged 400 watchmen to help the police to protect the city.[22] This continued until 1858.

The year 1858 witnessed the end of the Town Wall Fund Committee. In its place was established the municipal commission, a prototype of a municipality along modern lines, with a well-defined constitution and powers by virtue of Act XXVI of 1850, styled "an Act to enable improvements to be made in Towns". A petition dated August 10, 1852 was presented to the government for the application of Act XXVI of 1850 to their city by 269 leading men of Ahmedabad.[23] Bureaucratic delays and the outbreak of the 1857 war of independence postponed the establishment of the municipal commission to 1858. In this municipal commission, the members of the newly emerging middle class and government officials, both European and Indian, in addition to the traditional elite were included. Various castes, creeds and occupational groups came together, giving rise to new social and political relationships among the citizens of Ahmedabad. Significantly, this was the first town in the Bombay presidency where local people voluntarily came forward to tax themselves in order to provide civil amenities.

In the beginning, the British government continued many old privileges such as the traditional offices and those related to religious institutions. Even the pensions and charitable allowances to individuals and religious shrines started by the Muslim and the Maratha rulers continued. The *padshahi dewan* Ali Mahmud Khan continued his claim of three-quarter per cent on goods imported into and exported from the city. The *nagarseth* of the city, the chief of merchants, had been collecting an *ad valorem* fee of a quarter per cent on the octroi revenues since 1725. The British government converted both these claims into annual pensions in 1819. These and other allowances were continued in the form of fixed cash allowances which helped the government in systematising the octroi collection.[24] The British government liberally continued the allowances and privileges of the individuals and institution of *panjrapol*, Natwarji, Shyamji and other temples and the institution of *lungarkhana* of Sultan Ahmed Shah Pir at Ahmedabad. All these amounted to a total expenditure of Rs 37,905–1–05.[25] The *lungarkhana* provided 41 individuals with monthly allowances, which the government continued by giving a sum of Rs 2,894–7–3 annually from the collector's treasury.[26] The *kazi* of the city received two shawls each for Bakri Eid and Ramzan Eid, for which the British government agreed to spend Rs 150 from the treasury. The British government also gave annual allowances to both the

Hindus and the Muslims to celebrate festivals like Eid, Dussera, Ramnavami, Shivratri and Janmashtami. As mentioned earlier, the *nagarseth* and the *kazi* were respected by the British officials and were appointed to all the important government committees set up to deal with city matters. Both these persons acted as spokesmen for their communities and as mediators between the government and their people. Thus, the government not only was able to gauge public sentiments and feelings from them but gained their invaluable support when needed. Until 1842, the British were liberal in continuing their allowances, but in 1842, the collector was directed by the governor-in-council to seek his sanction before renewing the allowances and pensions.[27]

Once securely established, the British government in 1850 authorised the collector to strike off the list those pensions and charitable allowances which had not been claimed for five years and also all hereditary allowances not claimed for ten years.[28] After the enactment of Act XIX of 1844, many hereditary privileges and traditional usages were discontinued. The rights of *marphatias*, the intermediaries between the merchants and the government, ceased to exist. Their petition was turned down.[29] The *nagarseth's* right to import goods duty-free for his own consumption was disallowed; so were the exemptions given to the Vaishnav gurus and the institution of Jain *panjrapol*.[30]

In the initial stage, however, the British by and large made efforts not to disrupt the traditional power structure and not to alienate the traditional leaders and communities. They understood the mercantile character of the city and sought the cooperation of the traditional business leaders in administering the city.

Thus, it is not surprising that the people of the city initially considered the British as the saviours who had freed them from the Maratha tyranny. The emerging western educated middle class and the mercantile community of Ahmedabad found British rule to be the most benign and progressive rule in the history of the city. British rulers had assured them of law, order and the security of person and property, thus gaining the loyal support of the citizens.

In 1851, the chronicler Maganlal Vakhatchand, who wrote *Amdavad no Itihas* praising the rule of the British, described the British regime as *Ram Rajya*. Another historian, Edalji Dosabhai, a student of the Government English School in Ahmedabad who wrote *Gujarat no Itihas* in 1850, hailed the British government as *Dayalu Sarkar*, or kind government, and praised the security they had established. He wrote that under British Rule "the tiger and the goat drink together at the same waterhole."[31] Dalpatram, editor of a leading periodical *Buddhi Prakash*, eulogised the British regime in his poems and articles. The loyalist feelings of the people are illustrated by the fact that when the Crimean war was being fought in West Asia, the leading citizens of the city raised "patriotic funds" in 1855, collecting at the end of one public meeting a sum of Rs 5,375 to help the British.[32]

Even during the upheaval of 1857, businessmen and the nascent middle class demonstrated the same loyalty. This revolt was not a major event in the history of Ahmedabad since the city was not affected. When mutineers blocked the Indore–Mhow road, stopping the mail from Indore and Ratlam to Ahmedabad, it was Hemabhai Nagarseth who communicated the news of the mutiny to British officials four days before the government despatch agency brought the news to Ahmedabad. He also helped the government to get information from Central India through a private dak, or postal, service during the entire period of the mutiny. The nagarseth's service was greatly appreciated by the local British officials.[33] Another such instance was that of Bechardas Lashkari, a leading businessman who gave financial help to the Europeans trapped in Ahmedabad during the mutiny.[34]

The upheaval of 1857 convinced the intellectual elite that British rule was beneficial to the people of India. In the personal diary of Bholanath Sarabhai, a note dated May 23, 1857, expressed the hope that the final outcome of this conflict would be in favour of the British. According to him, British rule was the best of all previous regimes.[35] The periodical *Buddhi Prakash* also reflected similar sentiment. It hoped that the British would remain forever in India.[36]

When, in 1858, the British crown took over the administration of India from the East India Company, Dalpatram sang praises of Queen Victoria in his famous poem "Victoria Ranina Chhand", which includes these lines: "Long live Queen Victoria: We all are happy and jubilant to have now a wonderful regime of the Queen. We pray to God that her rule will last forever".[37]

The city's businessmen also celebrated the advent of crown rule. Seth Maganbhai Karamchand, on November 8, 1858, gave a big feast to the European officers and the leading men of the city to celebrate Queen Victoria's rule. Later Sethani Harkunvar, the widow of Hatesingh Kesarising, also gave a feast in her *haveli* to the *sahibs*. This was a formative period in which the local roots of the moderate and loyalist political culture of Ahmedabad were developed. In fact, this loyalist stance set the tone of the political culture of the city. There was no mass revolt in Ahmedabad against the British rule in the 19th century. In 1844, while the city of Surat reacted sharply to the increased tax on salt and resorted to mass agitations and protests across caste and class divisions, the city of Ahmedabad resorted to the politics of petitions. In 1844, when the government of the Bombay presidency was mooting a house tax to raise funds for town improvement schemes, the people of Ahmedabad protested by sending a petition to the government which was signed by the *nagarseth* and 2,145 other inhabitants of the city on September 23, 1844.[38]

The imperial strategy had thus shown excellent results. The British, by strengthening the traditional mercantile community and bolstering the emerging middle class, had successfully made them the instruments through which they themselves could function.

II

The city's trade and industries had suffered a setback during the turbulent times of the 18th century, but its indigenous civic and business institutions such as the *mahajans*, the *nagarseth* and the family and partnership firms, called *pedhis*, had survived and remained intact. A large numbers of artisans continued manufacturing various textiles and other goods and were organised into guilds.

Tired of the Maratha rule which had interfered with their business and property matters, the businessmen of Ahmedabad welcomed the new legal administrative measures which established peace, security, law and order in the city. The strict police measures freed the city and its neighbourhood from robberies. Pax Britannica and collector Dunlop's measures to remove vexatious duties on trade stimulated trade and commerce. Dunlop also wanted to encourage the indigenous crafts of Ahmedabad, not only to bring back to the city its past glory but also to bring considerable profit to the East India Company, as there was great demand for these products in European markets. During the Muslim rule, the town duties were five per cent for the Hindus and 2.5 per cent for the Muslims. After the Marathas took over the city, the town duties were raised and reached a high level when, in 1755, the Peshwa and the Gaikwad divided the city revenues between them. Each government collected a share through its own agents and constantly introduced fresh exactions. The system of rates was intentionally kept as complicated and as secret as possible, resulting in the rise of an intermediate class of persons known as *marphatias* who tried to understand the rates and conducted the transactions for the merchants. They asked for a percentage for themselves which increased the intricacies of their mode of collection. Every luxury or necessity from the *kinkhab* to a humble bundle of firewood or even greens, either brought into or sent out of the city was subjected to the imposition of this system. A small toll was exacted at every *chowkee* on the way to the market. Raw materials needed for manufacture were also charged import duties. Manufactured silk, before being exported, had already paid a fourth of its selling price, while the average burden on other manufactured exports was estimated at 20 per cent. Even necessities like vegetables and fruits attracted a duty of 15 to 20 per cent on entry.[39]

Dunlop, the first collector, found these heavy town duties an impediment to the growth of trade and manufacture in the city.

He had observed that traders evaded these duties and resorted to smuggling. *Kinkhab* was the staple product of the place, but the duty actually paid was only on Rs 10,000 worth of *kinkhab*, whereas the real value of the *kinkhab* manufactured in the city was about Rs 1,64,305.[40] In October 1819, Dunlop took the liberal step of reducing town duty on all items except opium, ganja and salt to 2.5 per cent from the previous 15 to 20 per cent in order to revive the city's trade and manufacture. He abolished all duties on the raw materials needed for manufacture.

The British rulers created certain infrastructural administrative facilities which also provided a stimulus to trade. The district *dak*, or postal service, established in April 1841, was used substantially by the mercantile community of Ahmedabad.[41] Other facilities like rest houses, drinking water facilities for caravans and police *thanas* on the main trade routes gave a boost to trade. Post, and later telegraphic facility in the 1850s, linked Ahmedabad with other parts of India and traders soon realised the importance of this new communication network.

All these infrastructural facilities, trade concessions and the peace and order gave an impetus to the economic activities of the city. As early as 1820, Dunlop wrote to Bombay that, in spite of the adverse economic conditions, "the people have been saved from the most deplorable distress and starvation. There was enough work for weavers who otherwise would have been thrown out of employment".[42] He added that trade had increased from the previous year, 1818–19, by Rs 24,51,280.[43] The import of raw silk increased more than three-fold, from 300 *maunds* to 1000 *maunds*, in that year. In 1830, Dunlop, then the revenue commissioner of the northern division of the Bombay presidency wrote in his observations on the circuit that the liberal steps of the district government had excited a spirit of commercial activity and enterprise scarcely to be surpassed. The surrounding countryside also benefited, and the cultivators' favourite expression was "we live upon Ahmedabad".

When the British took over Ahmedabad, the city had been depopulated and deurbanised. Many silk manufacturers and other

1. Bhadra Fort

2. Jama Masjid

3. Parwadi in the Pol

4. Hemabhai Nagarseth

5. Hatesingh Kesarising

6. Maganbhai Karamchand

artisans had left the city as they had not received encouragement from the previous rulers. Since 1817, the population slowly increased in the city. As early as 1820, Dunlop wrote in his report, "Many families of merchants and manufacturers who had quitted the place have returned and the population has obviously increased considerably, though many of the military classes who do not find much encouragement under our government have gone to seek employment elsewhere."[44] As trade revived and weaving industries in silk, *kinkhab* and cotton textile thrived, many artisans immigrated to the city. Dunlop, in his Commissioner's Report of 1830 wrote that around 2,000 manufacturing families had settled in the city according to the estimate given by the *sethias* of the city.[45] Khatri weavers from Patan and Kanbis of the Kadi region immigrated to Ahmedabad.[46] Cultivators and artisans from the Gaikwad's state and other native states also flocked to Ahmedabad district to avoid the oppressive treatment by native princes.[47] The steady increase in the population was due to the revival of trade and indigenous industries. The waves of urbanisation became stronger after the industrialisation of the city, especially after the arrival of the railways.

Under Dunlop, the city thrived and prospered and its population increased. Dunlop took pride in the fact that he had transformed a declining city into a prosperous one. The thriving and flourishing condition of the city and its economy described in official reports is just one part of the picture. On the basis of these official reports, Kenneth L Gillion, the urban historian of Ahmedabad, has exaggerated the role of the British in reviving this decaying city's trade and industries.[48] He has overlooked the fact that the apparent prosperity of the city was only skin-deep and benefited a few traders. By and large, the city was gradually adversely affected by the capitalistic colonial policy of the British. In fact, "the colonial character of the British Raj arrested the urban economic potentialities and traditions of Ahmedabad to make a meaningful transition into the modern industrial stage." "Very few contemporaries noticed how the city, though seemingly glittering, was developing scars".[49] There was, however, no immediate dislocation in the economy. Though indigenous industries survived until the end of the 19th century, it cannot be denied that Ahmedabad's economy bore the brunt of imperial colonial capitalism. Gradually, the growth of indigenous industries was arrested as a result of the British government's policy of allowing unrestrained imports of cheap machine-made English goods. Artisans, in particular, underwent rapid impoverishment in the later part of the 19th century.

It was a part of the colonial policy of the British government from the very beginning to encourage the cultivation of raw materials like cotton and indigo to feed their cotton mills and other industries. It was with this end in view that the British government helped to set up experimental farms to develop better varieties of cotton and other raw materials. As early as 1818, Dr Gilder was given permission to cultivate bourbon cotton. For that purpose, he was given a part of Shahibag in the vicinity of the city.[50] But the experiment did not prove successful and had to be given up.[51] Again, in 1823, John Vaupell of the commercial firm Messrs Gilder, D'Souza & Co. also attempted indigo cultivation for the European markets and was able to manufacture indigo of a superior quality. However, the people of the city were averse to the destruction of insects this method involved, which was against Jain doctrines, and the experiment had to be abandoned.[52] Vaupell also prepared a report on the prospects of manufacturing saltpetre as an exportable commodity in the district of Ahmedabad.[53] Later, in the early 1830s, Heerabag was leased rent-free to Dr Johnson, the district surgeon, to conduct experiments in cultivating bourbon cotton, fruits, mulberry plants, potato and tobacco of the Persian and American quality. He was given financial help to carry out the experiments. He laid out extensive mulberry plantations for sericulture and introduced a new item, the potato, to the Ahmedabadi palate.[54] The cultivation of cotton increased in the district as it was gaining a firmer footing in the European market. As a result, many business agencies were established to purchase and ship cotton for the use of Glasgow and Manchester.[55] In 1851, cotton experiments were started in the district of Ahmedabad by the British, under Price who was appointed superintendent of cotton experiments. To facilitate the export of cotton, gin sheds for cleaning cotton were set up. In three years, Price was able to sell 13 gins to local parties.[56] Daley, who succeeded him, found people enthusiastic about the gin mills.[57] It is interesting to note that Ranchhodlal Chhotalal, the founder of the first textile mill in Ahmedabad, bought 20 saw-gins from Daley in 1858 to set them up in Viramgam because he wanted to control the cotton market.[58] Thus, the city and its hinterland were reorienting their trade and cultivation pattern to feed raw materials to British industries.

In 1818, the very first year of British rule in Ahmedabad, the city witnessed an influx of textile goods made in England. In the course of time, the import of foreign goods increased to a great extent. Dr Gilder, a senior partner of the firm Messrs Gilder, D'Souza & Co., introduced European Medappllam and yarns into this part of Gujarat, which dealt the deathblow to the manufacturing interests of the country. It is significant to note that English textiles and yarn were known as *docteri* in the Ahmedabad bazar.[59] Dunlop wrote to Bombay on August 29, 1820, "Government will be gratified to learn that about Rs 25,000 worth of the quantity (imported cloth) was of British manufacture which is quite a new article in the trade of the place."[60] On July 20, 1830, Dunlop, who had then become the commissioner of the northern division, wrote a letter to Bombay in which he gave statistics of thread imported in the city (Table 2.1).

Table 2.1: Amount of Thread Imported into Ahmedabad (in rupees)

Type of Thread	Samvat 1877–79	Samvat 1880–82
Country thread	31,704	20,797
European thread	23,505	56,340

These statistics reveal that the import of European yarn more than doubled in the period mentioned. The demand for country yarn continued only because the European thread could not be used in making *mashru* cloth.[61] Fortunately, the demand for *kinkhab* silk and printed cotton cloth in the local and outside market continued and, as a result, the indigenous textile industry was not immediately dislocated. However, cheapness of the European cloth had increased its popularity. Fawcett, the collector, wrote in 1849 in his report, "Weaving is at present very little resorted to as an employment to what it used to be, owing to the large importation of English cloths, which almost entirely superseded the Native manufacture, except dongaree of coarse description".[62] He further wrote:

> The manufacture of thread in England has materially tended to depress the condition of the poor classes so that they earn a very precarious livelihood. At the present time it is far cheaper to get English yarn of long cloth than to get the thread and coarse cloth, the manufacture of the country. The native looms are now used for working on such cloth as is suited to the poor classes.[63]

Spinning cotton thread had long been a source of livelihood for women, an important home industry. There was a popular Gujarati proverb: "*Bapni punji ma na samay te mana rentiima samay*"—a person may not get support from the capital of his rich father but may be easily supported by the spinning wheel of his poor mother. The import of European yarn must have dealt a blow to many poor women, especially widows who supported themselves on the spinning wheel. Muslim women especially suffered as they were not allowed to go out of their houses to earn a livelihood but were only allowed to work at home, where they had engaged in spinning cotton thread.[64]

However, the influx of machine-made English goods, especially textiles, did not immediately affect the well-established textile industry of Ahmedabad. Its branches withstood foreign competition until as late as the 1850s, and the indigenous textile industry even lingered on until the beginning of the 20th century.

As we saw earlier, the silk and *kinkhab* industries had declined during the turbulent 18th century but were revived by the liberal British taxation policies.

In 1818, 300 *mans* of raw silk was imported, rising to 1,000 Indian *mans* in 1820 and reaching 2,955 *mans* in 1847. But after that, it steadily declined. The decline of the demand for silks and *kinkhabs* was ascribed to the changing fashions among the rich who took to Chinese silk.[65] Also, the deposition of the Peshwa led to the decline of the *kinkhab* trade. The demand from the Gaikwad and the native kings and nobles for silk and *kinkhab* also declined. Since 1820, the Government of Persian Gulf changed its policy and stopped the import of *mashru* and *chintz*.[66] Though the foreign trade in brocade declined, the product maintained its popularity among Indian people well into the early 20th century. The *kinkhabs* and silks of Ahmedabad were celebrated for their durability and bright colours and remained in demand in Baroda, Poona, Gwalior, Bombay, Sindh, Saurashtra, China, Thailand, Iran and Afghanistan. *Kinkhab* and silk textiles of Ahmedabad were thus less vulnerable to English competition.

The local chronicler of Ahmedabad, Maganlal Vakhatchand, has given a detailed description of the various local indigenous manufactures of 1850 and observes that the indigenous textile industry and trade were prosperous at this time. The weaving of different kinds of textiles continued in and around the city. The excessive use of *docteri sutar*, a machine-made imported yarn, enabled the weaving of a superior quality of cloth.

Various traders like *tagias* (silk dealers) traded in raw materials for the industry. *Kinkhab* and *mashru* (cloth with cotton weft and silk warp) required tremendous division of labour and specialised skill to bring out the final product. The *tagias* imported the silk into Ahmedabad, gave it to Ahmedabad workmen, paid them for their labour and sold the finished goods.[67] Maganlal Vakhatchand observed that the final product of *mashru* required the skill of 30 different artisans. Around 1850, there were around 300 shops selling *mashru*, 275 shops selling products of silk and brocade, 300 shops dealing in coarse *dhotis*, *thepadas* and other coarse cloth, 50 shops dealing with turban weaving, 50 shops selling *sapeti*, a superior *dhoti* with a silk border, and 60 shops selling superior quality sarees. Also, there were many establishments selling *khadi*, cotton *sarees*, durries, and other textiles. The picture which emerges from this description shows that the indigenous textile industry was still not dead in Ahmedabad, though it had suffered a definite setback.[68]

The same picture reveals, interestingly enough, that the handloom weavers of coarse cloth were not affected by foreign competition. HG Briggs, a British traveller, observed that in Gujarat the poorer class preferred to purchase local products, however inferior and proportionately expensive they may be to European fabrics.[69]

The cotton textile industry was not the only manufacturing sector which received a severe blow from the influx of European textiles. The colonial policy of the British to allow unrestrained import of cheap machine-made English goods also arrested the growth of various indigenous industries. Blacksmiths, printers, paper manufacturers all experienced rapid impoverishment. By 1848, the indigo manufactures of Ahmedabad ceased doing business, despite the fact that a number of villages within ten miles of the city had indigo vats. [70]

The indigenous paper industry also suffered a setback due to large imports of machine-made English paper. The city had a large paper manufacturing industry which gave employment to about 800 people, including women. The art of making paper was a particular craft of Muslim artisans known as *kagdis*. This artisan community consisted of Sayeds, Pathans, Sheikhs and Mirzas.[71] The Bohras traded in paper and had 10 to 15 warehouses in the Kalupur area of the city where they sorted, tied and packed the paper.[72] Ahmedabad had been reputed for its glossy and white paper. At one time, paper was exported to Kutch, Kathiawad, Baroda State and Malwa. Briggs wrote in 1848 that *kagdis* earned handsome dividends as their paper was used for the government stamp, but this practice was later stopped.[73]

This flourishing industry succumbed to the *laissez faire* principles of the alien government. To withstand foreign competition, the indigenous paper manufactures introduced some time and labour-saving innovations in the 1840s so that four men's work could be done by one man in the same time.[74] In spite of this, the paper industry deteriorated rapidly after 1870 and completely lost its importance by the end of the 19th century.

Blacksmiths who manufactured hardware like nails, screws, hinges, locks and building material had to face foreign competition and suffered badly.

Shops selling European goods mushroomed in the city. Many shops of *vilayati* cloth and *docteri* yarn were established.[75] The Parsis set up shops selling European articles such as guns, wines and spirits, cloth and hardware. Briggs saw a large shop selling European manufactured goods at Karanj.[76] Thus, Ahmedabad, in keeping with other traditional urban centres of Gujarat, experienced the strain produced by the capitalist colonial policy of the British in the 19th century. Gradually, the influx of foreign goods corroded indigenous industries and many industries declined and gradually disappeared because they did not receive any protection and encouragement from the alien rulers.

To combat foreign competition, some innovations in production were introduced by enterprising artisans and merchants in the 1840s. As observed earlier, innovations were made in the manufacture of paper by some *kagdis*. One Bohra merchant developed a new process for weaving *mashru* which resulted in a better quality product. Again, to increase yarn production, an indigenous cotton spinning machine was invented. Unfortunately, the yarn it produced tended to break off during the process of manufacturing. Maganlal Vakhatchand wrote in 1851 that efforts were being made to remove these defects.[77] The climate of enterprise which still existed in Ahmedabad was manifested in these innovative measures which were noted by contemporary chroniclers.

III

One of the important reasons why Ahmedabad could withstand foreign competition in the early colonial phase was the poor transport and road system that existed in Gujarat in this pre-railway period. Ahmedabad being located at a great distance from the sea, the intensity of the colonial capitalism of the conquerors was not felt too strongly by the city in this early phase. The influx of foreign goods increased only after the railway line came to Ahmedabad and the grip of colonial capitalism tightened.

Fawcett, a collector, wrote in 1849, "Little has been done in road-making except in Ahmedabad and its immediate vicinity. The longest of these extends from the city to the camp for about four miles." He adds, "The roads through the country are merely the tracks formed by the carts passing." The general means of transport were carts drawn by bullocks, camels and pack bullocks, while during the monsoon, traffic was suspended as the roads become unusable.[78] Nothing was done to improve land communication until 1850. Later, some improvement was made in land transport and communication to facilitate the movement of raw cotton from the interiors to the ports where ships sailed for England. The British also increased port facilities and spent large government sums and local funds on building roads leading to ports. A road was built from port Ghoga via Dhanduka to Ahmedabad, which facilitated trade tremendously. A road also joined Ahmedabad to Viramagam via Sarkhej.

Enthusiastic officials like Captain George Fulljames initiated a project to construct a tramway between Dholera town and its port in 1851. It was "the first specimen of railway".[79] It was a private enterprise in which two Europeans, Major Fulljames and Major Wallace, and the capitalists of Ahmedabad, including Premabai Hemabhai, Maganlal Karamchand, Umabhai Rupchand, invested a capital of about Rs 70,000. The company finally expanded this to Rs 74,600 for construction. But since little or no profit accrued to the company while the expenses of maintenance continued to rise, the capitalists of Ahmedabad, in the absence of European entrepreneurs and their guidance, decided to close down the company in 1857.[80] This only goes to show that if guided properly, the merchants of Ahmedabad were open to new avenues for the investment of their capital.

The traders of Ahmedabad reoriented their commercial activities to utilise the new opportunities generated by the British regime. Many of the highly respected merchants in pre-British times had financed princes and armies and maintained branches in Delhi and Pune, which were then the seats of government. Since the establishment of British rule, many of these capitalists diverted their capital to the lucrative opium trade. The capital employed in the opium trade assumed "such dimension that in one year they are said to have netted a crore of rupees".[81] In 1849, Rs 50 lakh were invested in this trade.[82] This amount was much larger than the five or six lakh rupees employed in the cotton export trade. Until the 1850s, the opium trade remained a source of wealth for the Ahmedabad merchants, after which it shifted to Viragam, Sidhpur and other towns of Baroda State.

The merchants of Ahmedabad became involved in the opium trade as early as 1818, supplying huge amounts of opium to the East India Company.[83] In 1830, John Dunlop in his Commissioner's Report observed that the opium trade had lately increased tremendously, but he also lamented that a great portion of this trade was illicitly carried on through non-British ports such as the Portuguese port of Daman. He complained that instead of selling Malwa's opium to Bombay merchants, the merchants of Ahmedabad exported opium on their own account, thus reducing government profit in opium.[84] Most of the merchants of Ahmedabad had agents or branches of their firms in Malwa who procured opium for them. This was sent on camel pack from Palee via Jaisalmer to Karachi and Daman. The illicit trade in opium assumed such a regular and established character that, in 1829, 7,000 boxes were sent from Daman to China.[85] In 1843, about 14,000 boxes were exported from Daman after Sindh was captured by the British and the earlier opium smuggling route via Jaisalmer to Sindh was abandoned.[86] The most extensive dealers in the opium trade were nagarseth Hemabhai Vakhatchand, Maganbhai Karamchand and Hatesingh Kesarising, all of whom amassed great wealth. Hatesingh Kesarising was a Shravak Vania. He was the son-in-law of Hemabhai Nagarseth. His father traded in raw silk and textiles. His broker at Bombay was Motisha Seth, who asked Hatesingh's uncle to procure opium for China to be exported from Daman on their own account and consequently made a good fortune.[87] Opium trade thus helped the merchants of Ahmedabad to amass great wealth. The capital formation for the future machine-operated textile industry was to a great extent generated by this lucrative opium trade.

When the opium trade lost its lustre after 1850, the pragmatic merchants of Ahmedabad diverted their attention to the cotton trade. Raw cotton became the chief item of trade in the latter half of the 19th century. Its demand increased in England in order to feed her textile mills. The merchants of Ahmedabad acted as agents in the purchase of cotton for firms in Bombay and at times speculated in that item on their own account. Many bought saw-gins to clean the raw cotton for export. Thus, the trade of Ahmedabad merchants was shaped by colonial and imperial needs.

At the same time, the trading in textile continued and many merchants carried on with the indigenous system of banking and insurance. The economic institutions of the pre-British period continued during this phase. The pattern of commerce, trade and industry did not undergo many changes. The *mahajan's* and *nagarseth's* arbitration in trade disputes continued. Though the company rupee was introduced in 1837, the first bank was set up in Ahmedabad only in 1862. The uniform currency introduced by the British facilitated trade and commerce.

To summarise, although Ahmedabad had become a victim of the colonial system, the grip of colonial economy was not viciously tight on this interior city during the pre-railway period. As a result, its indigenous industries were not immediately dislocated. The lucrative opium and cotton trade, initiated by imperial needs, made some of the merchants of Ahmedabad very rich. The trade of the city had picked up under liberal tax measures. Consequently, the city not merely survived but also prospered.

One indication of this prosperity was that people built better houses. In 1847, there were 32,322 houses in the city, of which only 784 were thatched houses and the rest had tiled roofs. Edalji Dosabhai, a contemporary historian, wrote in 1850 that even the common man was building a good house.[88] Another contemporary historian, Maganlal Vakhatchand, writing in 1851 observed that people were extending their houses and were even adding upper stories. Some of the new houses were built in the English style with glass or Venetian windows. Such houses were furnished with Chinese curios and western furniture.[89] The wealthy merchants built 'ornamental' garden houses in the 'European style' in the vicinity of the walled city. Hatesingh Kesarising had built a large European style mansion with western style furniture just outside Delhi gate at a cost of one lakh rupees. He also began building a Jain temple near his house. There was a *dharmshala* and other buildings in the establishment which was known as Hathipura. Maganbhai Karamchand, *nagarseth* Hemabhai, Lalhubhai Panachand also built garden houses in and around the city in the 1840s.[90]

The rich who had hidden their wealth during the Maratha regime now became fearless and began to display it. As a result, many prosperous men of the city, as collector Fawcett wrote in 1849, "set up carriages, and several have built country houses, and enjoyed themselves in the ease and comfort which characterizes a peaceful and civilized life".[91] Maganlal wrote that those people who had been wearing dirty coarse clothes in the time of the Marathas, now wore finer and cleaner clothes. He added that the city looked brighter with well-dressed people. Maganlal also noted the change in the style of clothing. He said that many western fashions of the *sahib* were adopted, and a section of the people even wore socks and waistcoats in winter.[92]

Rich merchants built temples, *vadis* (caste lodges) and *dharamashalas* (rest houses) to gain merit in traditional society. However, they also gave rich donations to build schools, colleges and hospitals and won the government's acclaim in the form of awards and titles. Maganbhai Karamchand, the prosperous merchant, built a big *vadi* for his caste in Shahapur in 1839.[93] He also built an Ashtapadji temple in 1816 in Dosiwada *pol* at the huge cost of Rs 65,000.[94] The same Maganbhai generously donated Rs 20,000 for the cause of female education. Similarly, Harkunvar Sethani, widow of Hatesingh, completed building the grand Jain temple, the construction of which was started by her husband, outside Delhi gate at the cost of Rs 10 lakh. She also gave generously to a girls' school and a hospital. Thus, charities to traditional and modern institutions by the same person were quite a common phenomenon.

During this period, *vadis* and *dharamashalas* built by rich merchants and caste guilds proliferated. This reveals the prosperity of the city. The *tanias* (gold thread drawers), *mashruvalas* (*mashru* dealers), *tagias*, *gajanivalas* (silk weavers) not only built and maintained *vadis* but also kept *sadavrats*, or alm houses, which distributed uncooked food to the poor. However, by 1879 some of these *sadavrats* were closed down owing to the declining trade of the donors.[95] Even the *kadias* (brick-layers), *suthars* (carpenters), *luhars* (blacksmiths), *kandois* (sweetmeat makers), *mochis* (cobblers), *golas* (labourers), and *ghanchis* who enjoyed prosperity during this period, built their *vadis*.

While the merchants of Ahmedabad and their *pedhis* continued the traditional pattern of commerce, trade and industry, a young Nagar Brahmin administrator, hailing from Ahmedabad, perceived the challenge posed by the colonial policy of the British. This young man was Ranchhodlal Chhotalal, who, since 1847, had made efforts to start a textile mill in the city.

His efforts bore fruit in 1859 when he established his first mill in Ahmedabad.

Notes

1. Bombay Government, *Gazetteer of the Bombay Presidency*, Vol. IV, *Ahmedabad*, Bombay, 1879, henceforth cited as Ahmedabad Gazetteer, p. 260
2. Revenue Department, 125/1818, p. 40.
3. *Ahmedabad Gazetteer*, pp. 267–68.
4. Judicial Department, 105/1818, p. 2685.
5. Revenue Department, 126/1818, p. 650.
6. Revenue Department, 303/1817, pp. 43–48, 254.
7. Revenue Department, 125/1818, pp. 44–45.
8. Judicial Department, 105/1818, pp. 2680–8.
9. Judicial Department, 3/3/1821–23, pp. 21–32.
10. *Ahmedabad Gazetteer*, pp. 196–97.
11. *Ibid.*, p. 192.
12. *Ibid.*, p. 195
13. Revenue Department, 6/138/1826, not paged: EG Fawcett, "Report on the Collectorate of Ahmedabad". 1849, Selections from the Records of the Bombay Government, Vol. V, new series, Bombay, 1854, p. 88. Henceforth cited as *Fawcett's Report*.
14. Makrand Mehta, 'Ranchhodlal Chhotalal and the Ahmedabad Cotton Textile Industry – A study in Entrepreneurial History' Doctoral Thesis, Gujarat University, 1979, p. 29.
15. Judicial Department, 120/1820, p. 1372.
16. *Ibid.*, p. 1577.
17. Bombay Government, *Reports of selected cases decided by Sudder Dewanee Adalat*, Bombay, 1862 Case No. 16, pp. 60–65.
18. AF Bellasis, *Reports of Civil Cases Determined in the court of Sudder Dewanee Adalat of Bombay*, 1840–48, Bombay, 1850, Case No. 1894, pp. 25–32.
19. BK Boman Behram, (Ed.), *The Rise of Municipal Government in the City of Ahmedabad*, Bombay, 1937, p. 69.
20. *Ibid.*, pp. 77–89.
21. General Department, 85/1846, p 191, quoted in Boman Behram, *op.cit.*, p. 149.
22. Boman Behram, *op.cit*, p. XXV.

23. Quoted in Boman Behram. *op. cit.*, pp. 74–75.
24. Revenue Department, 137/1819, pp. 1154–56.
25. Revenue Department, 21/153/1826, p. 179.
26. *Fawcett's Report*, p. 73.
27. Revenue Department, 26/1359/1842, p. 179.
28. Revenue Department, 44/1855, p. 7.
29. Revenue Department, 163/1854, p. 89.
30. *Ibid.*, pp. 61–66 and pp. 85–86.
31. Edalji Dosabhai, *Gujarat no Itihas* (in Gujarati), Ahmedabad, 1850, p. 26.
32. *Buddhi Prakash*, February 1855, p. 45.
33. *Ibid.*, January 1858, p. 18; John Houston, *Representative men of the Bombay Presidency* (2nd ed.), London, 1900, p. 197.
34. *Ibid.*, p. 91.
35. Krishnarao Bholanath, *Bholanath Sarabhainu Jivan Charit*, (in Gujarati), Bombay, 1888, p. 66.
36. *Buddhi Prakash*, July, 1857. pp. 115–16.
37. *Ibid.*, December, p. 198.
38. Revenue Department, 32/1689/1844, pp. 115–16.
39. Dunlop to Bombay, December 28, 1817, this letter is in "Revenue System in Ahmedabad and Kaira", a collection of documents in manuscript form in the library of Bombay University (Fort) under the call Number 352 and Accession Number 27630.
40. Revenue Department, 30/1818, pp. 2836–38.
41. Revenue Department, 5/1339/1842, p. 155.
42. Revenue Department, 159/1820, pp. 4971–82.
43. *Ibid.*, p. 4973.
44. Revenue Department, 6/138, 1826, not paged.
45. Revenue Department, 12/293/1830, p. 146.
46. Maganlal Vakhatchand, *Amdavad no Itihas*, (in Gujarati), reprint, Ahmedabad, 1977, p. 54.
47. Revenue Department 6/138/1826.
48. Kenneth Gillion, *Ahmedabad*, Berkley, 1969.
49. Makrand Mehta, "Business Environment, Urbanization and Economic Change in India: A Case Study of Ahmedabad in the Nineteenth Century" *Vidya*, vol. xxiv, No. I, January 1981, p. 6 and p. 9.
50. Revenue Department, 129/1818, pp. 2516–17.
51. Revenue Department, 152/1820, pp. 1684–89.

52. Revenue Department, 206/1828, p. 1940.
53. Revenue Department, 12/293/1830, p. 121.
54. Revenue Department, 28/356/1831, pp. 113-1929/1488/1833, 27/420/1832, pp. 327–39 and 155–62, 84/1168/184, pp. 13–18; HG Briggs, *The Cities of Gujarashtra*, London, 1849, pp. 316–18.
55. Revenue Department, 11/769/1837, p. 40.
56. Revenue Department, 76/1851, p. 193.
57. Revenue Department, 37/1054, pp. 77–78.
58. Revenue Department, 53/1859, p. 7.
59. H Briggs, *op.cit.*, p. 317.
60. Revenue Department, 159/1820, p. 4978.
61. Revenue Department, 12/293/1830. p. 144.
62. *Fawcett's Report*, p. 70.
63. *Ibid.*
64. *Ibid.*, p 70: *Ahmedabad Gazetteer*, p. 80.
65. *Ahmedabad Gazetteer*, p. 135.
66. Revenue Department, 5/137/1826, not paged; Revenue Department, 6/1563/1844, not paged.
67. Maganlal Vakhatchand, *op cit.*, pp. 69–70; *Ahmedabad Gazetteer*, pp. 135–36.
68. Maganlal Vakhatchand, *op.cit.*, pp. 76–82.
69. H Briggs, *op. cit.*, p. 400.
70. *Ibid.*, p. 317.
71. Fawcett's Report, p. 81.
72. *Ibid*, p. 82.
73. *Ibid.*, pp. 266–67.
74. Maganlal Vakhatchand, *op.cit.*, pp. 65 and 77.
75. *Ibid.*
76. H Briggs, *op.cit.*, p. 296.
77. Maganlal Vakhatchand, *op.cit.*, pp. 65 and 77.
78. *Fawcett's Report*, p. 89.
79. James Robertson (Ed.), *Western India Reports Addressed to the Chambers of Commerce of Manchester, Liverpool, and Glasgow by their Commissioner the Late Alexander Mackay Esq.*, London, 1853, p. 224.
80. Revenue Department 194/1857, pp. 221–223.
81. *Ahmedabad Gazetteer*, p. 64.
82. *Fawcett's Report*, p. 82.

83. Revenue Department 132/1818, p. 3542.
84. Revenue Department 12/293/1830, pp. 115 and 170.
85. *Ibid.* pp. 166–169.
86. Anonymous, *Hindustan Ane Chin Vachena Affinna Veparni Tawarikh*, (in Gujarati), Bombay, 1854, p. 42.
87. Maganlal Vakhatchand, *op.cit.*, p. 118.
88. Edalji Dosabhai, *op.cit.*, p. 27.
89. Maganlal Vakhatchand, *op. cit.*, pp. 65–66.
90. Revenue Department, 120/1847, pp. 141–73.
91. *Fawcett's Report*, p. 70.
92. Maganlal Vakhatchand, *op-cit.*, pp. 65–66.
93. *Ahmedabad* Gazetteer, p. 296.
94. *Ibid.*, p. 301.
95. *Ibid.*, pp. 296–98

3

British Rule in Ahmedabad (1818–1861) Cultural and Social Changes

The British rulers in Ahmedabad initially did not make any conscious efforts to change society. However, in 1848, Alexander Kinloch Forbes and some other British officials founded the Gujarat Vernacular Society (GVS) to promote education and the Gujarati language. The GVS, the first major voluntary association of the city, played a pivotal and modernising role not only in the city but also in the entire province of Gujarat. The GVS, western education and the press generated social consciousness in Ahmedabad and brought about some important changes in social and cultural life.

I

In the 19th century, western education and the printing press, complementing each other, were two powerful instruments of modernisation in India. In Ahmedabad, too, these two potent agents of social change contributed to the modernising process of the city. Western education, with its secular, liberal content and scientific world view, exposed the younger educated generation to western values and the shortcomings of their own society. As a result, many western educated young men in the city pioneered socioreligious reform movements. The reform leaders of Ahmedabad were products of western education. Prominent among them were Mahipatram, Bholanath Sarabhai, Lalshankar Umiashankar, Hargovinddas Kantawala, Ramanlal Nilkanth and Navalram.

In the Bombay presidency, Mountstuart Elphinstone, with his reforming zeal and liberal ideas, laid a firm foundation of western education. He wanted to make this education available to Indian people through the medium of their own vernaculars, that is, Indian languages. Consequently, the Native Education Society of Bombay launched a programme for preparing books in Indian languages based on English texts and for training vernacular teachers. In 1826, the first two batches of 14 Marathi and 10 Gujarati teachers trained by the Society were ready to be sent to outstations in the districts of the presidency at government expense. These vernacular schools were controlled by the collectors. Thus, schools were opened outside the city of Bombay based on a regular plan of expansion of native education. The year 1826, therefore, was a significant milestone in the history of modern education in Bombay presidency.[1]

As result of this plan, two government vernacular schools were established in 1826 under two trained masters—Tuljaram Sukhram, a Nagar Brahmin, and Gaurishankar Kripashankar, a Motala Brahmin—in the crowded areas of Raipur and Kalupur in Ahmedabad. The schools gradually attained popularity. The revenue commissioner in his report dated April 9, 1834, wrote to Bombay that boys from the 'best' families attended them, and that the principal people of the town showed no prejudice but seemed to take a considerable interest in their welfare.[2] But the number of students attending these two schools was not large in the beginning.

Fawcett, the collector of Ahmedabad, in his annual report of 1844 noted that parents in Ahmedabad were interested only in primary education for their children.[3] Until the mid-1840s, there was apathy and indifference towards English education. It was only among the Deccani inhabitants of the city that there was a small movement in 1833 demanding an English school in the city.[4]

The missionary G Piggot started the first school in 1838 which taught English[5] and later Rev. GL Allen, in the early 1840s, opened an English school in the buildings of the Old Dutch Factory where, in 1844, about 30 to 40 students were studying.[6]

Ahmedabad's initial indifference to English education faded from the mid-1840s. The people of the city realised the importance of the English language and western education for administrative and business purposes. Knowledge of English was required to obtain a situation in any government office. The first Government English School was established on January 1, 1846, at the request of important inhabitants of the city. The demand for the first Government English School arose because Rev. GL Allen admitted a Dhed, an untouchable boy, into his school. The Hindu students strongly resented this action and boycotted the school. The missionary tried to conciliate them by making the untouchable student sit outside the classroom, but to no avail. Some of the leading men, such as Hatesingh Kesarising and the *nagarseth* Hemabhai, sent a petition to the board of education to start an English school in Ahmedabad. Government conceded the people's demand, as it came from the influential section of the city, and started a school on January 1, 1846, in the *nagarseth's haveli.*[7] The inhabitants of the city also raised a large sum of Rs 4,397 to construct a school building, which was erected near Bhadra.[8]

The board of education appointed a promising and highly accomplished teacher Bhogilal Pranvallabhdas as school master in 1845; his efforts and patience made the school very popular.[9] Later, under Curtis, the English teacher, the school became even more popular. Table 3.1 shows how the number of students increased rapidly from 47 in 1846 to 236 in 1860.

Table 3.1: Students in Government English School of Ahmedabad

Year	Boys
1846	47
1847	73
1848	97
1849	99
1850	101

Table 3.1 continued

Year	Boys
1851	104
1852	122
1853	148
1854	188
1858	200
1860	236

Sources:

1. *Buddhi Prakash*, June 1854, p. 87.
2. *Ibid*, November 1861, p. 245.

In the 1850s, there was a rapid rise in the number of students, which meant that the school building had to be extended. Leading citizens of Ahmedabad offered generous loans to meet the contingency. This reveals their appreciation of the importance of western education for their progress. In an article in *Buddhi Prakash*, Dalpatram wrote in 1861, "Day by day the people's interest in English education is increasing".[10] This school taught boys up to college entrance and was one of four such schools in the Bombay presidency. One of the first students to pass the college entrance was the chronicler Maganlal Vakhatchand, who wrote the history of Ahmedabad in Gujarati in 1851. He later became assistant master in the high school. The number of government vernacular schools remained the same until 1847, but the number of students kept rising. Two more vernacular schools were added to the city in 1848 and 1849. Gujarati indigenous schools also existed alongside of the English schools. In 1850, for instance, there were 32 indigenous schools, which continued to exist right up to the end of the 19th century. Marathi and Persian schools also existed in the city. A Sanskrit *pathshala* was maintained by the *nagarseth*. The GVS adopted the indigenous mixed school for boys and girls run by Mehtaji Karunashankar Dayashankar, which flourished under his care.[11]

Though the first western education school had been established in 1817 in Surat, it was Ahmedabad which pioneered women's education in Gujarat. As early as 1846, Tuljaram Sukharam, the Nagar Brahmin school master of the Government Vernacular School, persuaded parents of his caste to send their daughters to his school. As a result, four Nagar Brahmin girls were admitted.[12] In 1850, a separate school for girls was set up under the care of the GVS, with Harkunvar, the rich widow of Hatesingh Kesarising, giving generously towards its maintenance. Later, she also donated money to erect a building for the girls' school. The original co-ed school started by the GVS was closed in 1853.[13] It had been conducted and supervised by the Society.[14]

In December 1850, Rao Bahadur Maganbhai Karamchand, a wealthy merchant, donated Rs 20,000 for the purpose of founding two native girls' schools in the city, desiring to place them under the superintendent of the board of education.[15]

The textbooks used in the girls' schools were the same as those in the boys' schools, with the exception of mathematics. Apart from geography, history, grammar, *Aesopniti*, *Balniti* and elements of arithmetic, they were also taught singing and stitching. The schools prospered and the number of students was gradually increasing. The schoolmaster Bhogilal Pranvallabhdas took a keen interest in the welfare and progress of women's education.[16]

Thus, Ahmedabad was far in advance of progressive Surat in women's education. Durgaram Mehtaji of Surat, for instance, found it impossible to evoke more than a lukewarm response when he endeavoured to raise funds for a girls' school.[17]

In Ahmedabad, the custom of child marriages, the stigma attached to women's education and the lack of women teachers prevented parents from sending their daughters to school. Consequently, at this stage, girls' education was confined to the primary level. To combat these social constraints, reformers such as Dalpatram and Ranchhodram Uderam wrote articles and plays to encourage parents to send their daughters to school. Thus, the society of Ahmedabad, conservative in many ways, did make considerable headway in the field of women's education.

In the field of higher education, too, there was a severe shortcoming. To eliminate this, Hope, educational inspector of the northern division, set up a committee to raise subscriptions for a provincial college. The committee was set up in 1856 and was composed of officials and leading citizens of Ahmedabad. A sum of Rs 54,543 was collected. Maganbhai Karamchand gave the generous sum of Rs 12,000. Premabhai Nagarseth, Vakhatchand Khusalchand, the Kazi Saheb, Hatesingh also contributed liberally to the fund.[18] The Provincial College was started in 1861 and a law lectureship was established. Classes in history, mathematics and Sanskrit were added later. As the College did not get affiliation to the Bombay University at first, it was not very popular. A few promising students had earlier left for Bombay in order to obtain higher education. Among them was Babarao Bholanath, the son of the famous Bholanath Sarabhai. He was honoured by the Vidhyabhysaka Mandali when he left in 1857 to obtain higher education, demonstrating that this was a rare phenomenon.[19]

Another landmark in the history of education in Ahmedabad was the opening of the normal class in 1857 to train teachers for vernacular schools. Initially, there were only 15 students who were given scholarships of five rupees each. This small class later developed into the large Premchand Raichand Training College, which soon became an important centre of enlightened and reformist ideas under the principal Mahipatram Rupram. The teachers trained in this college disseminated their progressive and reformist ideas in the rural areas where they were sent. Playing a significant role in bringing social change not only to the city but also to the *mofussil* areas of North Gujarat, this institute became the nucleus of the city's educational and intellectual activities.

Ahmedabad was thus gradually becoming an active educational centre of the northern division of the Bombay presidency, with one English high school, the provincial college, the normal class for training teachers, three female schools, four vernacular government schools and many indigenous schools. From the late 1840s onwards, the initial apathy and indifference to western education were replaced by a keen enthusiasm and positive response.

The generous donations of traditional business elite such as Maganbhai Karamchand, Premabhai Nagarseth, and Harkunvar Hatesingh towards the cause of education show their interest in western education. The change in their attitude is clearly seen in an incident noted by HG Briggs. When Briggs visited Ahmedabad in 1847, he met Hemabhai, the *nagarseth*, and his son Premabhai. The former showed a preference for the teaching of Sanskrit and Pali languages, while his young son Premabhai told Briggs, "the traditional education system could produce beggars profoundly versed in this dead language and that such a foundation would prove a waste of labour and expense without any essential good being derived".[20] The people of the city had realised the importance of English education, it being the language of administration. The attitude towards women's education was also changing. The advanced tone and positive response of the people of Ahmedabad were largely due to the enthusiasm of accomplished and devoted school masters like Bhogilal Pranvallabhdas, Mr Curtis, Tuljaram Mehtaji and Lalbhai Rupram. Even British officials like Alexander K Forbes encouraged western knowledge and the liberal outlook. The activities of the GVS and the articles in the influential periodical *Buddhi Prakash* emphasised the importance of education and western knowledge. Dalpatram, though not a product of western education, understood its importance and repeatedly emphasised in his articles in the *Buddhi Prakash* the advantages to be gained through education. He urged people to send their children to government schools.

The GVS played a significant role in modernising Ahmedabad, as did several persons who contributed greatly to the advance of education. Bhogilal Pranvallabhdas, a Meshri Vania from Surat, was one such person. He had studied under Balgangadhar Shastri in the Elphinstone Institute in Bombay. After a brilliant academic career, he was appointed assistant master at the Elphinstone Institute in 1844 on a salary of Rs 50. Later, he was appointed headmaster of the New Government English School at Ahmedabad and remained there until 1853. He retired as superintendent of schools of Kathiawad. He was the first Indian to be appointed on the committee of the GVS. He promoted the cause of women's education in Ahmedabad. When he left Ahmedabad for Rajkot, a public meeting was called to honour him, where a sum of Rs 400 was collected and later used for a library.[21]

In 1846, Bhogilal and others like Tuljaram Mehtaji founded a group called Pustak Vriddhi Karnar Mandali, association to develop books, which was set up even earlier than the GVS. Its purpose was to publish and popularise useful books. The credit for establishing the first press in Ahmedabad goes to this Mandali.[22] The first book published by this press was *Sansar Vehvarni Chopdi* in 1847, which contained practical topics like multiplication tables, alphabets, model application forms, rent bills and bills of exchange. It was intended as a textbook to prepare students to work in any business firm or government office and possessed a practical orientation.[23]

Bhogilal was also the main spirit behind another very important association called Vidhyabhyasak Mandali, association for the acquisition of knowledge, which was founded on February 2, 1851. Initially, it was meant for the students of the Government English School. The object of the Mandali was to encourage its members to write essays and participate in discussions on important topics, the activities being conducive to the gaining of new knowledge.[24] The Mandali was to refrain from discussions involving politics and religion. Punctuality and regularity were expected from its members. Thus, the educated youth of Ahmedabad was now getting familiar with association procedures and activities, a completely new experience. Later, the teachers of the government schools, students of the Normal Class and even the business elite joined this association, giving its activities a broad base. The activities of the association expanded under Curtis, who succeeded Bhogilal as the headmaster of the school in 1854. Curtis was also the honorary secretary of the GVS. Hc procured some laboratory apparatus and demonstrated experiments to the members, which popularised the association. For one and a half years, it also published the periodical *Buddhi Prakash*, but this was closed down due to lack of funds. Talks and discussions were organised on subjects as varied as geography, the steam engine, cotton in India, the advantages of learning, telegraph, electricity and more by well-known scholars and teachers like Dalpatram, Mahipatram, Lalbhai Rupram and Bhogilal. In 1858, so great was the response to the activities of this association by the people of the city that about 210 members attended one of the meetings. By 1860, the activities of this Mandali were merged with the activities of the Hemabhai Institute. This Vidhyabhyasak Mandali, like the Buddhi Vardhak Sabha of Bombay, attracted the western educated section of the city, becoming an important forum for talks and discussions on social issues and academic topics by leading reformers, writers and educationists. The Mandali's activities were supported by the GVS, which was directly or indirectly associated with it. It supplemented the social, cultural and academic activities of the GVS. Thus, Vidhyabhyasak Mandali not only played an important role in modernising people's thoughts, but also inculcated a scientific outlook among the people of Ahmedabad in this formative period.[25] Unfortunately, the Muslim community remained aloof from higher education.[26] As late as 1869, there were only three to four Muslim boys in the English school.[27]

The new education laid the foundation of a new social ethos. It created a critical attitude towards religious beliefs and social practices. Higher education was not confined to the Brahmin castes alone. The Vanias, Kanbis and even artisan castes like Mochis, Durjis and Sutars availed of the new education and acquired good posts in government departments.[28] This created upward social mobility for the lower castes. However, the stigma of ritual pollution attached to the Dhed kept them out of schools meant for caste Hindus. British officials were compelled to accept the casts prejudices at this early stage and even as late as 1879. The Dheds were not admitted to any government school.[29] When the Brahmin teacher Karunashankar of the GVS school refused to admit a Dhed boy sent by Seward, the secretary of the GVS, the latter was very angry and threatened to dismiss the teacher and appoint a Muslim or Parsi teacher in his place. When the teacher complained to Forbes who was aware of the customary caste prejudices, Forbes laughed and wrote a note to Seward explaining the customs of the country and telling him that his wishes would take another 200 years to be fulfilled. Seward had to concede and compromise.[30]

Western education was slowly but steadily gaining ground in the city. Even so, only a small percentage had access to it as the number of schools was still minimal. But certainly, it created a small group of western educated intelligentsia which cut across caste and creed lines, shared intellectual and social interests, and participated in the activities of the newly established associations such as Vidhyabhyasak Mandali and the GVS. However, the subculture created by the new education remained limited to the intelligentsia in this early phase. The educated youth who stayed in a *pol* with people of his caste was not completely detached from the traditional society. Caste still dominated his life. The educated youth, a torch bearer of new values and ideas, gradually tried to influence his caste members and bring modernisation through castes organisations or *panchayats*.

In Ahmedabad, the press played a major role in shaping public opinion and generating social awareness among the people at this stage. Periodicals such as *Buddhi Prakash* and *Gujarat Shalapatra* spread reformist and progressive ideas not only in Ahmedabad but all over Gujarat. Maganlal Vakhatchand wrote in 1851 that the newly started weekly newspaper *Vartman* of Ahmedabad had created interest among the people in the outside world and had helped to develop reading habits. People now willingly spent money to get interesting news from the *Vartman*.[31]

In Gujarat, the first printing press was established in 1820 in Surat by the London Missionaries and was known as the Mission Press. Ahmedabad's first litho printing press was established only by about 1846 by the Pustak Vriddhi Karnar Mandali and, as mentioned earlier, the first book published in Ahmedabad was *Sansar Vehvarni Chopdi*, published in 1847. Thereafter, Bajibhai Amichand and the GVS started two new presses which published many books. All these three early presses were later closed down as many other presses began proliferating in Ahmedabad.[32]

II

The establishment of the Gujarat Vernacular Society (GVS) on December 26, 1848 was a major landmark not only in the social history of Ahmedabad but also in that of Gujarat. GVS was established by Alexander K Forbes and his European friends Captain George Fulljames, Captain Wallace and collector EG Fawcett. Leading merchants in the city and members of the western educated middle class willingly cooperated with the European officers who founded this association. It was the first major voluntary association of the city, providing an organisational base for educational, literary and social reform activities in the city. Through its multifarious activities, it became the harbinger of the new age in Gujarat. It played a pivotal role in modernising Gujarati society by bringing about social change through the propagation of new ideas. Though the initial inspiration came from the Europeans and all the members of the first executive committee were Europeans, it was gradually Indianised. It became a forum where the local business and professional elite made an informal but close contact with English officials and European missionaries. This contact with Europeans had a profound influence on the city's elite.

AK Forbes (1821–65), the moving spirit behind the GVS, came to Ahmedabad in 1846. He was a Scotsman who in his childhood had wanted to be an architect, but later he changed his mind and was trained for the Indian Civil Service. He came to India in 1843 and started his career as assistant collector of Ahmednagar and Khandesh in the Bombay presidency where he learnt the Marathi language. In 1846, he was transferred to Ahmedabad as an assistant judge. This 'scholarly' administrator wanted to prepare a history of Gujarat like Col. James Tod who had earlier written *Annals and Antiquities of Rajasthan*. He started learning the Gujarati language from Bhogilal Pranvallabhdas.[33] He needed a full-time literary scholar to assist him in his literary and historical pursuits, and Bholanath Sarabhai, a leading citizen, recommended the poet Dalpatram Dahyabhai to him. In November 1848, Dalpatram was asked to come down to Ahmedabad from his native place Wadhwan and meet Forbes. The friendship between the bardic poet Dalpatram and the scholarly Scotsman, which flowered during the next 17 years, was to prove very beneficial to the cause of social reform in Gujarat. Forbes' influence on Dalpatram was profound, and despite his lack of western education, Dalpatram was able to guide the reform movement through his poems and prose works which propagated many new ideas conducive to social change in Gujarat. Dalpatram, on his part, taught Forbes the Gujarati language and accompanied him in his long, painstaking search for old manuscripts and other source materials for his work. Forbes was thus able to prepare a history of Gujarat entitled *Rasmala* (1856).

Gujarat was fortunate in enjoying the enlightened presence of Forbes for almost eight years. He left his imprint in the form of schools, libraries and associations in Ahmedabad, Surat and places in Saurashtra where he had been stationed. He was a utilitarian liberal in outlook who took a deep interest in Indian culture and customs. Though a devout Christian, he never forced his religious ideas on anyone. He reserved two per cent of his salary for poor and needy Indians. His warmth and courteous manners endeared him to Indians.[34] The biographer of Forbes, Mansukhram Tripathi paid tribute to him in a meaningful poem:

> Without Colonel Tod, the Kshatriya glory would have vanished;

Without the mediation of Forbes, Gujarat would not have progressed.[35]

The GVS was established to raise the Gujarati language from its ignoble condition, to encourage Gujarati literature, to spread knowledge and to promote and encourage education. The founders of the Society appealed to the people through advertisements to contribute generously to the growth of the proposed association. As a result, English officials, the business and professional elite of the city as well as some of the native princes contributed handsomely, and a sum of Rs 9,601 was collected.[36]

The GVS opened the first library in Gujarat near the gateway of Bhadra Fort early in 1849.[37] Initially, this library was known as the Native Library, but later when it had its own building, it became known as the Hemabhai Institute as Hemabhai Nagarseth had donated a handsome amount for the construction of the library building. In 1850, there were 76 members of the library.[38] By 1859, the number of members had increased to 227 which included English officials, businessmen, Brahmins, Parsis and Muslims. The library subscribed to 20 English periodicals and 14 Gujarati ones.[39] Interestingly, a rich man's daughter had become a member of the society, obtaining her books through her *gumastas*.[40] The increasing number of members suggests that interest in reading was spreading among the educated people of the city.

The Society also started a weekly newspaper called the *Vartman* in May 1849, which was the first newspaper of Gujarat. As it was published on Wednesday, or *Budhvar*, it was nicknamed *Budhvaria*. AK Forbes was the moving spirit behind this newspaper.[41] However, the newspaper had a short life. Having criticised the jail administration, it invited the wrath of government officials. Also, it made some derogatory remarks about *nagarseth* Hemabhai and other leading *sethias*. As a result, it alienated the rich of the city, and the GVS had to abandon it. It was taken up by one Babibhai Amichand who ran it until 1864.[42] In 1851, Maganlal, the local chronicler, wrote that before the establishment of the Society and the newspaper *Vartman*, people were not fond of reading. It was the *Vartman* that inculcated the interest in reading. Even illiterate people like Vanatias (weavers) bought this newspaper and had it read to them by others.[43] It spread news and modern ideas to the people of Ahmedabad. The Society had also started its own litho press to print this newspaper and books. However, when other presses started in the city and when the newspaper *Vartman* was abandoned, the press was closed down.[44]

The GVS's educational activities were praiseworthy. As mentioned, in 1849, it took charge of a private Gujarati school run by a private teacher, Karunashankar Dayashankar Mehtaji. This school was co-educational. However, boys and girls sat in separate classes. In 1850, Harkunvar Sethani's girls' school was brought under the management of the GVS. In 1853, the GVS decided to close down the boys' school as, by that time, a few more government schools for boys had been established in the city.[45]

The GVS had been established chiefly to raise the Gujarati language from its degenerate condition and to encourage Gujarati literature. It, therefore, encouraged translation of English works into Gujarati. Essay competitions on practical, historical or social reform topics were held, and the best works were printed by the Society. It published booklets on banks, famines, local self-government, agriculture, cotton and silk, the books *Amdavad no Itihas* and *Gujarat no Itihas* and a few school textbooks. It published Dalpatram's and Sankleshwar Joshi's books *Bal Vivah* (child marriage), *Bhut Nimband* (essay on ghosts) and on other social reform subjects. The GVS did commendable service in perpetuating and spreading knowledge. The Society's educational and literary activities were blended meaningfully in the publication of a reasonably priced series of readers known as *Hope Vanchan Mala* and other useful textbooks. In 1857, Hope, the educational inspector of the Gujarat division was entrusted with the job of preparing a series of readers graded from the first to the seventh standard, intended to give some integrated general knowledge of the world to school students. The content emphasised the new liberal, rational and scientific attitudes. As a result, these books also spread modern ideas which were imbibed by young students. The GVS cooperated with and supported the activities of the education department and helped to get its books written and published. Dalpatram, the poet and assistant secretary of the GVS, lent his services for a few months to prepare these readers. The Society acquired four litho presses for this purpose.[46] These textbooks were used in Gujarat until 1908. The activities of the Vidhyabhyasak Mandali, an associate body of the Society which has been reviewed, also supported the cause of western knowledge and reformist ideas and reinforced the Society's activities.

It is interesting that, for nearly the first five years, the business elite of Ahmedabad remained aloof from the activities of the GVS except to take an interest in the educational activities for which they gave generous donations. This aloofness was due to some slanderous remarks published in the Society's weekly *Vartman*. However, the situation changed when Dalpatram Dahyabhai joined the GVS as its full-time assistant secretary in June 1855. Within a short period, he established rapport with the leading businessmen of the city. He met *nagarseth* Hemabhai, Maganlal Karamchand, and Hatesingh, three leading *sethias*, and urged them to support the activities of the GVS and to help it financially. He praised the activities of the Society and convinced them of its achievements. As a result, Hemabhai agreed to donate a handsome amount for the construction of the new building and other rich people also renewed their interest in the Society. They started attending the talks organised by the Vidhyabhyasak Mandali.[47]

One of the GVS's objectives was to diffuse knowledge and new ideas and create a new social outlook. Its weekly newspaper *Vartman*, started in its first year in May 1849, had to be abandoned in 1852. In 1854, the GVS took charge of the monthly *Buddhi Prakash*.

Buddhi Prakash was started as a bimonthly magazine in May 1850 in Ahmedabad by the Buddhi Prakash Mandali. It was short-lived and was discontinued as the members of the Mandali dispersed. In March 1854, with a view to spread knowledge through a periodical, Vidhyabhyasak Mandali revived it, and the cost of printing and publication was borne by the GVS. However, within a month, from April 1, 1854, the GVS took direct charge of the publication. It decided to publish articles on history and biographies, poems, news and general knowledge.[48] From this time, *Buddhi Prakash* became one of the most influential periodicals, spreading new knowledge and advanced ideas in Gujarat. The tone of *Buddhi Prakash* always remained progressive. It became the mouthpiece of the GVS through which it helped to create social awareness and a scientific outlook. It propagated advanced technology, such as the steam machine, electricity, electric telegraph and the sewing machine. It provided information about the latest industrial developments. It was instrumental in starting an information revolution in Gujarat.[49]

From its very inception, *Buddhi Prakash* supported reformist ideas and exhorted the people to welcome western education. It advocated women's education and foreign travel. When Mahipatram Rupram went to England in 1860 for educational training, the magazine wholeheartedly supported him[50] and praised his bold decision. The GVS also published a small booklet on Mahipatram's foreign travel. When he returned to India in 1861, *Buddhi Prakash* observed, "There is a need to go to England to improve the condition of our country."[51] The same article also appealed to Mahipatram's caste to accept him after he performed the ceremony of *dehshuddhi prayaschit* (repentance for body purification). The GVS, through *Buddhi Prakash*, also crusaded against social evils such as child marriage, high marriage expenses, superstitions, caste dinners given on the street, obscene wedding songs, the dowry system and more. However, it was not radical in its reformist ideas. A policy of gradual change was more acceptable to the traditional city of Ahmedabad, where the businessmen tended to be conservative and resented radicalism. Moreover, Dalpatram, the editor and guiding spirit of *Buddhi Prakash* from July 1855 to 1879 except for brief intervals, was a strong advocate of gradualism. His slogan was "*dhire dhire sudharno sar*"—reform introduced gradually is effective. He believed that it was not prudent to introduce sudden and sweeping changes in a society that has deep-rooted traditions. The magazine's stance may have been apolitical, but it showed its awareness of the economic exploitation caused by the colonial policy of the British and advocated *swadeshi*.

After Dalpatram took over the editorship of *Buddhi Prakash*, not only did the number of subscribers double but his poems and articles made it the most popular and informative magazine in Gujarat. It was to Dalpatram's credit that the circulation of *Buddhi Prakash* was surprisingly widespread even in its early period. Copies of *Buddhi Prakash* were available in Bombay, Surat, Baroda, Broach, Kheda, Nadiad, Cambay, Gwalior, Jodhpur, Prantij, Kapadvanj, Borsad, Idar, Palitana, Bhavnagar, Rajkot, Bhuj, Karachi, Hyderabad (Sindh), Calcutta, and even in London, because of AK Forbes.[52]

Poet Dalpatram had become an assistant secretary of the GVS and the editor of *Buddhi Prakash* in June 1855. He galvanised the activities of the GVS, consolidating the institution and putting it on a very firm foundation. Mahipatram said while felicitating him on his retirement that "AK Forbes gave birth to the GVS, but Dalpatram nursed it and brought it up".[53] It was Dalpatram who set the tone of Ahmedabad's social reform movement through his writings in *Buddhi Prakash*.

Dalpatram Dahyabhai (1820–98) was a Shrimali Brahmin from Wadhwan situated 85 miles north-west of Ahmedabad. His father was a staunch Vedantist, while his mother belonged to the Swaminarayan sect. Thus, Dalpatram was brought up in a conflicting religious environment. He was sent to an indigenous school for three years after which his father gave him some training in religious rituals and Vedic texts. Dissatisfied with this training, Dalpatram left his home and was brought up in his maternal uncle's family which followed the Swaminarayan faith. Naturally, Dalpatram was influenced by this faith and embraced it. Dalpatram had absolutely no background of western education. He was trained in poetics in the Swaminarayan temples and was appointed as a poet of the *Satsang* in 1844 by the Swaminarayan temple of Ahmedabad. He became famous for his talent for composing spontaneously.

In Ahmedabad, Sarabhai Munshi employed Dalpatram as a tutor for his son Bholanath. Dalpatram left Ahmedabad in 1846 for Wadhwan, but was recalled, as mentioned earlier, by Bholanath to teach Forbes the Gujarati language and to assist him in his research work. This meeting with Forbes in 1848 changed the course of his life; the contact between the two grew into a close friendship. Dalpatram's views were influenced by the liberal thought of his employer, from whom he imbibed the modern values of individualism, secularism and rationalism. As a result, his perceptive mind could recognise the shortcomings of Indian society. He spoke and wrote against marriage and death expenses, superstitions, the dowry system, child marriages and the bans on foreign travel and widow remarriage. Through his powerful editorials in the *Buddhi Prakash*, he became an agent of social change. He exhorted people to send their sons and daughters to schools. He wrote in a simple style that blended tradition with modernity, using familiar idioms and symbols. Thus, he gained people's support for the GVS to which they gave donations for the construction of libraries, schools and other institutions.

Perhaps Dalpatram's most enduring contribution was his poems in the textbooks he wrote for Hope, an education inspector in the northern division. Dalpatram was a member of the textbook committee formed by Hope. In a simple, direct and entertaining manner, using commonplace imagery easily understood by children, he inculcated modern ideas and values. With his philosophy of gradualism and his stress on the continuity of tradition, he could appeal to the common man. His poems became a part of the popular culture during his own lifetime. His poems touched almost all aspects of social and cultural life. His long poem *Venacharita*, advocating widow remarriage and abolition of child marriage, can easily be considered the Bible of the reform movement. In his other poems, too, he urged people to change their rigid social and religious attitudes.

Dalpatram did not want to uproot tradition or alienate people from the indigenous culture. His was the middle path; he wanted to bring about change by removing evil and redundant practices, but retaining deep-rooted traditions. He believed in progress and gradual adaptation to the 'New Age'. Though he praised British rule in his poems, he did not hesitate to criticise it. He criticised the prolonged and costly litigation in the courts of justice and the complicated laws. He also recognised the economic exploitation by the British rulers. In Surat, he recited as early as 1851 the widely known poem *Hunnarkhan ni Chaddhai*, or the invasion of the king of industry. In this poem, he has allegorically described the disappearance of Indian crafts and industries under the onslaught of the king of industry of England and China, with the help of his minister *Yantrakhan*, the lord of machines. He exhorted the people of India to be receptive to new and modern ideas and advised them to embrace new machine industries, new technology and means of communication, and to shed their sluggishness, for otherwise prosperity would elude them forever. Dalpatram, even after he gave up working for the GVS in 1878, remained closely associated with it. He continued to educate and entertain the people of the city through his poems and speeches.

III

During the early British phase of its history, the society of Ahmedabad enjoyed great occupational mobility, which in its turn resulted in social mobility.

The expansion of trade and commerce created many opportunities for employment. By this time, various communities like the Kanbis and Parsis had entered the field of commercial activity in the city, thus broadening the social base of the business community. In the pre-British period, *Shravak* or Jain Vanias had dominated the business life of the city. They were able to impose their will on the rest of the mercantile community and had even appropriated the corporate taxes on trade for the support of the *panjrapol*. Soon after the establishment of British rule, the hegemony of the *Shravakas* was challenged by the Meshri (Vaishnava) Vanias and the wealthy Kanbi traders. By the mid-19th century, the Meshri Vanias had emerged as a dominant, well organised textile dealers' group. Their chief was known as the *chautano seth* (head of the cloth market). The *nagarseth*, the head of the *sharafi mahajan* (bankers' guild), was a *Shravak* Vania and was traditionally regarded as the leader of the city and of all the business groups. The *nagarseth* now considered it necessary to consult the *chautano seth* on all important matters affecting the city. The Meshri Vanias protested the imposition of taxes by the *Shravaks* for the support of the *panjrapol*. As a result, they diverted their contribution to their own religious head and to their local temples.[54]

Various fresh occupational opportunities emerged in the new elaborate administrative and legal set-up and in the educational system, where recruitment was not based on the hereditary principle any more, but on merit and qualifications. Thus, the doors to many occupations that were earlier reserved for certain castes were opened for educated youth, thus stimulating occupational mobility. As a result, an educated artisan, like a carpenter, tailor or even a Koli youth, had access to high posts in government services.[55] However, in this early phase, education was pursued only by the upper castes like Brahmins, Vanias, Kayasthas, Brahmakshatriyas, to a limited extent Kanbis and some artisan castes.

At this time, the Kanbi castes acquired great occupational mobility. The Kanbis migrated to the cities in pre-British times. In Ahmedabad, the Kanbis formed a large segment of the city population. They were mostly weavers and traders, and the revival of the indigenous weaving industry allowed many Kanbis to continue with their silk and *kinkhab* spinning and weaving. But many of them also took to trading and money lending.[56] For example, Ambaidas Lashkari—father of Bechardas Lashkari, the founder of the second textile mill in Ahmedabad—was the proprietor of a banking firm that did business with the Peshwas of Poona, the Gaikwads of Baroda and the military department of the East India Company.[57] Mansukhram Kahandas Biladivala owned a big *sharafi pedhi* (banking firm) and carried on cotton business on a large scale.[58] Some Kanbis, apart from manufacturing silk and *kinkhab*, also traded in them. Educated Kanbis rose to high positions in government services.[59]

Despite all these changes, Jain business leaders and merchant bankers formed the core of the business elite in the city. Hemabhai Vakhatchand, the *nagarseth* of Ahmedabad, was the most influential person in the city and an important link between the government and the inhabitants of the city. He was one of the five members of the Town Walls Committee. Petitions representing the people's aspirations, demands and grievances were signed under his leadership. For example, in 1842, the people delayed their reply to the government regarding the continuance and appropriations of the tax for the repair of the town walls because Hemabhai Vakhatchand was away from the city. He was also the head of *sharafi mahajans* and the leader of the Jain community.[60]

Hemabhai's family firm dealt in the extensive opium and textile trade. It lent money to big traders and native princes. His *pedhi* had branches in Bombay, Calcutta, Baroda, Ratlam, Bhavnagar, Dholera, Wadhvan, Limbdi, Palitana, Navanagar and other cities. He acted as an arbitrator and settled disputes of the *mahajans*, traders and princes. People were happy with his arbitration and preferred to go to him to solve their problems rather than to the government courts. He was a philanthropist, generously contributing towards the setting up of various institutions like libraries, colleges and schools in Ahmedabad. His charities even extended to institutes in Bombay. Being a devout Jain, he spent lavishly on the building of Jain temples and *dharmashalas*. As a leader of his Oswal Jain caste, he tried to reform his caste and get his community to lessen the expense on death ceremonies. His generosity, wisdom and able leadership had won him great popularity in the city.[61] The day he died, the city markets, school, and government offices were closed in respect to his memory.

Another leading *Shravak* Vania, Hatesingh Kesarising, the son-in-law of *nagarseth* Hemabhai, had amassed great fortunes in the opium trade. HG Briggs called him 'the Rothschild of Ahmedabad'.[62] His family firm was inducted by Motisha Seth, a merchant of Bombay, to procure opium for him from Malwa and send it to Daman to be shipped to China. Later, Hatesingh sent opium to China on his own account and made huge fortunes. It is said that when he died, he left almost Rs 80 lakh for his two wives.[63] Being a staunch Jain, he organised a *sangh* or pilgrimage to the five holy places (*teerths*) in 1836 and in 1843. He started building a beautiful Jain temple at an expense of Rs 20 lakh near the Delhi gate, but died in 1846 before it was completed. His widows completed it. The consecration ceremony was attended by several eminent guests, including the eldest son of Sir Jamsetjee Jeejeebhoy, baronet, and Nana Shankar Seth, who came from Bombay and even more distant cities.[64] Like Hemabhai, Hatesingh Kesarising, too, endeared himself to the people of Ahmedabad by his generosity and religiosity. His widow, Sethani Harkunvar, was most munificent in donating a large sum for the girls' school and for a hospital in the city.

The third wealthy Jain merchant banker was Rao Bahadur Maganbhai Karamchand, a Dasha Shrimali Shravak, who amassed great wealth through opium trade and banking. He founded the well-known firm of bankers called Karamchand Premchand of Bombay and Ahmedabad. Maganbhai visited Bombay, where he made the acquaintance of the first Jeejeebhoy whose love of charity he imbibed. He was inspired to establish a girls' school in Ahmedabad in 1851 at the expenses of Rs 20,000, despite the prejudices then existing against the education of girls. He also made a handsome contribution towards the funds of the Gujarat Provincial College. In recognition of all these charities, the government conferred on him the title of 'Rao Bahadur'.[65] He was the first citizen of Ahmedabad to receive this honour. Like his two contemporaries, he generously donated to religious institutions. He founded a Jain *shala* and built shrines and *dharmashalas*. He spent considerable money on building a Jain temple in Ahmedabad called the temple of Ashtapadji and a *vadi* or caste lodge to accommodate people giving caste dinners.[66]

The merchant princes of the city not only had great influence but were on good terms with the British government which sought their cooperation in governing the commercial city and recognised their meritorious services by conferring titles on them.

During this period, the emergence of the new middle class was a very significant social phenomenon. In Ahmedabad, it emerged as a result of changes introduced by the British rule in the system of law, administration, economic system and western education, which in turn generated social mobility. This middle class was a heterogeneous intermediate layer consisting of many different occupational interests. It was composed of educated government officials such as Bholanath Sarabhai (*sadar amin*), Mahipatram Rupram (deputy educational inspector who later became the principal of the Government Training College), and Ranchhodlal Chhotalal (government official in the Rewa Kantha); advocates such as Maneckchand Motichand; litterateurs and journalists such as Dalpatram, Ranchhodlal Uderam and Maganlal Vakhatchand; school teachers such as Bhogilal Pranvallabhadas, Tuljaram Mehtaji and Lalbhai Rupram; and small traders who arose in the wake of new commercial opportunities. It was a vertically aligned class which cut across the horizontal caste lines.

The western educated intelligentsia was the most influential amongst the middle classes and was considered as the middle class elite. In Ahmedabad, this was a progressive class holding liberal values which were expressed in the literary and social reform activities of the GVS and other reform associations. It was more receptive to new ideas and provided the necessary leadership to reform movements. It was an articulate class which expressed its views in periodicals like the *Buddhi Prakash*. Members of this class hailed innovations like the railways, telegraph, machine operated industries, science, electricity, western education and female education. They stood for the modernisation of the economy, social reforms, social justice and other such ideas, thus becoming the agents of social charge. At the same time, they were rooted in

Indian traditions and wanted to preserve them in their essential forms, consequently experiencing a feeling of ambivalence between tradition and modernity. In this period, the middle class was a very small one, but it gradually enlarged as a result of industrialisation and the spread of education.

The emergence of the middle class did not greatly disturb the caste-ridden society, since the members of the new middle class were not alienated from their castes. Caste remained important to them in matters regarding marriage, family and inheritance. Mahipatram, the leading social reformer and educationist, was ostracised by his Vadnagara caste of Surat when he returned from England. As he did not want to alienate himself from his caste, he underwent the expensive ritual of *deshuddhi prayaschit* (self-purification). Since members of the middle class remained attached to their castes, they could play an effective role as agents of change in their own castes by diffusing liberal ideas to their caste members and providing enlightened leadership to their castes. In the Audichya Brahmin caste of the city, educated middle class leaders influenced by liberal ideas made efforts to stop the bigamy prevalent in the caste.[67] The Sathodra Nagars of the city, for example, started a movement to weed out evil social practices in the caste.[68] *Buddhi Prakash*, the monthly journal of the GVS praised the castes for their reformist efforts. The Kadva Kanbis also reformed their marriage rules to stop the dowry system and prevent the inhuman practice of infanticide. The reformist trends set during this period by the middle class became stronger in the later industrial phase.

The strength of the caste is also seen in the proliferation of caste lodges which were built either by the caste organisation or the rich members of the caste for the use of caste members.[69] Thus, the caste continued to remain strong and the caste structure stayed unchanged.

The position of women, by and large, remained the same as in the pre-British period. Though Ahmedabad was more advanced than many cities in India in the field of women's education, the number of literate girls was minimal, as people in general jeered at girls receiving education. Many parents could not send their daughters to school, since this would invite the wrath of the people.[70]

The most illustrious woman of this period was Harkunvar Sethani, the widow of Hatesingh Kesarising. In 1849, this enlightened woman financially supported the girls' school run by the GVS and also donated a generous amount for building a hospital in the city. Her religious endowments were many. The Bombay government conferred on her the title of 'Nek Namdar Sakhavati Bahadur'.[71] Hatesingh Kesarising's mother Surajba was another bold woman who actually went to Bombay as early as in 1824 to see the leading merchant Motisha to settle his dispute with her son.[72]

At this point, an examination of the elite of Ahmedabad is necessary as it played a very important modernising role in the city at this formative stage. In this commercial provincial town, the elite structure was pluralist in character. The elite were composed of the business elite, the professional intelligentsia, and the ruling elite (the officials). These three elite classes generally cooperated with each other in public life. The GVS and the municipality became a common platform where their activities converged. Dalpatram, the poet and editor of the *Buddhi Prakash*, acted as a subtle link between these heterogeneous elite groups. He lauded the scholarly and professional achievements of the intelligentsia, eulogised British rule and praised the generosity of the businessmen towards modern institutions. With his emphasis on gradualism in reform activities, he could reconcile the conservative group of the business magnates who had earlier been alienated from the GVS. There was no conflict or competition between the *sethias* (business elite) and the intelligentsia (the professional elite), which was so marked in the city of Bombay. In Ahmedabad, both these elite showed their allegiance and support to British rule. British officials, too, sought the city elite's cooperation in governing the city. All three elite groups cooperated in the social, educational and economic activities of the city.

It is interesting that in Ahmedabad, the presence of the Europeans was never very strong. Until the establishment of the GVS, the relationship of the city elite with the British administrators remained formal and official. The GVS brought the British socially closer to the city elite. As seen earlier, Forbes moulded Dalpatram's world view and inculcated in him liberal and reformist ideas. Fawcett, Curtis and Captain Fulljames took keen interest in the activities of the GVS and guided Indians on various aspects. It was Capt. George Fulljames, a geologist, who guided and helped the entrepreneur Ranchhodlal Chhotalal to found the first textile mill in Ahmedabad. He was a founder member of the GVS and keenly interested in the educational activities of Ahmedabad. He was also the moving spirit behind the construction of the tramway between Dholera town and port as mentioned earlier. Thus, the contact with well-meaning Europeans exercised significant modernising influences on the city's elite.

IV

In this early British period, Ahmedabad's population increased due to the orderly rule of the British. The population became more heterogeneous in composition. The Hindus still formed the largest section of the population, while the second largest section was composed of Muslims. The 1824 survey indicates that there were 22,282 Hindu, 6,913 Muslim and four Parsi houses in the city.[73] By 1872, the city's population of 1,16,873 consisted of 80,895 Hindus, 23,491 Muslims, 11,724 Jains, 264 Christians, 446 Parsis and 40 Jews.[74] The new entrants, the Parsis and Jews, came to Ahmedabad to make use of the new opportunities which arose from British rule.

The Muslims of Ahmedabad lived in obscurity and poverty. Many of them lived on charities and pensions provided by the *lungurkhana* of Ahmedabad. Briggs, who visited Ahmedabad in 1848, observed that many Muslims sold their valuables such as illuminated manuscripts to make ends meet. He ascribed this poverty to their physical indolence and their intellectual apathy.[75]

The *kazi* and *padshahi dewan* were the prominent Muslims of the city. Fawcett, the collector, wrote in 1849:

> There are a few wealthy Mussalmans, who trade in silk and piece goods, but the majority of Mussalmans seek for employment as peons and weavers or as labourers. They will not permit their women to stir out of doors to assist them in earning a livelihood, and their time is spent in spinning cotton thread, earning a poor pittance of about one pice for the day's work.[76]

Bohras and Memons being traders were prosperous, but other Muslims were poor. Many poor Muslims sold their houses in the richer quarters of the city to thrifty Vanias and shifted to the poorer quarters of the city. They sold off their land in the walled city.[77] In this period, the Muslims did not take up English education. As a result, they remained backward and failed to acquire better posts in government offices.

Briggs noted in 1848 that there were about 42 Parsi families in the city and that they were chiefly engaged in trade of some kind.[78] They built their *dokhma* or Tower of Silence in the Jamalpur area in 1843 and a small *agiary* or fire temple in 1845. The *dokhma* was financed by general subscription, while the *agiary* was built by one Kharsedji Bairamji Nanavati.[79] The *Parsi panchayat* was established to look after these two Parsi institutions. The moving spirit behind the establishment of the *panchayat* was Mancherji Karanjwala, a merchant who dealt in European goods and had built a bungalow in Karanj. He was one of the oldest Parsi residents of the city.[80] Another senior prominent Parsi resident of the city was Pestonji Vakil who started a "European" shop in 1826, thriving so well in business that he gradually undertook government contracts.[81] He was a trustee of the *Parsi panchayat*. Edalji Dosabhai, a Parsi resident of the city, wrote *Gujarat no Itihas* in 1850 when he was a student in high school. The Parsi community thus formed a small but prosperous segment of the city's populace.

The Marathi-speaking Bene Israel Jews came to Ahmedabad to seek government jobs. They were employed as clerks and hospital assistants.[82] Abraham Benjamin Erulkar was appointed house surgeon in the Civil Hospital of Ahmedabad in 1848. He started congregational prayers for the Jews of Ahmedabad in his own house and also induced other Jews to settle in Ahmedabad.[83] Both these communities—Parsi and Jewish—were minuscule in size, but became an integral part of city life and continued to remain in the forefront of public life.

The number of Christians in Ahmedabad was also very small, around 264. Among them only 31 were native Christians and the rest either Europeans or Eurasians.[84] The Christian missionaries did not make much impact on the society of Ahmedabad, as Christianity could not penetrate the strong bulwark of the traditional society.

In Gujarat, evangelising activities commenced in the early 19th century. In 1815, the London Missionary Society launched an organised programme to spread the Gospel in the city of Surat. Surprisingly, the missionaries did not arrive in the capital of Gujarat until 1830, and only in 1861 did regular and organised missionary activities commence, initiated by the Irish Presbyterian Church. By 1861, they founded a Christian colony at Shahavadi, four miles south of Ahmedabad. The Society for the Propagation of the Gospel (SPG) commenced its operations in Ahmedabad in 1830. The early activities of the SPG were sporadic. Around 1838, the missionary G Piggot started a school. Later, Rev. GL Allen, who arrived in 1842, activated the operations of the Society. He acquired charge of the Old Dutch Factory and opened an English school and also began to learn Gujarati. About 30 to 40 children attended the school in 1844.[85] It was due to his efforts and initiative that the first Protestant church was built in Mirzapur in 1848.[86] Earlier, the small and plain Roman Catholic Church had been built in 1842 and enlarged in 1846.

It was not easy for the missionaries to break into the traditional society of Ahmedabad. Rev. Allen was able to convert only 11 persons during 1842–44.[87] Though there was no apparent hostility towards this alien religion, the people of Ahmedabad remained apprehensive of Vishwasis (Christians). They dreaded forcible conversions to Christianity. As a result, they did not like the Christians using their water reservoirs as they thought it was polluting. They petitioned the local magistrate to forbid converts from using the public wells. However, this petition was turned down by the government.[88] Thus, in the early period of British rule, Christianity hardly touched the society of Ahmedabad.

The rising population, the increasing prosperity, the changing values of the people and the improvements to the city by the Town Wall Committee had brought about several changes in the city. Ahmedabad had been a melancholy sight with dilapidated walls and ruined public building when it was first taken over by the British. It was only in the early 1840s that the city's face started changing for the better. Until 1839, this extensive town had only one or two small roads and no water carts to spray water on the dusty roads. The city came to be known as *Gardabad*, or a city of dust, a name given to it by the Emperor Jehangir. There were no drains to carry away dirty water and filth. As a result, the roads remained dirty throughout the year, while during the rains, the roads in some parts were reduced to knee-deep mud. There was no public aqueduct to supply water to the city. Thus, Ahmedabad was not a very habitable and pleasant place.[89] The wall repairs were completed by 1842 and the Town Wall Fund Committee continued to raise money for the city's improvement. As a result, the principal roads were watered twice a day and were lit at night. The Committee built some new roads, maintained city walls and roads and improved the scheme of water supply.

The people of Ahmedabad, the rich and the poor, still preferred to stay in their houses in the *pol* where they found security of life and property. The houses became taller and better as the people became prosperous. Some rich people built mansions in the European style outside the city walls. But they continued to stay in their houses in the *pols*. There were quite a few such mansions outsides the Delhi gate on the way to Shahibag, so that this place that had been deserted just a few years earlier now became a heavenly abode or

Indrapuri, with beautiful ornamental villas.[90] The deserted *puras* in the western part of the city within the walls, such as Jamalpur and Khanpur, were now being repopulated. Vacant plots were sold by Muslim owners to rich merchants who built houses there for rental purposes. The *sahibs* built their bungalows on vacant plots in Shahpur. The demand for land so increased that the historian Maganlal Vakhatchand in 1850 forecast that land prices would soar high very soon.[91] The new entrants, Parsis and Christians, built their houses in the Jamalpur and Khanpur areas.

Bhadra remained the seat of authority where the former public building was utilised by British administrators who did not add any impressive new public buildings. The public buildings constructed just outside Bhadra Fort were the Hemabhai Institute or the Library and the Government English School, all symbols of the modern age in the city. In 1849, the town clock with two dials was placed between the twin towers over the Bhadra gate at a cost of Rs 8,000.[92] The clock heralded a new era in the city. During this period, two impressive temples were added. One was Hatesingh's Jain temple near the Delhi Gate while another was the Swaminarayan temple, both completed by 1850. A number of small Jain temples were built or renovated by the rich *Shravakas* in Jhaverivada and in Khadia. Two small churches, the Roman Catholic Church and the English Church, were built in Mirzapur.

Though the main roads were cleaned, watered and maintained, the *pol* streets were still dirty. The people threw their garbage and dirt on the road. Caste feasts were held on the streets of *pols* which increased the filth. Dalpatram, in his essay on city improvement, jeeringly commented that dirt and filth removed from the roads by the government had entered the *pols* and sarcastically congratulated those who could stay on in the stinking and dirty *pols*.[93]

Ahmedabad, during these 40 years, grew and thrived. British rule added a new dimension to the socioeconomic environment of the city. It laid the foundation of a new social ethos. Ahmedabad changed in many significant ways from 1817 to 1861. The textile mills and the railway would bring greater changes to the city in the next 50 years.

Notes

1. RV Parulekar & Bakshi (Eds.), Selections from Educational Records (Bombay), Part II, 1815–1840, Bombay, 1955, p. xx.
2. Cited in Parulekar & Bakshi, *op. cit.*, Part III (1826–1840), Bombay 1957, pp. 120–21.
3. Cited in Parulekar & Bakshi, *op. cit.*, Part III, pp. 71–73.
4. Revenue Department, 00/8/1846, pp. 37–38,
5. Rev. Alishabhai Prabhakar, *Suvartanu Parodh* (in Gujarati), Ahmedabad, 1982, p. 177.
6. Revenue Department, 00/8/1846, pp. 37–38.
7. Maganlal Vakhatchand, *Amdavad no Itihas* (in Gujarati), reprint, Ahmedabad, 1977, pp. 84–86.
8. Fawcett's Report, p. 72.
9. Maganlal Vakhatchand, *op.cit.*, pp. 85–86.
10. *Buddhi Prakash*, November 1861, pp. 245–47.
11. Maganlal Vakhatchand, *op. cit.*, p. 63.
12. Fawcett's Report, p. 73.
13. Hiralal Parekh, *Gujarat Vernacular Society no Itihas*, Vol. I (in Gujarati), Ahmedabad. 1932, pp. 27–29.
14. *Buddhi Prakash*, July 1854, p. 77–78.
15. Government of Bombay, Report of the Board of Education Bombay, From May 1852 to April 30, 1853 Bombay, 1853, p. 73.
16. *Ibid.*, p. 78.
17. Government of Bombay, Report of the Board of Education Bombay, From May 1852 to April 30, 1853 Bombay, 1853, p. 75.
18. *Buddhi Prakash*, April 1856, pp. 78; Government of Bombay, *Report of the Director of Public Instruction 1855-56*, Bombay, 1856, p. 278; *Gujarat Shalapatra*, June 1872, pp. 81–84.
19. *Buddhi Prakash*, August to December 1857, pp. 131–32.
20. HG Briggs, *The cities of Gujarashtra*, London, 1849, p. 234.
21. Girdharlal Uttamram Parekh, *Rao Saheb Bhogilal Pranvallabhdasnu Jivancharitra* (in Gujarati), Ahmedabad, 1925, pp. 12–23.
22. *Buddhi Prakash*, January 1864, p. 4.
23. Hiralal Parekh, *op. cit.*, Part I, pp. 4 and 36.

24. *Buddhi Prakash,* April 1859, p. 57.
25. *Buddhi Prakash,* January 1858, p. 35; *Ibid.,* April 1859, pp. 57–58; *Ibid.,* August 1859, pp. 126–32; *Ibid.,* January 1864, pp. 8–10.
26. *Ibid.*, November 1861, p. 247.
27. *Gujarat Shalapatra*, April 1869, p. 86.
28. *Buddhi Prakash*, April 1864, p. 95.
29. *Ahmedabad Gazetteer*, p. 211.
30. *Buddhi Prakash*, October 1865, pp. 230–31.
31. Maganlal Vakhatchand, *op. cit.*, preface.
32. *Buddhi Prakash*, January, 1864, p. 11.
33. Mansukhram Tripathi, *Forbes Jivan Charitra* (in Gujarati), Bombay, 1869, p. 7.
34. *Buddhi Prakash*, October 1865, p. 231; *Ibid.*, April 1866, p. 88.
35. Mansukhram Tripathi, *op. cit.*, p. 7.
36. *Buddhi Prakash*, January 1878, pp. 8–10.
37. Hiralal Parekh, *op. cit.*, Vol. I, p. 230.
38. Maganlal Vakhatchand, *op. cit.,* p. 86.
39. *Buddhi Prakash*, March, 1860, p. 58.
40. *Ibid.*, September, 1855, p. 144.
41. Maganlal Vakhatchand, *op. cit.*, p. 86; Hiralal Parekh, *op. cit.*, Vol. I, p. 14–15.
42. *Buddhi Prakash*, February 1878, pp. 31–34.
43. Maganlal Vakhatchand, *op. cit.*, preface.
44. *Buddhi Prakash*, January 1864, p. 4; *Ibid.*, February 1878, p. 34.
45. Hiralal Parekh, *op. cit.*, Vol. I, p. 29.
46. *Buddhi Prakash*, May 1878, pp. 99–104.
47. *Ibid.*, April 1878, pp. 80–82.
48. *Ibid.*, April 1854, p. 1; *Ibid.*, April 1859, pp. 57–59; *Ibid.*, April 1878, p. 76.
49. Makrand Mehta, *The Ahmedabad Cotton Textile industry: Genesis & Growth*, Ahmedabad, 1982, p. 25.
50. *Buddhi Prakash*, March 1860, pp.52–53.
51. *Ibid.*, April 1861. pp. 74–75.
52. *Ibid.*, July 1855, p. 98; *Ibid.*, September 1855, p. 146.
53. *Ibid.*, December 1880, pp. 227–28.
54. *Ahmedabad Gazetteer*, pp. 112 and 114.

55. *Buddhi Prakash*, April 1861, p. 95.
56. *Ahmedabad Gazetteer*, p. 64.
57. John Houston, *Representative Men of the Bombay Presidency* (2nd edition), London, 1900, p. 91.
58. Vallabhji Sunderji Punjabhai, *Rajnagar na Ratno* (in Gujarati), Rajkot, 1918, pp. 95–96.
59. *Ahmedabad Gazetteer*, p. 36.
60. BK Boman Behram, The Rise of Municipal Government in the City of Ahmedabad, Bombay, 1937, pp. 132–34.
61. *Buddhi Prakash*, January 1858, pp. 17–18.
62. HG Briggs, *op, cit.*, p. 190.
63. Maganlal Vakhatchand, *op. cit.*, p. 122.; Edalji Dosabhai, *History of Gujarat from the Earliest Period to the Present Times*, Ahmedabad, 1894, p. 283.
64. Ibid.
65. Maganlal Vakhatchand, *op. cit.*, p. 123–24;, John Houston, *op. cit.*, p. 166; Edalji Dosabhai, *op. cit.*, p. 283.
66. *Ahmedabad Gazetteer*, p. 296.
67. *Buddhi Prakash*, August 1856, p. 151.
68. *Ibid.*, October 1859, p. 231.
69. *Ahmedabad Gazetteer*, pp. 295–300.
70. *Buddhi Prakash,* May 1860, p. 117
71. *Ibid.,* June 1856, p. 139.
72. Maganlal Vakhatchand, *op. cit.,* p. 119.
73. *Ahmedabad Gazetteer*, p. 317
74. The Government of Bombay, *Census of the Ahmedabad Collectorate,* Bombay 1973, pp. 38–39.
75. HG Briggs, *op. cit,* pp. 249 and 255.
76. Fawcett's Report, p. 70.
77. *Ahmedabad Gazetteer,* p. 323; Maganlal Vakhatchand, *op.cit*, pp. 249 and 255.
78. HG Briggs, *op. cit,* p. 270.
79. *Ibid.*, *Ahmedabad Gazetteer*, p. 327.
80. HG Briggs, *op. cit.,* p. 270.
81. FC Davar, *Sir Navroji P. Vakil: A Biographical Sketch*, Ahmedabad, 1955, pp. 25–26.
82. *Ahmedabad Gazetteer*, p. 294.

83. Chandrakant Patel, 'Amdavadna Yahudiono Purva Itihas Ane Sanskratik Jivan' (in Gujarati), *Vidypith,* May-June 1972, p. 164.
84. Census of Ahmedabad Collectorate, 1872, p. 39.
85. HG Briggs, *op. cit,* p. 265; Revenue Department, 00/8/1846, p. 38.
86. *Ahmedabad Gazetteer,* p. 279; HG Briggs, *op. cit,* pp. 267–68.
87. Alishabhai Prabhakar, *op. cit.,* p. 179.
88. GA Oddie, *Social Protest in India: British Protestant Missionaries and Social Reforms 1850–1900*, New Delhi, 1979, pp. 70–71; *Buddhi Prakash*, November 1862, p. 243.
89. Revenue Department, 106/1069/1839, pp. 76–81.
90. Maganlal Vakhatchand, *op. cit.,* p. 60.
91. *Ibid.,* p. 61.
92. *Ahmedabad Gazetteer*, p. 276.
93. Dalpatram Dahyabhai, *Saher Sudhara Vishe Nimbandh* (in Gujarati), Ahmedabad, 1858, pp. 14 and 20–21.

4

Ahmedabad Responds to British Colonial Policy

The year 1861 is a turning point in the history of Ahmedabad. It was on May 30 of this year that Ranchhodlal Chhotalal turned the giant wheel of the steam machine 'Adventure', thus establishing the first textile mill of Ahmedabad and ushering the city into the industrial age. The next 55 years witnessed the metamorphosis of Ahmedabad into the "Manchester of India", with no less than 60 mills producing one-fourth of the cotton goods made in India.[1] Far-reaching changes in the economic and social life of Ahmedabad and its hinterland were brought about when the steam operated industry introduced a new mode and a new process of production.

Within two years, in January 1863, the Bombay-Baroda and Central India Railway linked the city to Surat; in 1864, Ahmedabad was linked to the port city of Bombay. The railways, on the one hand, enhanced the importance of Ahmedabad as an entrepot while, on the other hand, it helped the British to tighten their colonial grip on this inland city. The British colonial capitalist system now offered an extremely intense challenge to industrial Ahmedabad. The mercantile city responded to this challenge, with two weapons—machine industry and *swadeshi*, that is, encouragement to indigenous industries and non-purchase of foreign articles. The response of Ahmedabad to the British colonial policy was the spontaneous outcome of its commercial ethos.

I

A favourable milieu for enterprise had been created in the city in the middle of the 19th century. Trade and industry had revived under the liberal trade policy of the British rulers.

Opium and cotton trade had generated considerable capital in the city for reinvestment. A sociocultural regeneration was brought about by western education and the establishment of the Gujarat Vernacular Society (GVS). *Buddhi Prakash*, the monthly journal published by the GVS, enlightened the people on new developments in science and technology. The very first issue of *Buddhi Prakash* featured an article on the steam engine.

The location of Ahmedabad was not really suitable for the textile industry, which nevertheless flourished in the city. There were various adverse factors which should have in the course of things gone against Ahmedabad. First, being an inland city, it lacked port facilities. It was also situated at considerable distance from coal mines, and its dry climate tended to disintegrate thread while it was being spun. Though raw cotton was easy to procure in the vicinity, it was of a mediocre quality. Despite these unfavourable factors, the city was to become the Manchester of India. The reason for this lies in its cultural strength. Kenneth H Gillion, in his history of Ahmedabad, has rightly emphasised that the cultural milieu played an important role in the development of the modern textile industry. Ahmedabad had a rich business culture and long experience in the indigenous textile industry. The city had a well-developed financial infrastructure to support the industry. Its dominant ethic of frugality and hard work suited it to the rigors of industrialisation.[2]

The entrepreneurial initiative was taken by a young Nagar Brahmin, Ranchhodlal Chhotalal (1823–98). He did not belong to the business community but to a community which was known for its administrative and diplomatic skills. Nagars, by and large, were educated people and lived in cities. They were among the earliest Gujaratis to acquire a knowledge of English and had access to western ideas. Ranchhodlal's ancestors on both his father's and mother's side had held high administrative positions under the Mughals and Marathas. After completing his formal education in 1842, he joined government services. He had attained high proficiency in Persian and English and rapidly rose to the position of assistant superintendent of Pavagarh in Panchmahal, the highest position to which an Indian in the political department of government could aspire at that time.[3]

While still in government service, Ranchhodlal took a keen interest in establishing machine industries. He was encouraged by the Act of 1843 which repealed the prohibition against the export of English textile technology. With the help of an army officer, Major George Fulljames (commandant of the Gujarat Irregular Horse and then the political agent of Rewa Kantha), Ranchhodlal investigated the possibilities of establishing a textile machine industry. Fulljames was not only well informed about machine industries but had excellent contacts with reputed English manufacturers. Moreover, he was very willing to help Indians start a modern industry. Earlier, Fulljames had gathered information to help merchants of Surat to set up a textile unit. But the Surat plan not having materialised, he handed over his information to Ranchhodlal in 1847, who was strongly convinced that the project was not only feasible but had sound profit potential. Needing financial support, he approached the merchants of Ahmedabad and Baroda but found a lukewarm response. They were not ready to plunge into an untried and novel enterprise.[4]

To attract the notice of the wider public, Ranchhodlal published the prospectus of his proposed company in the weekly *Vartman* on November 21, 1849. This weekly newspaper was published by the GVS and had a wide circulation. Ranchhodlal appealed to the citizens of Ahmedabad, showing the profit potential of the mill project and stating that it would increase the prosperity of the nation. However, the hard-headed capitalists of Ahmedabad refused to be convinced.

Not deterred, Ranchhodlal contacted Landon, the British planter who had successfully set up two steam engines for cleaning and pressing cotton in Broach, which was the first machinery of its kind in Bombay presidency. Happily, Landon was willing to join him in his venture and contribute half the capital if Ranchhodlal could get the other half.[5] Ranchhodlal convinced Gaurishankar Oza, the Nagar *dewan* of Bhavnagar, the Raja of Rajpipla, and

Shamal Bechar and Gopalrao Mairal, both Baroda merchant bankers, to form a company. English machine manufacturers were also contacted, but as the investors insisted on a formal guarantee from British manufacturers, the plan did not materialise. However, Landon continued in his efforts and succeeded in establishing a cotton spinning mill in Broach in April 1855, which worked very well.[6]

Meanwhile, three mills had come up in Bombay during 1854–1857, all of them proving successful. Ranchhodlal was even more convinced of the feasibility of his plan and continued making efforts. The success of the Bombay and Broach mills had tremendous psychological impact in convincing the *sethias* of Ahmedabad of the profit potential of such a plant. Ranchhodlal was now able to get financial support from the merchants of Ahmedabad. In 1859, the Ahmedabad Spinning and Weaving Company was floated on the joint stock principle, with an authorised share capital of three lakh rupees divided into 60 shares of Rs 500 each.[7] Only one-third of the authorised capital was to be initially subscribed. The early promoters were Maganbhai Karamchand, Nagarseth Premabhai, Jesangbhai Hatesingh, three renowned Jain Vanias, Dr White (an Englishman), Achratlal Girdharlal Veragi, Damodardas Manoharlal (all Vaishnav Vanias), Bholanath Sarabhai (a Vadnagara Brahmin and government officer) and Ranchhodlal himself. Interestingly, they were all from diverse castes and professional groups.[8]

Ranchhodlal purchased machinery from Dadabhai Naoroji, who was then in England. The machinery was unfortunately lost at sea, and the English engineer who had been sent to install it suddenly died of cholera in Ahmedabad. The machinery had been insured, so Dadabhai sent another lot of machinery which reached Bombay safely and was shipped to Cambay and then brought on bullock carts to Ahmedabad under the supervision of Ranchhodlal.[9]

Finally, with the help of the English engineer Edington, the machinery was installed in the mill at Shahpur. The mill opened on May 30, 1861 with a workforce of 63 men who had also been trained by Edington.[10] The Company made enough profit in the first year to declare a 6 per cent dividend. In 1864–65, the number of spindles in the mill was increased from 2,500 to 10,000, and a weaving plant with 100 looms to produce coarse cloth was set up. In 1864, the number of workers increased to 300.[11]

No further mills, however, were established in Ahmedabad until 1867. The fever of speculation in cotton and in shares started with the onset of the American Civil War. Ahmedabad, too, participated in the speculation. Even the common man speculated. The price of cotton rose very high and traders made huge profits in the cotton trade. But when the civil war ended, the price of cotton crashed and many speculations failed.[12] In Ahmedabad, about 28 new bubble companies and banks had been established. People bought shares in order to make quick money.[13] The poet Dalpatram initially made a fortune, but, overcome by greed, he did not stop speculating and as a result lost heavily. Premabhai Nagarseth also lost money. Shares fever diverted the attention of the investors, obstructing the growth of the mill industry.

In 1867, a second mill, the Bechardas Spinning and Weaving Mill, was promoted by Bechardas Lashkari (1818–1889), another industrialist who did not belong to the traditional business community. Bechardas was of the Kanbi caste, and his father Ambaidas was a leading banker of Ahmedabad. Bechardas also supplied groceries to the military department of the East India Company, thus the name "Lashkari" which means military. Bechardas had been brought up in Ahmedabad and joined the military services of the English East India Company, where he acquired proficiency in English. After his father's death, he joined his father's banking business. His firm had branches in Bombay, Broach, Dholera and Wadhwan. Apparently, he profited through speculation. With his friend Ranchhodlal's help, he established a mill with 10,000 spindles and 100 looms.[14] Enterprise had entered the blood of the citizens of Ahmedabad, and in 1876, Bholanath Sarabhai, a close friend of Ranchhodlal, floated the Ahmedabad Calico Printing Company with Ranchhodlal and Maganbhai Karamchand as partners. Unfortunately, the printing company did not do well and went into liquidation in September 1880.[15]

In 1877, Ranchhodlal started his second mill with some Vaishnav Vania partners in the Sarangpur area. It was known as the Ahmedabad Ginning and Manufacturing Company Limited. It was a spinning mill and soon surpassed his first mill in profits and reputation. In 1882, he added a weaving plant.

The management of the first three textile mills in Ahmedabad was in the hands of members of non-trading castes or 'outsiders'. The traditional commercial castes preferred to remain investors but not be directly associated with the management of the mills.[16]

The progress of the modern textile industry was much slower here than in Bombay. There were only four textile mills in Ahmedabad in 1879.[17] The fourth mill was promoted by Mansukhbhai Bhagubhai, a Jain Vania. He was the first of the commercial community to start an industrial mill. He came from a wealthy and established family. He and his brother Jamnabhai were the first Jains in Bombay presidency to enter into a manufacturing venture in the teeth of opposition from their Jain relations and caste fellows, who believed that machines would entail the loss of insect lives. Their mill had both spinning and weaving plants.[18] Another wealthy Jain family that entered the textile industry was the successor of Karamchand Premchand. The family firm under Sarabhai *seth*, an adopted son of Maganbhai, acquired the Ahmedabad Calico Printing Company which had earlier that year gone into liquidation. Ranchhodlal became the chairman of the board. The Calico mill was rescued and turned into a prosperous concern.

The five years between 1882 and 1887 saw a halt in the opening of new mills. However, the period which followed witnessed a proliferation of new textile mills. All the new entrants were Vaishnav or Jain Vanias. They had immense capital and entered the textile industry with great vigour. The 'old money' started flowing into the successful new industry, and in a few years, they had taken over the textile industry. They did not divert their funds to uncertain new ventures until they were assured of the soundness of investing in new industries. They then plunged, though cautiously, into them.

Trikamlal Harilal was the first Vaishnav Vania to promote a mill in 1889. He was followed by Motilal Hirabhai, a Modh Vaishnav Vania, a trader. Two of the most influential Vaishnav families to enter the textile industry were the Parekhs and the Shodhans, who rapidly rose in prestige.

Mangaldas Girdhardas Parekh's father was a poor clerk who saved his money and established a yarn business. Mangaldas helped his father in this business while he was still studying. He passed his matriculation examination in 1882 and joined Ranchhodlal's mill as a store clerk with Rs 20 as monthly salary. He acquired sound experience in the mill business and started a mill store business of his own in 1886 and later, with the financial backing of Ranchhodlal and Mansukhbhai in 1892, he founded a textile mill in partnership with Balabhai Damodardas.[19]

Balabhai Damodardas Shodhan, Mangaldas's partner, was a Vaishnav Vania. His father Damodardas was a clerk in a *sharafi pedhi*. During the American Civil War, he had arranged to get cotton market quotations from New York and London. For this search or 'shodh', he was known as 'Shodhan'. Balabhai also served in Ranchhodlal's mill as a store clerk and gained experience in the textile industry. He and his brother later promoted the famous Bagicha mill.[20]

After the 1890s, the mill industry grew rapidly. The large number of Vaishnav Vanias who entered textile manufacturing cooperated with each other during this formative stage, financing and managing companies and serving as directors on the boards of one another's companies. Ranchhodlal was the guiding spirit and mentor of the textile industry. When he died in 1898, Ahmedabad had gained a reputation as an important textile manufacturing centre. The city then had 25 mills. Just before 1898, an important

Jain family, that of Lalbhai Dalpatbhai, entered the mill industry. Lalbhai floated the Saraspur Mill in 1897.[21] His father, Dalpatbhai had made a good profit in cotton speculation and had established a banking firm. Another entrant into the textile industry was Sorabji Karaka, a Parsi spinning and weaving master in one of the mills of Ahmedabad who started his own mill in 1898.

The *shravak* (Jain) and *Meshri* (Vaishnav) Vanias had tremendous support from their caste and religious organisations and, being very close knit, co-operated with each other. The *Meshri* Vanias had organised themselves into the Gujarat Vaishya Sabha, which had cut across narrow caste and sub-caste lines since 1903. The Vaishya Sabha promoted cooperation, which was conductive to the growth of trade and business. The Jain Vanias established the Jain Swetambar Conference in 1902 with a view to achieving solidarity among the Jain in social, economic and religious spheres. In this formative period of the textile industry, such organisations provided the necessary cohesiveness to the mill industry.

Ranchhodlal dominated the textile scene until his death in 1898. He was revered by the mill agents as the mentor and guiding force of the industry, presiding over the inaugural functions of all new mills. In fact, until his death, he remained the president of the Ahmedabad Mill Owners' Association, founded in 1891. He helped those who wanted to set up new mills. Ranchhodlal is rightly thought of as the father of modern Ahmedabad and as one who inaugurated not only Ahmedabad's mill history but, more generally, its modern history. Ranchhodlal proposed and carried out other projects as enterprising as his mills. As member and sometime chairman of the municipal committee, he pushed through several novel and necessary programmes of water works and drainage despite powerful opposition and even physical attacks. He was truly the maker of modern Ahmedabad.

The last few years of the 19th century were lean years for Gujarat's economy. A famine of great intensity, popularly known as *Chhapanio*, struck Gujarat. Cholera and plague in the city aggravated the situation. As if this were not enough, the British government imposed heavy excise duties on the indigenous production of yarn in 1896, adversely affecting the mill industry. Despite this, new mills came up during this period. In 1890, there were only seven mills having a total of 2,266 looms and 1,77,147 spindles.[22] In 1895, six new mills were added, and the total of looms and spindles rose to 4,931 and 2,74,439, respectively.[23] In 1905, on the eve of the launch of the *swadeshi* movement, there were 32 mills with 7,061 looms and 5,37,928 spindles.[24] These statistics indicate the rapid growth of the textile industry from the last decade of the 19th century. The *swadeshi* movement of 1905 resulted in the growth of the domestic market, which gave the mill industry great impetus. During this time, the social base of the textile industry expanded as new entrants came from different castes and communities. Established mill owners took advantage of the situation to expand their mills or open new mills.

Apart from the Vaishnav Vanias with a trading background, there were middle class, educated persons like Hargovindas Kantawala, Lalshankar Umiashankar and Ambalal Sakarlal who entered the textile industry. Ambalal Sakarlal was a Brahmakshatriya. He was an educationist, social reformer and political leader, and an ardent supporter of *swadeshi*. He entered the textile industry in 1902. Even *nagarseth* Premabhai's family, which had kept aloof from the textile industry, floated a mill in 1905. One Dahyabhai Kripashankar, a Brahmin, promoted a mill. Parsis also appeared on the scene. Sorabji Karaka had set up a mill towards the end of the 19th century. JN Tata became the second Parsi to own a textile mill in Ahmedabad. He bought a sick mill and put it on a sound footing. The Jehangir Vakil Mill was promoted in 1905 by two Parsi residents of Ahmedabad, Rustamji Jehangirji Vakil and Navroji Ratanji Divecha.

During the period of *swadeshi* fervour, there seems to have been even more intercommunity cooperation in the textile industry. Mafatlal Gagalbhai of the Kadva Kanbi caste floated a mill in collaboration with Chandulal Mahadevia, a Kanbi textile dealer, and Arthur Shorrock, the first Englishman to float a textile mill in Ahmedabad. Mafatlal was the second Kanbi to enter the industry.

After 1908, the fervour of the *swadeshi* movement subsided. Under its impact, however, the Ahmedabad mill industry had expanded considerably. It had become the Manchester of India in a very real sense.[25] At the end of 1908, there were 49 mills, 12,779 looms and 8,71,703 spindles.[26]

Before 1912, Muslims were conspicuous by their absence in the textile industry. In 1912, a Dawoodi Bohra Muslim family, the Taiyabajis, floated a mill. The Muslims of the city, by and large, were not very enterprising. However, as early as the 1870s, they had set up a steam-operated paper mill, which unfortunately was damaged in the great Sabarmati flood in 1875. The proprietors dismantled the machinery and equipment and brought it all to Shaibag. For some reason, the machinery was never reinstalled.[27] In 1897, an enterprising Muslim Munshi named Fateh Mohammad Fakir Mohammad, set up the Gujarat Islam Match Manufacturing Company with a small capital of Rs 97,000. The founder had himself invented the compound to be used in the matches. The company had 132 workers in the factory in 1897.[28] This enterprise received wide publicity during the days of the *swadeshi* movement.[29] The founder, a dealer in wood, was a matriculate who had earlier taught in the Training College and had served as joint secretary of the Anjuman-i-Islam. Altogether, he was an excellent and encouraging example of Muslim enterprise.[30]

By 1914, the celebrated medieval textile centre was transformed into a modern industrial city with 61 textile mills, two iron works, two hosiery factories, one dye works, one match factory and three oil mills in the city and 25 ginning, cleaning and pressing units in its environs.[31] The first two decades of the 20th century saw very rapid industrialisation. The modern textile industry became the nerve centre of the economy of Ahmedabad and the main source of its prosperity.

In pre-British times, the trade and commerce of the city were in the hands of the people of Ahmedabad, that is, the locals rather than outsiders. Similarly, locals also controlled the city's modern industry. Industries were financially and managerially controlled by local men of the Gujarati merchant and banking community. Local men of Ahmedabad—not Marwadis, Parsis or the British—built Ahmedabad into the Manchester of India.[32] Every person of Ahmedabad directly or indirectly was connected with the textile industry.[33] Ahmedabad's money was generated by and re-invested in this industry.

II

New patterns in financial institutions and managerial organisation developed in the wake of industrialisation. Machine industries needed a large amount of capital and a different type of organisation. Some part of the pre-industrial heritage seems to have continued so that the Ahmedabad mill industry developed a unique pattern of finance and management. Many of the pre-industrial traditions and institutions, such as *mahajans* and *pedhis*, were carried over and blended with the modern industrial system.[34]

In management, the first textile mill of Ahmedabad set the trend for the future. Ahmedabad mill owners adopted the managing agency system from the British industrialists in India. They modified it to suit their needs. The companies responsible for managing industry were called managing agency firms. In Ahmedabad, the promoters of mills, holding the controlling shares, organised themselves into a managing agency, earning not only dividends on their investment but also commissions from those mills. In Ahmedabad, agents, once employed, usually held the rights of management hereditarily and in perpetuity. As a result, the traditional hereditary structure of the family business or *pedhi* continued. The business and the family continued to be conterminous. This was quite different from the British pattern in which the family name marked the continuity of the managing agency while the actual management was left to career men promoted to key posts on the basis of merit.[35]

The financial management of the mills also developed some peculiar features. With outside capital being unattainable and no help forthcoming from the British colonial government as protection or financial help, the mill owners perforce had to seek financial support in the city itself. In Ahmedabad, modern banking had been slow to develop. A branch of the Bank of Bombay was established in 1862 in the city. Later, the Royal and the Central banks opened branches. All three banks, however, were soon closed down. In 1870, the New Bank of Bombay opened a branch in Ahmedabad.[36] Until the close of the 19th century, Ahmedabad had only one bank which extended loans to its rapidly growing industry. As a result, the mills had to depend on the indigenous *sharafi pedhis*. As *sharafs* and the trading communities entered and dominated the mill industry in the 1890s, finance easily flowed into the industry. They were experts in finance and their good reputation made it easy for them to attract capital from the citizens. Ahmedabad evolved a system of deposits for borrowing money on interest. This money was used to finance working capital needs and sometimes for expansion. Other sources of capital were the sales of shares and investment by the managing agents, loans from banks and debentures. The public deposit system brought many people of the city into the orbit of the textile industry. The fortune of the city now depended on the textile industry.

The corporate spirit which pervaded the history of this commercial city was evident in its industrial life. The mill owners assisted each other. The market was large enough to prevent competition, so the mill owners cooperated with one another. A system of interlocking directorships connected the various managing agencies and created a close-knit group of managing agents. This spirit of cooperation led them to establish the Ahmedabad Mill Owners' Association (AMA) in 1891. It was founded to increase coordination among the owners of machine industries and to safeguard the interest of the industry against the colonial government's policies on the one hand and against workers' strikes on the other hand. In addition, it protested against factory legislations.[37]

Initially, the AMA had members from both the textile industry and other industries. By 1918, however, the membership was restricted to textile mills in and around Ahmedabad and mills up to Baroda and Broach. All major decisions were taken by the executive committee aided by a president and vice-president, who were nominated by consensus. The opinion and recommendations of the AMA were considered by the government when framing its textile policies. The AMA formulated rules and regulations for maintaining discipline among labourers, and these were put into practice in February 1909.[38] Some of the rules were strict and exploitative and intended to establish the domination of the mill owners.

AMA also undertook various charitable works, especially in times of natural calamity. This concern for charity was an obvious continuation of the guild tradition. From 1892, the AMA had one seat reserved in the Bombay legislative assembly for its representation. Later, it was also granted a reserved seat in the central legislature and one in the municipality of Ahmedabad.[39]

The tradition of *mahajans* was so strongly entrenched in the economic life of Ahmedabad that it continued even when the city was industrialised. Guilds and *mahajans* adapted their functions to the new situations. *Mahajans* and *panchs* became modernised. Various new *mahajans* such as AMA, cloth merchants' *mahajans* and, later, *majoor mahajan* emerged with the development of the modern textile industry.

Three new guilds of cloth merchants now emerged in the city. In 1897, the Panchkunva Kapad Mahajan was founded by 20 traders in cloth. Afterwards, *rangati mahajan* (piece-goods and silk merchants) joined this *mahajan*. The main purpose of the *mahajan* was to arbitrate and decide disputes among the members. The *mahajan* also undertook many charity works.[40] The second cloth traders' *mahajan* was the Mercantile Association of Madhupura, whose members had shops in Madhupura.

The third *mahajan* was the Maskati Mahajan founded in 1906 by the independent traders in the Kalupur area and some traders in the Madhupura area. To begin with, there were a hundred members. It was an association chiefly engaged in the wholesale indigenous cloth business. It soon became the premier cloth association of Gujarat. The Mahajan was named after the owner of the shops at Kalupur, Seth Taiyabbhai Mulla Mehmudali Maskati, a Bohra. He was a business magnate who charged a low rent for shops, furnished the facility for warehouses and provided loans at a low rate of interest. Members of the Mercantile Association also traded in this market. Over the years, the Mercantile Association merged with the Maskati Mahajan. The main object of the Maskati Mahajan was to provide suitable facilities for smooth distribution of cloth all over the country. It also wanted to safeguard the interest of members in their dealings with merchants of other centres.

Like the traditional guilds, the Maskati Mahajan exercised its authority in fixing trade rules, deciding holidays and administering common funds and arbitrating in matters under dispute. Arbitration to settle all disputes arising out of commercial dealings was one of the salient features of its constitution. The Maskati Mahajan was heterogeneous in composition and comprised of Jain and Vaishnav Vanias, Kanbis, Bohras, Parsis and later Marwadis, Sindhis and Sikhs. However, it was dominated largely by Jain traders. The Maskati Mahajan also continued in the guild tradition by showing great concern for charities. Being dominated by the Jain Vanias, a large sum went to the maintenance of the *panjrapol* and later funds were diverted to educational purposes and various relief works.[41]

The Maskati Mahajan as well as the Panchkuva Traders' Mahajan had very cordial relations with the AMA. The guild tradition continued even in the later Majoor Mahajan. Thus, the tradition of the guild, which was a primary pre-industrial institution, did not wither away with the onslaught of industrialisation, the

7. Alexander K Forbes

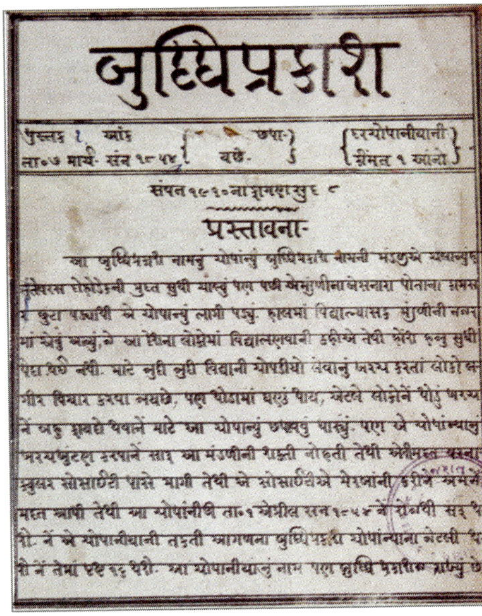

8.a: *Buddhi Prakash* - I

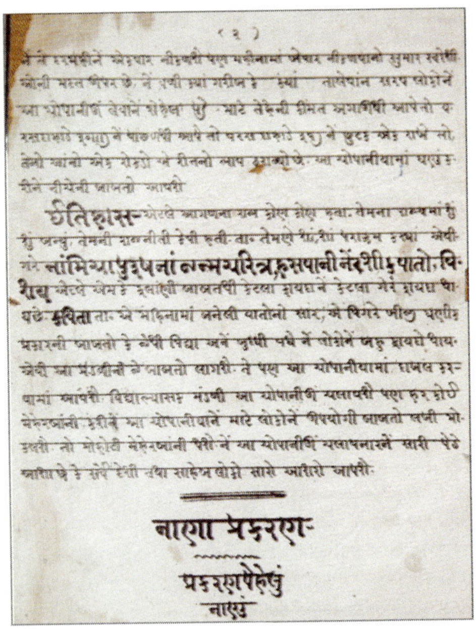

8.b: *Buddhi Prakash* - II

9. Dalpatram

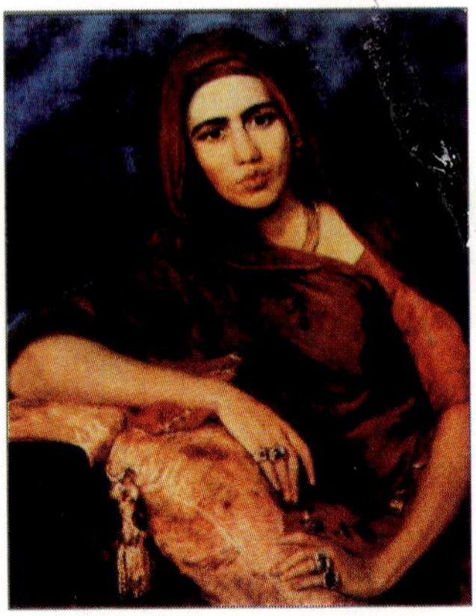

10. Harkunvar Sethani

11. Harkunvarbai Kanyashala

12. Hatesingh Jain Temple

advent of the railways or the British rule as had been predicted by Karl Marx. In 1853, Marx had seen the coming of modernity in India and prophesied the destruction of the objective conditions of tradition and their replacement by the objective conditions of modernity.[42] The hold of the guild on the economic life of Ahmedabad continued. New *mahajans* emerged in response to new forces. The AMA, cloth merchant *mahajans*, Majoor Mahajan were such examples. Another important *mahajan* which came into existence was the Share Market Merchants' *Mahajan*. As the investment in the cotton market increased, leading to a need for a local share market, the Ahmedabad Stock Exchange was established in 1894. The new *mahajan* of the share brokers was established along the lines of the older traditions of the *mahajans* and soon became a well organised *mahajan* of the city.[43]

Mahajans were still considered significant to the economic life of the city. The *Ahmedabad Gazetteer* recorded the existence of 29 *mahajans* in 1879.[44] In 1896, when E Washburn Hopkins, a professor at Yale University, undertook a study of the guilds in the city, he found no less than 40 guilds.[45] Interviewing the *seths* and *patels* of the leading guilds of Ahmedabad in 1896, he found that the leader of a guild was elected by its members. He was surprised to find guilds still vigorous in Ahmedabad despite the flourishing mill industry.[46]

Trade disputes were mainly settled by arbitration by the guild leaders so that very few disputes went to the courts. This is supported by the *Kapasia Bajarnu Khatpatra,* a legal document of the cotton market dated June 1892, which reveals that traders in cotton market preferred to settle internal disputes by arbitration through the five leading men of the *mahajan*, rather than go to court as they found the latter both ineffective and expensive. Fifty four cotton merchants agreed to arbitration by the *panch*, which was made up of five leading men of the *mahajan*.[47]

In the area of social and personal matters, however, the legal hold of guilds was loosened. The *mahajans* and *panchs* became more professional and less social in their orientation.

Thus, these traditional institutions had adapted themselves to the modern industrial age.

The other traditional institution of the city, that of the *nagarseth*, however, could not survive the emergence of the new industrial leadership and the introduction of the modern elected municipality. As a result, this informal institution gradually started losing its significance. The *nagarseth,* who had played an important role in civic affairs and had served as an informal link between the people and the government, now became redundant as the formal institutions of civic administration were firmly established by the last quarter of the 19th century. Simultaneously, with the growth of machine industries, those who ventured into new industrial enterprises prospered and rose in the esteem of the people. Ranchhodlal, the founder of the first textile mill, gained great prestige and honour both in business and in official circles. He was nominated the first president of the Ahmedabad municipality.

In 1896, E Washburn Hopkins wrote about the *nagarseth*, "he has already lost much of his power, which has been taken by a leading manufacturer, a man who does not belong to any guild, but by public gifts and wealth he has won in the business world a position of commanding influence—a fact indicative of the rapid passing away of the old order". He added, "In other towns this title has become a mere name, and even in Ahmedabad the *nagarseth* has now only a religious and social importance".[48]

The *nagarseth*'s family remained aloof from the mill industry until very late. As a result, their wealth and economic importance were surpassed by other capitalists who had entered the textile industry. Thus, the institution of the *nagarseth* was not able to meet the challenges of new political and industrial forces. The result was that the position lost all substance, though the title still continued as an irrelevant relic of the past and the reminder of the old order.[49]

The textile mill industry became the nerve centre around which the economic life of the city revolved. In spite of the British colonial capitalist policy, the textile mills flourished. Besides not giving any financial help or protection, the British government also cherished the *laissez faire* principles, which were beneficial to Britain. In India, the British government's policy was to encourage the export of raw cotton to England to feed its own textile industry. The Manchester textile lobby, through the British parliament, kept pressurising the British Indian government to introduce labour legislation such as cutting the working hours of labourers in order to stop exploitation of industrial labour. The AMA protested strongly against such labour legislation as they felt that such methods helped the British rulers to throttle the nascent textile industry. The British government continued to allow the influx of English-made yarn and textiles into India without any or with only a nominal excise duty. In 1896, the British government imposed duty on the indigenous production of the textile industry. This adversely affected the Indian textile industry.

In Ahmedabad, no major industries other than the textile industry developed owing to this colonial policy. For example, when entrepreneurs led by Ranchhodlal approached the Bombay government in 1884 with a proposal to develop the coal and iron deposits in the Panchmahal district, the Bombay government rejected it outright. In 1882, Ranchhodlal, Mansukhbhai Bhagubhai, Bechardas Lashkari, and Pestonji Vakil had already formed a joint stock company, the Gujarat Coal and Iron Company. When the Bombay government rejected their proposal, they took the matter to the viceroy, pleading that the development of such an industry would help the process of economic growth of the country. But the viceroy, Lord Dufferin, also turned it down. Thus, the project to develop a new type of industry remained still-born owing to the adverse British policy.[50]

III

The advent of the railways and the growth of modern industries accelerated the decline of indigenous handicraft industries. It is true that the railways increased the importance of Ahmedabad as a trading centre, but it also brought the city within the British colonial orbit. The BB & CI railway linked Ahmedabad to Surat in 1863 and to Bombay in 1864, though for the next seven years there was no further extension. In 1870, the railway was extended three miles to Sabarmati Station and in 1871, 15 miles to Sanand, 23 miles to Viramgam and a further three miles to Kharagoda. In 1872, it was extended to Wadhwan.[51] In 1879, Ahmedabad was joined to Delhi by the Rajputana metre gauge line. Between 1880 and 1897, Ahmedabad was connected to the native states of Saurashtra. It was also later joined to Prantij and Dholka.[52] Thus, Ahmedabad became a railway junction of considerable importance. The railway radiated from the city in all directions. The Rajputana–Malwa line opened up markets in Punjab and the North-West Frontier Province.[53]

The textile mill industry of Ahmedabad gave a further blow to the cotton home spinning and handloom weaving in the city. Moreover, the changing fashions and the increasing demand for *vilayati*, or foreign, articles among the urban educated classed led to the depression of various crafts of the city. The urban youth was dressed from head to toe in *vilayati*. Even the things on the youth's writing table—ink, paper, ink-pot, pen, pencil, envelopes, pins, blotting paper, paperweights, scissors, notebooks, glue—were *vilayati*. Hargovinddas Kantawala, the author of the famous book *Deshi Karigarine Uttejan* (Encouragement to Indigenous Craftsmanship), lamented in 1876 that in the preceding 10 years, the fondness for *vilayati* things had increased.[54]

The worst affected handicraft industry was home spinning which provided a livelihood to many poor women. The art of hand spinning was dead in Ahmedabad by the time Gandhi settled there in 1915. Gandhi wished to revive the spinning wheel and the production of *khadi* (handspun and handwoven cloth). However, he found it difficult to acquire a spinning wheel, or even a spinner, to teach the inmates of the *ashram* how to spin.[55] Another industry which suffered was handloom weaving. Both these indigenous industries succumbed to the machine textile industry of both England and Ahmedabad. The *Ahmedabad Gazetteer* stated in 1879 that the cotton textiles, paper, textile printing and hardware industries suffered severely from European competition.[56]

The first decade of the 20th century saw a sharp decline in the paper industry. By 1912, there were only about a hundred families left who made durable handmade paper used by the *sharafs* for account books.[57] The same was true of the silk industry. By 1911, the number of artisans engaged in silk and *kinkhab* spinning and weaving had dropped to 3,565 from 4,996 in 1901.[58]

The demand for silk and *kinkhab* decreased as Chinese and artificial English silk became popular among the rich. But both these industries continued to exist as demand for their products continued in the native states as well as in the countries of the Persian Gulf.[59] Though the city prospered owing to the mill industry and the railways, the artisan class suffered during this period. Some artisans joined mills while some educated themselves and took up government jobs, but many were rendered jobless.

The new machine industry and the railways brought about some other profound changes in the city. The prosperity of Ahmedabad increased, and its population grew rapidly as people from Saurashtra, Malwa and Rajasthan immigrated to the city. In 40 years, the city's population rose from 116,873 in 1872 to 213,727 in 1911. As a result, the city expanded.

The most significant social consequence of industrialisation was the emergence of the capitalist and working classes in the city. The middle class also expanded. The new classed superimposed on a caste-ridden society gave rise to new social relationships. Though the capitalist class was heterogeneous in its caste composition, it was dominated by the Jain and Vaishnav Vanias, the traditional commercial castes. The other castes and communities like the Nagars, Kanbis, Brahmakshatriyas, Parsis and Bohras remained marginal. The participation of the traditional commercial castes and their old established *pedhis* in industry gave continuity to the business culture of the city. It also put a distinct stamp on the way in which the capitalist class was formed and structured. The class had cohesion and solidarity which was manifested in managing agencies, partnerships and the interlocking directorships. As mentioned earlier, this cohesiveness was expressed in the formation of the AMA in 1891. The strength of the capitalist class was seen during the mammoth labourers' strike in 1895 when 8,000 labourers struck work and brought the mill industry to a standstill. The small but powerful class of capitalists could curb this strike with the help of the British government.

Another class which emerged was the working class which expanded with the growth of the machine industry. The working class of Ahmedabad is discussed in a separate chapter.

IV

The political culture of Ahmedabad was shaped by its commercial ethos. Since the medieval period, the mercantile city had developed conciliatory and pragmatic traditions, which valued peace, consensus and communal harmony above all other things. As a result, the business elite of the city had got along harmoniously with the Muslim and Maratha rulers in the past. Similarly, they developed an allegiance to the British rulers. The business elite and the newly emerged professional middle class were dazzled by the progressive and liberal values of the British. They hailed the British regime as Ram Rajya, or ideal governance, as it assured them of security and happiness. They had benefited from colonial patronage in the form of government jobs, titles, lands and educational and civic facilities. The newly emerged capitalist class of mill owners also shared these same political attitudes and sentiments because this class had its roots in the traditional business class.

However, this loyalist attitude did not blind the people of Ahmedabad to the exploitative nature of British capitalist colonial policy. Their strong business sense and pragmatic outlook led them to realise how British rule was injurious to their economy.

To prevent the ruin caused by the colonial policy of British rule, Ahmedabad cultivated the spirit of *swadeshi*, that is, promotion of indigenous industries and non-purchase of foreign goods. In fact, this was the commercial city's spontaneous response to the challenge posed by colonial policy. In the early phase, owing to a loyalist stance, the *swadeshi* movement developed as a purely economic movement without any political overtones. It was an expression of economic nationalism. The *swadeshi* movement in Ahmedabad developed a political tinge only after the partition of Bengal. In Ahmedabad, the *swadeshi* movement was constructive, utilitarian and non-militant in character.

In Ahmedabad and in Gujarat, the idea of *swadeshi* in its rudimentary form can be traced back to as early as 1851 in Dalpatram's famous poem titled *Hunnar Khanni Chhadhai*. In this poem, he explained how the country was being drained of its wealth by the influx of foreign goods. He appealed to the people to start indigenous industries.

The articles in *Buddhi Prakash*, the monthly journal of the GVS, reflected the spirit of *swadeshi*. The articles exhorted people to start modern industries and use indigenous goods and thus prevent the draining of the country's wealth.[60] As early as 1857, the Vidhyabhyasak Mandali of Ahmedabad organised a lecture titled 'Why does the wealth of Hindus go out of the country?'[61] In 1861, the writer Ranchhodram Uderam, after visiting the first textile mill of Ahmedabad, explained in an article in *Buddhi Prakash* how the textile manufactures of England, in alliance with the British rulers of India, imported cotton from India and sent back finished goods. The author thought the development of indigenous textile industries would stop this drain of wealth from India to England.[62]

In 1870, when two iron bridges were being built over the river Sabarmati, an anonymous author of an article in *Buddhi Prakash* lamented the fact that the steel and building material were imported from abroad in exchange for Indian gold and silver. He also appealed to the people to discover iron ore mines and to manufacture steel and other building material in India.[63]

Gopalrao Hari Deshmukh became the honorary secretary of the GVS in 1872. He was a pioneer and advocate of *swadeshi* in India. In Ahmedabad, he was a judge in the small causes court for about 12 years from 1866 to 1877. His presence must have had a significant influence on the *swadeshi* movement of Ahmedabad. When he left Ahmedabad in 1877, the Gopalrao Hari Memorial Fund was raised in his memory and was administered by the GVS. The interest on the Fund was spent on activities connected with indigenous industries. Essay competitions on subjects related to indigenous industries and their encouragement were organised by the Society. It announced prizes from this Fund for those who could produce long staple cotton of Egyptian or American quality and for manufacturing scented soap, purified castor oil and other such products.[64]

Hargovindas Dwarkadas Kantawala was a life member of the GVS, educationist, social reformer, ardent advocate of *swadeshi* and founder member of the Swadeshi Udhyog Vardhak Mandali. He delivered an effective lecture on *swadeshi* on October 8, 1876 at the Hemabhai Institute, when he exhibited indigenous soaps, locks and knives to the audience.[65] These products, according to him, were superior to foreign ones. Later, he also lectured in Baroda and Rajkot.[66] The activities of the Mandali inspired common people to use indigenous goods in a spirit of patriotism. A large number of people took vows not to use foreign goods if similar Indian products were available.

A part of Hargovindas Kantawala's invaluable contribution to spreading the *swadeshi* spirit was the powerful book *Deshi Karigarine Uttejan* (Encouragement to Indigenous Craftsmanship) published in 1876 which he authored anonymously. This was the first attempt to present the idea of *swadeshi* systematically and to suggest concrete measures to encourage indigenous industries and agriculture.

The GVS, too, took up the cause of *swadeshi* and published a series of articles in *Buddhi Prakash* titled *Deshi Karigarine Uttejan* in which various practical measures to encourage industries and agriculture were suggested. The Society also published books on the manufacture of various goods. In 1878, the book *Gujaratna Utkarsh Thavana Sadhano* (Measures for the Development of Gujarat) by Vithaldas Dhanjibhai, a school teacher, was published. In 1889, the GVS published another practical book titled *Pardeshi Mal Deshma Taiyar Karva Sha Upay Yojva Joiye?* (What Measures Should Be Taken to Manufacture Foreign Goods in Our Country?) by Bhavanishankar Joshi, a teacher at the Vernacular School of Ahmedabad. In the 1890s, *Buddhi Prakash* published a series of articles titled '*Kala Kaushalya*', in which it advised people to emulate advanced western countries and manufacture consumer articles like the ones produced abroad and so make foreign goods unnecessary. The propagators of *swadeshi* believed that handicrafts should continue and machine industries should be encouraged alongside. Great emphasis was laid on technical education. The example of Meiji Japan's rapid industrialisation was a great source of inspiration to the *swadeshi* movement in India.

The *swadeshi* movement in the country received a great impetus when the unfair and countervailing excise duty on Indian cloth was levied in 1896. This roused the anger of political leaders as well as of mill owners in the entire country. It was at this time that Maharashtra, under the leadership of Bal Gangadhar Tilak, gave a new dimension to the movement by organising for the first time a boycott of foreign goods on a large scale. Ahmedabad, the centre of the Indian textile industry, however, responded in a non-aggressive way. The leaders of the city protested only verbally. Ranchhodlal, the champion of *swadeshi* strongly protested the unfair duty on Indian cloth in the legislative council of the Bombay presidency of which he was a member.[67] Thus, Ahmedabad remained isolated from the countrywide agitation politics of the time even during this widespread movement against the excise duty on cloth. Thus, in Ahmedabad in the 19th century, the *swadeshi* movement remained largely economic in its content but in the long run contributed greatly to promoting patriotism and politicising the people of the city who were by nature apolitical.

Political consciousness and modern political activities were slow to develop in Ahmedabad. In 1871, the people of Ahmedabad did form a public association, the Ahmedabad Association, on the model of the Pune Sarvajanik Sabha to represent their demands to the government. But it soon became inactive and moribund.[68]

In 1884, another political association, the Gujarat Sabha, was founded to safeguard and promote political and socioeconomic interests. This was the only major political association which undertook any systematic political activities before Gandhi's arrival in Ahmedabad. Founded by rich and influential local people, who were mostly middle class professionals, the Gujarat Sabha dominated the political scene of the city. The first honorary secretary of the Sabha was MP Modi, a Parsi lawyer. Thereafter, Govindram Appaji Patil, a Maharashtrian lawyer, and Dr Joseph Benjamin, a Bene-Israeli (Indian Jewish community) doctor, worked as honorary secretaries. Other active members were Lallubhai Asaram (lawyer), Bhaishankar Nanabhai (solicitor), Mulchand Asaram (lawyer), Ramanbhai Nilkhant (lawyer), Jivanlal Desai (lawyer), Hargovindas Kantawala (educationalist) and Ambalal Sakarlal (an educationist and retired chief justice of Baroda State). Ranchhodlal Chhotalal remained active and was the president of the Sabha from its inception until he died in 1898.[69]

The Sabha not only made representations to the government of public wants, opinions and complaints in the form of petitions and memoranda but also tried to democratise the municipal administration. After the establishment of the Indian National Congress in 1885, the Sabha regularly sent delegates to the annual sessions of the Congress. Its stance from the very beginning was moderate, cautious, conservative and mild. It showed leanings towards the moderate politics of the early Indian National Congress leaders. It was also too loyalist to attack the British government's policies. It is not surprising, therefore, that the local newspaper *Prajabandhu* denounced the Sabha as 'timid' and 'ultra loyalist', criticising its sporadic and secretive activities.[70]

It caustically stated that the Sabha would perhaps rise once in a while like a phoenix but then would fall asleep like Kumbhakarna.[71] The Sabha nominated delegates to the Indian National Congress. Though the *Sethia* members extended financial help to the Sabha, they kept aloof from active participation for a long time. At the Sabha's annual general meeting, the prescribed quorum of five members was quite often difficult to achieve.[72]

Since the Sabha's annual subscription was high at Rs 12, a sum beyond the common man then, it remained an elitist and exclusive association. The *Prajabandhu* suggested that, if the subscription were lowered to five rupees, many politically aware people would participate in its activities. The Sabha made the mistake of pampering the rich mill owners and kept aloof from the masses, thus failing to mobilise public opinion. When the people of the city took a procession to the collector's office in 1899 to protest the increased income tax, not a single member of the Gujarat Sabha was present.[73]

The entry of Ambalal Sakarlal Desai in Ahmedabad activated the Sabha and subsequently the political scene of Ahmedabad. He was an ardent advocate of *swadeshi* and was one of the founder members of Ahmedabad's Swadeshi Udhyog Vardhak Mandali. He was the first Gujarati to obtain MA and LLB degrees and became the headmaster of the Government High School of Surat and Ahmedabad. He joined the judicial department of Baroda State in 1876 and rapidly rose to the position of chief justice in 1886. After, retirement in 1899, he returned to his home town of Ahmedabad, where he entered the textile industry and also took an active interest in public affairs. He was closely associated with most of the public institutions of Ahmedabad such as the municipality, the GVS and the Gujarat Sahitya Sabha. He wrote prolifically on *swadeshi*, education and politics and was a great advocate of technical education. He was a staunch opponent of the extremist elements in politics and, instead, followed in the footsteps of his mentors, Dadabhai Naoroji, Ranade, Gokhale, S Banerjee and Pherozeshah Mehta.

In 1900, the government conferred on Ambalal Desai the title of 'Dewan Bahadur'. In the midst of severe famine and plague, the Gujarat Sabha held a function in January 1900, in collaboration with the Gujarat Club, to felicitate Ambalal Sakarlal. Later, the Sabha even celebrated the victory of the British in South Africa and organised a show at the Shanti Bhuvan Theatre to collect a fund for the British.[74] As against this, the Sabha remained surprisingly indifferent to the suffering of the famine-struck people of India.

There had always been a close alliance between the textile mill owners and the middle class professionals in political matters. The middle class professionals had large investments in the form of deposits and shares in the mills. They also rendered professional services to the mill owners and thus shared with the latter many economic and political interests. The two groups cooperated and collaborated in economic, social and political life. By the turn of the century, the mill owners had become active in political matters.

In 1902, the eighteenth session of the Indian National Congress was held in Ahmedabad, a provincial town, largely due to the efforts of Ambalal Sakarlal. The mill owners actively participated in the session. Mangaldas Girdhardas was inducted into the Congress working committee and many other mill owners became members of the reception committee of which Ambalal was the chairman. JN Tata was requested to make available the premises of his Advance Mills for the Congress session.[75] It was decided to display mill-made yarn and textile goods with handmade products at the industrial exhibition which was to be held as an adjunct to the Congress session. The exhibition was inaugurated by Maharaja Sayajirao Gaikwad of Baroda, a champion of *swadeshi*. His brilliant inaugural address demonstrated his intense involvement in *swadeshi*.

Ambalal Desai, in his speech, criticised the unjust imperialistic economic policy of the British on the one hand and, on the other, praised British political institutions to show his loyalty to British rule. This was typical not only of the political leaders of Ahmedabad but of the Congress, which too was a loyalist organisation at that time.

The Congress Session of 1902 was memorable in the history of Ahmedabad. Until then, Ahmedabad had remained aloof from national politics, but now its citizens were brought closer to it.

A few days later, as an outcome of the enthusiasm generated by the Congress session, the Indigenous Articles Protection Association (IAPA) was founded on January 1, 1903, under the leadership of Ambalal Desai.[76] The aim of this Association was to promote and encourage indigenous industries. Indian industries could not flourish because the British government followed a free trade policy for India and did not extend protection to them. The only way to promote these nascent industries was through self-help, by people using only indigenous products and rejecting foreign products. The Association gave equal importance to machine-run industries and to handicrafts. This association was the first of its kind in India.

The partition of Bengal gave a fresh impetus to the *swadeshi* movement, one result being a public meeting called by the *Deccani Samaj* of the city.[77] Even the Gujarat Sabha followed its example and called a meeting on October 3, 1905, at the Premabhai Hall in order to consider ways of encouraging indigenous industries. The outcome of these meetings was the birth of the Gujarat Industrial Association. Ambalal Desai was made its president, and the IAPA merged with it.[78] Its members were required to sign a pledge that they would abstain from buying foreign goods. It opened *swadeshi* shops at Ahmedabad, Bhavnagar, Broach, Surat and Baroda.

Another important development at the height of the protest against Bengal partition was the establishment of the organisation the *Swadeshi Mitra Mandal* in 1906 by Maganbhai Chaturbhai Patel, Dr Hariprasad, Professor Swaminarayan and others of Ahmedabad.[79] Aimed at spreading the *swadeshi* spirit among the masses, this significant movement undid the negative attitude of the Gujarat Sabha which had remained aloof from masses. This was the first political association of the city which tried to arouse political consciousness among the urban as well as rural masses. A member of the *Mandal* had to take a pledge that he or she would not use foreign goods. The *Mandal* also started a campaign for signed pledges not to buy foreign goods. The *Mandal* published a book of songs on *swadeshi* and organised *swadeshi kirtan* programmes. It regularly observed Bengal Partition Day. The popular local newspaper, the *Prajabandhu*, hailed its activities and wrote on the observance of the first anniversary of Bengal Partition Day:[80] "It is no doubt a significant sign of the times that the people of the city, who are proved apathetic in matters political, should realize the necessity of suitably celebrating the first anniversary of the Bengal Partition Day."[81]

The *swadeshi* movement was now developing political overtones. The *Mandal* invited Annie Besant, Lala Lajpatrai and other national leaders to the city. The *Mandal* instilled patriotism and the spirit of *Swadeshi* into the people of Ahmedabad through public meetings and public lectures. The *Mandal* published the monthly journal *Udbodhan* for a few years. The *Mandal* composed a picture of Mother India—Hind Devi—which was placed on the stage at the public meetings and was later printed and the prints sold all over the country.[82] The *Mandal* also started night classes for labourers under the auspices of the Gujarat Paisa Fund. The fund was to be used for education and technical training, while the aim of the night classes was to spread literacy among labourers in order to increase political consciousness among them.[83] The *Mandal* started the Gokhale Society which organised debates on political issues. It also opened the Dadabhai Naoroji free reading room.[84] Working in all these directions, enthusiastically cultivating grassroots activities, the *Swadeshi Mitra Mandal* was able to politically awaken the people of Ahmedabad.

The enthusiasm and fervour with which people took up s*wadeshi* subsequent to the agitation against the partition of Bengal gave an impetus to the textile industry of Ahmedabad. Many new textile mills were established, resulting in the textile industry and *swadeshi* reinforcing each other.

Despite all this, Ahmedabad still remained a stronghold of moderate politics. The political leaders of the city supported the moderate group of the Congress. At the Surat session of the Congress in 1907, moderate leaders of Ahmedabad, under the leadership of Ambalal Desai, made an organised attempt to defeat the extremist cause.

The leaders of Ahmedabad strongly disapproved of the militant revolutionary activities of Shyamji Krishna Verma and his friends. When Maganlal Dhingra murdered a British official and a Parsi in London, a protest meeting was called by the people of Ahmedabad to show their disapproval.[85] When Lord and Lady Minto visited the city in November 1909, an unsuccessful attempt was made to hurl a bomb at them. Such an incident in a peace-loving city surprised everyone and cast a gloom over the whole city. A meeting was immediately called under the chairmanship of Sir Madhavlal to show the city's disapproval of such actions and to affirm its loyalty towards the British Empire.[86]

This was the political milieu of Ahmedabad before Gandhi arrived in the city.

Notes

1. Indian Industrial Commission, *Report of the Industrial Commission 1916–18*, Calcutta, 1918, p. 30.
2. Kenneth L Gillion, *Ahmedabad: A Study in Indian Urban History*, Berkeley, 1968, pp. 74–81.
3. SM Edwards, *Memoir of Rao Bahadur Ranchhodlal Chhotalal, C.I.E., Late Member of the Legislative Council, Bombay and Father of the Mill Industry of Gujarat,* London, 1920, p. 13.
4. Makrand J Mehta, *The Ahmedabad Cotton Textile Industry: Genesis and Growth,* Ahmedabad, 1982, p. 41.
5. Bhagwanlal R Badshah, *Life of Rao Bahadur Ranchorelal Chhotalal, C.I.E*, Bombay, 1899, pp. 15–16.
6. *Ibid.*, pp. 17–18.
7. *Ibid.*, pp. 39–40 (Gujarati version).
8. MJ Mehta, *op. cit.*, pp. 51–52.
9. B Badshah, *op. cit.*, pp. 39–40 (Gujarati version).
10. *Ibid.*, *Buddhi Prakash*, July 1861, pp. 156–57.

11. SM Edwards, *op. cit.*, pp. 21–22.
12. Bombay Government, *Gazetteer of Bombay Presidency*, vol. 4, *Ahmedabad,* Bombay, 1879, p. 63. Henceforth cited as *Ahmedabad Gazetteer.*
13. *Buddhi Prakash*, September 1865, p. 63; Shankarrai Amritrai, *Amdavadno Jivan Vikas* (in Gujarati), Ahmedabad, 1921, pp. 203–206.
14. Vallabhji Sundarji Punjabhai, *Rajnagarna Ratno* (in Gujarati), Rajkot, 1918, p. 221; John Huston, *Representative Men of the Bombay Presidency* (2nd ed.), London, 1900, p. 91.
15. *Ahmedabad Gazetteer*, p. 133.
16. MJ Mehta, *op. cit.,* pp. 75–76.
17. *Ahmedabad Gazetteer*, p. 133.
18. Vallabhji S Punjabhai, *op. cit.*, p. 249.
19. Bansidhar G Parekh, *Sheth Mangaldas Girdhardas; Jivan ane Karya* (in Gujarati), Ahmedabad 1955; Vallabhji S Punjabhai, *op. cit.*, p. 46–48.
20. Vallabhji S Punjabhai, *op. cit.*, p. 65–67.
21. Dwijendra Tripathi, *The Dynamics of a Tradition; Kasturbhai Lalbhai and Entrepreneurship*, Delhi, 1981, pp. 48–50; *Prajabandhu*, June 9, 1912, p. 8.
22. Bombay Government, *Statement Showing Statistics of Cotton Mills in the Bombay Presidency for the Year Ending 31st March 1890*, Bombay, pp. 24–25.
23. Bombay Government, *Cotton and Jute Mills Statistics Relating to the Bombay Presidency for the Year Ending 31st March 1895*, in General Department 41A/1895.
24. Bombay Government, *Bombay Presidency Cotton Mills the Year Ending 31st March 1905*, pp. 1–7 and 20–21.
25. MJ Mehta, *op. cit.*, pp. 124–131.
26. Bombay Government, *Bombay Presidency Cotton Mills the Year Ending 31st March 1908*, pp. 2–9, 22–23, 26–37 and 58–59.
27. *Ahmedabad Gazetteer*, 308.
28. Shankarrai Amritrai, *op. cit.*, Ahmedabad, 1921, p. 198; Bombay Government, *Annual Factory Report of the Presidency of Bombay, 1897*, p. 1. Henceforth cited as *FA* and the year.
29. *Prajabandhu*, July 1, 1906, p. 25.
30. Vallabhji S. Punjabhai, *op. cit.*, pp. 133–37.
31. *FA* 1914, pp. i–xxiv.
32. Kenneth L Gillion, *op. cit.*, p. 6.
33. Ratnamanirao Bhimrao, *Gujaratnu Patnagar Amdavad* (in Gujarati), Ahmedabad, 1929, p. 498.
34. Howard Spodek, 'Traditional Culture and Entrepreneurship: A Case Study of Ahmedabad', *Economic and Political weekly*, February 1969, pp. M-27–31.

35. *Ibid.*, p. M-29.
36. *Ahmedabad Gazetteer*, p. 65.
37. *Prajabandhu,* September 20, 1908, p. 2.
38. *Prajabandhu*, February 21, 1909, p. 12.
39. Jal S Ratnagar (Ed.), *The Indian Text*ile *Journal Special Souvenir Number to mark the Centenary of the Cotton Textile Industry of India—1854–1954,* Bombay, 1954, pp. 520–23; Kapilrai Mehta, *Ahmedabad*, 1959, pp. 221–23; *Report of the Mill Owners Association of Ahmedabad* from the year 1920 onwards.
40. Kapilrai Mehta, *op. cit.*, pp. 247.
41. Jal S Ratnagar, *op. cit.*, pp. 553; Kapilrai Mehta, *op. cit.*, pp. 227–28; Maskati Mahajan, *Navi Market Udghatan Smaranika* (in Gujarati) Ahmedabad, 1962, pp. 5-15; articles of *Amrit Mahotsava Souvenir* (in Gujarati and English), Ahmedabad, 1982, pp. 1–21; *Atmaram Bhogilal Sutarianu Nivedan* (in Gujarati and English), Ahmedabad, 1962, pp. 1–4; Shirin Mehta, 'The Continuity and Change in an Urban Institution: A Case Study of Maskati Cloth Mahajan of Ahmedabad 1906–1947', a paper presented at the Seminar on Urban History at Gujarat University, Ahmedabad, 1985.
42. Lloyd Rudolph and Susan Rudolph, *The Modernity of Tradition,* Chicago, 1967, pp. 21–23.
43. Ratnamanirao Bhimrao, *op. cit.*, p. 554.
44. *Ahmedabad Gazetteer*, p. 108.
45. E Washburn Hopkins, *India Old and New,* New York, 1902, p. 182.
46. *Ibid.*, pp. 199 and 204.
47. *Kapasia Bajarnu Khatpatra,* dated June 1892, is at the BJ Institute of Research and Learning, Ashram Road, Ahmedabad. It is in Gujarati and no accession number has been given to it.
48. E Washburn Hopkins, *op. cit.*, p. 179.
49. D Tripathi and M Mehta, 'The Nagarsheth of Ahmedabad: The History of an Urban Institution in a Gujarat City', *Proceedings of the 39th Session of Indian History Congress*, Hyderabad, 1978, p. 492.
50. B Badshah, *op. cit.*, pp. 20–36.
51. *Ahmedabad Gazetteer*, p. 97.
52. Bombay Government, *Report of the Administration of the Bombay Presidency for the Year 1911–12*, Bombay, 1913, p. 64.
53. Rotary Club of Ahmedabad, *Ahmedabad*, 1940, pp. 64–66.
54. Hargovindas Kantawala, *Deshi Karigarine Uttejan* (in Gujarati), Part I, Ahmedabad, 1876, pp. 47–50.
55. MK Gandhi, *An Autobiography or the Story of My Experiments with Truth*, Ahmedabad, 1989, pp.407–09.

56. *Ahmedabad Gazetteer*, p. 140.
57. Bombay Government, *Report of the Administration of the Bombay Presidency for the Year 1911–12*, Bombay, 1913, p. 66.
58. Government of India, *Census of India – 1901*, Vol. IX, *Bombay,* Part II, Bombay, 1902, p.1 xxxii and p. xxiv; *Census of India – 1911*, Vol. VII, *Bombay*, Part II, Bombay, 1912, pp. 412 and 453.
59. His Majesty's Secretary of State for Indian in Council, *The Imperial Gazetteer of India*, Vol. V (New Edition), Oxford, 1908, p. 109.
60. *Buddhi Prakash*, April 1860, p. 82.
61. *Ibid.*, June 1857, p. 102.
62. *Ibid.*, December 1861, pp. 282–88.
63. *Ibid.*, August 1870, p. 174.
64. *Ibid.*, June 1883, p. 124.
65. *Ibid.,* January 1876, p. 20–21.
66. *Ibid.*, November 1876, p. 263.
67. SM Edwards, *op. cit.,* p. 46.
68. *Ahmedabad Gazetteer*, p. 271.
69. *Prajabandhu*, November 13, 1898, p. 1.
70. *Ibid.*, December 17, 1899, p. 2.
71. *Ibid.*, May 29, 1898, p. 6.
72. *Ibid.*, February 19, 1899, p. 2.
73. *Ibid.*
74. *Ibid.*, January 28, 1900, p. 50; *Ibid.*, March 11, 1902, p. 8.
75. *Ibid.*, May 11, 1902, p. 8.
76. *Buddhi Prakash*, March, 1903, pp. 92–93; *Prajabandhu*, January 18 (English columns); February 15, 1903, p. 1.
77. *Prajabandhu*, October 1, 1905, pp. 7–11.
78. *Ibid.*, October 8, 1905, p. 2.
79. *Ibid.*, September 30, 1906, p. 18.
80. *Ibid.*, October 14, 1906, p. 11. Shankarrai Amritrai, *op. cit.*, pp. 103–104.
81. *Prajabandhu*, October 21, 1906, p. 2.
82. Indual Yagnik, *Atmakatha*, Part I, Reprint, Ahmedabad, 1967, pp. 127–31.
83. *Prajabandhu*, October 10, 1909, p. 12; November 14, 1909, p. 10.
84. *Ibid.*, September 8, 1912, pp. 2–3.
85. *Ibid.*, July 25, 1909, p. 7.
86. *Ibid.*, November 21, 1909, pp. 6 and 12–14.

5

Manifestation of Change: Growth of Voluntary Associations and the Press

Since the mid-19th century, apart from its rapid development as a centre of the textile mill industry, Ahmedabad had gradually emerged as the hub of educational and socioreligious reform movements in Gujarat. The middle class, a powerful section of Ahmedabad society, set up various associations to bring about specific reforms. In this, it was helped by the growth of industrialisation and the consequent prosperity. In turn, the association used the nascent press to diffuse new ideas. New periodicals which furthered reformist ideas were encouraged and sponsored by the middle class. The press, which began as a handmaiden of the associations, now started growing independently. Newspapers helped to mould and mobilise public opinion.

The reformist associations and the press played important transformational roles and shaped the change which had been set in motion by British rule. Where the press created an information revolution, the new set of socioeconomic and cultural organisations provided a platform to discuss vital issues.

During this period, the city of Ahmedabad also witnessed the popularity of public meetings. Such meetings had become a vital part of the public life of the city. They were convened to solve social, civic and political issues, to support various causes, and to protest against the municipality or the government when necessary.

These three—voluntary associations, the press and public meetings—played a positive role in changing the attitudes and even the lifestyle of the people. They generally helped to promote a progressive outlook and encourage the inhabitants of Ahmedabad to discover a strong identity as citizens of the city.

I

One important agent of change was education. As the educated class had established the voluntary associations and participated actively in them and as they also formed the major reading group, a brief review of the growth of education during 1861–1914 would be useful at this point.

The city of Ahmedabad had emerged as a centre of education in the northern division of the Bombay presidency. After 1861, the growth of education in the city of Ahmedabad was rapid. In 1877–78, there were 23 government schools with 2,709 names on the rolls. Of these, one was an English medium high school, three Anglo-vernacular schools, nine vernacular schools for boys and one for girls, three Urdu schools, four night schools and two training colleges, one each for men and women.[1] In addition to the government schools, there were six private schools, which included one mission high school, one Anglo-vernacular school, two vernacular schools for boys and two for girls. There were 829 students on the rolls of these private schools. From 1863 to 1878, about 136 students passed their university entrance examination from the high schools of Ahmedabad.[2]

In 1882, the management of primary education had been transferred to the municipality. Under the guidance of Mahipatram Rupram, a well-known educationist and the first chairman of the school committee of the municipality, primary education flourished in the city and primary schools multiplied rapidly. As a result, in 1914, there were 41 municipal primary schools for boys with 7,731 students on the rolls and 22 primary schools for girls with 2,411 students on the rolls. Besides these, there were 19 primary schools for boys and 10 for girls. Some of these, including six of the girls' schools, were run by the Irish Presbyterian Mission.[3]

Compared to primary education, the growth of higher education was slow. There were only seven high schools in 1914, with 3,030 students in the six boys' schools and 130 students in the one girls' school, which was attached to the Mahalaxmi Training College for Women. In addition, there were one government middle school, two English middle schools and one Anglo-vernacular Anjuman-i-Islam school in Ahmedabad.[4] Until 1920, the city could boast of only one college, the Gujarat College. It had the arts as well as the science streams. In 1914, there were 494 students on the rolls of the college.[5]

In addition to the Gujarat College, there were two Training Colleges which were running successfully. The Irish Presbyterian Mission also had opened a normal school for women and men. The BJ Medical School attached to the Civil Hospital offered a four-year course and had 168 pupils on the rolls in 1914. In addition, there was Ranchhodlal Chhotalal Technical Institute with 73 students.[6] This technical institute was established in 1910 from the generous donation of Sir Chinubhai in memory of his grandfather Ranchhodlal, the founder of the textile industry in Ahmedabad. It taught useful subjects such as spinning, weaving and mechanical engineering.[7]

It is interesting to examine the growth of the Gujarat College which contributed greatly to the intellectual growth of the city. Its early history has been traced in Chapter 3. It was started in 1861 as the Provincial College but was closed down in 1871. In 1879, it was reopened with a class for the first arts examination of the Bombay University,[8] and was affiliated to the University of Bombay. In 1887, it became a full-fledged college teaching up to the BA degree. It was managed until 1913 by a special board instituted for the purpose. This board comprised six representatives elected by the body of the subscribers to the college fund, one representative of the municipality and the collector, the district judge and the education inspector of the northern division as government representatives.[9] Illustrious citizens such as RB Lalshankar Umiashankar, Seth Mansukhbai Bhagubhai, Seth Chimanlal Nagindas, Sir Chinubhai and KB Jehangirji Pestonji

Vakil served on the board as representatives of the subscribers. The college got a separate building in 1897.

In 1910, the Madhavlal Ranchhodlal Science Institute was established from the primary donation by Sir Chinubhai Madhavlal. Later, the George Hall and Sydenham Library were added. The number of students increased from 67 in 1888 to 293 in 1900. It reached 310 in 1898 owing to the influx of students from plague-stricken Bombay. In 1910, there were 278 students, of which 244 were Hindus, one Jew, 19 Parsis and 13 Muslims. Of the total, 122 students belonged to the city and others came from all over Gujarat.[10] Hostel facilities were provided for the latter. The hostel had three separate kitchens and dining rooms for the Hindu, Muslim and Parsi students, while the college had a large playground with facilities for games such as football, cricket and tennis. It also had a literary and debating society. In every way, the Gujarat College, had become a centre for various youth activities.

II

Besides being an important centre of education, Ahmedabad had also emerged as a centre of socioreligious reform movements in Gujarat. As a result, after 1861, different associations emerged to give institutional support to the city's educational, socioreligious, economic, literary and political activities and movements. The associations became a significant part of the city's public life. As mentioned earlier, they met the diverse needs of a society which was being gradually modernised.

Even before 1861, in the pre-industrial phase, the city had witnessed the emergence of some *sabhas*, *mandalis* and societies to fulfil the social and intellectual needs of the newly emerging middle class. However, except for the Gujarat Vernacular Society (GVS), other associations were short-lived. Since its establishment in 1848, the GVS had become the nucleus of literary and cultural activities. It played a significant modernising role not only in the city but in the whole of Gujarat. In fact, the establishment of GVS in 1848 and the beginning of the first textile mill in 1861 were the two major events in the history of the city which were responsible for ushering a new era into Ahmedabad.

By 1861, the Society, founded by the farsighted Englishman AK Forbes, had so strengthened and entrenched itself that it provided a forum for the diverse elite of Ahmedabad—European officials, businessmen, middle class intellectuals—to come together to participate in its multifarious activities. Under the able leadership of its European honorary secretaries, AK Forbes and Curtis, and the assistant secretary Dalpatram, it had become the pivotal organisation of reform and regeneration. The rich in and around the city of Ahmedabad extended generous financial help to the Society, as did the native rulers of Gujarat. Thus, with ample funds, able leadership and its own building, the Society survived right into the middle of the 20th century. It would be interesting to compare the Society with its contemporary sister association the Buddhi Vardhak Sabha of Bombay, which was established in 1851 but survived only up to 1880. The reasons for the early death of the Buddhi Vardhak Sabha were lack of funds and a proper infrastructure which its leaders never tried to develop.[11] In 1865, Dalpatram, the editor of the *Buddhi Prakash* wrote:

> Under the influence of Society, students have become clever in poetry and have become reformist in their thought. The influence is not only confined to Ahmedabad but has spread throughout Gujarat. The Europeans as well as Indians who come to Ahmedabad, visit the office of the Society. They feel happy to see the progress of the Society and some show willingness to help.[12]

The GVS not only continued the activities started in its earlier phase but extended its work from year to year, assimilating new ideas as it went along. Responding to the new social and economic needs of Ahmedabad society, it oriented its activities to suit them. In order to increase awareness among the people, progressive issues became the topics of articles in the *Buddhi Prakash* and also provided subjects for lectures, essays and elocution competitions organised by the Society. Through its influential periodical,

Buddhi Prakash, the Society campaigned against social evils. Issues such as women's education, *swadeshi* and economic uplift of the country, health and hygiene, the temperance movement and the progress of native states became the focus of its attention. Significantly, however, it abstained from the very beginning from discussing religious and political subjects.

Dissemination of knowledge and the promotion of education were the main objects of the Society. Therefore, it was deemed necessary to register it as a corporate body so that it may act as a permanent agency to hold trust funds for educational purposes. The Society was accordingly registered under Act XXI of 1860 in September 1880. Some trust funds were meant to institute scholarships for promising students. Some funds were endowed to prepare literature on specific subjects like science, health, education and women. In addition, the Society managed the funds of libraries, schools and institutes. It administered the funds of the Seth Manilal Ranchhodlal Library in Khadia and the Apparao Bholanath Library and of the Anjuman-i-Islam. The Society conducted the activities of the Ranchhodlal Chhotalal Girls' School at Khadia.[13]

From its very inception, the uplift of women was the prime concern of the Society. It had opened the first girls' school, the Harkunvarbai Kanyashala, in 1850. Later, it conducted the activities of two more girls' schools, the Ranchhodlal Chhotalal Khadia Kanyashala and Diwalibai Kanyashala. In the former school, subjects especially useful to women, as well as religion and ethics, were taught. By crusading against social evils such as the ban on widow remarriage and early marriage, dowry, bride price and polygamy, the Society tried to improve the status of women in society. In addition, GVS also managed eight trust funds which were instituted for the publication of books useful to women or concerning women, and other trust funds to endow scholarships to encourage girls to study. In 1908, a separate library for women was started in the Ranchhodlal Kanyashala, which again was managed by the GVS.[14]

GVS encouraged women's education by various schemes. Since 1894, in order to encourage women to speak in public, the Society started organising annual elocution competitions on subjects relevant to women such as child care, health, hygiene, women's education, how women should spend their leisure time and social customs. This scheme was quite successful and women from all over Gujarat participated. The women of the city of Ahmedabad flocked to attend the programmes in very large numbers.[15]

In 1901, the Society discontinued this particular scheme and launched a more ambitious scheme of examinations for those women who had for various social or personal reasons abandoned their studies but wanted to now continue. The scheme of 'continuing education' was indeed novel in those days. Examinations were held in Ahmedabad and had two levels, higher and lower. The subjects for examination were literature, health, hygiene, first-aid, home science, nursing and other such. The course content was utilitarian. The Society thus played a vital role in enlightening the women of Ahmedabad by raising their intellectual level.[16]

Among the Society's multifarious activities, literary activities were given high priority. One such was the preparation of a Gujarati dictionary. The Society encouraged authors by publishing or purchasing their books. By 1912, it had published 286 books. The Society also encouraged the writing of books on various subjects by awarding prizes and publishing the best books. In cooperation with the education department, the Society undertook the preparation of useful textbooks and the sale and distribution of these books. Rev. Taylor prepared a book of Gujarati grammar as part of this scheme. The Society also collected old books and manuscripts.

The Society initiated the library movement in Gujarat, helping libraries in the various towns of Gujarat, and had 127 libraries registered as its members. It had its own library, the Hemabhai Institute. Also, it maintained at its own cost a free reading room in Maneck Chowk for the benefit of merchants and traders. It managed three other libraries—the Seth Manilal Ranchhodlal Library in Khadia, the Apparao Bholanath Library and the Anjuman-i-Islam Library.[17]

While the policies of the Society were framed by the honorary secretary and the managing committee, the former administered its activities. It is, therefore, important to study the composition of the managing committee and briefly look at the life of the honorary secretaries for a useful insight into the leadership pattern of this pivotal organisation in particular and of the city in general.

In its initial stage, the work of the GVS was carried on by the Europeans who were ardent lovers of the vernacular and who earnestly wished the spread of education among the people of Gujarat. Besides AK Forbes who founded it, the Society enjoyed the services of Steward, TB Curtis and Scott, who served as honorary secretaries, as well as the cooperation of Maj. Fulljames, Sir Theodore C Hope and Rev. JVS Taylor. In the beginning, the managing committee was made up of only European members. Bhogilal Pranvallabhdas, the headmaster of the Government English School was the first Indian to be included in the committee in 1851. He also acted as the honorary secretary for a few months in 1852–53.[18] Later, Bholanath Sarabhai and Hemabhai Nagarseth were included in the committee in 1855 and 1858 respectively.

The European element in the committee was gradually reduced and the committee became Indianised. In 1872, Gopalrao Hari Deshmukh, known as Lokahitwadi (proponent of public welfare), a judge in the small causes court of Ahmedabad, became the first Indian honorary secretary of the Society. By 1877, the managing committee had no European member. Rev. Taylor and Buhler were the last European members of the committee. European officials and non-officials now remained aloof from the Society's activities. However, they continued their interest in its educational activities.

Leading businessmen and industrialists like Premabhai Nagarseth, the Hatesinghs, Ranchhodlal, Bechardas Lashkari were all actively associated with the Society as members of the committee or as presidents. However, it was the middle class intellectual elite which dominated the committee. Bhogilal Pranvallabhdas, Bholanath Sarabhai, Mahipatram, Ambalal Sakarlal Desai, Lalshankar Umiashankar, Ramanbhai Nilkanth and Anandshankar Dhruv were some of the prominent middle class leaders of the city who were closely associated with the Society and were members of its managing committee. It is interesting to note that the managing committee included the key elite of the city, who were also active in other important economic, social, educational and political associations. The overlapping membership and leadership of the different associations was a significant feature of the city's leadership pattern which encouraged harmony and cooperation among different associations and helped to avoid conflict and competition.

From the 1880s onwards, the business elite became less dominant in its representation on the committee. The composition of the managing committee of 1906 shows that out of 15 members, only two were *sethias*—Seth Chinubhai Madhavlal and Seth Lalbhai Dalpatbhai. The rest of the members were the professional middle class elite. Professor Anandshankar Dhruv and Kamlashankar Trivedi were teachers; Krishnarao Bholanath, Bhaishankàr Nanabhai, Ramanbhai Nilkanth and Navalshankar Shukla were lawyers; Dr Solomon Abraham Erulkar was a doctor.[19]

Though the Society was eclectic and broadminded, the committee was dominated by Hindus and Jains. Only an occasional Parsi, Jewish or Muslim name is to be found in the committee. Cawasji Mancherji Karanjwala, Nowroji Pestonji Vakil, Jehangir Edalji Tamanna were Parsi members of the committee in the 1880s. Dr Solomon Abraham Erulkar was a Jew who remained on the committee for a very long period. The only Muslim member on the committee during this period was Burhanudin Abdulla Kurezi, who remained a member for only two years in the 1890s. Even the Kazi, the leading member of the Muslim community, did not become a life member of the Society. He was quite happy to remain an annual member for a long time. This does not mean that

GVS was indifferent to the cause of the Muslim community. To promote education among Muslims, GVS took an active interest in the Anjuman-i-Islam, which was founded in 1884. The honorary secretary of the Society was also the honorary secretary of the Anjuman-i-Islam. The Society administered the Haji Mohammad Lodha fund, the purpose of which was to encourage literature on Muslim culture, history, society and reforms. Mahipatram and Lalshankar, honorary secretaries, took a keen interest in the welfare of the Muslims.

Surprisingly, GVS continued to remain an exclusive association and did not attract many life members for a long period. In 1870, there were only 30 life members.[20] In 1881, the number was 65, which increased to 143 in 1891.[21] Thus, the progress in the enrolment of life members was very slow. This slowness was due to the rather high membership subscription of Rs 50. As a result, the Society remained an exclusive association for a long time. In 1885, the subscription fee was halved to encourage school masters, whose monthly salary was less than Rs 30, to join.[22] Later, in 1896, the subscription was halved for women members, too. As a result, many women joined the Society. In 1906, there were as many as 110 women members.[23] The first woman member was Rukshmanibai of Petlad, who became a member as early as in 1892.[24] The number of life members increased rapidly in the first decade of the 20th century, rising to 583 in 1912,[25] perhaps due to the growth of the educated middle class as well as the reduction in the membership subscription for teachers and women members.

The Society was fortunate in having enlightened leaders such as AK Forbes, Gopalrao Hari Deshmukh, Mahipatram Rupram, Lalshankar Umiashankar and Ramanbhai Nilkanth as honorary secretaries to direct the activities of the Society. The contribution of AK Forbes and the poet Dalpatram to the Society has already been described. The presidents of the Society were also enlightened and influential leaders. As presidents, Premabhai, Ranchhodlal Chhotalal, Bechardas Lashkari and Ambalal Sakarlal gave support to the activities of the Society and increased its prestige.

In 1872, Gopalrao Hari Deshmukh (1823–1892) became the honorary secretary of the Society. A Maharashtrian Brahmin from Pune, he was a well-known social and religious reformer and a pioneer of *swadeshi* in India. He was appointed assistant judge in 1862 for 11 months and a judge in the small causes court in Ahmedabad for 12 years from 1867 to 1876. He injected new life into the socioreligious movements of the city. Though a Maharashtrian, he spoke fluent Gujarati and took an active interest in the public affairs of the city. Besides being the honorary secretary of the GVS, he was vice-president of the Ahmedabad Prarthana Samaj, the president of the Ballagna Nishedhak Mandali (society to oppose child marriages) and the founder member of the Deshi Udhyog Vardhak Mandali. He gained such great popularity in the city that when he left Ahmedabad, 'Gopal Utsav' was celebrated by about 10,000 people.[26] He wrote scholarly articles in the *Buddhi Prakash*. His presence in Ahmedabad strengthened the *swadeshi* movement in Gujarat, which the GVS under his leadership and inspiration strongly supported.

When Gopalrao left Ahmedabad in 1876, the reins of GVS were taken over by Mahipatram Rupram (1829–1891), another stalwart reformer who injected a radical spirit into the social reform movement of Ahmedabad that had hitherto followed the path of gradualism. He steered the activities of the Society for about fourteen and a half years. It was said that, if AK Forbes gave birth to the GVS, Dalpatram nurtured it in its childhood and Mahipatram brought it up in its youth. These three stalwarts strengthened the foundation of the GVS.

Mahipatram, a Vadnagara Brahmin, was not an Ahmedabadi but had made Ahmedabad his home since 1857. He had been born and brought up in Surat. The city of Surat in the 19th century was the pioneering centre of the reform movement of Gujarat. He came into contact with the two great reformers of Western India, Durgaram Mehtaji and Dadoba Pandurang and was deeply influenced by them. As a high school student, he attended meetings of the Manav Dharma Sabha, a reformist association. He was also the assistant secretary of Parhejagar

Sabha, a temperance association, and an editor of a fortnightly paper, *Parhejagar Patra*, published by the Sabha (1850–51). It was here that he came into contact with Dalpatram and AK Forbes. After working for some time as an assistant teacher in the English school, Mahipatram went to Bombay in 1852 and joined the Elphinstone Institution for further studies. In Bombay, he was actively associated with the Gnyan Prasarak Mandali, the Buddhi Vardhak Sabha and the Students' Literary and Scientific Society. In 1856, he was the secretary of the Buddhi Vardhak Sabha. Mahipatram was a close associate of Karsandas Mulji and Narmadashankar Dave, two leading social reformers of Gujarat. Along with them, he attacked social evils including the immoral lifestyle of the Vaishnav Maharaj. He was also in charge of the periodical *Satyaprakash* for a short period when Karsandas was away at Deesa, and this helped to maintain the tempo of the reform movement. Mahipatram moved to Ahmedabad where he was appointed acting headmaster of the government school and later made deputy educational inspector. After this, Mahipatram made Ahmedabad his home and became deeply involved in its variegated activities, educational, socioreligious, municipal and more.[27]

In 1860, Mahipatram was selected by the education department to visit England to be trained in the British normal schools. In those days, crossing the ocean to go abroad was prohibited by Hindu customs for higher castes. It was a bold step to go abroad. In his biography of his wife *Parvatikunvar akhyan*, Mahipatram wrote that his wife Parvatikunvar gave wholehearted support to him and encouraged him to go even when he and his family were threatened with excommunication by his Nagar community.[28] His foreign visit created ripples in the orthodox society of Gujarat. Only a few reformers like Bholanath Sarabhai, Narmad, Durgaram Mehta, and Nandshankar Tuljaram supported him in his bold step.[29] Bholanath, in fact, described him as *Himmat Bahadur*, the bold man, in his diary,[30] while Kavi Dalpatram praised Mahipatram for his bold spirit in a poem and in articles in the *Buddhi Prakash* in 1860.[31] GVS hailed Mahipatram's move in a small booklet *Mahipatram Vilayat Java Vishe*, or Mahipatram's Visit to Foreign Lands, in 1860.

Returning to India in April 1861, Mahipatram was welcomed by reformers. But his Vadnagara Nagar caste ostracised him. He could not even obtain the services of a shudra servant. People jeered at him and called him *Vilayati vandaru* (English monkey).[32] In Surat, he was not allowed to perform religious ceremonies after the death of his father. Meanwhile, his son fell sick, and he did not get any help from his relations. As a result, Mahipatram lost courage, but his wife remained steadfast.[33] In 1862, he was appointed the principal of the Male Training College of Ahmedabad, a position which he held until his death in 1891. Under him, the college flourished and became a leading educational institute in Gujarat. In 1863, he started a periodical *Gujarat Shalapatra* to spread ideas about the new educational system and to provide educational information to school teachers all over Gujarat. The college also became the centre for the social reform movement under his leadership. The teachers trained in the college were influenced by the reformist ideas of the principal and disseminated his ideas wherever they went. They established girls' schools, libraries and reform associations wherever they worked.[34]

To introduce reform more effectively, Mahipatram believed, one should not remain aloof from one's caste.[35] To re-enter his caste, he had to undergo a series of purificatory ceremonies on the banks of the Sabarmati in Ahmedabad and later on the banks of the Narmada at Shuklatirth in 1862. These ceremonies helped him to overcome social ostracism, at least in Ahmedabad. But the Nagars of Surat continued to oppose him. To please them, he underwent another round of ceremonies seven years later. This time he was cruelly jeered at and criticised by his reformist friends in Bombay for his feeble attitude. Mahipatram assured the reformers that at heart he was a reformist and that he had agreed to the ceremonies merely to appease his caste fellows. This aroused the wrath of his caste fellows who once again drove him out of the caste. But a few years later, he again went through the same purificatory ceremonies and was re-admitted into the caste after a lapse of almost 12 years. This whole story of Mahipatram's caste problems was a much debated issue in those days.[36]

Mahipatram provided leadership to various social and religious reform associations and remained in the forefront of public activities in Ahmedabad. In 1877, he became honorary secretary of the GVS, a post which he held until his death in 1891. He helped Bholanath Sarabhai to start the Prarthana Samaj in 1871 and after Bholanath' death in 1886, conducted the activities of the Samaj. He also made efforts to uplift the Muslim community of Ahmedabad. He started Urdu classes in his college in 1871 and helped in establishing the Anjuman-i-Islam in 1884. He was also closely connected with Vidhva Vivahuttejak Mandali (widow re-marriage promotion association), Ballagna Nisheddhaka Mandali (Anti-child-marriage association), Hindu Sansar Sudhara Samaj, the Apparao Bholanath Library, the Bholanath Ladies Institute and the National Indian Association. He was appointed municipal commissioner and later the chairman of the Ahmedabad municipality for three and a half years. Mahipatram's multifarious activities and leadership of the GVS provided strength and momentum to the reform movement in Gujarat.

After Mahipatram's death in 1891, his pupil and leading reformer Lalshankar Umiashankar Trivedi (1845–1912) took over the reins of the GVS as the honorary secretary for 22 years until his death. Under his leadership, the society made tremendous progress. His own life revolved round the GVS. After finishing school in Ahmedabad, Lalshankar was appointed a fellow in the Male Training College of Ahmedabad where he came under the influence of his mentor Mahipatram. He wrote a textbook on mathematics and was a teacher of mathematics in high school. Being a champion of widow re-marriage, he translated Ishwarchandra Vidyasagar's book on widow remarriage from its Marathi version into Gujarati in 1867. He worked as a clerk (1871–74) in the small causes court of Ahmedabad and was actively associated with the Prarthna Samaj and other reformist associations. When stationed as sub-judge at Pandharpur (1874–79), he started an orphanage for deserted children. Later, he worked in the courts of Dhanduka,

Gogha, Viramgam, Solapur, Ahmednagar and Nasik, reaching a judge's position in the small causes court at Ahmedabad. In Ahmedabad, he was closely associated with all the reform and educational institutions. In 1904, he established the Gujarat Sansar Sudhara Samaj. In 1907, he was appointed president of the Indian National Social Conference in Surat. Though an ardent reformist, he advocated gradualism. He was a great champion of women's education. Under him the GVS flourished, proof of which is seen in the following statistics.[37]

Table 5.1: Progress of the Gujarat Vernacular Society

	1891	1912
Trust funds	20	82
The amount of trust funds (Rs)	72,875	2,31,329
Capital of the Society (Rs)	52,473	1,70,370
Life members	143	583
Books published	113	286

III

The Prarthana Samaj started by Bholanath Sarabhai in 1871 was an important reformist association in Ahmedabad. Inspired by western thought and showing definite western influence, it pioneered the religious reform movement in Gujarat.

Bholanath was a Vadanagara Nagar Brahmin. His ancestors were administrators and from very early times, they had held high positions of honour during the rule of the Moghuls, the Marathas and the British in Ahmedabad. Bholanath acquired knowledge of Persian, Sanskrit, Marathi, Gujarati and English. He commenced his government career as a candidate in the court of the district judge at Ahmedabad. He successfully passed the judicial examination for the post of *munsif* and in 1844, was appointed *munsif* at Ahmedabad. From this, he gradually rose to the post of *sadar amin* and provincial *sadar amin* and was finally made a first class subordinate judge. During this period of government service, he lived at several places in Gujarat such as Umreth, Broach, Kheda, Ahmedabad, Surat and Thana. He retired in 1874. He was honoured with the title of 'Rao Bahadur' in 1875 and 'Kaiser-i-Hind' in 1879.

In Ahmedabad, Bholanath was closely associated with GVS and other reform associations. He was the president of the Ballagna Nishedhak Mandali and Vidhva Punarvivah Sabha. He supported foreign travel and was bold enough to dine with Mahipatram when the latter returned from England. For this act, his caste excommunicated him. He did not allow his children and grandchildren to marry at an early age. He also stopped some evil customs regarding death and marriage ceremonies within his family. He put into practice what he believed. After the death of his son Apparao, he donated Rs 10,000 to start a library in his memory. However, his prime interest was in the field of religious reform, rather than social reform.

The year 1855 was a turning point in Bholanath's life. In this year, he came across Dr Blair's sermons, a work which he greatly respected and admired throughout his life. The work was recommended to him by his childhood friend Ranchhodlal Chhotalal (1823–98). It had a tremendous impact on his perceptive mind. His close contact with several English officials and non-officials influenced his religious outlook. His deep study of the Hindu scriptures enlightened him to the true nature of the Hindu religion. Gradually, he outgrew his faith in idolatry and superstitions and led the protest movement against this degenerate form of Hinduism. In 1859, he noted in his diary that God being omnipresent should be worshipped only in the heart and not through rituals and ceremonies. He vehemently criticised the lifestyle of the priests of the Vallabhacharya Sect.[38]

In 1858, Bholanath and a few friends—among them Ranchhodlal Chhotalal and Ramprasad Laxmikant—started a religious association called Dharmasabha in Ahmedabad. The association met in the Hatkeshwar temple in Raipur once a week and discussed religious topics and organised discourses by *shastris*. In September 1859, it started publishing the periodical *Dharma Prakash*, which only survived for two years.[39] After about 12 years, the association disappeared through a process of natural decay.[40] This Dharmasabha was the forerunner of the Prarthana Samaj, a new religious association founded on a purely theistic basis in 1871. Before Bholanath established the Samaj with the help of his friend Mahipatram Rupram, he had come across some books published by the Brahmo Samaj of Calcutta, and reading these books appears to have strengthened his views against idol worship.

Initially, the Prarthana Samaj held congregational prayers every week on Sundays. Bholanath composed a large number of hymns and prayers that were later collected in the book *Prarthana Mala* in two parts. The Samaj was primarily established to weed out superstitious beliefs and idol worship from Hinduism. It intended to present to Indians the ideal form of pure worship of the one true God. Thus, the doctrines and aims of the Prarthana Samaj were similar to those of the Brahmo Samaj of Bengal. However, in the Prarthana Samaj of western India, the stress was on *bhakti* (devotion) and *prarthana* (prayer). Moreover, unlike the Brahmo Samaj, the members of the Ahmedabad Prarthana Samaj were not ready to lose their caste identities.[41]

Until 1872, Bholanath had no direct association with the Brahmo Samaj of Calcutta. But in December 1872, Pratapchandra Majumdar of the Brahmo Samaj visited Ahmedabad. He injected a new spirit and enthusiasm into the Prarthana Samaj. On his suggestion, sermons were added to the weekly prayer meetings.[42]

For the first five years, Prarthana Samaj did not have its own building. Its weekly service was held in the Training College building. Through the munificence of its members and sympathisers, particularly people like Bechardas Lashkari, the association's building called Prarthanamandir was built in 1876.[43] It is interesting to note that in the prayer hall, there was a women's gallery on either side, reached by a staircase in the tower and isolated from the rest of the hall by a row of bamboo screens.[44]

Towards the end of 1874, the reformer and founder of Arya Samaj, Dayanand Saraswati, visited Ahmedabad on his grand missionary tour. He had been invited there by Gopal Hari Deshmukh. During his stay in December 12–27, he delivered several discourses on religious and social topics. At a private meeting, Dayanand proposed to Bholanath and Mahipatram that the name of Prarthana Samaj be changed to Arya Samaj for both institutions had the same objectives, namely, the abolition of idol worship and promotion of monotheism. Krishnarao Bholanath wrote, "Bholanath promised to consider the question before he gave his assent. He passed the whole of that night anxiously revolving this point and finally decided to decline Dayanand's proposal." He further wrote, "for had Bholanath accepted the proposal of this diplomatic reformer, Dayanand would have lost no time in triumphantly announcing to the world that he had established an Arya Samaj at Ahmedabad". Bholanath had strongly disapproved of Dayanand's expediency in religious matters and the doctrine of infallibility and sole religious authority of the Vedas. As Dayanand's diplomacy failed, he founded the Arya Samaj in Ahmedabad, which was short lived and soon ceased to exist.[45]

Bholanath formulated four principles as the essence of the creed of Prarthana Samaj, which were adopted by the Samaj after some modifications. They were as follows:

1) There is only one God. He is the creator, preserver and protector of the world. He is distinct from things created. He is omniscient, omnipresent, omnipotent, just, merciful and perfectly holy, and he alone is the object of the highest worship.

2) Religion consists in worshipping God with complete devotion.

3) Religion consists in loving God, believing in him with implicit faith, holding communion with him, singing his praises, offering prayers to him and leading a life of moral rectitude.

4) Pious and religious life is acceptable to God and is conducive to the welfare of the soul here and in the life hereafter.[46]

These principles upheld a monotheistic faith and were against image worship. God was to be worshipped without a mediator or a spiritual guide.

In 1876, Satyendranath Tagore, the second son of Devendranath Tagore, came to Ahmedabad as district judge. His friendship helped Bholanath to galvanise the activities of the Samaj. In January 1877, Bholanath visited Calcutta. He made personal contact with Keshavchandra Sen, Pratapchandra Majmudar and Devendranath Tagore. After his return from Calcutta, Bholanath strongly felt that no trace of idolatry should be allowed among the members.

Bholanath was in close contact with Prarthana Samaj of Bombay and attended its annual functions. He also met Madam Blavatsky and Col. HS Olcott, the founders of the Theosophical Society. However, he was not impressed by their knowledge of the Hindu religion.[47] In 1886, two well known Brahmo Samajists, Devendranath Tagore and Pratapchandra, visited Ahmedabad and strengthened the ties of the Ahmedabad Prarthana Samaj with the Brahmo Samaj.

Throughout his life, Bholanath remained the life and soul of Prarthana Samaj. He went on 'missionary' tours in Gujarat and established branches of the Samaj in towns like Kheda, Baroda, Dhandhuka, Viramgam, Matar, Baroda, Petlad, Broach, Surat and Sojitra.[48] After Bholanath's death, Mahipatram and Lalshankar Umiashankar conducted the Samaj's activities.

In Ahmedabad, Prarthana Samaj used to hold prayer meetings in the Christian fashion. Thus, Prarthana Samajists were sometimes ridiculed as 'pseudo Christians' by the people of

Ahmedabad. At the congregational services on Sunday afternoons, the prayers were read in Gujarati. Then, a sermon was preached from the hymn book. Later, hymns were sung accompanied by music.[49] The meetings were even attended by women, who sat segregated in the galleries. Also, some women of Bholanath's family and Mahipatram's wife preached sermons.[50]

Nevertheless, the Samaj remained a small group of people which could not find a popular base. In Gujarat, where *Sanatan Dharma* was deeply entrenched, the Prarthana Samaj could not become a mass movement. Its pro-Christian stance, its sophisticated and radical religious ideas and the propensity of its members towards western thought, prevented it from being a popular association.[51] It remained exclusive and isolated from the mainstream thought of its society. Thus, it could not make much impact on the society of Ahmedabad. In December 1872, the Samaj had 34 members, which increased to 109 in March 1879 and to 114 in 1883. Though the Samaj was open to all castes and creeds, no one of the Dhed, Bhangi or other depressed classes was allowed to attend. No Hindu who joined the Samaj cut himself off from his caste or old faith or made any change in his marriage, funeral and other family rites.[52] Despite its limitations, the Samaj became the centre of religious and social reform activities. But unlike the Bombay Prarthana Samaj, the Ahmedabad Prarthana Samaj did not undertake many social reform activities or show any empathy to the labourers or untouchables. Its reform activities remained predominantly religious in character. It had started music classes and opened four theological classes in Ahmedabad to teach the main principles of the Samaj.[53] It also lent support to the orphanage Mahipatram Anathashram, which was built in the memory of Mahipatram. In 1886, the Prarthana Samaj started a periodical *Gnana Sudha* which discussed religious and social subjects.

IV

Although GVS was reformist in its outlook and encouraged publication on the subject of social reforms, there was a strongly felt need to establish separate associations to combat specific social evils like child marriage and the ban on widow remarriage. As a result, the leading reformers of Ahmedabad set up associations which would take concrete steps against such social evils.

To assist widows of the higher castes, social reformers like Gopal Hari Deshmukh, Mahipatram, Satyendranath Tagore, Jagjivan Khushal and Janardhan Gadgil founded Punarvivahottehjaka Sabha.[54] The first widow remarriage took place on August 6, 1872 under the aegis of the Sabha. The widow Jivkor of Vania caste wanted to marry a teacher Lallubhai of the same caste. The family members and the caste fellows opposed this vehemently and ostracised them. The couple sought the help of the Sabha which organised their wedding, attended by 150 leading people of Ahmedabad including officials. This event created ripples in the orthodox section of society who were scandalised.[55] Lalshankar translated Ishwarchandra Vidyasagar's book on widow remarriage in 1867.

In September 1874, the Sabha helped a young Jain widow Jadaubai to marry Lallu Khushal. This invited the wrath of the Jain community of the city, which excommunicated the couple. As a result, the Jains became great opponents of the reformers and their reform associations. Many Jain girls were prevented from going to school.[56] The Sabha became moribund after a few years. It was revived in May 1878 by Bholanath Sarabhai, Mahipatram and Lalshankar and renamed the Vidhava Vivahottejak Mandali. The Mandali appointed agents in Baroda, Umreth, Patan, Nadiad, Kheda and Rajkot to enrol new members.[57] The association helped to spread the movement all over Gujarat by creating a network of agents in all the major cities. It also accepted the applications of willing widows and of men who were ready to marry widows. By and large, widow remarriage took place within the same caste. Under the Sabha's auspices, six widow marriages took place during 1878–86.[58]

As the custom of child marriage was the root cause of various social evils, it drew the attention of social reformers in

Ahmedabad. Even revivalist reformers joined the campaign against this social evil through their poems, essays and plays. The evil of child widows stemmed from child marriage. Moreover, it was an impediment to female education and adversely affected the health of young couples. To combat this social evil, social reformers founded Ballagna Nishedhak Mandali in 1874. Its object was to strengthen the anti-child-marriage movement by not only preaching against it but also by chalking out action-oriented programmes. To set an example, every member who joined the Mandali took a pledge to allow his male children to marry only after they had reached the age of sixteen and to see that there was a difference of five years between the age of the bride and of the bridegroom. They also promised not to allow their daughters to marry very young.

The Mandali tried to open branches in other cities of Gujarat.[59] About 300 persons became its members. It published a periodical called *Ballagna Nishedhak Patrika* from January 1876.[60] Gopal Hari Deshmukh was its president and Ambalal Sakarlal Desai and Navalram Laxmiram Pandya worked as honorary secretaries. Navalram also published the book *Bal Lagna Batrishi*, a collection of poems, and composed *Bal Garbavali* to show the harmful effects of child marriage.

On April 1, 1888, a new reform association, Gujarat Hindu Sansar Sudhara Samaj came into existence in Ahmedabad to abolish child marriage, lessen the wedding expenses, enhance women's status and encourage women's education.[61] The Samaj was an extension of the activities of the Ballagna Nishedhak Mandali. Dayaram Gidumal, assistant judge at Ahmedabad, was instrumental in founding the Samaj. It was started on the lines of the association founded by him earlier in Sindh.[62]

It started a campaign against child marriage and social evils like bride price and dowry. To diffuse these reformist ideas, its leading members went to different towns and cities of Gujarat, such as Dahod, Kheda, Surat, Broach, Nadiad, Matar and Mehmdabad.[63]

In 1903, the Gujarat Sansar Sudhara Samaj came into existence as the Gujarat branch of the Social Reform Association. It subsumed the activities of the Hindu Sansar Sudhara Samaj and the Vidhava Vivah Uttejak Mandali. Lalshankar Umiashankar was actively associated with it.[64] Besides encouraging women's education and opposing customs like child marriage, polygamy, bride price and dowry that had obstructed the progress of women, the Samaj also intended to encourage widow remarriage and merge sub-castes for the purpose of marriage. The Samaj celebrated Karsandas Mulji Jayanti every year in July to express support to his reforms. For the uplift of the untouchables, the Samaj supported their schools in the city of Ahmedabad.[65] The Samaj had its own building, the foundation of which was laid by RG Bhandarkar in December 1904.[66] To break caste barriers, an associated club, the Sansar Sudhara Club was founded in July 1911. It organised cosmopolitan dinners and sports for the families of members.[67]

These social and religious reform associations gave an organisational base to the socioreligious movements in the city. Ahmedabad had become the most important centre of the reform movement in Gujarat by 1915. But the influence of its reformist associations was limited only to a small group of intelligentsia. Leaders and participants in the activities of the associations came from the educated middle class. Owing to the sophistication of these associations, they remained exclusive and could not reach the common people. However, the role of these voluntary associations was important in moulding the perceptions of their members, who in turn could influence their caste fellows by providing leadership to the caste associations emerging during the same period. Thus, new and modernist ideas spread by voluntary reform associations like the GVS and Prarthana Samaj could percolate down to the masses through caste movements led by their reformist leaders.

By the end of the 19th century, Ahmedabad had also become an important centre of educational and literary activities. In order to promote and organise these activities, various associations emerged. In 1898, the Social and Literary Association was founded by the students of Gujarat College. Litterateurs like Govardhanram Tripathi and Narsinhrao Divetia and philosophers like Virchand Gandhi delivered lectures under the aegis of this association. In 1904, the first literary association for the whole province of Gujarat, the Gujarat Sahitya Sabha, emerged from this association.[68] It provided the necessary platform for the litterateurs of Gujarat.

The Bandhu Samaj was founded in 1902 to encourage and promote literature for women. It also started publishing a women's magazine, *Sundri Subodh*.[69]

Foremost among educational associations was the Gujarat Kelavani Mandal, or the Gujarat Education Society, which was founded in 1913 to disseminate knowledge through Gujarati. In order to achieve this objective, the Mandal planned activities like publishing textbooks and opening libraries, gymnasiums and technical classes. Various educational conferences were also held in the city.[70]

Evans and Caine, the British advocates of the temperance movement, visited Ahmedabad in 1888 and delivered lectures on the harmful effects of drinking. They inspired the people of Ahmedabad to start an anti-alcoholic association. As a result, Madhyapan Nishedhak Mandali was founded in December 1888. Ranchhodlal Chhotalal, who had shown keen interest in this issue, was elected the president of the Mandali. Mahipatram, Keshavlal Motilal, Dr Nilkanth Dahyabhai and Krishnarao Bholanath became the committee members.[71] The work of this association continued right into the 20th century. It regularly organised public lectures and also arranged magic lantern shows for all, including mill labourers.

In keeping with the Jain tradition of the city, which had shown compassion to animals and had supported the institution of the *panjrapol*, the Society for the Prevention of Cruelty to Animals was founded in 1881 at the initiation of collector Richey. Mahipatram, Bholanath, Bechardas Lashkari, Sarabhai Maganbhai, Nowroji Pestonji Vakil and Professor Kathvate were its founder members.[72]

Ahmedabad was the bastion of orthodoxy. The majority of the Hindus were entrenched in their *Sanatan Dharma*. As a result, the western-oriented reform movement spearheaded by the GVS, Prarthana Samaj and other reformist associations did not make much impression on them. In fact, a few associations even emerged to defend age-old traditions. The leading one was the Sanatana Bharat Dharma Mahaparishad, which was founded in 1896 to protect *Sanatan Dharma*. It believed in the protection of cows, encouragement of religious education about Hinduism and Ayurvedic Medicine. Pandit Din Dayal Sharma, the leader of the all-India *Sanatana Dharma* movement, visited Ahmedabad in 1903 and impressed the people of the city with his oratory. The Ved Sanatan Dharmottejak Mandal was founded in the city in 1904.[73]

In 1906, the Vaishnav Parishad was founded in Ahmedabad to regenerate and reform Vaishnavism under the leadership of Pandit Gatulalji and Goswami Devkinandacharya. In the city, the Vallabhachari sect of Vaishnavism had a large following. The Parishad decided to start the Vallabhiya Sabha in the city and to translate the sect's literature into Gujarati. It also planned to start a periodical discussing religious matters and a class to impart the sect's teachings.[74]

Among reformist religious associations, the Arya Samaj and the Theosophical Society established their branches in the city in the last decade of the 19th century. However, they did not receive much support from the populace of the city.

V

The Muslims, who formed a substantial segment of the city's population, did not participate in the activities of a cosmopolitan and eclectic association like the GVS. During the 19th century, very few Muslims took interest in public affairs. Nor did they have any associations to support the reform activities of their community. Lack of education and poverty were among the major reasons for their backwardness.

The economic conditions of the Muslims of Ahmedabad deteriorated from the 18th century. Muslim aristocracy had lost their fortune and status and were reduced to poverty as they continued their indolent habits and spendthrift lifestyles. Many sold their precious possessions to make ends meet. Contemporary literature and reports speak of their poor condition. Only the Bohras and the Memons engaged in trading. The rest were weavers, constables, shopkeepers, artisans, government messengers and labourers and were generally very poor.[75] A contemporary article written by Hargovinddas Kantawala in the periodical *Gujarat Shalapatra* stated that a large number of Muslims lived by begging. Many who were engaged as constables led such a wasteful life that they remained poor. Also, they did not take to English education and thus could not make use of the new opportunities which arose in the wake of British rule.[76] In 1869, there were only four Muslims studying in the high school of Ahmedabad.[77] Without higher education, they could not get good positions in government departments. Their poverty and indolence kept them backward in outlook. As a result, the Muslim community could not produce an educated, administrative or commercial middle class which could provide leadership to the community and spearhead their reform movements. Only towards the last decades of the 19th century did education increase in the Muslim community.

The initial efforts to introduce reforms and modern education among Muslims were made collectively by non-Muslim leaders such as Mahipatram, Lalshanker Umiashankar, Edalji Dosabhai, MC Gibbs and some local Muslim leaders who founded the Anjuman-i-Islam in December 1884. In 1862–63, an Urdu primary school was started thanks to the efforts of Curtis and principal Sadar Amin Ghulam Mohuddin. By 1868, there were three Urdu schools in the city.[78] Anjuman-i-Islam started a library, an English school for boys and Urdu schools for boys and girls. In the beginning no fees were charged, but later nominal fees were levied. The moving spirit of this Muslim association was Mahipatram. It was later nurtured by Lalshankar Umiashankar.

The GVS administered its funds. During the period of 1887–1893, 24 Muslim boys went for higher education in the government high school. The Anjuman also organised talks on various reformist subjects.[79]

Gradually, the number of Muslim schools increased. Many Muslims even sought higher education. In an annual function in 1903, Talati, the headmaster of the government high school stated in the report that the number of Muslim boys was increasing.[80] A few Muslims, by the end of the 19th century, also went to college and acquired high posts in government departments. The number of Muslim students in the Gujarat College was small. In 1891–92, there were five Muslim students out of the total 106 students. The situation was no better in 1910 when there were only 13 Muslim students out of the total 278 students.[81] The report of the director of public instruction (1900) states that, though the Gujarat College was close to a large Muslim population, it was ignored by them.[82]

Abdulla Kureshi was the first Muslim of Ahmedabad to receive the MA degree in 1899[83] and Narma of Ahmedabad was the first Muslim in Gujarat to become a barrister in 1909.[84] Many others obtained higher education and acquired good positions. For example, Sayed Kadri was a BA and was appointed a sub-judge. Thus, in the first decade of the 20th century, an awakening was observed among the Muslims who had become a part of the rising middle class and provided leadership to the Muslim reform movement of the city. The Anjuman-i-Islam extended its activities, and new libraries and schools were opened for Muslims. New associations such as the Young Men's Mohammedan Association and the Ahmedabad Bohra Union Society were founded for encouraging educational activities among Muslims. These associations also tried to introduce reforms regarding marriage and death customs.[85] Muslim education conferences were arranged in Ahmedabad in 1895 and in 1904. The conference of 1904 was particularly important in the history of the Muslim community. It was attended by 45 representatives from all over Bombay presidency. Lalshankar Umiashankar, the honorary secretary of Anjuman-i-Islam, was the vice-president of the conference. Curiously, on the one hand, members laid stress on education for women and, on the other hand, also advocated the *purdah* system for them. Thus, the conservative outlook of the Muslims slowed down the reform movement among them.[86]

This detailed discussion of voluntary associations reveals that, by 1914, Ahmedabad abounded in associations of all hues through which the leading men of the city fostered an environment conducive to reform. In fact, the membership and leadership of the voluntary associations overlapped. Mahipatram, Lalshankar, Ambalal Sakarlal were simultaneously members and leaders of a number of organisations. This overlapping leadership encouraged harmony and cooperation among various voluntary associations instead of generating competition and conflict. Secondly, these associations institutionalised various reform and literary and educational movements of the Ahmedabad society and gave educated Indians valuable experience of organisational activities in support of specific goals.

VI

Voluntary associations spread their new ideas by using the press effectively to further their cause. Voluntary associations, together with the press, played a significant role in changing the society of Ahmedabad.

The first weekly newspaper *Vartman* and the monthly journal *Buddhi Prakash* published by the GVS started in 1849 and 1854 respectively. The *Vartman* was soon abandoned by the GVS but continued to be published for a few years by a private agency. However, the *Buddhi Prakash* has remained an influential monthly of Gujarat until today.

In 1864, there were six litho presses and one type press in Ahmedabad. The latter was at that time a recent introduction and published three newspaper and three periodicals.[87]

In 1879, Ahmedabad had three newspapers. The *Hitechhu* (well-wisher) was an Anglo-Gujarati weekly which had been in existence for seven years and had a circulation of 450 copies. The *Ahmedabad Samachar* of 19 years' standing and the *Samsher Bahadur* of 24 years' standing were the other two Gujarati weeklies. The former had 60 copies and latter 200 copies in circulation.[88]

In 1886, there were 19 presses in Ahmedabad which published 13 periodicals and five weekly newspapers. In 1895, there were 20 presses, nine periodicals and five newspapers. The total circulation of newspapers was 2,100 out of which 1,000 copies were of the *Hitechhu*. In 1900, Ahmedabad had 25 presses, seven periodicals and nine newspapers. The total circulation of newspapers was 3,450 copies, out of which the *Prajabandhu*'s share was 1,500 copies.[89] On January 1, 1914, there were six Anglo-Gujarati papers and three Gujarati papers published in Ahmedabad, with a combined circulation of 11,500 copies.[90] Most of the newspapers published in Ahmedabad were weeklies. Until 1914, no successful daily newspaper had been published.

From these statistics, one can discern a slow but steady growth of the press in Ahmedabad. This indicated the growth of a reading public and an increasing prosperity and development of education. The Congress meeting of 1902 in Ahmedabad had stimulated the interest of Ahmedabad citizens in public and political affairs, which in turn, gave an impetus to press and public activities. The growth of the press was a sure sign of social change and increasing social awareness in the city as it generally advocated progressive ideas.

The press of Ahmedabad, as elsewhere in India in this period, catered to the needs of the educated middle class. The newspapers, periodicals and literature dealt with the interests of and issues concerning the intelligentsia and the higher castes. Sadly, they overlooked the issues and interests of the depressed castes and the working class. Thus, the press had an elitist stance and manifested the aspirations and attitudes of the middle class and higher castes.

Except for the *Prajabandhu* (1898), none of the old newspapers of Ahmedabad have been preserved. Therefore, one has to rely on *The Reports of Native Newspapers* of the Bombay presidency, which were compiled from 1868 onwards to discover the contents and tone of the newspapers of Ahmedabad.[91]

The *Vartman* was the first newspaper of Ahmedabad. The second newspaper was the *Khabar Darpan*, which was a biweekly started in July 1851.[92] As it severely conflicted in opinion with the *Vartman*, it vanished by 1854. The third newspaper was the *Samsher Bahadur*, which was launched in July 1854 by Lallubhai Raichand, a reporter of the *Vartman*. However, in 1855, it was closed down as it indulged in defaming prominent citizens of Ahmedabad. It was fined for libelling the clerks of Maganbhai Karamchand, a rich and influential merchant. For about 11 years, it was published in Bombay and was then revived in Ahmedabad in 1867.[93] For about the next 40 years, it remained an influential newspaper of Ahmedabad. Meanwhile, the *Ahmedabad Samachar* was started in 1860 by Lallubhai Surchand. The influential *Hitechhu* came into existence in 1873. There were several other papers during this early phase, that is prior to the launching of the *Prajabandhu* in 1898. However, these newspapers were short-lived. During this early phase, the standard of journalism was not very high. The three leading newspapers of this phase were the *Samsher Bahadur* (1854), *Hitechhu* (1873), and the *Ahmedabad Samachar* (1860).

As observed earlier, Ahmedabad was largely apolitical before Gandhi came to the city. Ahmedabad's political activities were few and moderate. The Congress session of 1902 held in Ahmedabad brought the people of the city close to national politics. Since 1905, the *swadeshi* movement had aroused their political interest. The press, too, matched the general ethos of the moderate politics of the city. The press, in this period, remained non-militant in its political outlook. In social matters, the newspapers represented two divergent viewpoints—reformist and conservative. However, in social matters, the press avoided radical viewpoints. Thus, moderation was the main feature of the press of pragmatic Ahmedabad that reflected the social and political ethos of the city.

At this point, it is interesting to compare the press of Surat, the other major city of Gujarat, with the press of Ahmedabad. The social and political ethos of Surat was different. It had shown signs of political consciousness as early as 1844 and later had reacted very sharply to unpopular taxes in 1848, 1860 and 1878. In social matters, Surat had shown a more radical outlook than Ahmedabad. The press of Surat, as a result, was politically alive from the beginning. It was bold, vociferous and militant in its criticism of the British government.

The range of topics and viewpoints in Ahmedabad newspapers in the early phase (before 1898) can be gauged through the *Reports on Native Papers*. The earlier papers mainly focused their attention on local matters and social issues. The target of their criticism was the municipality of Ahmedabad. This attack continued even in the later period. Though newspapers were bold and critical in their views on certain government policies, they were not militant. The *Samsher Bahadur* compared the municipality of Ahmedabad with the *panjrapol* (an asylum for useless beasts).[94] Local government officials were frequently attacked. Similarly, Hill, the English headmaster of the government high school, was severely censured by all the newspapers for his irregularity and inattention to his teaching duties.[95] The newspapers pointed out the *zoolum*, or oppression, by the city survey office.

The *Hitechhu* and *Samsher Bahadur* were progressive in outlook. Both opposed the practice of caste dinners, which were held in the streets of the city.[96] *Samsher Bahadur* showed its awareness of the decay of Indian arts and manufacture and exhorted the wealthy classes to introduce machinery and thereby improve the economic condition of the country.[97]

The Bombay Act VIII of 1870 on female infanticide stimulated a debate among the newspapers of Ahmedabad. *Samsher Bahadur* supported it while *Chandrodaya*, another newspaper, opposed the Act as an intrusion of the government into social matters.[98]

However, in 1873, all the newspapers of Ahmedabad raised a hue and cry against the BB & CI Railway Company because it allowed untouchables to travel in the same carriage with caste Hindus. They also objected to the order issued by the educational inspector of the north division to admit the children of Dheds, Bhangis and other untouchables into government schools.[99]

The newspapers also opposed any increased taxation. The people of Ahmedabad specially detested the house tax, which they found unjust and humiliating.[100] *Samsher Bahadur*, though a loyalist paper, condemned Lord Lytton's autocratic policies and disapproved of the proposed Factory Act, which, according to this newspaper, was formulated to stifle the young textile industry of India.[101]

The introduction of the drainage system by Ranchhodlal Chhotalal, the president of the municipality of Ahmedabad evoked unanimous strong criticism from the newspapers of Ahmedabad.[102]

However, the Ahmedabad press was divided into two camps on the issue of the Bill on the Age of Consent in 1890–91. The Bill stimulated a lively debate between the reformists and the orthodox of the city. Both the groups called public meetings to express their views. The *Hitechhu, Samsher Bahadur* and *Hindustan* supported the Bill and approved of government intervention in social matters, while the *Prajamat* and *Nyaydarshak* were equally vociferous in showing disapproval. Until 1898, the *Hitechhu* remained the most popular newspaper of Ahmedabad.[103] Interestingly, the early newspapers showed little interest in nationalist movements.

The birth of the *Prajabandhu* on March 6, 1898 was a landmark in the history of the press in Ahmedabad. It soon became a popular and widely read newspaper that also maintained a high standard of journalism. As this is the only newspaper available today, a detailed study of its content and tone is possible. Its popularity can be gauged by the fast growth in its circulation. The circulation of its copies increased from 1,530 in 1899 to 2,400 copies on January 1, 1914.

Prajabandhu was an Anglo-Gujarati weekly started by Bhagubhai Fatehchand Karbhai with the help of Jivanlal Vrajray Desai, the prominent lawyer of Ahmedabad. In its first issue, the introductory article "Prarambh", or the beginning, specified the weekly's objectives and policies. Service to the country was the primary goal of the paper. The editor wrote, "Though the paper is new and has new blood, it is not radical in its viewpoint. Though it has a new format, it will be judicious and will discriminate between good and bad." Its main purpose, the article indicated, was to impart knowledge on various issues to the people.[104]

The new publication soon became a first-rate Gujarati paper. It gave coverage to international, national, regional and local news. It published social, political, economic, cultural and literary news and greatly influenced the public opinion of Ahmedabad.

In politics, *Prajabandhu* held moderate views. However, it was highly critical of the apathetic attitude of the people of Ahmedabad to politics and the Congress movement and condemned the inertia of the Gujarat Sabha, the dominant political organisation of the city. But being moderate, it denounced revolutionary political activities. It supported the *swadeshi* movement, praised the programmes of the Indigenous Articles Protection Association, the Gujarat Industrial Association and the Swadeshi Mitra Mandal. The paper showed very keen interest in local municipal affairs and regularly featured constructive and critical articles on the subject. The suggestions made in the articles influenced the decisions of the municipality.

The paper had a reformist outlook in social matters but avoided radicalism in reform. When Madhavlal gave a dinner to the Brahmins of the *Chorasi* or 84 castes after the death of his father Ranchhodlal Chhotalal, the paper criticised him for spending Rs 15,000 on a dinner when he could have spent it in a better cause.[105] It supported foreign travel and opposed the levy of a fine on those who travelled abroad.[106] However, it was not in favour of the Aryan Brotherhood Movement of Bombay. Also, it did not show any sympathy for the issues of the depressed castes before Gandhi's arrival in the city.

Advertisements figured in the paper from the very first issue and increased in the course of time. Illustrated advertisements for umbrellas, Singer sewing machines, typewriters and spectacles appeared. These advertisements manifested the changing lifestyle and increasing consumerism in the city.

Prajabandhu, true to its name, became a friend of the people of Ahmedabad. Important personalities of the city like Ambalal Sakarlal Desai wrote editorials and articles. It echoed the people's wishes and breathed the spirit of the city.

Another very influential Anglo-Gujarati newspaper weekly was the *Gujarati Punch*, which was started by Somlal Mangaldas Shah on May 10, 1901. Initially, it was illustrated with caricatures in imitation of the *Hindu Punch* of Bombay. It wanted to generate interest in politics among the people of Gujarat in general and Ahmedabad in particular. It supported the Congress movement, and, through its efforts, the annual session of the Congress was held in Ahmedabad in 1902. It opposed Curzon's oppressive policy and criticised the sentence of Lokmanya Tilak in 1908. As a result of its critical attitude, it incurred the wrath of the government. It criticised the municipality and supported the Rate Payers' Association founded in 1904.[107] It also supported the *swadeshi* movement.

Like the newspapers, the periodicals of Ahmedabad, too, catered to the needs and tastes of the educated middle class. Most periodicals of this period were mouthpieces of the organisations which sponsored them.

Buddhi Prakash was the first periodical not only in Ahmedabad but also in the whole of Gujarat. It was started in 1850, and, after the GVS took it over in 1854, it became the most instructive and influential magazine of Gujarat. Under the editorship of Dalpatram, the magazine gained popularity. It contained diverse matter such as history, religion, philosophy, serial stories, poems, articles on literature, general knowledge, geography, geology, science, mathematics, travel, economics, education, book reviews and the annual reports of the GVS. It enlightened and entertained its readers. Its contents were so varied that it became a family magazine. It maintained a high literary, intellectual and moral standard. Though it was apolitical in its views in the early phase, it openly showed its allegiance to the *dayalu*, benevolent, English rule. It discussed religious topics in an eclectic spirit without being sectarian. In social matters, it held reformist and advanced views but never expressed radical views. It was an advocate of gradualism with regard to the introduction of reforms and of middle class values such as thrift, hard work, morality, self-help and progress.

Its progressive viewpoints and scientific outlook made *Buddhi Prakash* the leading reformist magazine of Gujarat, and it played an important role in modernising the outlook of the people of Gujarat. In 1863, its editor wrote that the *Buddhi Prakash* had inculcated reading habits in the people of Gujarat and had encouraged reformist activities.[108]

Another important monthly published in Ahmedabad was the *Gujarat Shalapatra*, which was a semi-government magazine. Its main objective was to spread knowledge and modern teaching methods to school teachers in Gujarat. It was started in July 1862 by Mahipatram Rupram, principal of the Male Training College of Ahmedabad, on the model of Bombay's *Elphinstone School Paper*.[109] The magazine contained educational news and information, writings on teaching methods, reports of the educational departments and articles on educational subjects like history, science, geography, mathematics, grammar and examination papers.

Though primarily an educational magazine, *Gujarat Shalapatra* contained various subjects like literature, history, social issues, news and book reviews. Again, the editors of this educational journal were prominent reformers like Mahipatram, Navalram, Madhavlal Harilal and Kamlashankar Trivedi. As a result, the tone of this periodical was advanced and reformist. It supported foreign travel, widow remarriage and women's education. It opposed child marriage, dowry, caste feasts and other such practices. It diffused reformist ideas. By doing so, it played a vital role in modernising teachers in Gujarat. Navalram Laxmiram took over the editorship of this periodical in 1870 and continued until his death in 1888. Under his editorship, the journal gained great popularity and its circulation increased to 2,500 copies. He wrote critical book reviews and analytical articles on social issues like child marriage and widow remarriage. From September 1888, the periodical gradually became more educational in its content and, with the growth of education, its circulation increased.

Gnyan Sudha was another significant periodical, which was launched by the Prarthana Samaj in December 1886. This Anglo-Gujarati fortnightly became an organ of the Prarthana Samaj. Though a religious magazine, it was not sectarian in its outlook. When Ramanbhai Mahipatram Nilkanth became its editor, it started discussions on literary subjects.

Two other important periodicals of the early 20th century were *Vasant* and *Sundri Subodh*. *Vasant* was a highly scholastic magazine started by Professor Anandshankar Dhruv in 1902. Though literary subjects dominated *Vasant* in the earlier period, social and miscellaneous subjects were also included later. In politics, it held moderate views. Owing to its high literary and scholarly standard, it became the most prestigious magazine of Gujarat. In 1914, 600 copies of *Vasant* were issued. Gandhi read it regularly and was influenced by it. However, the elitist stance of *Vasant* was criticised by *Buddhi Prakash*.[110]

Sundri Subodh was the first monthly journal of Ahmedabad entirely devoted to women's interests. It was founded in September 1903 by the Bandhu Samaj, the association of Ahmedabad which had been established to create literature for the uplift of women. Its main purpose was to entertain as well as educate literate Gujarati women. It aimed at social, religious, moral and intellectual uplift of women. It also invited women writers to contribute articles and poems to the magazine.[111] The magazine discussed women's education, home decoration, child care, home medicine, household tips and other such topics. It was reformist but not radical in its outlook. It visualised an ideal woman as a mother and housewife who was devoted to her husband, home and family, but her separate identity as an individual was never thought of. A good housewife was preferred to a good orator.[112] It became one of the most readable family magazines, but its irregularity was criticised by contemporary periodicals.

Towards the end of the 19th century, various caste and community journals proliferated in Ahmedabad. They were sponsored by the caste or community associations. Their main purpose was to uplift their castes. They usually contained caste news and articles on social issues, caste histories and such other material. *Tolak Shubhechhak Patrika* was the first caste journal and was founded as early as 1876. It was followed by *Audichya Hitechhu Patra* in 1880. *Jain Hitechhu*, *Kadva Vijay*, *Shrimali Subhechhak* and *Vaishya Patrika* were some other caste journals published in Ahmedabad. Thus, the press was active in the city and played a role in shaping the perceptions and opinions of the people.

VII

In pre-British times, the people did resort to collective action. But this action was not in the form of public meetings as we understand them today. The collective action was an extreme step to protest the misrule of the state. But no one met again to ventilate grievances after the problem was solved. On the other hand, the public meetings from the second half of 19th century onwards were aimed at educating common people about burning social issues ranging from child marriage and death and marriage expenses to the problems of education. In this sense, the public meetings of this period were qualitatively different from the mass action of the earlier period. The earlier mass action was not designed to change old habits, whereas the public meetings were designed for precisely this purpose.

In the last few decades of the 19th century, the city's public scene was enlivened by public meetings convened to solve public issues—social, civil and political. This new avenue was increasingly used by the people to express their sentiments. The increasing use of this modern medium manifested rising social awareness and interest in public issues and was an important means of moulding public opinion. People could vent their dissent and grievances through such meetings.

In the 1870s, increased municipal taxes and the excessive interference of municipal inspectors aroused the indignation of the people, who assembled at meetings to protest these acts. The drainage issues evoked hostile reactions among the conservative people of Ahmedabad. The people feared added taxation for the construction of the drainage system. Various protest meetings were called in June 1888. Even social reformers like Mahipatram, Bechardas Lashkari, Keshavlal Motilal resisted the change.[113] The resistance to drainage and water pipes continued up to 1899 when the drainage work started in Kalupur. A public meeting was called in which about 2,000 men protested the increased taxation which would follow on the construction of drainage. This shows that the process of modernisation was not smooth in the conservative society of Ahmedabad. The drainage issue created a kind of civil war between the progressive group and the conservative group. The latter was larger, but the former was more influential and hence stronger.

The Age of Consent Bill also generated a conflict between tradition and modernity. Educated people were divided on the issue, and the orthodox and the reformist groups both called meetings. Such conflicts were a part of the process of social change in a traditional society.

Public meetings were held frequently in the early 20th century. In 1900, when a European hide merchant from Kanpur established a slaughter house in the vicinity of the city, the religious feelings of the Jains and the Hindus were deeply hurt. To show their indignation, a protest meeting was called by the *nagarseth*, the leader of the Jain community. A memorial was prepared for submission to the commission of the northern division. About 5,000 people of all castes and creeds had assembled at this meeting. The unrest culminated in a general strike by the shopkeepers of the city. Consequently, the government had to concede the demands of the people.[114] As the people of Ahmedabad became politically conscious and active, many meetings were called to support the *swadeshi* movements in 1905 and 1906.

Through public meetings the people of Ahmedabad expressed their sentiments and voiced their opinions and grievances. These meetings generated awareness of contemporary issues among the people of the city.

* * *

Thus, voluntary associations, the press and public meetings facilitated change. In spite of their limitations, they enhanced the social interaction among different castes and creeds and kept public opinion alive and strong.

Notes

1. Bombay Government, *Gazetteer of the Bombay Presidency*, Vol. IV, *Ahmedabad*, Bombay, 1978, p. 216, p. 309. Henceforth cited as *Ahmedabad Gazetteer.*
2. *Ibid.*
3. Government of Bombay, *Supplement to the Report of the Director of Public Instruction in the Bombay Presidency for the Year 1913–1914*, Bombay, 1914, pp. 7, 36, 47.
4. *Ibid.*, pp. 18–28.
5. Government of Bombay, *Report of the Director of Public Instruction in the Bombay Presidency for the Year 1913–1914*, Bombay, 1914, p. 3.
6. *Supplement to the Report of the Director of Public Instruction in the Bombay Presidency for the Year 1913–1914*, pp. 52–54.
7. *Prajabandhu*, October 30, 1910, p. 9.
8. *Ahmedabad Gazetteer*, p. 309.
9. *Annual Report of the Principal of the Gujarat College, Ahmedabad for 1894–95 with Statement of Accounts*, Bombay, p. 18. Henceforth cited as *The Annual Report of the Gujarat College* and the relevant year.

10. *The Annual Report of the Gujarat College for the Year 1909–10*, pp. 2, 11.
11. *Buddhi Prakash*, February 1879, pp. 31–32.
12. *Ibid.*, January 1865, p. 3.
13. *Ibid.*, February 1898, Supplement, pp. 2–4.
14. Hiralal Parekh, *Gujarat Vernacular Society no Itihas*, Vol. III (in Gujarati), Ahmedabad, 1934, p. 6.
15. *Buddhi Prakash*, December 1901, Supplement, p. 27.
16. Hiralal Parekh, *op.cit.*, Vol. III, p. 206.
17. *Buddhi Prakash*, October 1912, p. 317.
18. *Buddhi Prakash*, March 1878, p. 54.
19. The Gujarat Vernacular Society, *The Gujarat Vernacular Society no Report 1906,* Ahmedabad, 1907, p. 1.
20. *Buddhi Prakash*, July 1877, p. 185.
21. *Buddhi Prakash*, October 1882, Supplement, pp. 17–18.
22. *Ibid.*, October 1891, p. 317.
23. *Ibid.*, September 1886, p. 120.
24. The Gujarat Vernacular Society, *The Gujarat Vernacular Society no Report 1906* (in Gujarati), Ahmedabad, 1907, pp. 3–5.
25. *Ibid.*, October 1912, p. 317.
26. *Ibid.*, April 1877, pp. 88–91; Narsinhrao B Divetia, *Smaran Mukur* (in Gujarati), Bombay, 1926, pp. 47–55.
27. Bhanusukhram Nirgunrai Mehta, *Mahipatram Charitra* (in Gujarati), Baroda, 1930, pp. 1–30. *Buddhi Prakash*, July 1891, Supplement, pp. 2–4.
28. Mahipatram Rupram, *Parvatikunvar Akhyan* (in Gujarati), Ahmedabad, 1881, pp. 12–15.
29. Dalpatram Dahyabhai, *Mahipatram Vilayat Java Vishe* (in Gujarati), Ahmedabad, 1860, p. 7.
30. Krishnarao Bholanath, *Bholanath Sarabhainu Jivan Charitra* (in English and Gujarati), Bombay, 1888, pp. 89–90.
31. Dalpatram, *Mahipatram Vilayat Java Vishe*, p. 26.
32. Bhanusukhram Mehta, *op. cit.*, p. 59.
33. Mahipatram, *Parvatikunvar Akhyan*, pp. 17–20.
34. *Buddhi Prakash*, April 1864.
35. Mahipatram, *Parvatikunvar Akhyan*, p. 20.
36. Bhanusukhram Mehta, *op. cit.*, pp. 76–77, Navalram Trivedi, *Sansar Sudharanu Rekha Darshan* (in Gujarati), Ahmedabad, 1974 (reprint) pp. 81–82.

37. *Buddhi Prakash*, October 1912, pp. 310–18; Hiralal Parekh, *Gujarat Vernacular Society no Itihas*, Vol. II, pp. 248–57.
38. Krishnarao Bholanath, *op. cit.*, pp. 92–96, English Text pp. 9, 108.
39. *Ibid.*, English text, pp. 6, 113; *Buddhi Prakash*, September 1859, p. 170; June 1876, pp. 129–30.
40. Krishnarao Bholanath, *op. cit.*, English text, p. 3.
41. *Ibid.*, pp. 11, 6.
42. *Ibid.*, p. 116.
43. *Ibid.*, *Buddhi Prakash*, September 1874, pp. 217–222; June 1876, pp. 128–139.
44. *Ahmedabad Gazetteer*, p. 326.
45. Krishnarao Bholanath, *op. cit.*, English text, pp. 7–8.
46. *Ibid.*, p. 9; *Buddhi Prakash*, September 1874, pp. 217–222.
47. Krishnarao Bholanath, *op. cit.*, pp. 19–22; *Ibid.*, English text, p. 9; *Ibid.*, pp. 54–55.
48. *Gujarat Shalapatra*, April 1884, p. 90.
49. *Ahmedabad Gazetteer*, pp. 326–27.
50. Narmadashankar Dave, *Dharmavichar* (in Gujarati) (2nd ed.), Bombay, 1900, p. 35; *Buddhi Prakash*, April 1878, p. 95.
51. Vijay Singh Chavda, *Modern Gujarat*, Ahmedabad, pp. 155–56.
52. *Ahmedabad Gazetteer*, p. 326.
53. *Buddhi Prakash*, April 1883, p. 95.
54. *Gujarat Shalapatra*, October 1886, pp. 222–25; *Buddhi Prakash*, November 1886, pp. 247–48.
55. *Buddhi Prakash*, October 1872, pp. 230–340.
56. *Ibid.*, November 1874, p. 264, Navalram Trivedi, *op. cit.*, pp. 77–78.
57. *Gujarat Shalapatra*, September 1879, pp. 214–16; *Buddhi Prakash*, November 1878, pp. 263–64; September 1886, pp. 230–40.
58. *Buddhi Prakash*, September 1886, p. 239.
59. *Gujarat* Shalapatra, May–June, 1874, pp. 65–66.
60. *Buddhi Prakash*, September 1888, p. 224.
61. *Ibid.*, July 1888, pp. 163–68.
62. *Ibid.; Buddhi Prakash*, September 1888, Supplement, p.2.
63. *Ibid.*, pp. 1–6; January 1889; pp. 23–24.
64. *Ibid.* February 1889, pp. 44–48; March 1889, pp. 71–72.
65. *Prajabandhu*, November 1, 1903, p. 10; October 24, 1909, p. 12.
66. *Buddhi Prakash*, January 1905, p. 28.

67. *Prajabandhu*, July 23, 1911, p. 14.
68. Shankarrai Amritrai, *Amdavadno Jivan Vikas* (in Gujarati), Ahmedabad, 1921, p. 100.
69. Shankarrai Amritrai, *op. cit.*, p. 101.
70. *Buddhi Prakash*, May 1913, pp. 129–30.
71. *Gujarat Shalapatra*, December 1888, pp. 282–83.
72. Dahyabhai Derasari, *Society for the Prevention of Cruelty to Animals*, Jubilee Number, Ahmedabad 1931.
73. *Prajabandhu*, March 29, 1903, p. 9.
74. *Ibid.*, July 22, 1906, p. 5.
75. *Ahmedabad Gazetteer*, p. 294.
76. *Gujarat Shalapatra*, January 1865, pp. 3–9.
77. *Ibid.*, April 1869, pp. 80–81.
78. *Ibid.*, September 1868, p. 230.
79. *Buddhi Prakash*, February 1885, p. 43; *Ibid.*, December 1893, pp. 264–67.
80. *Prajabandhu*, February 8, 1903, p. 11.
81. *The Annual Report of the Gujarat College for the Year 1891-92*, p. 7; *Ibid.*, for the year 1909–1910, p. 11.
82. Government of Bombay, *Report of the Director of Public Instruction in the Bombay Presidency for the Year 1899–1900*, Bombay, 1900, p. 54.
83. *Prajabandhu*, December 24, 1899, p. 3.
84. *Prajabandhu*, January 7, 1909, p. 14.
85. *Prajabandhu*, March 8, 1903, p. 10.
86. *Gujarat Shalapatra, December 1904, pp. 359–60; Buddhi Prakash*, December 1904, pp. 352–53.
87. *Buddhi Prakash*, January 1864, p. 4.
88. *Ahmedabad Gazetteer*, p. 311.
89. Government of Bombay, *Report on the Administration of Bombay Presidency for the Year 1886–87,* Bombay 1887, p. 237, for the year of 1894–95, Bombay 1895, p. 345, for the year of 1899–1900, Bombay 1901; p. 532; Government of Bombay, *The Report on Native Newspapers of the Bombay Presidency.* (Henceforth cited as *RNP*) for the week ending January 6, 1900, p. 3.
90. *RNP*, for the week ending January 3, 1914, pp. 3–5.
91. *The Reports on Native Newspapers of the Bombay Presidency* (*RNP*) printed weekly the official summaries or reproductions of the editorial comments and articles which appeared in the vernacular newspapers

and periodicals. They were close and careful translations of the contents of the vernacular newspapers. They were strictly confidential and were made available only to officials of the rank of divisional commissioner and above, to keep them informed about native opinion.

92. *Buddhi Prakash*, February 1878, p. 32.
93. *Ibid.,* March 1878, pp. 77–78.
94. *RNP* for the week ending October 17, 1868, p. 10.
95. *RNP*, for the week ending July 24, 1869, p. 7; October 16, 1869, p. 8.
96. *RNP* for the week ending March 18, 1871, p. 8.
97. *RNP* for the week ending June 10, 1869, p. 11; April 23, 1870, p. 61, April 12, 1873, p. 10.
98. *RNP* for the week ending June 1, 1872, p. 7.
99. *RNP* for the week ending September 11, 1880, p. 89; September 21, 1880, p. 13.
100. *RNP* for the week ending April 1, 1882, p. 17.
101. *RNP* for the week ending December 27, 1879, pp. 10–11.
102. *RNP,* for the week ending May 5, 1888, p. 13; May 19, 1888, p. 13; December 7, 1889, p. 15.
103. *RNP* for the week ending January 18, 1890, pp. 7–8; September 18, 1890, p. 18; November 1, 1890, p. 9; January 24, 1891, p. 15; January 31, 1891, p. 11.
104. *Prajabandhu*, March 6, 1898, p. 1.
105. *Ibid.*, June 28, 1899, p. 6.
106. *Ibid.,* May 29, 1898, p. 1.
107. *RNP*, for the week ending September 3, 1904, p. 30; September 17, 1904, pp. 36–37.
108. *Buddhi Prakash*, January 1863, p. 4.
109. *Gujarat Shalapatra*, April 1870, pp. 97–98.
110. *Buddhi Prakash*, June 1902, p. 192.
111. *Sundri Subodh*, October 1903, inside of the front cover.
112. *Ibid.*, December 1904, p. 76.
113. *RNP*, for the week ending June 9, 1888, p. 12.
114. *Prajabandhu*, March 11, 1900, p. 417; *RNP*, for the week ending January 13, 1900, pp. 24–26; January 21, 1900, p. 23; February 3, 1900, p. 27; February 10, p. 23; February 17, 1800, p. 23.; General Department, Compilation File No. 360/1914, p. 7.

6

Caste in Transition

Social structures die hard. This is particularly so in a traditional Hindu setup where the caste system has had strong organic links with religion. It is chiefly because of this that the caste structure, with the power of hierarchy behind it, remained intact in Ahmedabad society throughout the period covered in this book. Nevertheless, an interesting phenomenon was that the 'caste' which earlier was the steel-frame of Hindu social life, began gradually to respond to the stimuli provided by the reformers. The castes, of course, fought against some of the reformist impulses, but they did also absorb some new values, especially those reflected in the demand for education for boys and girls and the lower age limit for marriage and other such matters. Caste groups evolved their own organisations—"caste reform associations"—to carry out these reforms. Perhaps this is why the two contradictory trends were equally strong—the efforts to retain the purity of the caste and, at the same time, the efforts to absorb within its fabric the values introduced by western education, the agency of the press and the voluntary reform organisations described earlier.

Being a malleable institution, the caste system, while retaining its vitality, also exhibited tremendous adaptability towards new forces. It assumed new roles and functions which gave momentum to the modernising process in the city. At the same time, it is evident that the various material and intellectual forces introduced by British rule did affect the caste system.

I

Though the British government recognised the customary rights of the different communities with regard to marriage, property and inheritance, the judicial powers of the caste *panchayats* in regard to criminal offences were restricted. Criminal offences like assault, adultery and rape were now dealt with by British law courts. Social legislations such as the Sati Regulation of 1829, the Widow Remarriage Act of 1856, the Anti-infanticide Act of 1870, and the Age of Consent Act of 1982 introduced by the British also undermined the authority of the caste. In addition, the Caste Disabilities Removal Act XXI of 1850 had a direct bearing on the caste system. This Act laid down that a person did not forfeit his rights to property if he happened to lose caste or change his religion. Moreover, the principle of equality before the law further affected the caste system. As a result, the special privileges enjoyed by castes like the Brahmin and the Rajput in judicial matters were withdrawn. However, as mentioned earlier, the government did not greatly interfere in caste matters and in the caste's civil jurisdiction as long as no malice or violence was involved under the Clause 1st Section XXI Regulation. Thus, the judicial powers of the caste were certainly reduced, but were not totally wiped out.

Modern education brought in new liberal ideology based on the tenets of rationalism and equality. As a result, the educated person could challenge the rigidity of the caste system if he wanted to reform and liberalise it. However, in the city of Ahmedabad, the social reformer might have wanted to change the caste system from within, but he definitely did not wish to abolish it altogether.

The modern educational system affected the caste system in yet another way. Earlier, higher education was the prerogative of the Brahmins, but new education was open to all castes and creeds. As a result, the Vanias, Kanbis and even artisan castes like the Mochis, Ghanchis, Bhavsars, and Durjees obtained higher education and acquired good posts in government departments since these did not consider caste and creed distinctions when recruiting a candidate. This created upward social mobility for the lower castes. Even the children of the Kolis and Bhils acquired the new education.[1] Mary Carpenter, a social worker from England visiting the Normal College of Ahmedabad in 1866, remarks on how she saw a very bright low caste Mochi (cobbler) boy who far outstripped all his fellow students.[2]

Dalpatram, the renowned litterateur of Ahmedabad, perceiving this occupational mobility in 1865, commented:

> At present, even the Ghanchi (oil pressers) and Durjee (tailors) and other such castes take English education. Therefore, in a decade or two changes would occur in hereditary occupations. This change is evident even today. Earlier, the teaching work was done only by the *Bhikshuk* Brahmins. It was insulting to ask the Vanias to teach. Today the children of the Vanias and the Nagars are teachers. In Ahmedabad, one Brahmin repairs watches and also does some work of Blacksmith. Some Vania and Nagar's children study engineering and work in the Government Departments.[3]

Until 1859, however, the fear of ritual pollution kept the untouchable castes out of the government schools.[4] When a circular was issued by the educational inspector of the northern division, in 1880, instructing masters of the government schools to admit the children of Dheds, Bhangis and other outcastes, it was severely criticised by the Gujarati Press. Even the reformist newspapers of Ahmedabad, *Samsher Bahadur* and *Hitechhu,* disapproved of this circular. *Samsher Bahadur* suggested that separate schools for the outcastes should be set up.[5] Later, the same paper observed that the circular showed disregard of the solemn royal proclamation of 1858.[6] As a result, from the last decade of the 19th century, separate schools for untouchables were started in Ahmedabad. Nevertheless, the Dheds and other untouchable castes themselves were apathetic to education and did not avail of the new opportunities created by British rule.[7] As a result, the untouchable castes continued to remain uneducated.

The teaching profession, too, was no longer the prerogative of the Brahmins. As early as 1869, the caste composition of the teacher trainees at the Training College of Ahmedabad revealed that among 61 trainees admitted, there were 39 Brahmins,

13. Bhogilal Pranvallabhdas

14. Maganlal Vakhatchand

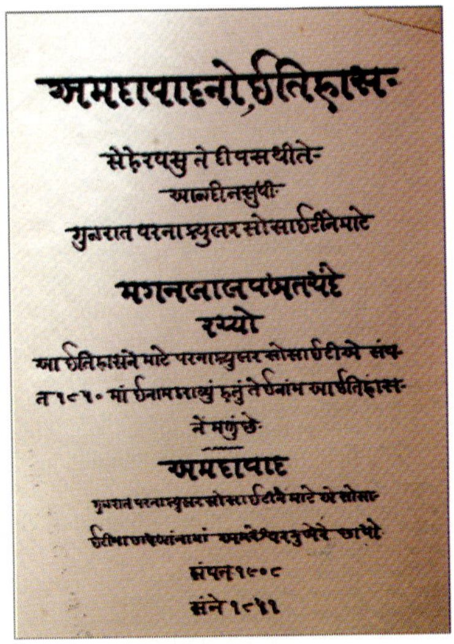

अमदावादनो ईतिहास.

शेहेर वस्युं ते दीवसथी ते
आज दीन सुधी.
गुजरात वरनाक्युलर सोसाईटीनी माटे
मगनलाल वखतचंदे
रच्यो
आ ईतिहासने माटे वरनाक्युलर सोसाईटीए संव-
त १९१० मां ईनाम ठराव्युं हतुं ते ईनाम आ ईतिहास-
ने मळ्युं छे.
अमदावाद
गुजरात वरनाक्युलर सोसाईटीने माटे ए सोसा-
ईटीना छापखानामां [illegible] छाप्यो.
संवत १९०८
सने १८५१

15. The first page of
Maganlal's book
Amdavad no Itihas

16. Premabhai Hemabhai

17. Gujarat Vernacular Society building

18. Premabhai Hall

19. Mahipatram Rupram

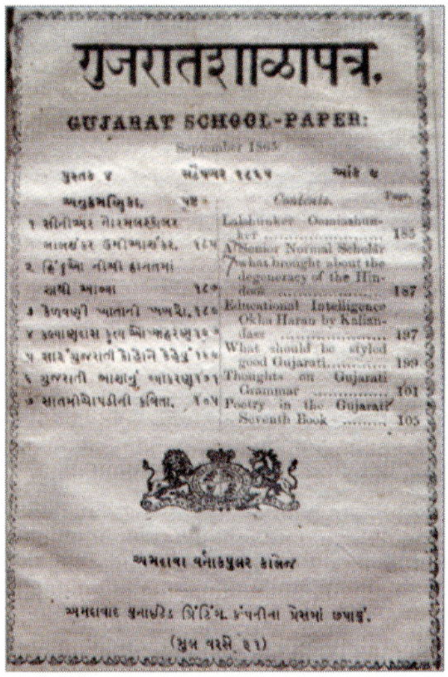

गुजरातशाळापत्र.

GUJARAT SCHOOL-PAPER:

September 1865

Contents.	Page.
Lalshanker Oomiashunker	185
A Senior Normal Scholar what brought about the degeneracy of the Hindoos	187
Educational Intelligence	
Okha Haran by Kalian-dass	197
What should be styled good Gujarati	199
Thoughts on Gujarati Grammar	101
Poetry in the Gujarati Seventh Book	105

20. *Gujarat Shalapatra's* First Issue

21. Premchand Raichand Training College

22. Bholanath Sarabhai

23. Prarthana Mandir

24. Interior of the Prarthana Samaj Building

12 Vanias, nine Patidars and two Barots. The caste composition of the trainees became more heterogeneous in the 1890s. The caste composition shows that various artisan castes and lower castes like Mochis, Ravalias, Kachhias and Kolis were candidates for the entrance examination of the Premchand Raichand Training College of Ahmedabad in 1896.[8]

The Directory of Vernacular Teachers of 1914, which listed teachers holding qualifying certificates recognised by the educational department and employed in the local board municipal schools in the northern division, shows that the teachers belonged to various castes. Although Brahmin teachers were the largest number, the number of teachers from the Vania and Kanbi castes was not small. Apart from Muslims, there were native Christian teachers and teachers of the Ghanchi, Rout, Valand, Kumbhar, Bhavsar, Mali, Bhojaka, Koli, Luvana, Rajput, Garasia, Durjee, Sutar, Sathvar and Bhangi castes working in Ahmedabad city schools. The most noteworthy new entry to the teaching profession was that of the Bhangi caste. Bulakhi Bhikha Bhangi was employed as a teacher in school No. 17 of Ahmedabad from 1905, but he was one single untouchable in the teaching profession until 1914. The fear of ritual pollution which gripped the higher castes, and the lack of education among the low castes, restricted occupational mobility among the untouchable castes.[9]

The caste did not, however, restrict any qualified individual from adopting new professions like medicine or law. Thus, education induced occupational mobility. The relationship between caste and occupation was no longer rigid.

Industrialisation gave a further impetus to occupational mobility, which in turn affected the socioeconomic position of castes. New occupations had emerged which did not fit neatly into the traditional caste hierarchy, so employers set aside caste considerations if required. Ahmedabad, by 1914, had become an industrial city with 41 textile mills and other industrial units and about 41,000 industrial workers. The new working class consisted of labouring castes like the Waghris, Kolis and Rawalias, artisan castes like the Kanbis, Muslims and Chhipas and a small number of workers even from the Brahmins and Vania castes. Similarly, the capitalist class which emerged as a result of industrialisation was a multicaste and multicreed group that included the Vania (Meshri and Shravak), Nagar, Brahmakshatriya and Kanbi castes and a few Muslims and Parsis. Thus, the economic basis of the caste was slowly but surely being undermined by industrialisation.

Railways, restaurants, hotels and factory work dealt a blow to the ideas of ritual purity and pollution which were at the base of the caste system. The advent of the railways was hailed by the people of Ahmedabad as it made travelling easy, fast and cheap. But as the higher castes soon realised, even untouchables could travel with them in the same carriage, so they strongly protested against the BB & CI Company.[10] An incident in 1873 sparked off public wrath against the BB & CI Company. Lallubhai Surchand, the editor of *Ahmedabad Samachar*, while travelling to Baroda by a train was compelled by a railway official to sit near a Dhed despite strong remonstrance on his part. Lallubhai brought a civil suit against the railway official in the Ahmedabad small causes court to recover damages. He alleged that he had suffered as a consequence of being forced into close proximity of a Dhed. The Gujarat press strongly censured the attitude of the railway officials for offending the deep-rooted religious feelings of caste Hindus. The newspapers *Ahmedabad Samachar* and *Samsher Bahadur* demanded a separate carriage for Dheds. However, Lallubhai lost the suit.[11]

Many high caste Hindus did not eat while travelling by train lest they be defiled by the presence of the low castes sitting in the carriage. Gradually, however, long train journeys forced these eating taboos to be relaxed.[12] The railway system posed the greatest challenge to the caste system.

Students of various castes and creeds from outside Ahmedabad came to study in the male and female training colleges in the city. The need for hostels for these students created quite a few problems for caste Hindus. In these hostels, students of high and low castes had to reside together. Although separate arrangements for cooking and eating were made for high castes, the stringent rules of ritual purity and pollution could not always be observed. In 1890, some Hindu women students were greatly offended when their food was polluted by being touched by Christian women students. Ideas of ritual pollution and purity were so strong that this episode created a great flutter among caste Hindus. The offended Hindu students complained to the educational authorities, but eventually they themselves were suspended on a charge of indiscipline. The press of Ahmedabad and the whole of Gujarat criticised the highhandedness of the woman superintendent of the college and the educational authorities and showed their sympathy towards the Hindu women students.[13]

Towards the end of the 19th century, lodging houses, hotels, restaurants and tea houses were opened in the city. Evening parties were frequently given by rich Parsis and Hindus, which were attended by Parsis, Muslims and various Hindu caste members who ate together. However, for caste Hindus, separate food arrangements were sometimes made in which only sweets and fruits would be served.[14] The drinking of aerated waters prepared by non-Hindus had become fashionable even among caste Hindus. Many young men drank tea and coffee in restaurants and railway canteens. Many caste Hindus had by this time put aside their ideas of purity and traditional food habits.

Thus, legal changes, industrialisation, the railways and modern education together and separately weakened the caste system in various ways. Caste was gradually being dissociated from its traditional occupations. However, the traditional economy based on handicrafts had not been completely dislocated by industrialisation or by British colonial policy during the period so that some of the traditional hereditary occupations continued. In addition, the sociocultural dimension of caste offered strong resistance to the change generated by the factors just mentioned. As a result, caste retained enough strength to dominate individual action. Each person still lived and worked within the limits of the caste traditions. The attitude of the social reformers of Ahmedabad had also strengthened the institution of the caste, as seen from the following viewpoints of the major social reformers of the city.

II

The social reformers of Ahmedabad followed the course of moderation and gradualism in bringing about social change. Adopting the line of least resistance, most of the reformers did not want to do away with the caste system. Instead, they wanted to remove the ills and shortcomings of caste from within, which they believed would reform society. Reformers such as Dalpatram, Hargovindas D Kantawala and Ambalal Sakarlal Desai did not consider the caste system as an impediment to the modernising process of society but rather as an agent of change from within, hoping to make the best use of the caste tradition. It was this belief which led to the formation of the caste associations in Ahmedabad, which played a vital role in bringing about social change at the grassroots level. The social reformers of the city also expected caste leaders to utilise caste councils or *panchayats* for introducing social reforms within the framework of the caste. This caste reform movement accentuated caste consciousness in the city's populace and thus strengthened the institution of caste.

Dalpatram (1820–1898), an important social reformer in Ahmedabad, believed in blending tradition with modernity and in introducing gradual change. He encouraged and supported the caste reform movement. As the editor of the influential periodical *Buddhi Prakash*, he praised the efforts of the Audichyas, Khedawals, Rayakwals and others who undertook caste reform programmes. He advised his own Shrimali Brahmin caste to emulate these castes.[15] He believed that reforms which could not be successfully implemented by the British king or the government could effectively be brought about by the caste organisations. He considered caste a useful institution which helped its members in times of need. He believed that caste organisation should be strong enough to introduce reforms within the caste.[16]

Mahipatram (1830–1891), the social reformer and educationist whose ideas were tinged with radicalism, did not, however, support the idea of an anti-caste association which was mooted by some reformers in western India. In fact, he warned them not to be hasty in taking steps that would arouse public wrath.[17] Mahipatram himself was harassed and excommunicated by his Surti Vadnagara Nagar caste because he had defied his caste laws in crossing the black seas to go to England in 1860. It took him seven years and self-purification to re-enter the caste, but he was expelled again when he affirmed his belief in reformist principles. It took another four years and another purification to re-enter his caste. He never again took the risk of defying the caste.

Gopalrao Hari Deshmukh alias Lokhitawadi, who was in Ahmedabad for more than 12 years (1866–1877), approved greatly of the activities of the caste reform associations of the city.[18]

Bholanath Sarabhai (1823–1886), the founder of the Prarthana Samaj of Ahmedabad, abhorred the restrictive character of the caste system. In his diary, he commented: "The abominable institution known as caste which is the greatest stumbling block in the way of all kinds of reform, exercises its binding forces equally on the educated and the uneducated."[19] He showed great courage when he wholeheartedly supported Mahipatram on his return from England. He even dined with him. As a result, he was expelled by the Vadnagara Nagar caste of Ahmedabad. He refused to undergo a self-purification ceremony and preferred to remain outside the caste for many years.[20]

Without taking the approval of his caste, Bholanath got rid of many unnecessary social customs connected with the ceremonies of marriage and death within his own family. For example, he stopped the women of his family from singing obscene songs or *phatanas* on wedding days. He also prevented them from weeping and breast-beating after any death in the family.[21] However, he could not totally break away from the caste system as the members of the Brahmo Samaj of Bengal were able to do. Though the Christians, Parsis and Muslims could attend the prayer meetings of the Prarthana Samaj, Dheds and the depressed castes were not allowed in the prayer hall in order to respect the caste feelings of the members.[22]

The most systematic and detailed exposition of the idea of reforming the caste from within and bringing about social change in the society through it was given by Hargovindas Dwarkadas Kantawala (1849–1931) in his booklet *Nat Sudharo*, which he distributed to his Khadayata Vania caste members on the occasion of his daughter Chanchal's wedding in 1886.[23] Kantawala was a social reformer, educationist and ardent supporter of *swadeshi.* As a student of Ahmedabad Training College, he had been strongly influenced by Mahipatram who was the principal of the college at that time. He also became a member of the Prarthana Samaj and was convinced that "caste custom could only be improved by caste organisation". A supporter of gradualism in introducing change in society, he contended that the most effective method of social reform was through the caste organisation. He did not have much faith in reform by legislation. He believed that educated young caste members and caste leaders could easily introduce reforms in the internal functioning of caste organisations and combat evil customs like child marriage, polygamy and the exorbitant expenses of marriage and death ceremonies.[24] They could also end unnecessary and bad customs like singing of obscene songs at weddings and weeping and breast-beating after a death. He argued that if each caste improved, the whole country would improve and progress.[25] He wrote, "Caste is a miniature republic. Caste leaders enjoy authority similar to the members of parliament or the council".[26] He felt that the younger educated elements should strive to gain the leadership in caste councils and adapt the functions and customs of the caste to modern times. He believed that each caste should promote education within the caste and all other castes should follow the example of the Khadayata, Khedawal, Vadnagara and Visnagara castes who had already started collecting educational funds in order to achieve the uplift of their caste members through education. He exhorted people to donate money generously to caste educational funds instead of spending it on caste feasts. His strong conviction was that "if the caste willed, it could remove all the evils."[27]

Similarly, Ambalal Sakarlal Desai (1844–1914), an eminent educationist and social and political leader of the city, felt that the caste system had a positive role to play in the improvement of Hindu society. With this in mind, he favoured introducing reforms through caste organisations. In his presidential address to the Sixth Brahmakshatriya Conference held in Ahmedabad in 1911, he observed that social reform could be successfully brought about only by the agency of caste and to regard the institution of caste as an evil was not a correct view.[28]

Lalshankar Umiashankar (1845–1912) of the Gujarat Sansar Sudhara Samaj established in 1904 was a supporter of the method of least resistance in introducing social reforms. He, too, advocated caste reform. Actively associated with his Visnagara Nagar association, he presided over the second Visnagar caste Conference held in Ahmedabad in 1911.

Anandshankar Dhruv (1869–1942), a Sanskrit professor of Gujarat College and editor of the prestigious Gujarat periodical *Vasant*, was a proponent of the revivalist movement in Gujarat. Convinced that some vital features of Hinduism could profitably be revived for the educational and social regeneration of Hindu society in a colonial setup, he argued that caste itself could serve as an agent of change.[29]

Ramanbhai Nilkanth (1868–1928) did not totally share the views of his contemporaries, such as those of Anandshankar Dhruv or Ambalal Sakarlal or Kantawala. A prominent lawyer and reformist writer, Ramanbhai, cherished western ideals and laid emphasis on rationalism and secularism. Though he found the method of introducing reforms from within the caste of some use, he doubted the overall efficacy of this method. His own radical views led him to attend a dinner party organised in Bombay under the auspices of the Aryan Brotherhood at which guests from all castes including untouchables ate together under the same roof. This event caused ripples in the conservative society of Ahmedabad. Ramanbhai was expelled from his Vadnagara Nagar caste, but he remained unruffled and did not perform the purification ceremony to re-enter the caste. Later, in one of his lectures at the Prarthana Samaj, he remarked: "The reform which you want to introduce, you yourself should practice first."[30]

Unlike Ramanbhai Nilkanth, the other social reformers of the city did not want to break away from their own castes. To introduce structural changes in Hindu society by getting rid of the caste system was too radical a step to be accepted and implemented. Thus, social reformers of the city ardently believed in the efficacy of the caste organisation in reforming society.

Fortunately, Ahmedabad being a city with the corporate spirit, caste tensions or conflicts did not arise during this period. In this mercantile city, cooperation between various castes was necessary for economic activities. Caste meetings and caste association programmes were attended and sometimes even presided over by members of different castes.

The Gujarat Vernacular Society (GVS), in spite of being a multicaste and multicommunity association, administered the trust funds which were meant for the uplift of each particular caste. For example, Ranchhodlal Chhotalal, the founder of the first textile mill, instituted a fund for his Sathodra Nagar caste, for the education of deserving boys and girls. Similarly, Bapuji Jagannath, a lawyer, donated Rs 2,500 in 1898 on the occasion of a wedding in his family for deserving students among his Audichya caste members. Such caste-based trusts and funds abounded in the GVS and reveal that caste consciousness was very strong in the city. It also shows that multicaste voluntary associations like the GVS, too, had accepted the method of introducing social reform through caste bodies.

In 1908, Kishanlal Ratanlal Daftary, a solicitor, started an anti-caste movement in Bombay. *Prajabandhu*, the most widely read and influential paper of Ahmedabad, expressed outright disapproval of this scheme. The long editorial in the issue of August 9, 1908, stated that Daftary's approach was diametrically opposite to the method adopted by the moderate leaders of Ahmedabad and other parts of Gujarat for over half a century, which according to the *Prajabandhu* had produced beneficial results in Gujarat. It wrote:

> It would be far better that the present castes which are small solid blocks of individuality should continue than that the Indian people should be reduced to a mere mass with no common sentiment at all.[31]

The newspaper was only echoing the public opinion of the city.

III

The social reformers of Ahmedabad found the method of introducing social reform through the caste and within the caste to be the most effective and suitable for the conservative caste-ridden society of the city. There were three types of caste organisations—*gnyati panchayat*, or the caste council, the caste reform association and the amalgamated caste federations—through which caste assumed significant new roles and functions necessary for the changing needs of society. Through them, the caste assumed the role of a moderniser and played a vital role in bringing about social change at the grassroots level in the city. The caste promoted social reforms and carried out educational and economic betterment programmes.

As mentioned earlier, the leadership for the caste reform movement was provided by educated members whose outlook was influenced by modern values, which they had imbibed through modern education and through their participation in voluntary reforms associations such as the GVS, Prarthana Samaj and Sansar Sudhara Samaj. Since the educated person was not alienated from caste, he or she tried to diffuse new ideas and values to fellow caste members through the three caste organisations by assuming their leadership. Such a person became the carrier of modern ideas and values to the caste. Thus, the person became the link between the generalised socioreligious movements started by the voluntary associations and the reform movements of his caste. The activities of the voluntary associations were mainly confined to the educated urban middle class, and thus their influence on society was marginal. It was only through the caste organisation that new ideas could percolate downwards to the common people. The caste could translate and define social issues in more meaningful terms at the grassroots level than could the voluntary associations. Thus, there were two stages in the process of social change. Social betterment begun by the voluntary organisations was taken up and reinforced by caste organisations in the second stage. They proved more effective and important than the voluntary associations in this transitional period.

It is necessary at this point to analyse, from the historical, social and cultural point of view, some of these caste organisations of Ahmedabad to trace the process of social change described above. As has been mentioned earlier, the caste reform movement had started as early as the 1850s in an informal manner. The Audichyas, Sathodra Nagars and Kadva Kanbis had tried to reform their castes from within since 1850.

The first organised caste reform association of the city was started in 1873 by the Audichyas Sahasra Brahmin caste. It was named Audichya Hitechhu Sabha (AHS). Audichya was the largest Brahmin caste of the city and was divided into two major sections, Sahasra and Tolakia. As the name indicates, they immigrated to Gujarat from the north during the regime of Siddharaj Jaisinha, the Solanki king. Most of the Audichya Brahmins were priests and lived on alms. They were particularly successful as exorcists, astrologers and magicians. Some also worked as cooks.[32] They were scattered all over Gujarat, but Ahmedabad was their stronghold. As early as 1856, some of the educated reformist Audichyas made efforts to curb the evil custom of polygamy which was widely prevalent in the caste.[33] In the 19th century, this caste was backward, being ridden with many evils such as illiteracy, child marriage, polygamy, dowry, begging, poverty and heavy expenses on ceremonial functions.[34] The educated Audichyas, who had imbibed the liberal spirit of the west through education and the reformist activities of the GVS, were motivated to start a reform movement within the caste to weed out caste evils by establishing the Sabha. The important founder members of the Sabha were Bulakhiram Chakubhai (poet), Prangovind Rajaram (teacher), Mansukhram Narbheram (teacher), Bapuji Jagannath (lawyer) and Bhovandas Bapalal Jani (teacher). All these men were educated. Bulakhiram was a poet trained by Dalpatram and had been influenced by Dalpatram's advanced and reformist ideas. In 1873, he wrote *Audichya Aniti Jamanvar Shatak* in one hundred verses with the intention of reforming his own caste.[35] Bapuji Jagannath was a lawyer and was associated with GVS activities, while the others were trained teachers who must have come under the reformist influence of Mahipatram Rupram, the principal of the Male Training College of Ahmedabad. The aim of the Audichya Sabha was to promote unity, education, morals and religion among the Audichyas. In the first four years, the meetings were organised every Sunday to enlighten caste members on various social and religious issues. In 1880, the Sabha also launched the monthly journal *Audichya Hitechhu Patra* (AHP) which became the mouthpiece of the Sabha. Through it, the Sabha spread reformist ideas throughout the province of Gujarat. The Sabha started a campaign against the evils of child marriage, dowry, polygamy, and the obscene songs and heavy expenses connected with death and marriage ceremonies. It also promoted women's education and tried to stop obscene songs being sung at weddings. The Sabha set up an educational fund from which financial help was given to needy children, and it also had its own library. It engaged a *shastri* to teach the children of the caste rituals like *sandhya* and *Gayatri* recitation.[36] The caste traditions were reinforced by such activities. Membership of the Sabha was optional. As the life membership subscription fee of Rs 10 was high, there were only 117 life members of the Sabha in 1889. But the facilities offered by the Sabha were utilised by all caste members. The AHP frequently lamented that though the caste was very large, very few Audichyas subscribed to this inexpensive periodical. However, as a result of the Sabha's endeavour, begging, singing of obscene songs and unnecessary expense of weddings were reduced while education among the Audichyas increased.[37]

The Sabha supported foreign travel. When a member of the Sabha, Ambalal Bapalal, returned from Paris in 1910, Audichya Mitra Mandal felicitated him. Later, he performed the purification ceremony and dined with his caste members.[38]

From the very beginning, the Audichya Hitechhu Sabha aimed at establishing unity and solidarity in the entire Audichya caste of Gujarat. To achieve this horizontal solidarity, branches of the Sabha were established in the major cities of Gujarat by 1888. The Audichya Sabha's journal was read all over Gujarat. In 1888, the first conference of the Audichyas of Gujarat was arranged in Bombay.[39] This became a regular annual feature. Such caste conferences contributed to the horizontal mobilisation of the Audichyas. In 1912, the Sabha went one step ahead and convened the Bharat Varshiya Audichya Samaj in Surat. Thus, in Gujarat, the credit for spearheading the movement for horizontal solidarity within the caste goes to the Audichya Sabha of Ahmedabad.

The second and smaller division of the Audichyas was known as the Tolakiya Audichyas. The Tolakiyas did not lag behind and formed their caste association Audichya Tolakiya Shubhecchak Sabha in 1876; the Sabha started its own Anglo-Gujarati monthly journal *Tolak Shubhecchak Patrika* as early as 1878, much before the Sahsras started theirs. It was the first caste journal not only in Ahmedabad but in the whole of Gujarat. The *Patrika* became the organ of the Sabha through which it spread reformist ideas amongst caste members all over Gujarat. Unfortunately, the first caste journal of Gujarat was short-lived and ceased publication in 1889. The Tolakiya Sabha also laid down rules and regulations with regard to marriage customs. To bring about horizontal solidarity among the Tolakiya Audichyas of Gujarat, they founded the Tolak Samaj in 1901.[40]

Both these Audichya associations were the earliest caste reform associations in the city. They strove hard to introduce reforms in the caste. However, since the education rate was low among them, both the castes were slow to progress. *Audichya Hitechhu Patrika* lamented that there was no Audichya graduate in Ahmedabad until 1902.[41] All the same, both these associations generated social awareness about evil caste customs and induced unity among caste members. They set an example for other castes.

Compared to the Audichyas, the Brahmakshatriyas organised their caste association as late as 1898, in spite of which they could make rapid strides in the field of social reform and education as the caste was by and large well-to-do and well educated. The Brahmakshatriya caste was small in number but enjoyed a high status in Hindu society as its members were well educated and held high positions in government departments. Many of the Brahmakshatriyas were lawyers, doctors, and teachers and were prosperous. The Brahmakshatriyas claimed to be of Kshatriya descent. According to caste traditions, they had migrated from Punjab about 600 years earlier and had settled in various parts of Gujarat. A sizeable Brahmakshatriya community flourished in the city of Ahmedabad.[42] The Brahmakshatriya caste of Ahmedabad was well advanced. To this caste belonged many public leaders associated with the various political, educational and social associations of the city. Ambalal Sakarlal Desai, a mill owner, educationist, political and social reform leader; Dr Nilkanthrai Dahyabhai, the principal of the Blind School; Dr Hariprasad Vrajrai Desai, the principal of the Male Training College; Jivraj Vrajrai, a foremost barrister of Ahmedabad, were among the prominent Brahmakshatriya personalities of the city. The women of this caste were educated and participated in the caste reform movement.

The Brahmakshatriya Association was founded in September 1898 to promote unity and progress among caste members. It started on a small scale with a debating society and a library and organised lectures by eminent scholars. In 1907, it began publishing the quarterly *Brahmakshatriya Trimasik Patrika*.

Every year, it organised sports and get-togethers for caste members. To promote higher education among Brahmakshatriya women, the association made arrangements for their conveyance in horse carriages to the Female Training College and its practicing school. The association had its own educational fund from which it gave books and financial help to needy children. It also supported foreign travel and felicitated those who travelled abroad. As a result, the caste's attitude towards those who travelled to foreign countries became very liberal and it did not ask them to pay a fine or perform self-purification rites. The Brahmakshatriya Association of Ahmedabad also started a movement for horizontal mobilisation of the Brahmakshatriyas of Gujarat and convened the Brahmakshatriya Conferences.

The Brahmakshatriya Association and Conferences together succeeded in eradicating many evil social customs prevailing in the caste such as child marriage. Restrictions on foreign travel were lifted. Heavy expenses on caste feasts and breast-beating after a death were controlled to a great extent. The education rate rose. As mentioned earlier, women of the Brahmakshatriya caste were well educated and actively participated in public life. From 1910 onwards, they held their own conferences as an adjunct of the general Brahmakshatriya conferences. However, the issue of widow marriage remained a sticky one with no easy solution.[43]

Some other early caste associations in the city were Sathodra Hitechhu Sabha, Vadnagara Nagar Swasudharak Mandal, Vadnagara Nagar Association and Raikwal Shubhechhak Sabha. Associations of Mevada Brahmins, Khadayata Vanias, Tapodhan Brahmins, Modh Vanias, Kadva Kanbis, Leva Kanbis, Shrimali Brahmins, Vanias and many other castes were very active from the last decades of the 19th century. Even low castes like the Valand (barbers) and the Tragalas and Bhojakas (performing artist castes) organised their associations.

As analysis of the Tragala Bhojak Hitavardhak Samaj reveals how even the illiterate and backward castes improved themselves through the reform activities of their caste associations. These two performing castes established an association in December 1900.

They founded a school to give free education to boys and special training in music and dancing to the children. In 1903, there were about 80 children studying in this school. The Samaj started a class for women where embroidery and sewing were taught. It had its own library. Its efforts were praised by the newspaper *Prajabandhu*. The Samaj was advised by a body composed of the city's leading men like Lalshankar Umiashankar, a social reformer, Mangaldas Girdhardas, a mill owner, Maganbhai Chaturbhai, a lawyer, and Dr Benjamin.[44]

Emulating the higher castes, the Valands (barbers) founded their own association called the Valand Hitavardhaka Sabha in 1907. The Valands of Gujarat met in the village Pansora in Kheda district. There they discussed the problems of child marriage, drinking habits and illiteracy prevailing in their caste.[45] Even the Dheds convened a Dhed Sabha to implement a self-uplift programme. At this Sabha, many Dheds took pledges to abstain from drinking and meat eating.[46] The higher castes extended generous help and guidance to such low caste associations.

By 1914, almost all the major castes had their own caste associations which implemented social uplift programmes for their members. The traditional institution of the caste had transformed itself into a modern voluntary association.

Another important caste organisation through which caste reforms were carried out was the caste council or *gnyati panchayat*, which introduced reforms for the whole caste under the able guidance of educated caste leaders. The Kadva Kanbi caste is a good example of this process. Kadva Kanbi was the largest caste in the city of Ahmedabad. Though originally agriculturalists, the Kadva Kanbis prospered in the city as traders, moneylenders and weavers.[47] Various social evils prevailed in this caste, of which the most serious was female infanticide, which was a consequence of the heavy expenses associated with marriage and the particular evil of the dowry system.

An early as 1848, caste reform movement began among the Kadva Kanbis. The early efforts to introduce social reforms in the caste were abortive. In 1869, Jorawarsinghji Kubersinghji, the Kanbi landlord of Patadi near Viramgam, convened a conference of Kanbis at Patadi. About 40,000 Kanbis gathered and passed resolutions, regulating various customs regarding marriage and limiting monetary and other exchanges at the time of marriages, births and other such occasions. These rules were known as *Kadva Kanbi Natna Dikriona Saurakshan Saru Niyam*, that is, rules for the protection of Kadva Kanbi daughters.[48]

It was Bechardas Ambiadas Lashkari (1818–1889), a textile mill owner, noted reformer, and member of the Kadva Kanbi caste from Ahmedabad, who played a major role in suppressing female infanticide among the Kadva Kanbis. He also regulated marriage expenses which were the root cause of many social evils in his community.[49] His efforts resulted in the Bombay government passing the Act VIII in 1870, making female infanticide a crime. From April 1871 onwards, the government, through another notification, regulated customary, monetary and other exchanges at the time of marriage. Bechardas called a conference of the Kadva Kanbis in Ahmedabad in 1889 which was attended by about 5,000–6,000 delegates from various parts of Gujarat. As a result of many and long deliberations, expenses to be incurred on occasions like birth, marriage and death were fixed. The orthodox section of the caste naturally protested against these changes and reforms, and many social abuses continued to be rampant.[50]

To reinforce the above caste reform movement, the Kadva Kanbi caste association Kadva Patidar Subhechhak Sabha was founded in the last decade of the 19th century. It started a periodical and had its own library near the Dariapur gate and a hostel for students near the Delhi gate.[51]

The progressive caste councils of Visa Oswal, Dasa Shrimali Shravak and Dasa Khadayata Vanias introduced reforms among their own castes. They prohibited the customs of weeping and breast-beating after death.[52] Some castes like the Visa Porwad relaxed some rules regarding marriage and even permitted a member to marry a Dasa Porwad girl.[53] The Dasa Khadayata Vanias caste council decided to utilise the funds received during any caste feast for the purpose of education.[54] Almost all the Shravak Vania castes were quite liberal in the matter of foreign travel. The reforms introduced by the caste councils were most effectively implemented as the members regarded the sanction of the caste in such matters as final.

During this transitional period, a significant dimension was added to the caste movement by the formation of amalgamated caste associations or federations of sub-castes which were known as Samaj, Parishad or Sabha, for example, Patidar Samaj, Audichya Samaj, Brahmansabha, Nagarsabha and Vaishya Sabha.

This movement of reform through caste associations was pioneered by the Audichya Sabha of Ahmedabad, which was renamed the Audichya Samaj of Gujarat in 1888. Later, this movement of the Audichyas of Ahmedabad was integrated into an All India Audichya Movement.

The Nagar was an important caste group of Ahmedabad. The Nagar caste was divided into various sub-castes—Vadnagaras, Visnagaras, Prashanoras, Krishnaraos, Sathodaras, Chitrodas, and more. Each sub-caste was further divided into *grahasthas* and *bhikshukas*. There was competition among the sub-castes, with each claiming a higher social status than the others and refraining from intermarriages. Even intercaste dining was not permitted.[55] All these Nagar sub-castes had lived in cities and been actively associated with administrative work ever since Muslim rule was established in Gujarat. They had acquired great proficiency in the Persian language and were employed in government departments in high posts during Muslim rule. The Marathas and later the British rulers also recognised their administrative abilities and employed them in the administration. They were among the first Gujaratis to acquire knowledge of English and to come in contact with western ideas. Therefore, it was not surprising that the Nagar sub-castes like Vadnagars, Visanagars and Sathodras of Ahmedabad had organised caste reform associations as early as the 1870s. They promoted education in their castes and introduced social reforms connected with marriage and death customs.[56]

To promote interaction and unity among the different sub-castes of the Nagar castes in the city and to relax sub-caste divisions among them, the Sabha of the amalgamated Nagars, or the Nagar Sabha, was founded in 1903 in Ahmedabad. It aimed at promoting interdining and intermarrying among the sub-castes. Social reformers belonging to the Nagar castes, such as Lalshankar Umiashankar, Keshavlal Harshadrai Dhruv, Krishnarao Bholanath, Chinubhai Madhavlal, Ramanbhai Nilkanth, participated in its meetings.[57]

Another noteworthy attempt in this direction was by the Meshri (Vaishnav) Vanias of the city who founded the Gujarat Vaishya Sabha in 1903 to unite and strengthen all Meshri Vania castes. This association emerged in response to their business needs. There was a strong need for cooperation among the different castes and sub-castes to nurture the growing textile industry in the city. The Gujarat Vaishya Sabha was a multipurpose organisation, aiming at promoting prosperity, trade, industry, education and social reform among the Meshri Vanias, with activities much wider in scope than those of other caste organisations. It encompassed the economic, social, religious and cultural life of the Meshri Vania castes and aimed at achieving their all-round development. At its first meeting, the following objectives of the Sabha were laid down:

1) To promote education, industry, trade and to increase prosperity among the Vaishnava Vanias.
2) To help the poor, invalids and orphans by setting up a home for destitute.
3) To put an end to child-marriage, polygamy and other social evils, practice of dowry, breast-beating and weeping after death, expenses on marriage, death and other ceremonies.

4) To promote community feeling among the Vaishnav Vanias.

5) To spread knowledge of Vaishanavism and ethics, to revive the old Vaishnava scriptures and have them translated into the Gujarati language.

6) To implement action-oriented programmes to achieve these objectives.

7) And finally, to collect and administer trust funds to achieve these objectives.[58]

Many textile mill owners and government bureaucrats of Vaishnava castes were actively associated with the Sabha, which effectively cut across the narrow caste and sub-caste lines of the Vaishya caste group.

The Vaishya Sabha's activities corresponded with its numerous objectives. In 1904, it set up a hostel which provided free board and accommodation to poor Vaishya students. In the first year, there were 49 orphans and poor boys in the hostel. In the same year, the Sabha started a class for women where sewing and embroidery were taught. Scholarships were awarded to Meshri Vania women studying in the Female Training College in Ahmedabad. The Sabha started the monthly journal *Vaishya Patrika* from July 1904 to spread progressive social and economic ideas in the Vaishnav community. The journal had a large circulation of 1,500 copies a month. In 1905, the Sabha also set up a library.[59]

The Gujarat Vaishya Sabha supported the *swadeshi* movement, foreign travel and encouraged foreign trade, urging traders to establish branches of their companies in foreign countries. The Sabha took steps to remove hurdles against foreign travel. Influential mill owners like Mangaldas Girdhardas and Balabhai Damodardas were able to pressurise the Vaishnava religious heads and *maharajas* to remove restrictions on foreign travel and got a resolution passed to permit the family members of a person who had returned from a foreign country to attend caste functions and dinners from which they had hitherto been excluded.[60]

The Gujarat Vaishya Sabha also took up the cause of social reform and campaigned against child marriage, dowry, ill matches, heavy expenses on caste feasts and other such practices. In an attempt to relax sub-caste restrictions, it favoured interdining and even intermarrying among all the Vaishnava Vania sub-castes.[61] It promoted the greatly needed unity and cooperation for the industrial development of the city among the Vaishnav Vanias of different sub-castes.

Other amalgamated federations of the city were the Jain conferences of the three major divisions of this community—Swetambar, Sthanakwasi and Digambara. Since Ahmedabad was the stronghold of the Jains, the Jains of Ahmedabad dominated these federations.

The ground for Jain unity was prepared by the non-sectarian Jain periodical *Jain Hitechhu*, which was started in 1898 to bring about religious and community awareness among the Jains. It suggested that the Jains hold conferences to bring about religious and social awakening in the Jain community. The periodical was against restrictions on foreign travel and against the subdivisions of Jains such as Dasa, Visa and Oswal Shrimali, which it argued should be removed and marriages among the subdivisions be permitted.[62] All three divisions of the Jains founded their federations and started periodicals for bringing about socioreligious awakening in their communities. The *sadhus* (monks) and the *shravakas* (householders) of each Jain sect combined their efforts. The most noteworthy federation was the Jain Swetambar Conference which was founded in 1902 and combined all the Swetambar Jain castes under its banner. This organisation had an all-India character but was mainly dominated by the businessmen and mill owners of Ahmedabad. Lalbhai Dalpatbhai, the owner of the Saraspur Mills, was the general secretary of this organisation from 1903 to 1908. Many rich Jain traders and mill owners of Ahmedabad were actively associated with the Swetambar Conference. It had its own funds and headquarters. The objective of the Jain Conference was to provide a common platform to the community for social and moral progress. Every year, the delegates met to discuss social, religious and economic issues such as female education, child marriage and vocational and technical education.[63]

The Conference started a monthly journal entitled *Jain Swetambar Conference Herald* in 1906.[64] The Jain Conference encouraged intercaste Jain marriages.[65]

The Brahmin castes traditionally numbering 84, or '*Chorasi*', were not far behind in starting a movement to amalgamate their castes into a federation so as to promote unity amongst them. In the first decade of the 20th century, efforts were made to dissolve sub-caste distinctions and promote interdining and intermarrying among the Brahmin castes in Ahmedabad.[66] It is interesting to note here that, in Ahmedabad as early as 1864, Bholanath Sarabhai and Mahipatram had actually started an abortive movement to amalgamate all the Brahmin castes into one new Brahmin caste.[67]

By 1908, the time had arrived for all the Brahmin castes of the city of Ahmedabad to unite and found the Brahmin Hitwardhak Association to protest the book *Brahmin Nirnay*, written by a Lohar (blacksmith) named Nagar Pitambar, which abused and criticised the Brahmins. This book enraged the Brahmins of the city who boycotted the blacksmith caste.[68]

Except for this particular episode, the city of Ahmedabad did not witness any anti-Brahmin movement such as that in Maharashtra or South India. This can be explained variously. First, in the mercantile province of Gujarat, the most dominant and influential castes were the Vania castes. Though in the traditional hierarchical set-up of the caste system, the Vanias were lower than the Brahmin castes, in Gujarat they were equated with the Brahmins. Second, many of the Brahmins of Gujarat were illiterate and poor and thus were not able to command the respect of the people. Third, sects like Swaminarayan, Pushtimarg and Kabirpanthis undermined the importance of the Brahmins. Fourth, the enormous influence of Jainism over the mercantile community in Gujarat may have been responsible for decreasing the dominance of the Brahmins. Fifth, the Brahmins themselves were not strong and united. As a result, the dominance of the

Brahmin castes over the society of Gujarat was not as strong as in Maharashtra or South India.[69]

All these caste federations and conferences—the Gujarat Vaishya Sabha, the Brahmin Hitwardhan Sabha, the Nagar Sabha—played a vital role in relaxing the caste subdivision distinctions. They advocated the liquidation of endogamous subdivisions within the caste and encouraged interdining among the sub-castes. They helped in bringing about a change in the attitude of the people towards these two matters. However, intermarriage among the sub-castes was still a rare phenomenon. As regards eating and drinking, the old restrictions were considerably relaxed. The Vadnagara Nagar caste of Ahmedabad earlier had made it a point to eat food cooked only by fellow caste members but had relaxed the rule and now openly employed cooks of other Brahmin castes.[70]

In a welcome manifestation of the changing role of the caste, these three types of caste organizations—the caste association, the caste council, and the amalgamated caste federation—were not isolated from one another; their activities were actually complementary to each other. It was through them that the traditional institution of the caste was transformed and adapted to modernity.

IV

The four major depressed castes in Ahmedabad were the Dheds, Chamars, Dabgars and Bhangis. They stayed within the walled city of Ahmedabad in their *vadas*, which lay on the outskirts of Jamalpur, Shahpur, Khanpur, Mirzapur and Khadia. Each *vada* was usually a cluster of mud huts. They were not allowed to reside in the *pols*. In 1872, there were 433 Chamars (tanners), 71 Dabgars (drum makers) and 4,166 Dheds and Bhangis. Together, they formed a substantial segment of the city's population.[71]

The depressed castes were poor and illiterate. All the depressed castes were considered to be outside the pale both of Hinduism and the caste system based on the four *varnas*. This was ironical because they worshipped Hindu gods and goddesses such as Ram, Hanuman, Ganesh, Devi and the tulsi plant. They also followed sects like Kabirpanth, Ramanandipanth and the Swaminarayan sect. However, these sects did not allow them to enter their temples. Following the caste system, each depressed caste had its own caste rules and regulations for matters such as marriage, divorce and inheritance. The caste leaders or *patels* punished those who did not observe these rules and even ostracized those who committed any major breach. They indulged in drinking and ate animal flesh. Many of the depressed castes assumed Rajput surnames like Solanki, Rathod, Chavda, Chauhan, Waghela, Makwana and Parmar.[72]

The Dheds occupied the highest position in the hierarchy of the depressed castes and were followed by the Chamars and Dabgars who made leather goods. The Bhangis were considered the lowest in this hierarchy. They were scavengers, sweepers and weavers of bamboo baskets. During the British regime, they had been employed by the Ahmedabad municipality and railways as sweepers. Earlier, Dheds had been weavers of *thepadas*, or coarse cloth, but machine-made cloth ousted them from this occupation. As their touch was regarded polluting, they were not even employed in the textile mills until the 1890s. Thus, the Dheds were hard-pressed in the 19th century. In the city of Ahmedabad, Dheds enjoyed the dubious privileges of picking up leftovers from the caste feasts which were frequently given in the city.[73]

British rule brought about some changes among the depressed castes. The railways proved to be a catalyst of social change. Earlier in this chapter, mention was made of how the advent of the railway caused a flutter among caste Hindus as they had to travel in the same railway compartment as the untouchables. The press of Ahmedabad was vociferous in its opposition to this and demanded that the railway authorities provide a separate carriage for untouchables. There was a popular saying in Gujarati: "God has gone to the hills, the *pirs* have gone to Mecca and, under British rule, Dheds are pushing us and knocking us down."[74]

Earlier in this chapter, it was stated that Dheds were kept out of government schools by caste Hindus who did not agree to the coeducation of the 'clean' and the 'unclean'. Some untouchables received education in missionary schools. The press raised a great clamour against the government circular in 1880 which ordered government schools to admit untouchables. A strong demand for separate schools was made. As a result, from the last decade of the 19th century, separate schools were started in Ahmedabad. In the first decade of the 20th century, there were four schools for the depressed castes in the city,[75] but there was only one Bhangi teacher employed in the city up to 1914. The stigma of untouchability was so great even until 1898 that the people of Gomtipura, a suburb of Ahmedabad, resisted a government order admitting Dhed children to the government school and submitted a petition to show their disapproval.[76] As a result of this attitude of caste Hindus and the untouchables' own apathy to education, the majority of untouchables in the city remained illiterate and poor.

Until Gandhi arrived in the city, the social reformers of Ahmedabad made no serious or conscious efforts to improve the conditions of the depressed castes of the city. To them, the social problems of the Dheds and other depressed classes did not exist, though some of them were actually in close touch with the Christian missionaries who had already started social uplift programmes for untouchables. The reform movement started by the educated middle class was restricted to higher caste problems so that their reforms institutions could do very little to improve the lot of the untouchable castes. The Prarthana Samaj of Ahmedabad was inspired by the Brahmo Samaj of Bengal, which erased caste distinctions among its members. However, the former not being radical enough in its outlook respected the caste feelings of its members, so it did not admit any untouchable into the Samaj for a very long time.[77]

This indifference and apathy to the downtrodden on the part of caste Hindus and even social reformers can be ascribed to the sociocultural milieu in which such issues were considered quite peripheral. This arose from the fact that in Hindu traditional society, ideas of family, caste, occupation, religion and bureaucracy were intertwined in such a manner that the institution of untouchability had become an acceptable and integral part of society. It was never considered a social issue or a problem by the elite or by the religious leaders.[78] The apathy among caste Hindus stemmed from the Hindus psyche which these leaders inherited and was noted by Mary Carpenter in 1866. She wrote:

> The inferior portion of the population is quite untouched by any educational institution, they do not feel the want of education for their children, and the higher classes do not appear to feel any sympathy for them, as in our country. A deep impassable gulf is between the different classes, arising chiefly from caste distinctions; never did I notice any friendly recognition of the lower by the higher nor hear of any effort being made to do them good or elevate their condition. When I urged upon a native gentleman the duty of trying to do something to diminish the ignorance of those who constitute the largest portion of the population, he replied "We have enough to do at present with the education of our own class, without thinking of these."[79]

This indifference persisted in the pre-Gandhian period. An interesting episode testifies to this. When the famous Parsi woman doctor Motibai Kapadia admitted a Bhangi woman into the Victoria Jubilee Hospital for Women, the caste Hindu patients vacated the hospital. Later, the hospital was forced to build a separate ward for the untouchables.[80]

By the early years of the 20th century, modern education had slowly spread among the untouchables. The efforts of missionaries in educating them were commendable. They had opened many schools in the city and had founded a Christian colony near the city as early as 1863. As a result, the depressed castes became aware of their backwardness and, to improve their lot like the higher castes, they started to introduce reforms from within the caste. In 1909, their Ramanandi priest Mohandasji and Nathaji Shamaldas, a

Dhed school teacher at the school for depressed classes at Raipur, initiated a caste reform movement by convening a Dhed Sabha where lectures were given on the benefit of temperance and caste reforms. At the first meeting, about 50 Dheds took a pledge to abstain from intoxicants. They also sought to improve their ritual status by claiming Rajput descent for themselves and called themselves 'Maiyavat Rajputs'. They claimed a higher status than the Waghris who, according to them, were lower than themselves because they ate wild animals. Dheds raised the question that, if the Waghris were not to be considered untouchables, the Dheds should not be so considered. They were becoming aware of the injustice meted out to them.[81] This movement was supported by social reformers like Ramanbhai Nilkanth and Lalshankar Umiashankar under the auspices of the Sansar Sudhara Samaj. At one of their meetings, Ramanbhai said that it was the duty of the educated to guide and help the downtrodden castes just as in America the educated had struggled to help the black slaves.[82]

Here, it is interesting to note that *Prajabandhu,* the influential and reformist newspaper of Ahmedabad, sounded a note of caution in commenting on this movement. It warned the radical social reformers to be cautious in dealing with the untouchables and thought it was not desirable to amalgamate the untouchables with caste Hindus.[83] In fact, this comment echoed the public opinion of the conservative Hindu society of Ahmedabad.

Gradually, an awareness regarding the conditions of the downtrodden was created among the social reformers of the city. In Ahmedabad in 1913, the Provincial Social Reform Conference met under President Narsinhrao Divetia, where the problem of untouchables was given eleventh place in importance on the agenda.[84] But, in fact, reformers' support to this movement was merely verbal. They never worked with the downtrodden. This is illustrated by an episode which occurred in 1911. The Bhangi sweepers employed by the municipality of Ahmedabad struck work as they had not received two months' pay. They also wanted a hike in wages. The municipality tried to crush the strike with the help of the police and arrested the strike leaders. The Bhangis continued to be on strike until the demand for the overdue wages was satisfied, but there was not to be any wage hike. During the strike, none of the reformers bothered to inquire into the circumstances leading to the strike.[85]

Another incident which occurred in 1912 reveals that Ahmedabad society still held strong ideas about ritual pollution. In November 1912, about 200 guests of diverse caste including the untouchables dined together under the auspices of the Aryan Brotherhood in Bombay. The Aryan Brotherhood organisation was against caste restrictions and wanted to put an end to the old system. Ramanbhai Nilkanth, a Vadnagara Nagar, was one of the participants at the dinner party. He was ostracized by his caste for this action. He was also boycotted by the conservative society of Ahmedabad. To show their disapproval and opposition to the movement started by Aryan Brotherhood, the leading Jain and Meshri businessmen and the middle class elite of Ahmedabad called a mass meeting in the city under the presidentship of a well-known Brahmin solicitor, Bhaishankar Nanabhai. This meeting passed a resolution endorsing the opinion that the caste Hindu eating with the untouchables was against the age-old caste tradition, and therefore, Ramanbhai should be boycotted by society.[86] The incident reveals that the caste Hindus of Ahmedabad, including the educated elite, had strong religious prejudices against the untouchables, preferring to keep them in their depressed condition.

Thus, as a result of the attitude of the caste Hindus towards the untouchables, the latter remained backward and hardly benefited from British rule. It was only when Gandhi came to Ahmedabad that their conditions improved.

V

The emergence of the new economic classes—the capitalist, middle and working classes—in Ahmedabad was a significant social phenomenon, which added a new dimension to the social stratification in the city. These new classes were multicaste and multicreed in composition and were vertically aligned and cut across horizontal caste lines. They had emerged under British rule, which induced occupational mobility. The middle class arose as a result of the rise of British administrative bureaucracy and western education. It comprised mainly government officials, clerks and professionals such as teachers, lawyers, engineers and doctors. In its formative years, before industrialisation commenced in the city, the middle class was constituted of higher castes like Brahmins and Vanias who had made good use of the new education. Nagar Brahmins like Mahipatram, Bholanath Sarabhai, Brahmakshatriyas like Ambalal Sakarlal, Vanias like Maganlal Vakhatchand and Bhogilal Pranvallabhdas were members of the new middle class. Later, even artisans and lower castes received education and acquired good posts in the government and the industries. The middle class expanded in numerical strength as the new textile industries generated jobs such as those of clerks, managers and storekeepers.

Two other classes—the capitalist and the working class—emerged in the wake of the industrialisation of the city. The higher castes dominated the capitalist class, which was mainly composed of Shravaka and Meshri Vanias, Nagar Brahmins, Kanbis, Brahmakshatriyas, and some Parsis and Muslims. The founding father of the textile industry, Ranchhodlal Chhotalal, was a Nagar Brahmin; Bechardas Lashkari was Kanbi; Ambalal Sakarlal was a Brahmakshatriya; Mangaldas Girdhardas was a Meshri Vania; Mansukhbhai Bhagubhai was a Shravak Vania; Rustamji Vakil and Sorabji Karaka were Parsis.

The working class was made up of low castes such as the Kolis, Waghris, Rawalias and artisan castes such as Kanbis and Khatris. Later, even Dheds were employed in the spinning department.

This caste composition of the new economic classes shows that the relation between the caste and traditional occupations was finally breaking down. However, the caste hierarchy had an impact on the formation of the new classes, and thus the caste system dovetailed into the emerging class system.

How did the traditional caste-ridden society of Ahmedabad react to the newly emerging classes? Did nascent classes loosen the city's caste structure? These questions are answered here. The members of the new classes did not lose their caste identity, retaining as they did strong ties with their castes and following caste rules and traditions. The caste feelings were too strong to obliterate caste consciousness. The members of the new classes were not alienated from their castes. Ranchhodlal Chhotalal, the founder of the textile industry and the president of the Ahmedabad Mill Owners Associations, had close ties with his Sathodra Nagar caste. His biographer Bhagwanlal Badshah says that he was keen on the uplift of his caste. He instituted scholarships for the boys and girls of his caste in the GVS. He wanted to reform his caste and tried to lower the expenses connected with death and other ceremonies. But the conservative members of his caste turned down his suggestion. This did not dampen his zeal in wanting to improve the condition of his caste. Badshah calls him the 'Crowning Glory' of his Sathodra caste.[87] Similarly Bechardas Lashkari, the Kadva Kanbi mill owner, did not neglect his duty towards his caste. He endeavoured to suppress evil customs such as female infanticide and dowry in his community. His son Shambhuprasad was the president of the Kadva Kanbi community by virtue of his benevolent gifts and his special interest in their education and progress.[88]

Bapuji Jagannath, the Audichya Brahmin, a notable lawyer of the city, was one of the founder members of the Audichya Hitechhu Sabha in 1873 and a well-wisher of his caste.[89] Ambalal Sakarlal Desai, the Brahmakshatriya educationist and mill owner, was very active in the movements of his Brahmakshatriya caste. These examples illustrate that the members of the new classes had continued having strong caste identities. But this does not mean that class consciousness did not exist.

The mill owners were organised into the Ahmedabad Mill-owners' Association as early as 1891 to represent collectively their rights and demands to the government on the one hand and to work together against the workers' strikes and protests on the other hand. In 1895, they were able to successfully control the massive strike of 8,000 textile workers which lasted a week. Similarly, the incipient working class was gradually developing class consciousness, which is clearly evident in their frequent strikes and protests against mill owners. The heterogeneous middle class came together to combat social evils. They shared many progressive ideas and worked together in various voluntary associations such as the GVS and the Prarthana Samaj. As a result, the caste and the class did coexist and overlap in the city of Ahmedabad.

Although caste as a system remained intact and caste identities were not obliterated, a more significant phenomenon was that people belonging to diverse castes and socioeconomic groups made closer contact. They began to feel that their existence was not limited only to their caste. There were other broader identities too—identities represented by the vocations, professions, educational institutions, libraries, municipality and voluntary associations. The caste was no longer a static entity. It was changing, although the change was gradual and slow.

Notes

1. *Gujarat Shalapatra*. August 1866, p. 187.
2. Mary Carpenter, *Six Months in India,* Vol. I, London, 1868, p. 157.
3. Dalpatram Dahyabhai, *Gujaratna Hinduoni Sthiti* (in Gujarati), Bombay, 1865, p. 72.
4. *Ahmedabad Gazetteer*, p. 211.
5. Bombay Government, *Reports on the Native Papers* (henceforth cited as *RNP)* for the week ending September 4, 1880, p. 9.
6. *RNP* for the week ending September 25, 1880, p. 13.
7. Bombay Government, *Report of the Director of Public Instruction for the Year 1885–56*, Bombay 1857.
8. *Gujarat Shalapatra*, January-February, 1870, p. 79.
9. Bombay Government, *Director of Vernacular Teachers Holding Certificates of Qualifications recognized by the Educational Department employed in Local Board and Municipal Schools and in Native States in the Northern Division, British Districts and Native States 1914*, Ahmedabad, 1914.
10. *Gujarat Shalapatra*, March 1863, p. 64; October 1864, pp. 235–38.

11. *RNP* for the week ending June 14, 1873, pp. 9–10.
12. Hargovindas Dwarkadas Kantawala, *Sansar Sudharo* (in Gujarati), Baroda (3rd ed.) 1923, p. 126.
13. *RNP* for the week ending September 27, 1890, pp. 15–16; October 4, 1890, p. 10.
14. *Prajabandhu,* June 21, 1899, p. 6.
15. *Buddhi Prakash,* December 1872, p. 268; February 1876, p. 48.
16. *Ibid.*, May 1873, p. 119; December 1877, p. 274.
17. *Gujarat Shalapatra,* October 1866, p. 229.
18. *Ibid.,* April 1877, p. 85.
19. Krishnarao Bholanath, *Bholanath Sarabhainu Jivan Charit* (in Gujarati and English), Bombay 1888, p. 86.
20. *Ibid.*, p. 23; Narsinhrao Bholanath Divetia. *Smaran Mukar* (in Gujarati), Bombay, 1926, p. 39
21. Krishnarao Bholanath, *op.cit.,* pp. 82–86.
22. *Ahmedabad Gazetteer*, p. 326.
23. *Gujarat Shalapatra*, August 1886, p. 169.
24. Hargovindas Kantawala, *Nat Sudharo* (in Gujarati), Ahmedabad, 1886, p. 18, p. 29.
25. *Ibid.*, p. 21.
26. *Ibid.*, pp. 21–23.
27. *Ibid.*, pp. 15–17,and 8–9.
28. *Prajabandhu*, April 16, 1911, p. 163.
29. Anandshankar Dhuruv, *Apno Dharma* (in Gujarati), Ahmedabad, 1942, p. 502.
30. Ramanbhai Nilkanth, *Dharma Ane Samaj* (in Gujarati), II, Ahmedabad, 1935, p. 33.
31. *Prajabandhu*, August 9, 1908, p. 12.
32. Bombay Government, *Gazetteer of the Bombay Presidency,* Vol. IX, Part I, *Gujarat Population: Hindus*, Bombay. 1901, pp. 6–7; *Ahmedabad Gazetteer*, p. 34.
33. *Buddhi Prakash*, August 1856, p. 151.
34. *Ibid.*, December 1875, p. 269; *Audichya Hitechhu Patra*, May 1884, p. 15.
35. *Buddhi Prakash*, March 1873, p. 63.
36. *Audichya Hitechhu Patra,* February 1886, pp. 22 and 27; June 1884, p. 27, August 1884, pp. 82–86, February 1886, p. 22, April 1888, cover page.
37. *Ibid.*, June 1890, pp. 27 and 32.

38. *Ibid.*, September 1910, inside cover; *Prajabandhu* July 3, p. 12; July 18, p. 14; July 22, p. 13.
39. *Audichya Hitechhu Patra*, April 1888, p. 5.
40. *Tolak Subhechhak Patrika*, February 1880, pp. 23–24.
41. *Audichya Hitechhu Patra,* June 1906, p. 36.
42. *Bombay Presidency Gazetteer*, Vol. IX, Part I, *Gujarat Population; Hindus*, pp. 55–59; Kashinath Govindji Brahmakshatriya, *Brahmakshatriyano Ujval Itihas* (in Gujarati), Panchora, 1927, pp. 4–6.
43. *Brahmakshatriya Patrika*, October 1909, pp. 10–11., January 1912, pp. 18–19; October 1909, p. 39; January 1912, p. 43; April 1912, p. 47.
44. *Prajabandhu*, November 15, 1903, p. 9.
45. *Ibid.*, January 24, 1909, pp. 7–8.
46. *Ibid.*, April 18, 1909, pp. 7–8.
47. *Ahmedabad Gazetteer*, p. 293.
48. Purushottam Lallubhai Parekh, *Kanabi Kshatriya Utpatti Ane Itihas* (in Gujarati), Ahmedabad, 1912, pp. 143–150.
49. John Houston, *Representative Men of the Bombay Presidency* (2nd ed.), Bombay, 1900, p. 91.
50. P. L. Parikh, *op.cit.*, pp. 151–67.
51. *Kadva Vijay*, November 1910, p. 71.
52. *Prajabandhu*, May 16, 1900, p. 293; January 6, 1901, p. 10; April 7, 1901, p. 10.
53. *Ibid.*, December 4, 1898, p. 2.
54. *Ibid.*, July 341, 1898, p. 7.
55. Dalpatram Dahyabahi, *Gnyati Nibandh* (in Gujarati), Ahmedabad, 1851, pp. 35–39.
56. *Buddhi Prakash,* February 1876, p. 10.
57. *Prajabandhu*, April 19, 1903, p. 10.
58. *Prajabandhu*, December 17, 1903, p. 7; *Vaishya Patrika*, May 1905, pp. 168–172.
59. *Vaishya Patrika*, August 1904, p. 27; July 1904, p. 1; April 1905; pp. 9–10.
60. *Prajabandhu*, April 30, 1905, pp. 11–12; *Vaishya Patrika*, May 1905, pp. 168–172.
61. *Prajabandhu,* August 9, 1908, p. 2.
62. *Jain Hitechhu*, April–May–June 1907, pp. 66–68.
63. Makrand Mehta, *The Ahmedabad Cotton Industry: Genesis and Growth*, Ahmedabad, 1982, pp. 101–102.

64. Dahyabhai Derasari, *Sathina Sahityanu Digdarshan* (in Gujarati), Ahmedabad, (reprint), 1964, p. 302.
65. *Prajabandhu*, August 9, 1908, p. 26.
66. *Ibid.*, October 14, 1906, p. 11.
67. *Gujarat Shalapatra*, October 1894, pp. 256–257; March 1865, pp. 47–48; Bhagvanlal Badshah, *The Life of Rao Bahadur Ranchorelal Chotalal,* Bombay, 1899.
68. *Prajabandhu*, January 26, 1908, p. 17; February 23, 1908, p. 10.
69. *Gujarat Shalapatra*, August 1864, pp. 176–177.
70. *Prajabandhu*, August 9, 1908, p. 2.
71. *Ahmedabad Gazetteer*, pp. 317–326 and 293–294.
72. Narmadashankar Dave, *Gujarat Sarvasangraha* (in Gujarati), Bombay, 1887, pp. 108–117.
73. *Gujarat Shalapatra*, October 1864, p. 238: Dalpatbhai Dahyabhai, *Shehar Sudhara Vishe Nibandh* (in Gujarati), Ahmedabad, 1858.
74. *Bombay Presidency Gazetteer,* Vol. IX, Part I, *Gujarat Population: Hindus*, p. 344.
75. *Prajabandhu*, October 24, 1909, p. 10.
76. *Ibid.*, July 10, 1898, p. 7.
77. *Ahmedabad Gazetteer,* p. 726.
78. Makrand Mehta, "Samajik Parivartan ane Gujaratna Asprushya", *Arthat*, October 1981, p. 42.
79. Mary Carpenter, *Six Months in India*, Vol. I, London, 1868, p. 47.
80. Ek Jankar Tabib, *Amdavadna Janita Banu Doctor (Miss) Motibai Rustomji Kapadia L.R.S.P.L.C., S.L.M. S.R.C.S. Ireland ni Jindagino Ehwal* (in Gujarati), Ahmedabad, 1938, pp. 8–9.
81. *Prajabandhu*, April 18, 1909, p. 12; p. 8.
82. *Ibid.*, October 24, 1909, p. 12; p. 8.
83. *Ibid.*
84. *Buddhi Prakash,* May 1913, p. 119.
85. *Prajabandhu*, September 17, 1911, p. 13; September 24, 1911, p. 13; October 1, 1911, p. 14.
86. *Prajabandhu*, November 17, 1912, pp. 6–9; December 22, 1912, p. 20.
87. Bhagwanlal Badshah, *op.cit,* pp. 266–269.
88. J. Houston, *Representative Men of the Bombay Presidency* (2nd ed.*)*, London, 1900, p. 91.
89. Vallabhji Punjabhai, *Rajnagarna Ratno* (in Gujarati), Rajkot, 1918, p. 105.

7

The Changing Profile of Women

Among the many and varied factors that affected the social and economic position of women in Ahmedabad were the social reform movement, the growth of women's education, British colonial policy and the industrialisation of the city.

The work of men such as Dalpatram, Bholanath Sarabhai and other social reformers in Ahmedabad has been discussed in detail earlier. It was such men of vision who made possible reform in the area of widow remarriage, polygamy, child marriage, dowry, women's education and other customs. Their strong conviction that the reform of women's condition was the only way that society could progress led to a perceptible rise in the status of women. These reformist men not only preached but also practiced what they believed. Bholanath, for instance, was among the first to educate his daughter and daughter-in-law. Pioneering the cause of women's education and therefore, of their social emancipation. Dalpatram, Bholanath, Mahipatram, Lalshankar Umiashankar, and Ramanbhai Nilkanth actively involved themselves in social reform to combat social evils. To do this, they instituted several major voluntary associations and caste organisations.

The earliest of these institutions was the Gujarat Vernacular Society (GVS) which, though founded to promote Gujarati language and literature, encouraged social reforms from its very inception. It soon became the pivotal point of social reform activities relating to women's issues. An interesting feature of its activities was the establishment of an annual elocution competition for women. This competition provided women with a platform where they would express their individual views on their problems. Thus, women acquired a voice that could be heard in a traditional society. The educational programmes instituted by the GVS allowed the women of Ahmedabad to participate in non-familial, non-caste and non-religious activities and in this manner afforded them an awareness of the social spaces outside the home.

Another great association, the Prarthana Samaj, primarily established for religious reforms, also took a liberal and reformist stance towards women's status. It was so successful in doing this that the first two women matriculates in Ahmedabad Yashodabai Thakur and Vidhyaben were members of the Samaj.

Among other associations which sprang up to fight discrimination against women and resultant social evils were the Ballagna Nishedhak Mandali, organised to prevent child marriages, and Gopal Hari Deshmukh's Punarvivah Uttejak Sabha, which helped widows of the higher castes to remarry. At the turn of the century, the Bandhu Samaj, started by a small group of Vadnagara Nagars, helped to develop literature for women. They published from 1893 the monthly journal *Sundri Subodh*, which was entirely devoted to women. This journal produced entertaining and educational Gujarati literature and, significantly, it encouraged women writers. However, the stance of this journal was not to perceive woman as an independent, self-sufficient person with her own identity but primarily as a homemaker, wife and mother. It even went so far as to feel that women should be given a different curriculum from that for men.

An important organisation aiming at improving women's status in Ahmedabad was the London-based National Indian Association (NIA) founded by Mary Carpenter in Bristol in 1870. Its main objective was to establish intelligent cooperation between the east and the west, thus promoting education and social reform all over India. A branch was set up in Ahmedabad in the 1880s, which took over the administration of the Bholanath Sarabhai Institute for women. This institution had a library and a women's club. It not only awarded scholarships to women in the Female Training College, but went on to extend medical help to needy women. The NIA attempted to bring together women of different castes and communities through its many programmes.[1]

The caste organisations in Ahmedabad were not far behind the voluntary associations in attempting social reforms. Their promotion of women's education within the caste and their reforms with regard to social evils such as polygamy, excessive dowry and wedding expenses and child marriage have been mentioned earlier. While the Kadva Kanbi Council tried to regulate marriage customs and expenses, the Brahmakshatriya Association made arrangements to transport their female students to and from the Training College. In Ahmedabad, the reforms initiated by the caste organisations brought about significant changes in the status of women. Other lower and artisan castes, with the exception of the scheduled castes, followed the examples of the upper castes. Though their aim to evangelise did not greatly succeed, the Christian missionaries did set up and run several excellent primary schools for untouchable girls and boys in Ahmedabad. Thus, the efforts of Christian missionaries in educating the untouchables and lower castes are certainly commendable.

All this goes to show that in the 19th century, it was essentially educated men of the upper classes who took the initiative in improving the status of women. It was not until the first decade of the 20th century that any liberating movement for women by women was begun. All the earlier reform movements were led by men who focused mainly on upper caste social evils. But in spite of this, the pioneers of social reform did manage to create awareness of the oppression suffered by women, at least among educated people.

I

The result of the efforts of social reformers and missionaries was to make Ahmedabad better advanced in women's education than any other city in Gujarat. Their efforts were reinforced by the generous financial support given by the city's mercantile community.

Initially a very small number of girls opted for education, partly because conservative society jeered at the idea of female education, and partly due to the custom of early marriage which impeded it. In 1864, there were 264 girls studying in Ahmedabad schools. Journals such as *Buddhi Prakash* tried to remove these hurdles, exhorting their readers to educate their daughters since this would enable them to keep household accounts, read and write letters, and most important, to shake off their superstitions.[2]

Some English officials and their wives took an active interest in female education. Mrs Oliphant, the collector's wife, along with her Indian and European women friends, frequently visited the schools. In the 1860s, Mahipatram's wife, Parvatikunvar used to invite her Indian and European friends home. Such interactions led to an active interest in women's education, especially among Indian women. Parvatikunwar even encouraged wives of school teachers to go to school.[3] In fact, when Mary Carpenter visited Ahmedabad in 1866, she was pleasantly surprised to find the educated elite of the city taking a keen interest in women's education. The group of women she met at the *nagarseth*'s house expressed a strong desire to educate their daughters. During her visit to the Harkunvar Sethani's school, where 80 girls between 6 and 11 years were studying, she met four widows who expressed great willingness to train as teachers. This was a welcome step, as most of Ahmedabad thought that the want of women teachers was the main impediment to the growth of women's education.[4]

As a result of Mary Carpenter's efforts and in response to the people's demands, a class for adult women was opened in the city in 1869, which was the origin of the Female Training College in Ahmedabad,[5] which was established in 1871 by the government. The institution was administered by a European woman superintendent. It trained women for primary school teaching. Soon the college became a stronghold of women's education, and, in 1875, had constructed its own building with a donation of Rs 10,000 from Rao Bahadur Bechardas Ambaidas. It was named after his deceased daughter Mahalaxmi and thereafter the Female Training College came to be known as the Mahalaxmi Female Training College. For resident students, hostel facility was provided in which women belonging to different castes arranged to cook their own food.[6] The number of scholars rose from six to 17 in 1879; in 1900, there were 116 students, and the number rose to 133 in 1908. The number of trained teachers who graduated from this college up to 1908 was 320.[7] In 1914, the number of students rose to 160 of whom six were Muslims.[8] A practicing school was attached to it, established in 1875 and maintained by the government. The training college conducted a three-year course, plus an entrance class. The wives of the vernacular teachers studying in the Male Training College were encouraged to study in the Female Training College.[9]

An Anglo-vernacular class for girls was started in 1882, attached to the Female Training College, which gradually developed into a fully fledged high school teaching up to matriculation. As mentioned earlier, the first two Ahmedabad women who passed the matriculation examination in 1892 were Vidhyaben Nilkanth and Yashodaben Thakur, both from reformist families. Vidhyaben recorded her reminiscences that there were no teachers for many subjects and that she and two other students had to study under private tutors. It was the enthusiasm and hard work of Superintendent Mrs MacAfee that enabled them to take the matriculation examination.[10] Higher education was slow to develop in the city so that, until 1908, only 12 women had passed the matriculation examination, two had passed the intermediate examination, two had passed the BA examination, and three had passed the previous examination of the Bombay University. Women students went on to study at Gujarat College after passing the matriculation examination.[11] The census of 1911 showed that, in the city of Ahmedabad, there were only 27 Hindu, 10 Jain, two Muslim and 64 Parsi, Christian and Jew women who knew the English language.[12] The custom of early marriage continued with the apathy of parents towards the education of their daughters and slowed down progress. Vidhyaben Nilkanth and Sharadaben Mehta were the first two Gujarati women who passed the BA examination in 1901. Vidhyaben, after passing her matriculation, took almost 10 years to complete her graduation as her studies were interrupted by pregnancies and household responsibilities. It was her determination, her husband Ramanbhai Nilkanth's interest and enthusiasm and her parent's support which enabled her to finally pass the BA examination. It was not easy for these pioneers to complete graduation. Sharadaben remembers that girl students had to put up with not only the teasing of boy students but also the hostility of the orthodox. When she was studying in the Gujarat College, there were only two women students. They had to sit separately from the boys and did not dare raise their eyes from their books.[13] The courage of these two women opened the doors to higher education not only for the women of Ahmedabad but also for the women of the rest of Gujarat.

If the progress of higher studies was slow, primary education for girls made rapid progress. After 1875, the number of girls' schools increased. The Irish Presbyterian Mission founded its first girls' school in 1876. The number of these girls' schools increased to six by the end of the period covered in this study, one among them being an Urdu medium school. The total number attending these missionary schools in 1908 was 314 girl students.[14] The Salvation Army had established an industrial school for girls in the city in the last decade of the 19th century.[15]

The Anjuman-i-Islam of Ahmedabad started its first school for Muslim girls in 1887 and another in 1893.[16] In 1908, there were 119 Muslim girls in primary schools. Though Muslim social reformers supported the cause of women's education, they were adamant regarding the strict observance of *purdah* even inside the school. It has been mentioned earlier that, at the Muhammadan Educational Conference held in Ahmedabad in 1904, Muslim reformers stuck to this stance, earning sharp criticism from contemporary newspapers for such a retrogressive outlook.

In 1892, Rao Bahadur Ranchhodlal Chhotalal, the founder of the first textile mill in the city, endowed Rs 12,500 to the founding of a girls' school in Khadia. This school imparted knowledge of Hindu religion and ethics, but was largely a primary school up to the sixth standard, including a kindergarten class. The funds and activities of the school were administered by the GVS. Various caste-based scholarships were given to deserving girls to induce them to study. In 1908, a separate library for women was started in the school and managed by the Society.

A Jain girls' school was established in Fatashani *pol* in 1894, soon becoming popular enough to have 395 girls on it rolls in 1908. Besides these schools, there were eight girls' schools maintained by the municipality and attended by 688 pupils in 1908.

In 1908, there were 2,241 students studying in the primary schools of the city. In a talk on the occasion of the *Stree Bodh* Jubilee Celebration in Ahmedabad in 1908, Lalshankar Umiashankar gave an account of the city's women's education. He presented an interesting caste and community composition of the girl students in primary schools, shown in Tables 7.1 and 7.2.[17]

Table 7.1: Girl Students in Primary School by Religion

Religion	Students
Hindu	1,486
Jain	570
Mohammedan	119
Parsi	57
Jew	12
Christian	15
Total	**2,241**

Table 7.2: Hindu Girl Students in Primary School by Caste

Caste	Students
Brahmin	357
Vania-Meshri	318
Kanbi	301
Ghanchi	133
Kshatriya	42
Khatri	36
Sutar	34
Soni	33
Luhar	26
Bhavsar	20
Kachhia	20
Durji	17
Rajput	11
Hajam	11
Maratha	10
Kumbhar	9
Bhojak	8
Khalasi	8
Ravat	7
Kadia	7
Mali	6
Gola	5
Kansara	4
Kayastha	3
Bhat	2
Vyas	1
Koli	1
Luvana	1
Rabari	1
Bava	1
Dhobi	1
Other Castes	37

The figures Umiashankar quoted show that primary education of girls had made considerable progress since 1849. Even girls from the artisan and other service castes took up primary education. However, in the field of higher education, progress was painfully slow. The break-up of girls studying in each standard of RC Kanyashala in 1898 indicates that the number of girl students steadily decreased from 43 in the first standard to 36 in the second, 29 in the third, 21 in the fourth, six in the fifth and two in the sixth standard. In the kindergarten, there were 29 girls.[18] By 1908, the situation had not changed greatly so that there were only four girls in the sixth standard, out of which only two appeared for the examinations.[19]

What is particularly interesting about the situation at the time is that the educationists of Ahmedabad, as elsewhere in India, thought that the main objective of women's education was to make them better wives, mothers and homemakers.[20] It was also felt that education could lessen the intellectual gap between an educated husband and his wife.

A debate over the curriculum for girls arose in the last decade of the 19th century among educationists in Ahmedabad. At the educational conference held in Ahmedabad in 1896, educationists like Nilkanthrai Dahyabhai Chhatrapati, Dr Joseph Benjamin and Lalshankar Umiashankar reiterated that female education should be useful to women and should make them better homemakers. Thus, they wanted to include subjects like home management, child care, hygiene and health care in the curriculum for women. Chimanlal Setalvad, a prominent lawyer, was also of the opinion that woman's education should be utilitarian and should suit the woman's temperament. He went so far as to argue that to train them as lawyers and to place them in competition with men would not benefit them greatly.[21]

On the other hand, there were some educationists in Ahmedabad who believed that woman's education should be intended to develop the women's intellect.[22] Vidhyaben Nilkanth and her sister Sharadaben too were of the opinion that women's education should not be different from men's.[23]

II

Though upper caste Hindu women of Ahmedabad did not observe *purdah* unlike their Muslim counterparts, their social life and mobility were restricted. They rarely stirred out of their homes, their social life being confined to visiting temples and relatives on formal occasions such as births, weddings and deaths. They attended caste feasts and religious festivals but had no opportunity to participate in non-kin, non-caste or non-religious activities. Their mobility was also limited by various restrictions. A woman had to travel in a closed vehicle. She was not allowed to carry an umbrella in the rain or wear sandals in the hot sun. Mixed gatherings were rare, so that she hardly met any men outside of her family.

In such a situation, social reform movement, female education and the emergence of women's organisations in late 19th century Ahmedabad helped women to emerge from the seclusion of their homes to participate in various non-familial and non-caste activities. This expanded their social space. This was a phenomenal social change.

When Mary Carpenter, the social reformer from England, visited the city in 1866, she found women of the city progressive. She even ate at the same table with the wives of some prominent men, which as she remarks was a 'solitary incident in my visit to India'.[24] Her host, Satyendranath Tagore, assistant judge in Ahmedabad, encouraged his wife to come out of the seclusion of their home. Their presence in Ahmedabad brought many women out to mixed gatherings. They gave a mixed party to the English and to the native elite of the city when Mary Carpenter was in Ahmedabad, a brilliant account of which appeared in the local newspaper.[25]

As mentioned earlier, in the 1860s, Mrs Oliphant, the collector's wife, had befriended many Parsi, Hindu and European women of the city and formed the first group of women in the city, which visited girls' schools regularly and helped the cause of women's education. This was a cosmopolitan group where Hindu women mixed and interacted with Parsi and European women. In 1868, when Mrs Oliphant died, a condolence meeting was held in the Hemabhai Institute. A memorial fund of Rs 84 was collected by her friends. It was decided to use this fund for prizes to be awarded to the best girl students. This group consisted of wives of Gopalrao Hari Deshmukh, Premabhai Hemabhai, Jagjivandas Khusaldas, Dalpatbhai Bhagubhai, Bechardas Ambaidas, Adarji Jiwanji and Kharsedji Palanji, and Parvatikunvar Mahipatram, Balaben Bholanath, Mrs Taylor, Mrs Sheppard.[26]

It is necessary here to dwell on the exceptional boldness of Parvatikunvar, the wife of Mahipatram, the foremost social reformer of the city, who vehemently protested against the injustices heaped on the women of Gujarat. Her biography, *Parvatikunvar Akhyan,* written by Mahipatram, depicts her courage and shows how advanced she was for her times. She had no formal education, but she could read and write and did not believe in superstitions. When her husband decided to go abroad for training, she supported his decision. When he returned from abroad and was ostracized for more than 12 years, she stood by him and gave him strength and courage, while relations and caste members snapped ties with them. Even Shudra servants would not work in her home. From 1861 onwards, she spent her life in Ahmedabad, where her husband worked as the principal of the Premchand Raichand Training College. She mingled with the Parsi, European and caste Hindu women. Wives of S Tagore, Oliphant, Newham and Ms Carpenter were among her friends. These relationships gave her a broad vision. When she went out, she wore socks and sandals and advised other Hindu women to follow her example. She argued that if men could use umbrellas and shoes, she didn't see why women should not use them. She also went out in an open carriage with her husband. She did not care about the criticism of the orthodox society of Ahmedabad. She argued that if high caste women were permitted to go about openly on the streets and even to bathe in the river, there was no need to draw the hood of the carriage, especially in Gujarat where the custom of *purdah* was not generally observed.[27]

However, Parvatikunvar's boldness was exceptional. Women generally took care to draw down the screens of their carriages while moving about the city. Vidhyaben Nilkanth, who also came from a progressive family, remembers that in her childhood she and her friends were severely reprimanded for putting down the hood of a Victoria carriage, though they had done so outside the city because they did not have the courage to do it in the city itself.[28] Even the unjust custom of women not being allowed to use umbrellas and sandals continued right up to the end of the 19th century. *Prajabandhu*, a reformist newspaper, wondered why a woman laden with ornaments walked in a wedding procession without an umbrella or footwear in the scorching heat of summer.[29]

The role played by the Prarthana Samaj and the GVS in improving women's condition was of primary importance, as both these organisations helped women to come out of their homes and participate in activities in the wider world. These organisations extended social space for women in a segregated society. Women attended the prayer meetings and lecture programmes of the Prarthana Samaj. When Dayanand Saraswati gave a lecture at the Samaj in 1875, a good number of women attended.[30] Members encouraged the women in their families to receive education. Parvatikunvar and Balaben even addressed women's meetings.[31]

The GVS organised various activities for women, of which the elocution competition drew a large number of women. As noted earlier, in order to encourage women to be life members, women's subscription fees were halved in 1896. Within a decade, in 1906, there were 110 women members of the Society.

III

The last decade of the 19th century saw several women's organisations emerging in Ahmedabad. This was significant as these organisations gave opportunities to women to participate in non-caste, non-kin and non-religious activities and thus helped to develop an interaction between women of different castes and communities. Secondly, they led to the rise of women's leadership in the city. Vidhyaben Nilkanth, Sharadaben Mehta, Sulochanaben Desai and Dr Motiben Kapadia were some prominent leaders who steered the activities of these organisations.

The first separate women's organisation came into existence in the form of the Gujarat Ladies Club in 1887. Miss Mary Sorabjee, the woman superintendent of the Mahalaxmi Training College, along with her two sisters and the wives of English officers in Ahmedabad, founded this club to promote social interaction between women of different communities. This club was the first of its kind in the province of Bombay presidency. The club's membership was open to all communities. European, Parsi, Jewish and Hindu women were members. In 1908, 60 women were members of this club.[32] Initially, when it had no place of its own, the members met once a week at the house of some members. They played games, sang and read. Later, they also started classes in painting, embroidery and music. When the building for the Bholanath Sarabhai Literary Institute for Women, built in memory of Bholanath on Oliphant Road, was completed in 1895, the Gujarat Ladies Club was housed in it.

The Bholanath Institute was established to improve the lot of women and to afford opportunities for women to meet other women in their leisure time. The institute intended to provide a reading room for women and to organise talks useful for them. It also planned to provide facilities for games and sports. The necessity for such an institute devoted to women's needs was realised by the members of the Gujarat branch of the National Indian Association (NIA) in 1881. The plan for such an institute was approved by the managing committee of the fund raised in memory of Bholanath, which had succeeded in collecting Rs 8,000. The committee decided to allot funds for this plan, and the institute was subsequently named after Bholanath Sarabhai, the great champion of women's education.[33]

The NIA took over the administration of the building of the institute, which also housed the ladies club and a library for the use of women.[34] The building became popularly known as the Ladies

Club building. The tennis court and other facilities for games were used by the members of the Ladies Club. Thus, the activities of the NIA and the Ladies Club were closely interlinked.

The activities of the Ladies Club were conducted by the women themselves. Manning, honorary secretary of NIA of London, visited the Club.[35] Vidhyaben was honorary secretary of both the institutes from 1902. The Club celebrated Sharadotsava every year when *garba* and *raas* were performed. The club revived the *garba*, a form of folk dance which had fallen into decadence.[36] This used to be a mixed gathering where English officials and their wives, and Parsi and Hindu women and men participated. Important newspapers like *Prajabandhu* reported these occasions.

In 1899–1900, Gujarat came under a cruel spell of drought and famine. During this time of distress, the Club took up relief work under the leadership of Lady Lely, the wife of the commissioner of the northern division. She initiated Vidhyaben Nilkanth into public relief work. Lady Lely took a keen interest in the activities of the Club and often invited members of the Club and the NIA to her house, especially during Diwali. She was moved by the poverty of the Muslim community of Ahmedabad and, to train Muslim women in work which would enable them to earn their livelihood, she started a sewing class in the building of the Ladies Club. She also managed to obtain a contract for the sewing of uniforms for the Civil Hospital and the Mental Asylum of the city. More than 100 Muslim women were employed in this work. Vidhyaben continued this work for a few years after Lady Lely left for England.[37]

Another noteworthy woman leader was Dr Motiben Kapadia, who worked as the joint secretary of the Club for many years. She was appointed doctor of the Victoria Jubilee Hospital for women and children in the late 1880s. Though she was from Bombay, she made Ahmedabad her home where she spent more than 40 years as a very popular doctor. She went to Britain in 1888 for higher studies in medicine. She was the first woman doctor from the Bombay presidency to have been awarded the FRCS degree. She was also the moving force behind the nursing school of the city where nurses were trained.

Motiben was a great connoisseur and lover of music and drama. She pioneered an amateur theatre movement in the city. She staged many amateur plays and concerts under the auspices of the Ladies Club, in which both Hindu and Parsi women and men participated. She thus awakened the interest of the citizens of Ahmedabad in the delights of drama and music.[38] She raised funds for relief work during emergencies such as famines and wars.

The Ladies Club became the centre of social and cultural activities for women. But for a long time it merely remained an exclusive club for the elite women of the city. Though Parsi and European women took a keen interest in the activities of the club, Hindu women did not make full use of it. They did not participate wholeheartedly in activities like reading, sports or drama. Kantaben, daughter of Sambhuprasad Lashkari, remembers that her in-laws did not allow her to participate in the activities of the club.[39] Thus, for a long time, the orthodox Hindu society of Ahmedabad stayed aloof from the Club. In fact, they ridiculed the Hindu women who visited it. The orthodox section found the club too forward and westernised. Mixed gatherings of the club were frowned upon by the orthodox. Despite this social disapproval, Vidhyaben had been a member of the club since 1890. Many women of the Bholanath family were also members. Krishnarao Bholanath encouraged women of his family to become members of the club.[40]

Since the activities of the Ladies Club were too westernised and advanced for the orthodox, Motiben Kapadia inspired Mahalaxmi Mansukhlal to start the Mahila Mandal in 1910 for Hindu middle class women belonging to the orthodox section of the city. Mahalaxmiben, the wife of the editor of *Hitechhu*, was a member of Prarthana Samaj and at the time already conducting a Prarthana Mandal for women in her home, where about 50 to 100 women gathered to listen to lectures on various subjects relating to women. The Mahila Mandal organised various activities such as talks on subjects of women's interest as well as *garba* performances and *bhajan* singing. Motiben and Vidhyaben took an active interest in the Mandal. Motiben even donated a generous sum to the Mahila Mandal for building a hall for its activities, which the Mandal named after her.[41]

An important milestone in the history of the women of Ahmedabad was the foundation of the Vanita Vishram in 1907 by Sulochanaben Desai. She was Brahmakshatriya by caste and the granddaughter of Ambalal Sakarlal, a social reformer, political leader and educationist of Ahmedabad. Sulochanaben studied up to the fifth English standard in the high school of Ahmedabad. She was married at the age of 15 to an educated young man. Unfortunately, she was widowed two years later. Her mother and grandfather advised her to start an institute to help widows to be economically independent. So she opened classes for widows where they were taught sewing, crafts, embroidery and other such useful skills. She also started a library for women. In 1906, an institute called Saraswatimandir was established at her mother's residence at Khadia in the city.

Sulochanaben later met the founders of Vanita Vishram of Surat, Baji Gauri and Naniben Gajjar. As the purpose and scope of both institutes were similar, the name of Saraswatimandir was changed into Ahmedabad Vanita Vishram. Sulochanaben, with untiring zeal, collected a large sum to construct a building for the Vanita Vishram where widows and destitute women could live and study. She also opened a class for adult women. In 1914, Sharadaben Suman Mehta opened the school Mahila Vidhyalay, affiliated to the Vanita Vishram, where she worked as honorary principal for five years. Its curriculum included English, Gujarati, Sanskrit, Hindi, history, geography, music, painting and sewing.[42]

Various other women's organisations were established in the first decade of this century. In 1909, a branch of the Seva Sadan was opened in the Bholanath Ladies Institute. The honorary secretaries were Dr Motiben Kapadia and Vidhyaben Nilkanth.

The sewing class was operated by the Seva Sadan to train needy women.[43] In Ahmedabad, Parsi ladies had founded the Stree Jarthosthi Mandal. They put up plays and concerts. Dr Motiben Kapadia was very actively associated with this organisation.[44]

The Bholanath Sarabhai Literary Institute for Women became the centre of women's activities. Its building housed the Gujarat Ladies Club, the Seva Sadan and the Gujarat branch of the NIA. No wonder Sharadaben Mehta, who spent her early life in Ahmedabad but resided in Baroda after her marriage, wrote in her memoirs that she found the Gaikwad atmosphere of Baroda stifling, dull and drab, as there were no clubs or institutes for women and there were no mixed functions.[45]

The women of Ahmedabad were advanced and enlightened and were aware of the social and political issues of the time. As early as 1891, a women's meeting was convened in Ahmedabad to support the Age of Consent Bill.[46] When Dadabhai Naoroji visited Ahmedabad in 1893, the women of the city felicitated him.[47] All this would seem to convey that women were politically active. But a closer look reveals that, in actuality, women's political activities were somewhat sporadic. Most of the women's organisations were apolitical, which is not surprising as the city itself, as noted earlier, was not very political. However, women did attend and participate in the Congress Session which was held in the city in 1902, where Vidhyaben and Sharadaben sang the Congress anthem.

Ahmedabad women showed an active interest in the *swadeshi* movement and organised meetings to protest the partition of Bengal. Later, under Gandhi's leadership, many women leaders like Sharadaben Mehta, Ansuyaben Sarabhai, and Vidhyaben came to the national political forefront.

Another interesting development can be observed in the first decade of the 20th century, when women of several castes started holding separate women's conferences to bring about awareness among the women of their castes. The women's movements in the caste were more meaningful as they could spread reforms at the grassroots level. In 1907, the Jain Mahila Parishad was held in the city, in which 7,000 Jain women took part. Ansuyaben Sarabhai delivered a lecture on the importance of women's education.[48] Since 1910, the Brahmakshatriya women had held their caste meetings as an adjunct to the Brahmakshatriya caste conference.[49] Brahmakshatriya women were educated and wanted to reform their caste by reforming their women. In 1907, women of this caste started a movement to prevent the social evil of bigamy in the caste. They made their men take a pledge not to commit bigamy.[50] Even Muslim women, who now interacted with women of other communities, organised a *purdah* party in 1914 in the city.[51]

The emergence of women's organisations shows that women were assuming new attitudes and new roles. Since the activities of the organisations were now conducted by women, leaders were being trained and women's cultural and social horizons widened. However, the number of women participating in these organisations was still small, its members belonging largely to the privileged social and economic castes and classes. The orthodox section of society did not look favourably on an organisation where the social relationships were new and unrelated to kin. This section feared that organisations like the Ladies Club would bring disruption and discord into family life.

A pre-eminent and pioneer woman leader in Ahmedabad was Vidhyaben Ramanbhai Nilkanth, whose career as a woman leader stretches from the last decade of the 19th century to the first half of the 20th century. She and her husband Ramanbhai were in the forefront of the public life of the city and were associated with all the major organisations—social, literary, educational and political—of the city. Vidhyaben was active in all the women's organisations in one official capacity or the other.

Vidhyaben was the granddaughter of Bholanath Sarabhai, an important socioreligious reformer of Gujarat. Her mother Balaben Bholanath and father Gopilal Dhruv were enlightened and staunch Prarthana Samajists, who encouraged their daughters Vidhyaben and Sharadaben to obtain higher education. Balaben herself took active part in the educational activities of the city. She compiled a book of the special songs sung by Nagar women on occasions like birth and marriage. Balaben also delivered speeches during the women's prayer meetings of Prarthana Samaj.

Vidhyaben was brought up in her maternal grandfather Bholanath's house in Ahmedabad in a progressive and enlightened but strict atmosphere, under the supervision of her great-aunt Jithuben. She regularly attended prayer meetings of the Prarthana Samaj and cultivated an interest in music, drama and intellectual pursuits. At 13 years, she was married to Ramanbhai Nilkanth, a son of Mahipatram Rupram, another renowned reformer. At that time, she was studying in high school. Strongly supported and encouraged by her husband and parents, she completed her matriculation in 1891 and was able to start further studies in college. Amidst her domestic difficulties, pregnancies and, worse, society's criticism, she studied for BA over a long span of 10 years and passed her BA examination with honours in 1901. Her younger sister Sharadaben also passed the BA exam with her that same year. As mentioned earlier, these two sisters were the first women graduates of Gujarat. The Social and Literary Association of Ahmedabad felicitated both sisters.

Vidhyaben became a life member of the GVS and took an active interest in its educational activities. Vidhyaben's associations with the Ladies' Club, Mahila Mandal, Seva Sadan NIA and Vanita Vishram have been described earlier. She took an active interest in almost all the public organisations of the city with which her husband was closely associated, such as the Prarthana Samaj, GVS, Mahipatram Anathashram and other educational and literary institutes of the city. After her husband's death, she closely associated herself with all these institutes and the municipality in an honorary position. In 1932 at Lucknow, she was the president of the All India Women's Conference. In this manner, her public life gradually expanded to the national level. Her name became synonymous with the Gujarat Kelavani Mandal. Later, she was also closely associated with institutes like

Harijan Seva Sangh. Her multifarious activities in public life did not prevent her from performing admirably her traditional roles of a wife, mother and homemaker. She became a role model for the women of Gujarat. Hiralal Parekh, the assistant secretary of GVS, paid her a rich tribute, saying that Vidhyaben was an inspiration, fire and torchbearer to modern women. Women of the new age, he observed, can appropriately call this age "an age of Vidhyaben".[52]

Vidhyaben was a charismatic person with literary skills and oratory flair, able to deliver inspiring speeches both in English and Gujarati. In December 1904, she spoke eloquently in English at the National Social Conference.[53] Her educational aspirations and her elite connections in society helped in making her a leader. She and her sister Sharadaben translated two books. One was Rameshchandra Dutta's *Sudhahasini* and the other *The Position of Women in India* written by Maharani Chimnabai Gaikwad.

Sharadaben Mehta, too, was to play a leading role in the social and educational life of Ahmedabad in the Gandhian period. Another leader in the making during this period was Ansuyaben Sarabhai, who was the first labour leader of Ahmedabad. She came from the enlightened Jain family of Maganlal Karamchand. Her father was a mill owner. Her mother Godaveriben read English and was fond of Shakespeare. Ansuyaben was educated at home. She was married at the age of 12 years but did not go to her husband's home as he was not educated. She left for England to study medicine but, influenced by Fabian socialist ideas, gave up medicine to take an interest in the labour movement and women's movements in England. She became aware of the poverty and difficult conditions of labour in Ahmedabad. When she returned, she started educational activities for the working class in 1914. She started a school in Amarapura for the children of labourers. Later, she opened nursery schools and night schools in the areas where labourers resided. Gradually, she won the confidence of the working class of Ahmedabad, who looked upon her as their leader. Her real career as a labour leader started under the guidance of Gandhi in 1917.[54]

IV

Traditionally, the woman's position was subordinate to men in a patriarchal family. She was perceived primarily in her traditional role of mother, wife and homemaker by society. Her life revolved round the family and home. Even active participation in public life did not succeed in challenging this traditional role. Vidhyaben Nilkanth, a public figure, never neglected her home and family.

Though the social evil of child marriage decreased and women's education became more popular in this period, a bride was still very young at the time of marriage. In the city of Ahmedabad, as elsewhere in Gujarat, the young daughter-in-law, inexperienced in household work, was dominated by the mother-in-law. Many a times, she was ill-treated and oppressed by her in-laws. The social reformer Mahipatram, in his famous social novel *Sasu Vahuni Ladai*, depicts the tensions existing in a joint family. Wife beating was also common. He wrote in his preface that, in Ahmedabad, the position of women was particularly degraded in the Kanbi and Audichya Brahmin castes where brides brought dowry.[55] It was quite common among men of the Audichya Brahmin caste to have two to three wives. In spite of the efforts of the Audichya Hitechhu Sabha to end polygamy, the practice continued. Ironically, some of the so-called reformers of the Audichya caste had more than one wife.[56] Only among a few castes such as the Dasa Porwad, was bigamy not prevalent because the caste rules prohibited it.[57] The custom of bride price, or *pallu*, prevailed among some Nagar Brahmin castes and Vania castes, while bigamy was still quite common among them.

Articles in periodicals such as *Sundri Subodh* and *Buddhi Prakash* reveal the prevalent middle class views of the role of women. The traditional role of woman as wife, mother and homemaker was emphasised by these articles. The ideal woman portrayed by the articles was sober, industrious, thrifty, clean, wise in worldly matters, good natured, adaptive and a *pativrata* (loyal to her husband). The articles written by women also upheld the ideals of *pativrata*, and of *pati parmeshwar* (husband as a God).[58]

Even *Buddhi Prakash*, enlightened and reformist in its stance as it was, only sporadically published articles advocating the ideals of equality of husband and wife or opposing the enslavement of women.[59]

The role of a mother was always strongly stressed in the curricula for women. Child care and health education received great attention during this period. The GVS held an elocution competition on the subject of how to rear children in 1895. The glut of books on child care shows the rising interest in the scientific approach to the rearing of children.

The woman was essentially perceived as a homemaker. An ideal housewife epitomised the middle class values of thrift, hard work and meticulousness. She must know how to keep household accounts systematically and to run her household economically and efficiently. She should use her leisure meaningfully in reading, stitching, knitting and such activities. At the turn of the century, house decoration received much attention and many articles focused on this aspect of a woman's domestic duties. An ideal picture of the middle class family portrayed in contemporary periodicals like the *Buddhi Prakash* and *Sundri Subodh* shows that an educated wife ran her house efficiently and kept her house clean and tidy. Her husband was sober and abstained from drinking. Education was designed to make a woman into an ideal wife, homemaker and mother.

Though the joint patriarchal family was the main form of family, nuclear families were found in large number in an urban centre such as Ahmedabad. The description of houses in the *khatpatras* reveals that some of the houses were too small for joint families. The onslaught of individualism played an important role in disintegrating families. Sharadaben Mehta and Vidhyaben remember that their maternal grandfather Bholanathbhai's family had 30 to 40 members who ate in the same kitchen. However, Sharadaben later commented that she perceived the growing trend of individualism in some members of her maternal family, which gradually led to the disintegration of the joint family.[60]

This individualism can be discerned in Bholanath Sarabhai's son Narsinhrao Divetia's diary in the entry dated December 15, 1892: "By and large, the institution of joint family is harmful and is one of the causes of the downfall of this country."[61]

Many educated young men were not in favour of the joint family. Govindrao Patil, then a budding young lawyer of Ahmedabad, delivered a talk in 1892 on the joint family. In his talk he proved that this institution was socially disadvantageous.[62]

Hindu tradition generally denied property rights to the woman except for her right over *stridhana,* that is, the gifts she received at the time of her wedding. However, the epigraphic and documentary evidence in Ahmedabad reveals that women of several Hindu and Muslim communities, in their role of wives and daughters, enjoyed extensive property rights during both pre-British and British times. They owned, bought, sold and mortgaged houses, shops and land. *Khatpatras*, or legal documents pertaining to real estate transactions, throw light on the property rights of women.[63]

Many women received property (houses) as gifts from their husbands. A particular *khatpatra* reveals that a person named Kubera renovated his house in *Lakha Patelni* pol and gifted it to his wife Lakhamaber, which she sold in 1817.[64] Similarly, a woman called Zamku received a house as a gift from her husband, which she sold for Rs 1,701 in 1725.[65] Many *khatpatra*s of the city reveal that property was received by women as *pallu*. The *pallu* was the money given by the bridegroom or the father-in-law to the bride as her personal property and over which she had full control. The *pallu* offered security against widowhood or other financial crises. The custom of *pallu* prevailed among certain Vania and Brahmin communities but varied from caste to caste, though it always bestowed valuable property rights on women. This custom continued right into the British period. Quite often, a house was given to a bride in lieu of *pallu*.[66] *Khatpatra* (Accession number 128) of 1901 reveals that the sum received as *pallu* was deposited in a business firm and the interest accrued to the owner's credit.[67]

Khatpatra (Accession number 212) is most interesting; it reveals that even granddaughters could inherit property. When Manji of Ahmedabad died, his daughter's daughter inherited his house. The sons of another daughter relinquished their claims on the property.[68]

Recall the incident of 1812, mentioned in Chapter 1. During the severe famine and epidemic in the year, the Maratha government interfered in property matters and confiscated the property in the case of any man who died leaving only female heirs. The people of Ahmedabad collectively pleaded with the British resident of Baroda. Consequently, an order was passed recognising the right of a daughter to inherit ancestral property in the absence of male heirs.

This documentary and epigraphic evidence shows that women were not denied property rights in Ahmedabad in several communities. The generous charities of Harkunvar Sethani, the widow of Hatesingh Kesarising, show that she was able to exert her right over her husband's property which was divided into two shares, of which she received one share and his first wife the other.

V

Pre-British Ahmedabad was a thriving industrial city, celebrated for its brocades, fine silk and cotton fabrics, wood work and paper, gold and silver articles. Women were extensively employed in the various manufacturing processes of textiles, paper and other goods and were well integrated into indigenous handicraft industries.

It was mentioned earlier that the city was gradually being adversely affected by the capitalistic British colonial policy. The influx of cheap machine-made cotton yarn, fabrics and other foreign goods depressed the textile and other indigenous industries. This de-industrialisation, or decline of indigenous industries, in its turn severely affected women as they had been involved in household production.

In Ahmedabad, spinning cotton thread was an important home industry in which women were preponderant. Many widows supported themselves through the spinning wheel. Many poor Hindu and Muslim women added to the family income by spinning cotton yarn. Even rich women spun to pass the time. *Retia*, or the spinning wheel, brought economic independence to women. The import of *doctri sutar*, or foreign yarn, dealt a severe blow to this home industry. As a result, women in general suffered. Until the end of the 19th century, however, many women still earned their livelihood by spinning. Vidhyaben Nilkanth, in her autobiographical essay '*Maru Balpan*' (My Childhood), remembers that there was a spinning wheel in every house in the city on which women worked in their spare time.[69] In the early morning, the *sutaria*, or cotton seller, sat at the end of the street. He supplied cotton to women and collected yarn from them. Women received four to five pies as daily labour charges and could earn up to 12 to 14 annas a month. Some women earned as much as two rupees a month.[70] However, home spinning dwindled rapidly as it could not withstand the competition of cheap foreign as well as Indian machine-made yarn. According to the census of 1901, there were only 133 spinners in the city, of which 100 were women.[71] Thus, women were deprived of an important source of livelihood.

Other manufacturing sectors where women of Ahmedabad were employed in substantial numbers, were the silk and *kinkhab* (brocade) industries. In the silk textile industry as late as 1881, women formed 48.5 per cent of those engaged in various manufacturing processes.[72] Women and girls of the Kanbi castes were employed in processes such as sorting, reeling and winding.[73] Many women worked either at home or at the traders' place of business and earned up to three rupees each a month.[74] In Ahmedabad, silk printing was done by knotting, which was carried out by *bandhnari* women who were generally of middle and lower caste Hindu and Muslim communities.[75] As Chinese silk became popular among the rich and the demand for silk and *kinkhab* from the nobles and native kings decreased, these industries declined after the 1850s. However, the industry survived into the 20th century because the designs and durability sustained demand in the native states and even more in the countries of the Persian Gulf. *The Imperial Gazetteer of India Vol. IV*, 1908, stated that all the processes connected with the manufacture of silk and brocade goods were carried on as Ahmedabad silk had a market in Bombay, Kathiawar, Rajputana, Central India, Nagpur and in the Nizam's dominions.[76] In the census of 1901, the number of women engaged in the silk spinning and weaving industry was mentioned as 1,922, which declined to 1,304 in 1911. There was also a decline in the number of male workers, which indicates the gradual decline of the silk industry in the city.[77]

The paper manufacturing industry of Ahmedabad declined sharply in the wake of the influx of paper made in England. Women had been employed in the various processes of paper manufacture. One can clearly discern the industry's decline by the decrease in the number of male and female workers. In 1901, there were 378 male workers and 106 female workers. In 1911, they were reduced to 113 and 33 respectively.[78]

The decline of indigenous industries spelt unemployment for many women who had been engaged in household production. Many women were displaced from their traditional occupations and were reduced to the status of dependents or unskilled or marginal workers. Census data indicates the decline in the number of actual women workers. In 1901, the female population of Ahmedabad was 88,549 and the total number of women workers was 24,016. In 1911, the total women population rose to 99,475, but the number of women workers was reduced to 20,442.[79] Even so, women were employed in grinding and husking grain, sweeping, domestic work, washing and other kinds of work. Some were engaged in tailoring, pot and tile making and silk and cotton dying and printing. In this commercial city, a large number of women were engaged in various trading activities such as selling grains, vegetables, fruits, opium and snuff.

The growth of textile mills in the second half of the 19th century opened a new work avenue for women. Though women were employed in the mills from the very beginning, their number remained relatively small compared to that of male workers. Table 7.3 shows that the number of women mill workers never exceeded one-seventh of the total number of workers.

Table 7.3: Total and Women Mill Workers

Year	All Workers	Women Workers
1892	8,175	1,077
1896	13,813	1,618
1902	20,669	2,793
1905	24,792	3,209
1909	33,749	4,676
1914	41,300	6,835

Source: *Annual Factory Reports: Statements.*

The rate of increase in the number of women workers was lower compared to that of the total number of workers. Women were employed in all departments of the mills except in the weaving departments. They were mainly employed in reeling, winding and cotton picking.[80] They worked steam-operated machinery and worked the same hours as men before the Factory Act XI of 1891 came into force. This Act restricted the working hours of women to 11 hours and led to the replacement of women by men as frame-minders. Women were gradually transferred to the reeling and winding departments. After 1891, the number of women workers decreased rapidly and it always remained smaller than that in the city of Bombay. Though textile mills rendered new work opportunities to women, in this early stage, only women of the labouring and low castes such as Waghris and Kolis took up factory work. Even the artisan and other intermediate castes did not work in the mills. As a result, artisan women who were left without occupation after the decline of indigenous industries could not make use of the new factory work. The wages of unskilled workers, as in the annual factory reports of Bombay presidency reveal the distressing fact of disparity between the wages paid to male and female workers.

A small but important development can be discerned in the last decade of the 19th century, especially among upper caste women who took up the teaching profession to earn livelihood. The Female Training College, established in 1871 in Ahmedabad, trained women for primary school teaching. It started with only six women students, but steadily the number increased. By 1908, 320 teachers had been trained in the college. These trained teachers were employed in various parts of Gujarat, in different districts and native states. Their work was highly regarded, as seen in the reports of the education inspectors.[81]

Looking into the social milieu of these new women teachers, it is evident that as a rule women trainees in the college were wives of school masters or of men who were being trained for the teaching profession. LR Collet, superintendent of the Ahmedabad Female Training College, stated this in her report to the Bombay provincial committee of the education commission in 1882. She added that government authorities make an agreement with the women trainees that after completion of training, they would be sent to the same places as their husbands. Miss Collet added: "Besides the wives of school masters, we admit respectable widows." According to her, there was initial apprehension about admitting widows into the college, but soon these fears and apprehensions died as widows succeeded in winning the respect and confidence of the residents in the villages where they were sent to teach. In 1882, there were 32 students on the college rolls, out of which 18 were Brahmins, three Kanbis, five Parsis and six Native Christians. The Native Christians were new entrants at that time because, as Miss Collet observed, "A short time ago, it was deemed inadvisable to admit Native Christians even to the Practicing School, or to have them sitting in the same classes with Hindu girls." The trained Native Christian teachers were soon absorbed in the schools of Mission Society and in the staff of the Female Training College of Ahmedabad.[82]

The caste and community composition of women teachers gradually became more heterogeneous. In 1901, female teachers trained and qualified in the Female Training College of Ahmedabad and employed in Ahmedabad district were 34 in number, out of which 23 were Brahmin, three Native Christian, two Kanbi and one each of Kshatriya, Valand (barber), Luvana, Vania, Ghanchi (oil-pressers) and Durji (tailor) castes. Brahmin teachers remained preponderant.[83] Until 1904, there were no Muslim trained women teachers working in the Ahmedabad district. One Nurbibi Gulabshah Dabhoya obtained the certificate from the Mahalaxmi Female Training College in 1900 and started working in school number 27 in Ahmedabad from 1904.[84] This was an unprecedented phenomenon in the *purdah*-observing Muslim community. In 1914, there were six Muslim students in the Training College. This was a sure sign of social change in the Muslim community.

In 1914, *The Directory of Vernacular Teachers* shows that there were 106 trained teachers employed in Ahmedabad district who were trained in the Mahalaxmi Female Training College. Out of 106 teachers, 57 were Brahmin, 19 Kanbi, four Native Christian, four Vanias and others belonging to the Jain, Bhavsar (printers) Luvana, Valand, Khatri, Kumbhar (potter), Rajput and Barot castes. Two Muslim teachers and one Jewish teacher also appeared on the list.[85] Thus the teaching profession, which paid from Rs 20 to Rs 40, attracted women from various castes and communities.

Another profession which opened up for women in the last decade of the 19th century was nursing. Since there was no school to train nurses, the municipality of Ahmedabad sent a woman named Jivi to study nursing at the Cama Hospital in Bombay in 1892. She returned with a certificate and was employed by the municipality in the Victoria Jubilee Female Hospital to care for poor women in their homes.[86] Dr Motiben Kapadia, the female doctor who joined the Victoria Jubilee Hospital in the late 1880s, took a keen interest in the training of nurses. Later, she started a nursing school in the premises of the Hospital. Sir Chinubhai Madhavlal gave a generous donation to construct a school for nurses and midwives at the Victoria Jubilee Dispensary.[87] In 1911, there were 31 nurses in the city. It is interesting to note here that, in 1919, the BJ Medical School in Ahmedabad admitted four women students for the first time.[88]

Though new work avenues for women opened up in the city, only a small number could avail of these opportunities at this time. By and large, women's productive role in the economic life of Ahmedabad decreased as a result of the British colonial policy.

* * *

In the pre-Gandhian period, as a result of the efforts made by social reformers in Ahmedabad, the social evils of child marriage and female infanticide had decreased and women's education and widow remarriages had increased considerably. Widow marriage no longer evoked either criticism or a flutter in society. Several widows remarried under the auspices of the Gujarat Samsar Sudhara Samaj and the Prarthana Samaj. About 52 widow remarriages were celebrated in the city until 1908. People showed greater sympathy towards the cause of widows. Also, it was common for a girl of 14 to be unmarried.[89] Female infanticide in the Kanbi community was brought under control by the Act VIII of 1870. The census data testifies that child marriages had decreased in the city. Girls' schools proliferated. Girls began going to schools and colleges in spite of the hostility of the orthodox sections of society. The emergence of numerous educational, political, social and cultural activities helped to bring women out of their homes. Upper and middle class women began to attend meetings to listen to lectures and to enjoy dramatic and other performance. The emergence of women's organisations increased women's participation in public life and widened their social and cultural horizons. These organisations also helped to shape women leaders like Vidhyaben Nilkanth and Sulochanaben Desai. It is true that the changes were limited to a small section of the upper and privileged economic classes and social groups, but what is more significant is that these changes set definite trends for the future.

Notes

1. *Buddhi Prakash*, February 1906, pp. 36–39.
2. *Buddhi Prakash*, November 1864, pp. 263–264.
3. *Gujarat Shalapatra*, September–October 1868, pp. 226–233; Bombay Presidency, *The Report on Native Papers* (henceforth cited as *RNP*), for the week ending October 17, 1869, p. 10; Mahipatram Rupram, *Parvatikunvar Akhyan* (in Gujarati), Ahmedabad, 1881, pp. 20–21.
4. Mary Carpenter, *Six Months in India*, Vol. I, London,1868, pp. 48, 69 and 53.
5. *Buddhi Prakash*, March 1870, p. 54.
6. Bombay Government, *Gazetteer of the Bombay Presidency*, Vol IV *Ahmedabad Gazetteer*, 1879, Bombay, pp. 309–10 and 325.Henceforth cited as *Ahmedabad Gazetteer*.
7. The Stree Bodh Office, *The Stree Bodh and Social Progress in India A Jubilee Memorial*, Bombay, 1908, p. 223. Henceforth cited as *Stree Bodh Jubilee Celebration Volume*.
8. The Government of Bombay, *Report of the Director of Public Instruction in the Bombay Presidency for the year 1913–14*, Bombay 1914, p. 29.
9. *Gujarat Shalapatra*, September 1883, p. 202.
10. Hiralal T Parekh, *Lady Vidhyaben Mani Mahotsava Abhinandan Granth*, Ahmedabad, 1936, pp. 220–23.
11. *Stree Bodh Jubilee Celebration Volume*, p. 223.
12. Government of India, *Census of India 1911,* Vol. VII, Bombay Part II, *Imperial Tables*, Bombay, 1912, p. 140.
13. Sharadaben Mehta, *Jivan Sambharna* (in Gujarati), Vadodra, 1938, p. 30.
14. *Stree Bodh Jubilee Celebration Volume*, p. 222.
15. His Majesty's Secretary of State for Indian in Council, *The Imperial Gazetteer of India*, Vol. V, New Edition, Oxford, 1908, pp. 98–99.
16. *Buddhi Prakash*, December 1893, p. 98–99.
17. *Stree Bodh Jubilee Celebration Volume*, p. 222.
18. *Buddhi Prakash,* April 1898, p. 114.
19. *Ibid.*, May 1908, p. 159.
20. *Gujarat Shalapatra*, September 1892, pp. 225–26.
21. *Ibid.*, January 1897, pp. 30-36, February 1897, p. 41.
22. *Buddhi Prakash*, August 1895, pp. 227–235.
23. *Sundri Subodh*, January 1912, pp. 169–173.
24. Mary Carpenter, *op.cit.,* p. 57.
25. *Ibid.*, p. 33.
26. *Gujarat Shalapatra*, January 1869, p. 16.

25. Ranchhodlal Chhotalal

26. Mangaldas Girdhardas

27. Lalbhai Dalpatbhai

28. Bechardas Lashkari

29. Sarabhai *seth*

30. Munshi Fateh Mohammad Fakir Mohammad

31. Vidhyaben and Sharadaben,
first women graduates of Gujarat

32. Balaben Bholanath

33. Ladies Club

34. Bholanath Sarabhai Institute's
Foundation Inscription

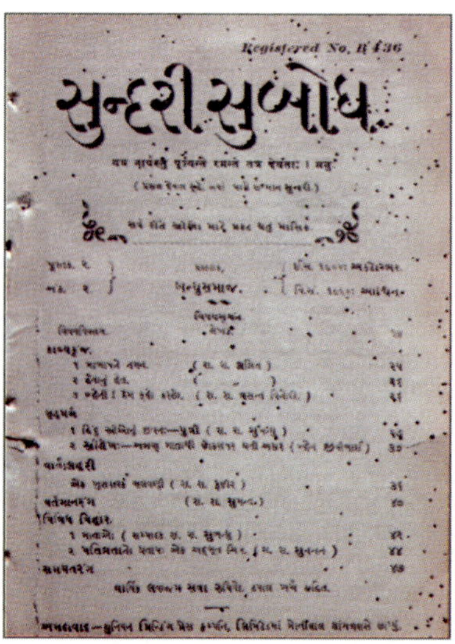

Registered No. B 436

સુન્દરી સુબોધ.

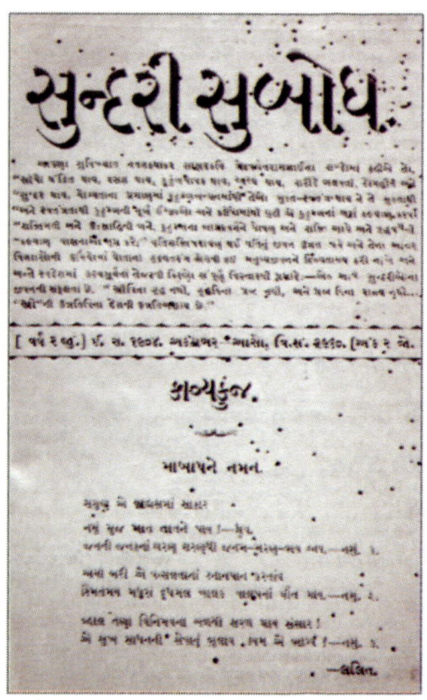

સુન્દરી સુબોધ.

કાવ્યકુંજ.

માબાપને નમન.

35. *Sundri Subodh*, Ahmedabad's First Women's Journal

27. Mahipatram Rupram, *Parvatikunvar Akhyan*, 1881, Ahmedabad pp. 30–31.
28. Lady Vidhyagauri Nilkanth, 'Progress of Women in Ahmedabad' in *Ahmedabad* published by the Rotary Club, Ahmedabad, 1940, pp. 60–61.
29. *Prajabandhu*, April 24, 1898, p. 6, May 1, 1898, p. 2.
30. *Buddhi Prakash*, April 1875, p. 67.
31. N Dave, *Dharmavichar* (2nd edition), 1900, pp. 35–36.
32. *Stree Bodh Jubilee Celebrations, Volume,* p. 223.
33. *Gujarat Shalapatra*, April 1890, pp. 90–92; *Twentieth Annual Report of the National Indian Association*, London, 1890, pp. 32–33.
34. *Stree Bodh Jubilee Celebration Volume*, p. 223.
35. *Prajabandhu*, January 1899, p. 3.
36. Sharadaben Mehta, *op. cit.,* p. 36.
37. Vidhyaben Nilkanth, *Phorum*, pp. 174–78.
38. *Prajabandhu*, February 18, 1912, p. 23; Vidhyaben Nilkanth, *Phorum,* pp. 101–105; Jyoti Sangh, *Jyoti Vikas Yatra* (in Gujarati), Ahmedabad, 1971, pp. 11–16.
39. An interview with Kantaben Shambhuprasad Lashkari (born in 1893) on January 28, 1987 in Ahmedabad at her residence.
40. Vidhyaben Nilkanth, *Phorum*, p. 125; *Sundri Subodh*, January-February-March 1913, p. 107; Sharadaben Mehta, *op. cit.*, p. 36.
41. Vidhyaben Nilkanth, *Phorum,* pp. 104–105; Jyoti Sangh, *op. cit.*, pp. 16–20; Kapilrai Mehta, *Amdavad Sarvasangha* (in Gujarati), Ahmedabad, 1948, p. 262.
42. Diwaliben Bhatt and Shridevi Budha, *Apna Nariratno* (in Gujarati), Bhavnagar, 1944, pp. 183–186; *Prajabandhu*, June 14, 1908, p. 15; Jyoti Sangh, *op. cit.*, pp. 59–61; Hiralal Parekh, *Arvachin Gujaratanu Rekhadarshan* (in Gujarati), Ahmedabad (revised edition), 1976, pp. 539–543.
43. *Prajabandhu*, May 2, 1909, p. 13.
44. *Ibid.*, April 2, 1911, p. 14.
45. Sharadaben Mehta, *op. cit.*, p. 63.
46. *RNP*, in the week ending March 7, 1891, pp. 9–10.
47. Sharadaben Mehta, *op. cit.*, p. 34.
48. *Sundri Subodh*, August 1907, p. 286.
49. *Ibid.*, June 1910, pp. 309–314.
50. *Ibid.*, August 1907, p. 286.
51. *Prajabandhu*, October 1914, p. 21.

52. Hiralal Parekh, *Gujarat Vernacular Society no Itihas* (in Gujarati), Vol. III, Ahmedabad, 1934, pp. 236–246; Vinodini Nilkanth, *Vidhyagauri Nilkanth*, Bombay 1976, Passim; Hiralal T. Parekh, *Lady Vidhyaben Mani Mahotsav Abhinandan Granth*, Ahmedabad, 1936, Passim.
53. *RNP* for the week ending January 7, 1905, p. 24.
54. Shivshankar Shukla, *Ansuyaben Sarabhaini Jivankatha* (in Gujarati), Ahmedabad, 1973, pp. 9–43; Leena Mangaldas, Akhand *Divo* (in Gujarati), Ahmedabad, 1979, pp. 5–18.
55. Mahipatram Rupram, *Sasu Vahuni Ladai* (in Gujarati), Ahmedabad (second edition), 1875.Preface.
56. *RNP*, for the week ending July 6, 1889, p. 11.
57. *RNP* for the week ending December 20, 1873, p. 3.
58. *Sundri Subodh*, March 1907, p. 6.
59. *Buddhi Prakash*, May 1882, p. 108; July 1899, p. 208.
60. Sharadaben Mehta, *op. cit.,* pp. 13–15.
61. Narsinhrao Divetia, *Narsinhraoni Rojnishi*, (in Gujarati), Ahmedabad, 1953, pp. 27–28.
62. *Ibid.*, p. 26.
63. *Khatpatras* at the BJ Institute, Ahmedabad, show that many sellers and buyers of houses in the city were women (Accession nos. 8836, 8852, 8907, 8911, 8912, 8896, 8874, 8916).
64. *Khatpatra,* Accession no. 8920.
65. *Khatpatra,* Accession no. 8911.
66. *Khatpatra,* Accession no. 8916.
67. *Khatpatra*, Accession no. 128.
68. *Khatpatra*, Accession no. 212.
69. Vidhyaben Nilkanth, *Phorum*, p. 4.
70. *Buddhi Prakash*, August 1874, pp. 169–71.
71. Government of India, *Census of India – 1901* Volume IX, Bombay, Part II, 1902, p. xxxii

    It would be interesting at this point to examine the use of census data as a source of information for women's economic activities. In India, the census started from 1871. Data about occupation was collected right from the beginning. However, in the first three censuses (i.e. of 1871, 1881 and 1891), the occupational data was recorded district-wise. Only from 1901 was the occupational data of each major city of the Presidency collected and recorded. Furthermore, in the censuses prior to 1901, women and children who were engaged in home production were not properly recorded and were placed in the category of dependents. Employment in such domestic occupations as spinning was not tabulated by the census authorities who felt that, considering the meagre earning, spinning yarn was not an employment worthy of mention as the women did not receive any independent or special remuneration for the work. (Government of India, *Imperial Census of 1881, Operations and Results of the Presidency of Bombay. Vol. I,* Text, Bombay, 1882, p. 187). In 1901, the information regarding occupations was recorded separately in three categories, one for actual workers, one for dependents and one for subsidiary occupations on the basis of sex. This method was followed in the census of 1911. The census of 1901 is important because, for the first time in census returns, particulars of the population employed by the power industries are recorded as distinct from those of the hand worker. In this study, the censuses of 1901 and 1911 are mainly used as sources of information on women's economic activities.

72. Government of India, *Imperial Census of 1881, Operations and Results of the Presidency of Bombay,* Vol. I, Text, Bombay, 1882, p. 197.
73. *Ahmedabad Gazetteer*, p. 136.
74. *Buddhi Prakash*, August 1874, pp. 169–171.
75. *Ahmedabad Gazetteer*, p. 136.
76. *The Imperial Gazetteer of India*, Vol. V, 1908, p. 109.
77. *Census of India 1901*, Vol. IX., *Bombay*, Part II, p. 1xxxii; *Census of India 1911*, Vol. VII, *Bombay*, Part II, p. 412.
78. *Ibid.*, 1901, p. 1xxiv; 1911, p. 453.
79. *Ibid.*, 1901, p. xcviii; 1911, p. 466.
80. Bombay Government, *Report and Proceedings of the Appointed to Consider the Working of the Factories in the Bombay Presidency,* Bombay 1885, p. 137.
81. Bombay Government, *Report of the Director of Public Instruction in the Bombay Presidency for the year 1888-89,* Bombay, 1889, p. 29.
82. Education Commission, *Bombay,* Vol.II, *Evidence Taken Before the Bombay Provincial Committee and Memorials Addressed to the Education Commission*, Calcutta, 1884, pp. 274–278.
83. Bombay Government, *Directory of Vernacular Teachers Holding Certificates of Qualification Recognized by the Education Department, Employed in Local Boards and Municipal Schools and in Native States in the Northern Division for 1901*, Ahmedabad, 1901, pp. 4-23. Henceforth cited *as Directory of Vernacular Teachers in the Northern Division and its year.*
84. *Directory of Vernacular Teachers in the Northern Division 1906*, pp. 52–53.
85. *Ibid.*, 1914, pp. 66–79.
86. Ahmedabad Municipality, *Administration Report of the Municipality of Ahmedabad. For the Official Year 1892-93,* p. 20.
87. Maharashtra State Archives General Department, Vol. 48/1913, pp. 77–87.
88. Maharashtra State Archives General Department, Compilation file No. 462/1919, p. 1.
89. *Stree Bodh Jubilee Celebration Volume*, pp. 223–224.

8

Emergence of Industrial Working Class

Among the several social consequences of industrialisation, the most important was the emergence of the industrial working class in Ahmedabad. Initially, this class had been small and inconspicuous, but with the expansion of the mill industry, it grew rapidly and soon became an important and prominent segment of the city's population. In 1861, the first textile mill had only 63 workers,[1] but by 1914, there were more than 40,000 industrial workers working in 61 textile mills, two iron works, two hosiery factories, one dye works, three oil mills, and 25 ginning, cleaning and pressing mills in and around the city.[2] In 1922, the number of workers further rose to 59,041.[3] From 1914 onwards, almost 20 per cent of the city's population was made up of factory workers. There was a steady increase in the number of industries and a corresponding increase in the number of workers.

The emergence of the industrial working class naturally added a new dimension to the life of the city. In the pre-British period, Ahmedabad had manufactured textile goods, but the manufacturers had been artisans who owned tools and implements and worked in their own homes. With the advent of the modern textile sector, the foundation of the old system was shattered. The workers in the machine industries did not own the means of production but sold their labour for wages.

As there is no reliable statistical data available on this nascent class, one has to rely on the scanty but valuable qualitative data provided by the *Ahmedabad Gazetteer* (1879) and the reports and proceedings of the Factory Commission of 1875, 1885, 1890 and 1908 and of the Royal Commission on Indian Labour of 1929–1930. *Annual Factory Reports 1892–1923* of the Bombay Presidency and inadequate census data of the city from 1901 onwards also throw some light on the formation of the working class in the early stage of industrialisation in the city.

I

From the very beginning, the working class of Ahmedabad was heterogeneous, composed of various castes and communities. As early as 1878, the 2,010 labourers working in four textile mills were drawn from various castes and from the Hindu as well as the Muslim communities, as mentioned by the *Ahmedabad Gazetteer*.

> Except a few Brahmin men employed as bundlers, Vania men as reelers and Kanbi men as weavers, the workmen were Mussalmans, Kolis, Marathas, Pardesis, Bauchas, Waghris, Marwadis and other labouring classes. The Muslims worked 'as binders and piecers' and in other capacities, whereas the Marathas and the Pardesis were rated as good workers. They were generally employed in the carding room.[4]

The bulk of the factory labour force was drawn from the local landless labouring castes like the Waghris, Kolis, Bauchas, Marwadis and Pardesis. This is corroborated by the evidence given by the mill owner Bechardas Ambiadas Lashkari to the Factory Commission of 1875 that most of the mill workers were of the Koli and Waghri castes.[5]

The Waghris were fowlers, labourers and beggars. They were poor, but their entire families worked in factories where they improved their financial status. As a result, they purchased ornaments and built better houses. The Kolis who were cultivators, labourers and husbandmen, came from the city and its vicinity. The Marathas and Bauchas were labourers and came from the Deccan but settled in Ahmedabad. The Marwadi labourers had already immigrated in large numbers to Ahmedabad district during the famine in Rajasthan in 1869. They were employed as unskilled labourers in the government public works, in the fields in the centres of cotton trade, in various crafts like carpentry and also in the textile mills. The Rawalias who were grain carriers, vegetable vendors and beggars found factory work more remunerative, while payment too was regular.[6] Thus, mills provided employment to the poor quasi-proletariat castes.

Another group which worked in the mills was the local artisan class, especially Muslim and Kanbi handloom weavers. The de-industrialisation process had displaced them from their traditional pursuits. Their artisan traditions and training set them apart from other unskilled labourers so that they were able to take some of the best paid and most skilled positions in the weaving department and were thus saved from the plight of unemployment. Mir Mohammad, a 25-year-old Muslim weaver working in a mill at Ahmedabad, in his evidence given to the Indian Factory Commission on October 16, 1890, stated that he was an inhabitant of the city of Ahmedabad and his parents were handloom weavers who earned about six to seven rupees a month.[7] Gibbs, the collector and district magistrate of Ahmedabad, wrote in his report on the strike of mill-hands at Ahmedabad in 1895 that the weavers were nearly all local Muslims belonging to the class of hereditary handloom weavers who had lost their trade because of the mills.[8] Higher and regular wages at the mill seem to have attracted many displaced handloom weavers to analogous factory occupations.

It is interesting to note that during this early stage of industrialisation, Dheds and other untouchable castes were not employed in the textile industry of Ahmedabad. Dheds, whose hereditary occupation was weaving, suffered economically, first, because they had been ousted from their occupation of weaving by the machine industry and second, because of the prejudice existing against employing them on farms and in steam mills. They were forced to seek employment in the public works as unskilled workers.[9] In fact, in one of the spinning mills of Ahmedabad, all the mill-hands struck work when they discovered that one of the Marwadi workers was really a Dhed who had passed himself off as a member of the higher caste.[10] This incidence in the initial stage of industrialisation reveals that the workers themselves resisted the employment of the Dheds in the mills.

The situation changed by 1908, when Dheds and other untouchables were found to be preponderant in the textile mills. The evidence from Ahmedabad placed before the Indian Factory Labour Commission in 1908 indicates that Dheds were recruited in large numbers for mill work.[11] This is somewhat extraordinary, especially because the presence of Dheds in textile mills was not mentioned by any of the 13 mill-hand witnesses who were examined by the Indian Factory Commission in 1890. Among these 13 witnesses, seven were Waghris, five were Muslims and one was a Rawalia.[12] Collector Gibbs, in his 1895 report mentioned earlier, observed that the spinners were mostly local and included Kanbis, Waghris, Kolis and Marwadis. He did not mention Dheds as spinners.[13]

It is difficult to guess exactly when the shift in the recruitment pattern occurred and at what point of time the Dheds made an entry into the mills. With the increase in the number of textile units in the late 1890s and thereafter, more workers were obviously needed. Dheds were after all skilled textile artisans and mill owners must have found it expedient to recruit them, particularly in the spinning section. Such economic compulsions obliged mill owners to shed their conventional prejudices against the untouchables and to recruit them as a necessary part of the recruitment policy. The mill workers' strike of 1895 may have helped Dheds and other depressed castes to enter the mills as strike breakers. Dheds were already working in the Surat mills as early as 1892.[14] In the first two decades of the 20th century, when labour was in short supply, the *mukadams* began recruiting Dhed boys from the neighbouring villages and entering into contracts with their parents for two or three years, paying them fixed sums annually.[15]

Economic necessity may have made mill owners employ Dheds, but the Dheds were not given access to the weaving department. They were only employed in the various spinning processes, where they worked side by side with the 'clean' castes. The explanation given for not admitting the Dheds to the weaving department was that whenever a weft bobbin was replaced, yarn had to be sucked on to the shuttle. This process would ritually defile the other 'clean' castes using the same shuttle. In Bombay, too, untouchables were prohibited from working in the weaving departments. In Ahmedabad, the weaving departments were largely dominated by the Kanbis and Muslims.[16] Strangely enough, ritual defilement by working with Muslim weavers was never feared by the higher castes such as the Kanbis or Brahmins or other castes working in the weaving department.

The textile workers, as noted, belonged to various castes and communities. The heterogeneous character of this 'working' class was emphasised in the report of the Bombay Labour Office, which conducted an enquiry into working class family budgets in Ahmedabad in 1926. It stated that, while Hindus and Mohammedans were found in large numbers, Jains and Zoroastrians were not found among the working classes. Among the Hindus, there were no less than 70 different castes in the workforce, of whom Chamars, Dheds, Thakardas, Patidars (Kanbis) and Waghris were predominant. Christians were also found among the working class.[17]

It is interesting that the regions which supplied the labour force in the initial phase of industrialisation in Ahmedabad were the city and its immediate neighbourhood. As the industry expanded, the area of recruitment was enlarged. As early as 1885, when there were only seven mills with about 4,000 operatives, the local supply of labour was not sufficient. We have the valuable evidence of Rao Bahadur Bechardas Ambiadas in this regard. Giving evidence before the Factory Commission of 1885, he stated: "In Ahmedabad, supply is hardly equal to demand. We have, for instance, to bring men from as far as Nadiad."[18] In 1890, the Indian Factory Commission examined 13 mill operatives in Ahmedabad. Out of these 13, two came from Kadi (Baroda State) and one from Palanpur, both places being within a radius of 50 miles of Ahmedabad. The rest belonged to the city and its immediate neighbourhood.[19]

There was little change in the policy of labour recruitment over the next 40 years. As late as 1929, 75 per cent of the labour force still came from the city of Ahmedabad, Ahmedabad district, Kathiawar and Baroda State.[20]

The movement to cities of rural people seeking employment was a common phenomenon in the 19th century. As occupational opportunities decreased for landless labourers, sub-marginal peasants, indebted agriculturists and village craftsmen, they left their villages to seek jobs in the Ahmedabad mill industry. Harsh economic conditions following famines, plague and other epidemics, increase in population and limited availability of land for cultivation also forced villagers to abandon their villages. The Kanbis were originally agriculturists, had been moving to Ahmedabad since the late 18th century and had first taken to handloom weaving and business. In the 19th century, with the reduction of opportunity in this area, they took jobs in the weaving departments of mills. The machine industries also ousted Dheds and Vankars from handloom weaving, who then migrated to Ahmedabad and sought work in the mills.

Many villagers from Kutch and Rajasthan came to Ahmedabad at the end of the 19th century for similar reasons. Maratha labourers were hired as early as the 1870s, who then permanently settled in Ahmedabad. The backwardness of the native states of Gujarat was also responsible for the migration of labour to Ahmedabad. Similarly, the flow from the United Provinces, Central Province and Madras was due to the fact that these provinces were not as industrially advanced as Bombay presidency and those who failed to secure employment in Bombay came to Ahmedabad. The ousted weavers from Jabalpur also came to seek jobs in the mills of the city.[21]

The in-flow of labour from the rural areas was continuous and constant, both in bad and good times. It is true that a temporary shortage of labour occurred whenever the mills expanded or proliferated very rapidly. This happened during the *swadeshi* movement (1905–1908) and later during 1912–14. But though such a shortage of labour was short-lived, during the shortage, demands for higher wages and several partial strikes took place.[22]

A large proportion of the workforce came from outside the city but settled permanently in Ahmedabad. In contrast to the immigrant and unsettled character of Bombay's working class, Ahmedabad had a substantial settled working class whose habits were less migratory than those of workers in Bombay. From the very beginnings of industrialisation in Ahmedabad, there was a distinct and separate class of factory workers, whose only source of livelihood was factory work. In 1892, an official report remarked:

> In Ahmedabad and Surat only does it seem to be a permanent class of factory workers who do not look forward to going back to agriculture. The Collector reports "most of the hands live by factory work only" and "the number of years that the workers continue to work may be taken at 30".[23]

Significantly, the same report noted that in the Bombay textile industries, there was no separate class of factory workers, for most of the workers were drawn from the cultivating classes and again got absorbed into them.[24]

The witnesses (mill operatives) examined by the Indian Factory Commission in 1890 were permanent residents of Ahmedabad. Those who came from the villages nearby or from Kadi and other regions had hardly any close ties with their villages.[25] Some of the mill workers who came from the villages of nearby districts returned to their villages only for weddings or in the festive seasons of Diwali or Holi, and very few returned for the sowing season. Those who came from distant regions like the United Provinces, Jabalpur, or Madras went for longer duration perhaps once in two or three years.[26]

Many of the workers brought their families to the city. The enquiry conducted into the budgets of working class families of Ahmedabad by the Bombay Labour Office in 1926 revealed that only seven per cent of the working class families in Ahmedabad remitted money to the dependents who did not actually live with them.[27]

The *mukadam*, or jobber, was the main recruiting agent for the labour force. He would go to the neighbouring regions to bring back workers for factory work from the villages. He extorted a commission from the workers when labour was plenty and took a commission from the mills when there was a shortage of labour. His main function was to see that the machines under his supervision were worked to full capacity.[28] During the first decade of the 20th century, when the mills faced a severe problem of getting an adequate supply of labour, jobbers from other mills enticed operatives away. In such cases, to retain a worker's services, it was the custom for successful mills to pay him his wages for a full month although he may have been in the new mill for just a few days.[29]

As a rule, workers did not pay bribes to jobbers in Ahmedabad. Out of the 13 mill operatives examined by the Indian Factory Commission of 1890, only two gave bribes of Rs 2 to 3 to the *mukadams* who got them work.[30]

In times of shortage, the jobbers offered inducements such as tea, cold drinks or cash to the workers under them. The mills used to defray these expenses.[31] At such times, the jobbers made journeys to distant places and brought recruits to mills.

II

The machine industry introduced a new mode of production in Ahmedabad based on factory lines, entailing a new type of discipline and coordination hitherto unknown to the artisans or peasants. In the early phase of industrialisation, they had to adapt themselves to tediously repetitious factory work just as the workers in England had.

The hours of work were long, from sunrise to sunset, with an interval of half an hour for rest. The collector of Ahmedabad wrote to the commissioner of the northern division on July 28, 1888: "The hours are just as long as the sun offers light." He added that in May and June, the work extended from 12 to 13 hours and 20 minutes, and, in that particular year, in spite of intense heat and a raging cholera epidemic, there was no relaxation allowed to the workers.[32]

The Factory Act XV of 1881 limited children's working hours to nine. The Ahmedabad mills devised a shift system of six hours for children—the first shift lasting from 6:30 a.m. to 12:30 p.m. and the second shift from 12:30 p.m. to 6:00 or 6:30 p.m. In the busy season, the ginning factories worked in shifts that lasted for one and a quarter day.[33]

Ever since their foundation, the Ahmedabad mills had granted four days in the month as holidays. Sundays were considered holidays, except when a native festival holiday occurred during the week, when the mills worked on Sunday to make up for the festival holidays. But actually, Sunday was not a complete holiday, because the mill-hands were expected to go to the factory and clean the machines in the morning. This work lasted from 10:00 a.m. to 11:00 a.m. The muster roll was taken on Sunday, but if an operative did not attend on Sunday, no fine was charged.[34] The Sunday holiday in Ahmedabad was significant because, before the Factory Act XI of 1891 was implemented, many of the mills in Bombay worked on Sundays, while some worked on alternate Sundays. Some factories in Bombay and elsewhere allowed only 15 holidays a year. In Ahmedabad, the mill-hands enjoyed altogether 59 to 63 holidays a year. For the festivals of Diwali and Holi, they got two days as holidays.[35]

The Factory Act VI of 1891 restricted women's working hours to 11. Before this Act was passed, many women worked as long as men because they worked on the power machinery. The restriction on women's working hours resulted in the removal of many women mill-hands from factory work and caused discontent and unhappiness amongst the women. This is discussed in detail later. They protested by sending a petition to the government, which was turned down.

The mill-hands were quite used to dawn to dusk working hours. But in 1905, when electricity was introduced in some of the Ahmedabad mills, mill owners ran the machinery for excessive hours from 5:00 a.m. to 9:00 p.m. The working hours were extended to fifteen. The evidence of Sheikh Dost Mahomad, a Muslim weaver aged 40, given to the Indian Factory Labour Commission in 1908 revealed the seething discontent of the mill operatives against the excessive hours introduced owing to the use of electric lights. He stated in his evidence:

> All the mill hands in Ahmedabad are unanimous in wishing that the hours of work should be restricted. At present we do not get a single hour of daylight at home. Those mills which have no electric light work from sunrise to sunset and those with electric light work on till 8:00 or 9:00 p.m. Often we find that the electric light injures our eyes but men in mills where it is installed have to work long hours by it, otherwise they would lose their places.[36]

Other mill-hands also complained to the Commission that they were exhausted by long hours of work and that their sight suffered. They emphatically stated their preference for a scheme of working hours from sunrise to sunset.

The Factory Act XII of 1911 restricted the working hours of male adults to twelve and the working hours of children to six. Though the Factory Acts restricted the hours, quite often, mill owners broke the rules. Throughout the period covered by this work, the hours were far too long for the operatives to enjoy any kind of leisure.

The manager of Ahmedabad Merchants' Spinning Mills, C Knowles, remarked in his written evidence given to the Indian Factory Labour Commission of 1908:

> The Indian Labourer is entirely of a different type from the labour one finds in England. He is very careless, independent and irregular and spends most of his time loafing about the mill compound smoking, talking, washing his teeth and so on.[37]

This evidence reflects the working style of the operatives. The operatives in Ahmedabad and elsewhere in India worked in a leisurely and casual manner. They did not work continuously but managed to do the minimum work in the time allotted. In 1907, the Textile Factories Labour Committee wrote in their report: "No legislation can alter the nature and ingrained habits of Indian workers. They have been in the habit of leaving their work at odd and uncertain periods throughout the nominal working hours."[38]

The operatives obviously counteracted the long hours by taking frequent spells of rest. They used the midday interval for rest and ate their meals at various times. About 10 per cent of the operatives were always out loitering, smoking or talking, and thus they wasted about two to three hours during working hours. Owing to these idling habits, the mill owner was obliged to employ 50 per cent more hands than needed in some departments and 30 per cent in others.[39]

Supervision was light. The mills were personally managed by the mill agents. Generally, however, technical supervision and management was initially placed in the hands of the European managers who were sent out by large firms in England such as Platts and Oldham.[40] Later, some of the managers appointed were Parsis and Hindus, but labour was largely recruited, trained, disciplined and supervised by jobbers or *mukadams*. The jobber himself hailed from the working class. He was illiterate and had the same social and economic background as the workers. He had tremendous hold over the labourers and, in effect, was the actual manager of the workforce. He maintained discipline among child labourers with the help of a small stick held in his hand.[41] He saw that work progressed well and that the machines worked on a full complement. He not only arranged the workloads and rest intervals, but had extensive power to fine or discharge workers for breach of discipline and bad work. Thus, he was the key figure in the supervision of work and maintenance of discipline, his powers being endorsed by the mill owners. He was thus the link between higher management and the labourers.

Fines were a device by which discipline was maintained at work. In the early phase of industrialisation, there was no code governing the norms of work. A system of small fines for bad work, insubordination and carelessness, destruction of machinery and absence without leave was in force in the mills in Ahmedabad.[42]

Absenteeism in the mills of Ahmedabad was fortunately not high as that in Surat or in other centres of industry. In Surat, it was as high as 18 per cent while in the mills of Ahmedabad, it was from 8 per cent to 10 per cent.[43] Among the operatives, it was common to take two to three days holidays in addition to Sundays. Illness, funerals, weddings and private business were some of the reasons for frequent absence. Occasionally, absenteeism was really a protest against the drudgery of factory work, especially as no other leave was granted except the four Sundays in the month and a few festivals. In every mill, about 10 to 15 per cent workers remained absent on the day after pay day. Prizes were given for regular attendance but mill owners complained that it was difficult to find anyone to deserve them.[44]

When new mills proliferated, *mukadams* would entice mill workers to the new mills by offering higher wages and other inducements, so the mill-hands changed jobs frequently to get more wages in the new mills.

Factory work was not always safe. Regular inspections were carried out by the inspectors jointly with the assistant collectors and the district magistrates to check safety measures in the mills. In spite of all these checks, serious and even fatal accidents did occur. Mill owners neglected fencing off the machinery; fire exits were defective or insufficient in many mills. Workers were maimed and killed in accidents. Cases of burning, suffocation, entanglement in the machinery and other such accidents occurred frequently.[45]

There was no compensation given for accidents except payment of wages until the worker was once again fit for labour. Sickness allowance was paid for two days in a month and only when it was a result of an accident in the mill. The injured workers were not always provided for.[46] Many were maimed and had to take to begging because there was no insurance system, pension or provident scheme for the workers.

Ventilation in the mills was defective. Sometimes, steam was used instead of water for humidification in weaving sheds, which made the atmosphere humid and oppressive, especially in hot weather. Mohammad, a mill worker, in his complain to the Indian Factory Labour Commission of 1908 said: "We have to work in that great heat and are exhausted, so much so that at times men faint in that hot weather and have to be taken home in carts."[47] The air in the mills being impure and unhealthy, the operatives often contracted respiratory diseases such as tuberculosis. Long hours and confinement in a polluted atmosphere impaired the health of operatives, who aged prematurely, becoming unfit for mill work at the early age of 40 or 45. There was, therefore, an absence of older operatives in the mills, for example in 1908, in spite of the shortage of labour.[48] The worker of Ahmedabad was underweight and undersized. The children examined by the Factory Labour Commission of 1908 were found to be in poor health, thin and listless due to the overtime and overwork that they did.

The insecurity of the worker was another adverse factor. If the mill stopped in the day for some reason, the workers were sent away without compensation. They could not leave the mill while the machinery was running. In none of the mills was there any definite system of insurance against accidents or old age.[49]

Medical facilities were provided in a few of the Ahmedabad mills. Ranchhodlal's mills were better equipped than most others in welfare measures for operatives. Fines and unclaimed wages were credited to saving funds from which sick and injured workmen were given a weekly allowance. There was a small dispensary in the mill which was attended by a doctor every day. This mill also had a night school which was attended by 75 boys employed in the mill and where a factory clerk taught, receiving an extra four rupees for his work. But many mills which started schools for mill children ran into trouble. If the education was made compulsory, the children left the mill, and if it was made optional, the children did not come to school at all. The children did not come even if inducements were offered to them. A large number of mill owners were not in favour of providing education to child workers, as they thought it would encroach on their playtime and increase their burden. Such workers were, therefore, illiterate and did not get the benefit of education.[50]

There were very few other amenities provided by the mills to the workers. Though toilets were provided in all the mills, they were not kept clean. Mills provided water for drinking and washing, but in many mills, drinking water from wells was more or less contaminated. The mills would very often shut off the supply of municipal water to save money. In June 1909, cholera broke out in one of the mills. The outbreak was attributed to the water supply, and it was found on investigation that the drinking water was being drawn from the backwaters of the river Sabarmati.[51]

Mill-hands in Ahmedabad received only moderate wages. Their wages were lower than wages in Bombay but higher than those of farm labourers and other labourers in the city. They were paid better than some of the artisans engaged in cotton textile manufacturing but less than the skilled silk and *kinkhab* artisans. Generally, they were paid in cash and both by piecework and by time. The operatives earned Rs 7 to 14 a month while *mukadams* received Rs 20 to 50 a month in 1875.[52] The collector of Ahmedabad stated in 1888 that mill-hands in Ahmedabad received only moderate wages. For example, a *mukadam* got Rs 15 to 20, hands at the frames or carding machine reeler Rs 7 to 9, winders Rs 6, warpers Rs 10 and so on. The ordinary rate of wages elsewhere for common coolies was Rs 3 to 5 a month, and the mill-hands were more or less skilled labourers. Beyond the fact that they were regularly paid, they had little or no advantage over ordinary labourers and certainly not over employees of the railway companies.[53]

The peculiarity of the Ahmedabad mills was that they paid their operatives weekly, unlike the Bombay mills, which paid once a month. For mill-hands on small wages, this was an important consideration.[54] However, from 1895, the Mill-Owners' Association of Ahmedabad decided to pay mill-hands fortnightly in spite of a strong protest by labourers expressed through the mammoth strike of 1895 discussed later in this chapter. Generally, wages were paid on piece work, so that earnings were higher in summer when hours were longer.

The wages remained steady, but when famine conditions in Kutch and Rajasthan led to an influx of labourers in 1899, mill owners reduced the wages, which resulted in strikes.[55] During the *swadeshi* movement (1905–1908), the demand for labour rose. As a result, the wages of labourers were raised.

Tables given in the annual factory reports of the presidency of Bombay showing the wages of skilled and unskilled labourers in the important factories show that there was great disparity in wages between skilled and unskilled labour. They also show that wages of unskilled women workers were lower than that of unskilled men workers. There was no definite system of granting bonuses or other allowances. Bonus was given for excellence of work, regular attendance or for extra production.

Women and children were used extensively in the mills of Ahmedabad since they provided cheap and manageable labour. The children were employed in the cotton mills as piecers and doffers. There was a demand for bigger boys and young adults due to the nimbleness of their fingers, so essential for piecing, and for their lower height which enabled them to work at the spinning frames without fatigue.[56]

Before the Factory Act IX of 1881 was implemented, small boys of 5 to 12 years worked from sunrise to sunset and stayed on the premises for the whole day. They took frequent intervals for rest and play and thus worked for about nine hours. As mentioned earlier, after 1881, Ahmedabad mill owners evolved the shift system of six hours for the children for administrative convenience. The mill owners Ranchhodlal Chhotalal and Bechardas Ambiadas favoured the shift system.[57]

Many abuses regarding child labour prevailed in Ahmedabad factories. Of these, the employment of children on a full-time basis and the employment of underage children were the most serious. Double employment of the same child in different mills was common in Ahmedabad.[58] To control the abuse of double employment, the mills were asked to maintain a bound register of children's certificates. The certificate contained elaborate personal details and identification marks of the children to make identification easy. In Ahmedabad, a duplicate of this certificate was carried in a small tin case worn by the children when at work.[59] Even so, abuses persisted. During the course of its inspection, the Indian Factory Commission of 1908 found that in Ahmedabad seven per cent half-timers were underage, while children under 14 years worked as male adults, because there was great demand for such children owing to their nimbleness.[60] In Ahmedabad, about 10 to 12 per cent of the total workers were children. Many times, half-timers were retained for longer hours under the pretext of attending school on the mill premises. Sometimes, even small underage children who accompanied their mothers to the mills were employed as labourers. The long hours of work, the noise of the machines, poor ventilation, excessively hot rooms impaired the children's health and stunted their growth. Many of the abuses regarding child labour, such as double employment, continued throughout the period covered in this work. Children were employed in the mills of Ahmedabad in a larger number than in Bombay.

Before the Indian Factory Act XI of 1891 came into force, women were extensively employed in all the departments of the mills, except the weaving department, in Ahmedabad. They were employed in card and throstle rooms and in reeling, winding and cotton picking.[61] They generally worked as frame-minders. A team of two women, an old woman and a young one, tended one frame.

They worked at the steam-operated machinery and worked the same hours as men before the Factory Act of 1891 came into force. This Act restricted the working hours of women to 11 hours. This led to the replacement of women mill-hands by men as frame-minders, while women were generally transferred to the reeling and winding departments. The welfare measures of the Act proved injurious to skilled women mill-hands who were thus deprived of their livelihood.[62] The mill owners of Ahmedabad ruthlessly discharged many of the female labourers as the new 11 work hours laid down for women caused administrative difficulties. After the Act was passed, some 259 women were thrown out of employment, and the wages of the rest were reduced by 25 per cent. Even after the women strongly protested, the Government Resolution General Department No. 2815, August 13, 1892, decided that it would be unnecessary to exempt the Ahmedabad mills.[63] The Act of 1891, thus, had an adverse effect on the women labourers of Ahmedabad. Only those women in the reeling and winding departments who worked shorter hours and came and went at their convenience were not affected.[64]

Before 1891, women workers were not allowed to bring their infants and non-working children to the mills with them. They would either go home to feed their infants or had their babies brought to them at the mills by relatives. Gujjee Sukku, aged 22, employed on the roving frame, would go home to feed the child at noon and her mother-in-law would bring the child twice a day to the mill. Ballee and Hurri Passee, both Waghris and working on the roving frame, also stated in their evidence to the Indian Factory Commission 1890 that their infants were brought to them during working hours.[65]

The restriction on bringing infants and young children to the mills was not in force when the Indian Factory Labour Commission visited the Ahmedabad factories in 1908. There were no crèches in the mill, so infants and small children stayed with their mothers in the workrooms. It was not uncommon for women to administer opium to their children to lull them to sleep. The government of Bombay presidency appointed a woman doctor to enquire into the question of maternity benefits, and her investigations showed that opium was given to 78 per cent of the children of factory workers. The family budget enquiry by the labour office in Ahmedabad stated that opium was administered to children both in Sholapur and Ahmedabad.[66] Occasionally, women workers left small children with their elderly relatives or neighbours, paying them small amounts. Later, in the 1920s, some of the mills finally provided crèches.

Women employed in the factories were usually married, carrying the double burden of caring for home and children and working in the factory. Women workers were generally from lower castes, as women from the upper castes and Muslim women did not work in factories. After 1891, the number of women workers decreased and was smaller than that in Bombay.

III

The mill industry provided new opportunities of employment to various labouring classes, artisans and peasants. This was particularly true of the Kolis, Waghris, Rawalias and other such communities, who were very poor and had quite often to depend on begging for their livelihood. Now with factory work, which gave regular pay, they could build better houses, wear brighter clothes, eat better food and invest in ornaments.[67]

The factory worker in Ahmedabad lived by factory work alone. The wages were not high but enough for subsistence and a few amenities. The collector of Ahmedabad observed about mill workers that they were "frequently better off and less involved in debt."[68] *The Administration Report of the Working of the Municipality of Ahmedabad 1892–93* noted that there was a continual excess in the consumption of clothes and metal ware by the labourers, who were getting comfortable wages in the mills.[69] Though life was without frills and left no margin for saving against bad times, this class was certainly not the most deprived segment of the urban population of Ahmedabad.

The mill workers' standard of living was low. Their diet was simple. The worker spent more than half of his income on food. In addition to grains—wheat, rice and bajri—pulses, vegetables and *ghee*, or clarified butter, were the main items on his diet. Tea, milk and sugar were also included in the household budget. The enquiry conducted from February to August in 1926 into working class family budgets in Ahmedabad showed that a worker spent nearly 58 per cent on food, 12 per cent on house rent, seven per cent on fuel and lighting, 10 per cent on clothing and 13 per cent on miscellaneous items.[70]

Drinking and smoking were quite common among factory workers. Even the Waghri and Bhangi women workers and children smoked. *Bidikhanas* mushroomed near the mills, frequented by workers during working hours. At home, the workers smoked a *hukka*. Betel chewing was also common, though opium and drug taking was not very common.[71]

The workers preferred to live in the vicinity of the mills. Their quarters were overcrowded. Their houses were close and confined, being small, damp and ill-ventilated. The predominant type of housing in Bombay and Ahmedabad was the single room tenement, or *chawl. Chawls* around the mills accommodated the workers who poured in from outside Ahmedabad. Ventilation and lighting were so poor that the majority of tenements had no windows at all while some had one, while hardly any had more than one window. The workers used common privies which either belonged to the municipality or to the *panch.* Municipal water taps supplied water shared by eight to ten tenements. The surroundings were filthy. The narrow gutters for carrying off waste water and sewage gave out a strong stench. The natural result of such an environment was epidemics and a high rate of mortality among the workers. The furnishing in a worker's house was minimal, but there was invariably a cot or a *charpoy* with a thin mattress on it. In Ahmedabad, there was a distinct attempt by the mill owners to provide accommodation to the mill workers in the compounds. They built *chawls* for them from the second decade of the 20th century.[72]

The long factory hours disrupted family life, leaving no time for leisure. Quite often, husbands and wives worked in different factories. Often enough, an agriculturist, having left his family back in the village, would come to the city to seek his fortune in the mills. Such disruption quite often led to temptations and to broken marriages.

However, compared to the workers in Bombay, more workers in Ahmedabad managed to bring their families to the city and enjoy a permanent family life there. But once a worker left his village, his links with it ended. He rarely visited it except occasionally for a few festivals. Only seven per cent of workers remitted money to their villages. Families of mill workers were joint families or nuclear families, the average family consisting of four members.[73]

The worker was not alienated from his caste by his factory work and followed caste rules and traditions. Caste feasts during weddings and after the death of a member were an important part of his social life. Religion, too, had a strong hold over him. Though long hours did not leave much time for recreation or leisure, his favourite mode of recreation was religious gatherings where the *manbhattas* sang *bhajans* or devotional songs, and recited *kathas* or stories from religious scriptures, with songs. Folk dances and plays were other forms of entertainment.[74]

Two evils which occasionally destroyed a happy family were drunkenness and indebtedness. There was more drunkenness among mill-hands than among those in other employments. One reason was that they were better paid, and the other was that they believed that they required some kind of stimulant to keep up their strength. The drinking habit was not uncommon even among women workers. This habit ruined the health of mill-hands.[75] In his written evidence to the Indian Factory Labour Commission of 1908, Vaikunthbhai Ambalal Desai wrote: "He is the best paid coolie and but for the ruin brought by drinking and reckless expenditure on pay days, he would be richer, healthier and happier by far than the middle class man of India."[76]

The drunkenness and extravagance rampant among the mill-hands gave rise to the evil of heavy indebtedness. Though they earned more than a subsistence wage, they always remained in debt. The official report of 1901 says: "In Ahmedabad, both debt and drink are the rule rather than exception."[77] Many times, both husband and wife earned well, but they hardly ever saved, as they had to pay heavy interest to the moneylenders on the money borrowed for weddings or ceremonies. Social customs and religious observances were responsible for great waste of money, often out of proportion to the income. Once the worker got into debt, the high interest rate kept him forever in debt. The household budget left but a small margin for emergencies and extraordinary expenses. In 1890, Sanker Seva Raval earned Rs 2 a week but gave 12 annas a week to the moneylender. He found his pay insufficient for his wife, child and himself. Ballee, a Waghri woman, also stated in her evidence to the Indian Factory Commission in 1890 that though both husband and wife worked, they hardly saved. They were in debt to an amount of about Rs 80 to Rs 100, which they had borrowed at the time of their marriage for expenses.[78] Payment of high interest to *sahukars* (moneylenders) was one of the major causes of their poverty.

However, some labourers were thrifty. For instance, the Kanbi weavers saved money as did the Dheds. The higher caste worker's habits were more sober, and his higher wages as a skilled worker enabled him to save some money to meet emergencies. Even so, such savings were hardly sufficient to support retirement. Muslims, on the other hand, spent extravagantly on luxuries and clothes and hardly ever saved money.[79]

The amount of debt varied from a few rupees to, many a times, the whole of the monthly income. The rates of interest ranged from one to four annas per rupee per month. Generally, the rate of interest varied from 12 per cent to 24 per cent. Usually, workers borrowed from the local *sahukars* or pathans.[80]

IV

The first recorded strike occurred in 1878, to which reference is found in the *Ahmedabad Gazetteer* (1879). It stated: "A short time ago all the hands in one of the Ahmedabad spinning mills struck work on finding out that one of the Marwadi workmen was a Dhed who had passed himself off as a higher caste."[81]

Thus, the first known strike of Ahmedabad was sparked off by a social grievance. Strikes were common in the 1890s, but they were sporadic, short-lived, unorganised and small-scale. Until 1917, there was no union or organisation of the operatives. There was no system of arbitration or conciliation or any other means of settling industrial disputes. Ahmedabad workers did not have representatives, unlike the middle class Lokhande in Bombay, to guide them. But an unnamed and unwritten bond of union did exist among the workers.[82] This helped them to come together for collective action. They usually expressed their discontent by striking work, stopping work until their disputes were settled. In 1892, the mill owner Ranchhodlal Chhotalal, in his replies to the Royal Commission on Labour's (RCL) questionnaire, stated: "There have been no strikes in the last 10 years, in the sense in which they take place in England. Occasionally, the hands stop away for a day or so, when they are fined for absence or bad work, and when a reduction of wages is attempted.'[83] He added that, owing to many new mills which had come up at the time, industrial disputes had increased, but such disputes lasted at the most for a day and therefore were not recorded.

GG Pandit, the secretary of the newly born Ahmedabad Mill-Owners' Association in 1892, in his replies to the RCL, stated:

> As far as our Indian work-people are concerned, the occasions for strikes are very rare and far between, and even then they are not general. Even these few and far between strikes can be avoided if employers of labour in the cotton-spinning industry are more sympathetic than they are at present and pay more attention to the improvement of the work-people.[84]

The early strikes were mainly caused by social and economic grievances. These were purely local and mainly affected one mill or one of its departments. However, such strikes were significant in that they reflected an emerging class consciousness in the nascent working class, which cut across caste and community barriers. The strikes also show that, in this initial phase of industrialisation, a "perfect harmony" did not exist between the employers and the employed.

Striking work was not the only form of protest known to this incipient class. In 1891, when the proposed Factory Act intended to restrict the working hours of women to 11 hours, the female operatives of Ahmedabad who worked at the 'moving' machinery sent a petition to the Bombay government pleading for removal of this restriction on working hours, otherwise they would soon be dismissed by the mill owners and lose their source of livelihood. As mentioned earlier, mill owners ruthlessly removed about 259 women workers and reduced the pay of others by 25 per cent. This caused great discontent among the female workers of Ahmedabad. It is interesting to speculate on who could have led these illiterate women workers to protest in such an organised manner. It appears that Sorabji Dinshaw Karaka, the Parsi manager of Trikamlal Harilal Spinning & Weaving Co., who had been associated with the Ahmedabad mill industry since 1882, was sympathetic to the cause of female workers and must have helped them. He wrote to the leading papers advocating the claims of the mill-hands for consideration. In his opinion, the decrease of working hours for women would mean great hardship for them.[85] He may well have guided the female operatives to send a petition to the government. Public opinion, reflected in the contemporary native newspapers of Bombay presidency such as *Gujarati* and *Gujarat Darpan*, sympathised with the cause of female operatives in Ahmedabad. But the petition was turned down by the government. This action of the government was severely criticised by contemporary newspapers. For instance, *Gujarati*, a newspaper noted for its strong opinions, in its issue of the August 21, 1892, exclaimed: "They asked for bread but have been offered a stone instead."[86]

Working class solidarity was evidenced in Ahmedabad when one of the largest strikes of the mill operatives ever known in Bombay presidency occurred during July 5–13, 1895. All the weavers in the 13 mills struck work without notice and workers in other departments joined them. The cause of the strike was the resolution by the Mill-Owners' Association to pay the weavers fortnightly instead of the weekly payment, which had been in force ever since the first mill was started in Ahmedabad.

The notice conveying this change in the schedule of payment was put up in all the mills in the first week of June. Only a week's notice was given before the change would be implemented. On July 1, 1895, the weavers of all the mills struck work. The observance of Mohurrum fell on July 3 and 4. These two days passed quietly. But on Friday, July 5, a mob of 2,000 mill workers proceeded to Ranchhodlal's mill at Shahpur and smashed the windows and destroyed some of the machinery. The police of Ahmedabad could not check the mob. Collector Gibbs, with the help of army troops, controlled the mob and arrested 33 rioters. Through the intervention of the collector, a settlement was reached between the mill workers and the mill owners. About 10,000 workers took part in this strike. The strike was crushed and wages continued to be paid fortnightly. The strikers could not achieve their goal, but this was the first time that the mill owners experienced the united power of the mill-hands.

Gibbs, blamed the mill owners because they gave only a week's notice to the workers before introducing such an important change in their payment and that, too, on the eve of Mohurrum.[87] The *Kathiawar Times*, a weekly Ahmedabad newspaper, in its issue of July 10 gave a detailed account of the strike as follows:

> The Mill-Owners' Association at Ahmedabad having declined to yield to the threats of the mill-hands, they have continued the strike, but no further mischief has been done. The police have been taking precautionary measures by placing police guards at the mill. *Sowars* are patrolling near the mills and the grain market. Mr Reid,

> the Commissioner, Mr Gibbs, the Collector, Messrs Kabraji and Robertson, Assistant Collectors, the Police Superintendent and Mr Grey, Police Inspector, are all going round the mills. Yesterday, all the mills were closed. Today four mills were opened but without weavers. Thirty-four of the ring-leaders have been arrested. The mill-hands appealed to the Collector to intercede to keep to the old system. Today, the mill-hands met at Kankaria Talao, but the police dispersed them.

Ahmedabad Times, in its issue of July 7, reported that the number of mill-hands on strike was very great and they were greatly excited. The paper requested the police to take prompt steps to prevent them from causing a disturbance.[88]

These contemporary accounts show that the strike was of great magnitude and shook the city. The accounts just quoted also indicate that the excited workers became violent and rioted at the beginning. Though the police suppressed the riots, the concern of the officials and their vigilance and that of the people showed that the working class had emerged as a strong social force to be reckoned with. This massive strike also revealed that though workers came from different socioeconomic backgrounds, they could combine to protest against the mill owners when the need arose. A rudimentary class-consciousness among the workers had finally emerged.

During the next two decades, there were no general or massive strikes like the 1895 strike. But strikes by mill workers were common and frequent. In the years 1898 and 1899, the famine in Rajasthan and Kathiawar brought many labourers to Ahmedabad so that the supply of labour often became greater than the demand. When mill owners took the opportunity to reduce wages, mill workers protested and struck work.[89]

In 1905, the introduction of electric light and the boom in textile markets prompted many mill owners to work the mills for excessive hours. This caused resentment and discontent among the workers who agitated, causing mill owners to concede their demands and stop the use of artificial light in the mills.[90] During the first decade of the 20th century, many new mills were started in Ahmedabad, increasing the demand for labour. There was a temporary shortage of labour in the city. Mill-hands took the opportunity to demand higher wages. On several occasions, mill owners had to concede this in view of the shortage of labour and their fear that other mills would snap up their workers.[91] The workers were almost masters of the situation.

Though mill workers had learnt the mechanism of local strikes and forced employers to comply with their demands in many cases, they could not establish any permanent organisation or union during this early phase of industrialisation. This class was illiterate and poor and they had neither the leisure nor, more importantly, the proper leadership needed for organised activities. Caste, religion and regional barriers also impeded the formation of any proper union.

During this period, the middle class did not provide any leadership to the nascent working class. The Ahmedabad working class did not have any representatives, unlike Lokhande and Kelkar who led the contemporary labour movements in Bombay and gave advice on workers' problems. The literate middle class elite of Ahmedabad during this phase were indifferent and apathetic towards the working class, as the latter was too small in size to attract attention. However, some of the issues and problems of this new class, such as illiteracy, drunkenness, lack of thrift, sexual immorality, did draw the attention of the middle class. In the leading journal *Buddhi Prakash*, many articles highlighted these problems and also suggested solutions. Such articles insisted that the mill owners should adopt a paternalistic attitude towards the illiterate workers and orient them to virtues like thrift, temperance and good behaviour.[92] In the 1890s, the temperance movement had gained momentum among the middle class of Ahmedabad. Many lectures were organised under the aegis of the Gujarat Vernacular Society (GVS) on the virtues of temperance. Mill owners in particular were exhorted by the speakers to save their labourers from the grip of this evil by removing liquor shops from the vicinity of the mills and to inculcate temperance by giving prizes to those who abstained from drinking.[93]

On the whole, there was very little sympathy for or understanding of the working class on part of mill owners. Dr Nair, a member of the Indian Factory Labour Commission of 1908, in his minute of dissent, observes:

> Even some of the most enlightened and educated Indian gentlemen with whom I discussed industrial questions, had not a single word of sympathy with the labourers to express. They were all anxious to make up for the lost time and to push industrial venture and to accumulate wealth. As for the workers, they were part of the machinery of production and nothing more.[94]

This was true of the capitalists of Ahmedabad, too. There was hardly any direct contact between the worker and the mill owner. The only link between them was the jobber, who himself hailed from the working class. The mill owners' ignorance of the conditions of this class made them quite apathetic towards it. This point was also emphasised by collector Gibbs in his report on the strike of 1895.[95] Welfare measures in this early phase were minimal. It has been mentioned earlier that medical facilities were scarce, while compensation for injured mill workers was not always paid. Living conditions were unsanitary as were working conditions. The attitude of mill owners lacked both sympathy and humanity.

The evidence given by the mill owners of Ahmedabad to the Factory and Labour Commissions of 1875, 1885, 1890, 1892 and 1908 revealed their exploitative tendency. The majority of mill owners justified the long hours of work and did not want any legislation which would restrict the hours or interfere with factory work. As Dr Nair observed, they were mainly interested in achieving maximum profits. All the mill owners united to achieve this purpose and established the Mill-Owners' Association in 1891. In this way, this class organised and united itself much earlier than did the working class.

The lack of sympathy and of humanitarian considerations by mill owners gave rise to feelings of disharmony between mill owners and workers. Mill owners did not make any attempt in this period to improve the conditions of the working class. The protests staged by labour during this period were a clear symptom of this feeling of disharmony. But the class consciousness among the workers was not strong enough in this period to generate any intense feeling of class conflict.

As mentioned earlier, the working class of Ahmedabad was a heterogeneous group which comprised various castes and communities. Though caste or religion was not generally an impediment to the recruitment of workers, initially, as observed earlier, Dheds and untouchables were not permitted to work in the mills for fear of ritual defilement. Later, when they were permitted to work, they were not given an entry into the better paid weaving department where higher classes like Kanbis and Khatris were preponderant.

Some caste attitudes persisted at work. The age-old sociocultural dimension of the caste, such as the restriction on inter-dining and ritual notion of pollution and purity, persisted. Many caste Hindu workers did not eat any meal in the mill lest they be ritually defiled, preferring to eat at home either before or after their shift.[96] Covered sheds were provided where meals could be eaten, but workers of the same caste and religion chose a particular corner and ate together at the same place. Two Kanbi weavers complained to the Factory Labour Commission in 1908 that they were put to great inconvenience to look for a place to eat their food where they could avoid contamination by lower castes.[97] Thus, the ingrained ideas of purity and pollution persisted and determined behaviour in the mills.

Factory work created a new work situation in this caste-ridden society. In a factory, different castes had to work side by side and do similar kinds of work. This was a vital socioeconomic change. However, the emergence of this new class did not obliterate the caste identity of the worker. In his private life, he continued to follow caste rules and traditions; his ties to his caste remained strong.

Notwithstanding the persistence of caste identity among working class people, one can perceive a rudimentary class consciousness emerging in this period. They struck work and protested against unjust demands of mill owners. They shared a common lot and often united to solve common problems. Thus, a proto-class had emerged, later to be developed into a fully conscious working class.

Notes

1. Bhagwanlal Badshah, *The Life of Rao Bahadur Ranchorelal Chhotalal, C.I.FE.*, Bombay, 1899, p. 39.
2. Bombay Government, *Annual Factory Report of the Presidency of Bombay for the year 1914*, pp. i–xxiv. Henceforth cited as *FA* and its year.
3. *FA 1922*, pp. iv–xiii.
4. *Ahmedabad Gazetteer*, pp. 132–139.
5. Bombay Government, *Report of the Commissioners appointed by the Governor of Bombay In Council to inquire into the Condition of the Operatives in the Bombay Factories and the Necessity or Otherwise for the Passing of a Factories Act, Bombay,* 1875, p. 99. Henceforth cited as *FC 1875.*
6. *Ahmedabad Gazetteer*, p. 39 and 48.
7. Government of India, *Report of the Indian Factory Commission, 1890,* Calcutta, 1890, p. 60. Henceforth cited as *FC 1890.*
8. Judicial Department, 222/1895, p. 248.
9. *Ahmedabad Gazetteer*, p. 80.
10. *Ibid.*, p. 48.
11. Government of India, *Report of the Indian Factory Labour Commission 1908*, Vol. II, Evidence, Simla, 1908, pp. 1–27. Henceforth cited as *FC 1908* and its volume.
12. *FC 1890*, pp. 58–67.
13. Judicial Department, 222/1895, p. 248.
14. *FA 1892*, p. 6.
15. Bombay Government, *Royal Commission on India Labour, Memorandum from the Government of Bombay, 1929*. Bombay 1929, p. 10. Henceforth cited as *RCL 1929, Memorandum*.
16. The witnesses whose evidence was taken by the Indian Factory Commission,1908, were working in the weaving departments, being

either Kanbis or Muslims; Shankarrai Amritrai, *Amdavad no Jivan Vikas* (in Gujarati), Ahmedabad,1921, p. 210.

17. Government of Bombay Labour Office, *Report on an Enquiry into Working Class Family Budgets in Ahmedabad,* Bombay, 1928. p. 3.
18. Bombay Government, *Report and Proceedings of the Commission Appointed to Consider the Working of the Factories in the Bombay Presidency*, Bombay, 1885, p. 136. Henceforth cited as *FC 1885.*
19. *FC 1890*, pp. 858–69.
20. *RCL 1929, Memorandum*, p. 2.
21. *Ibid.*, pp. 2–7.
22. *FA 1906*, p. 3; *FA 1913*, p. 4; *FA 1914*, p. 5; *FA 1908*, Vol. II, p. 10.
23. *FA 1892*, P. 5.
24. *Ibid*, p. 13.
25. *FC 1890*, pp. 58–67.
26. *RCL 1929, Memorandum*, p. 6.
27. *RCL 1929, Memorandum*, p. 6.
28. *Ibid.*, p. 9.
29. *FC* 1908, Vol. I, p. 3–4.
30. *FC 1890*, pp. 58–67.
31. *RCL 1929, Memorandum*, p. 9.
32. Government of India, *Return to an Address of Hon. House of Commons, Dated April 15, 1889 for a Copy of Reports on the Working of the Indian Factories Act Made to the Government of India in Reply to Inquiries Recently Directed by the Secretary of State for India,* London, 1889, pp. 70–71.
33. *FC 1885*, pp. 136–37.
34. *FC 1890*, pp. 58–67.
35. *FC 1875*, p. 96.
36. *FC 1908*, Vol. II, p. 28.
37. *Ibid.*, p. 15.
38. Government of India. *Report of Textile Factories Labour Committee Appointed by the Government of India on the 17th December 1906 to enquire into the Conditions of Factory Labour in India with Appendices*, Bombay, 1907, p. 16. Henceforth cited as *IFLC 1906.*
39. *FC 1908*, Vol. II, p. 12.
40. *Report on the Working of the Indian Factories Act Made to the Government of India 1889,* p. 71.
41. *FC 1890*, p. 620.

42. Government of Great Britain, *Royal Commission of Labour, Foreign Report, Vol. II, The Colonies and the Indian Empire With An Appendix on the Migration of Labour,* Parliamentary Papers1892, XXXVI, Part V, p. 117. Henceforth cited as *RC 1892.*
43. *FA 1896*, p. 20.
44. *FC 1908*, Vol. II, p. 17.
45. *FA 1892–1914.*
46. *RCL 1892*, pp. 117-18; *FC 1890*, pp. 61 and 63.
47. *FC 1908*, Vol. II, p. 28.
48. *Ibid.* Vol. I, p. 26.
49. *FC 1890*, pp. 61 and 65.
50. *Ibid.*, pp. 62 and 2–27.
51. *FA 1909*, p. 2.
52. *FC 1875*, pp. 99–100.
53. *Reports on the Working of the Indian Factories Act made to the Government of India 1889*, p. 71.
54. *FC 1890*, p. 59.
55. *FA 1899*, p. 3.
56. *FC 1908*, Vol. I, pp. 14–17.
57. *FC 1875*, pp. 95-97; *FC 1890*, pp. 3 and 6.
58. *FC 1908*, p. 3.
59. *TFLC 1906*, p. 11,
60. *FC 1908*, Vol. I, pp. 16–17.
61. *FC 1895*, p. 137.
62. *FA* 1892, p. 6; FC 1890, pp. 3–5.
63. *FA 1892*, p. 6.
64. *FC 1890*, pp. 63–64.
65. *Ibid.*, pp. 58–67.
66. *RCL 1929, Memorandum*, p. 10.
67. *Ahmedabad Gazetteer*, p. 79, p. 133.
68. *FA 1896*, p. 3.
69. Ahmedabad Municipality, *Administration Report of the Working of the Municipality of Ahmedabad 1892–93*, p. 43.
70. Government of Bombay Labour Office, *Report of an Enquiry into the Working Class Family Budgets in Ahmedabad*, Bombay, 1928, pp. 14–16; Mahadev Desai, *A Righteous Struggle*, Ahmedabad, 1951, pp. 75–82.

71. *FC 1908*, Vol. II, pp. 13–14; *The Enquiry into the Working Class Family Budgets of Ahmedabad*, p. 22; *FC 1890*, p. 63.
72. *The Enquiry into the Working Class Family Budgets of Ahmedabad*, pp. 17–27; FC 1908, Vol. II, p. 1.
73. *Ibid.*, pp. 5–8; Shankarrai Amritrai, *op.cit.*, p. 212; RCL 1929, Memorandum, p. 10.
74. Shankarrai Amritrai, *op. cit.*, p. 212.
75. *Buddhi Prakash*, May 1887, pp. 113–168.
76. *FC 1908*, Vol. II, p. 17.
77. *FA 1901*, p. 2.
78. *FC 1890*, p. 65.
79. *FC 1908*, Vol. II, p. 13.
80. Mahadeo Desai, *op.cit.*, pp. 56–57; *RCL Memorandum*. pp. 164–165.
81. *Ahmedabad Gazetteer*, p. 48.
82. *RCL,* 1892, p. 132.
83. *Ibid.*, pp. 117–118.
84. *Ibid.*, p. 120.
85. *FC 1890*, p. 65.
86. *RNP* for the week ending August 27, 1892, p. 9.
87. The account of the strike is based on the report of the district superintendent of police, Ahmedabad, dated July 1895, and collector Gibbs, dated July 18, 1895, in Maharashtra State Archives, Judicial Department of Vol. No. 222/1895, pp. 237–263. *FA 1895*, pp. 5–6.
88. *RNP* for the work ending July 13, 1895, p. 22.
89. *FA 1899*, p. 3.
90. *FA 1905*, p. 40; *FC 1908*, Vol. II, pp. 1–28.
91. *FA 1906*, P. 2; *FC 1908*, Vol. II, p. 1.
92. *Buddhi Prakash*, May 1887, pp. 113–116.
93. *Ibid.,* October 1, 1889; March 1895, p. 89; February 1983, p. 30.
94. *FC 1908*, Vol. I, p. 104.
95. Judicial Department, 222/1895, pp. 261–262.
96. *FC 1885*, p. 137.
97. *FC 1908*, Vol. I, p. 104.

9

The Changing Face of Ahmedabad

The process of the urbanisation of Ahmedabad was given a strong impetus by the growth of the textile mill industry and by the coming of the railways, helping the city to emerge as the second largest city in Bombay presidency. Ahmedabad had never looked back, whereas other cities of Gujarat, even Surat, had shown diminishing returns. The population of Ahmedabad had almost doubled in 40 years, from 1,16,873 in 1872 to 2,16,667 in 1911[1], rising further to 2,70,775 in 1921 and 3,10,000 in 1931.[2] This population growth, as well as the prosperity of the city, was largely the result of the textile industry, a growth somewhat steadier than that of any other city in the presidency, never having been interrupted by a severe epidemic of plague.[3]

I

In the last decade of the 19th century—in fact, soon after the 1880s—the city's population grew rapidly, following the growth of the textile industry. By 1921, almost one-third of the city's population was supported by cotton industries, which included cotton ginning, cleaning, pressing, spinning, sizing and weaving. There were 43,763 factory workers and 2,386 higher-ranked workers employed in the textile mills that had proliferated in the first two decades of the 20th century. As against this, there were only 1,469 home workers engaged in handloom weaving and spinning. Thus, there were 47,618 workers and 40,347 dependents making a total of 87,965 people entirely supported by the textile industry.[4]

Population statistics show that the female population as a proportion of male population decreased from the 1890s onwards owing to the influx of male factory workers from the provinces of Marwad, Kathiawad and other parts of Gujarat. The immigration of male labourers, sometimes without their families, affected the sex ratio in the city. The extension of the railway from Ahmedabad to Rajasthan, Malwa and Kathiawad facilitated immigration from these parts.

With the growth of the population, all the segments of the city's heterogeneous population—Hindus (including Jains), Muslims, Christians, Parsis, Jews—expanded in size. The Hindu segment remained preponderant. The second largest segment was the Muslim, but this grew more slowly than the Hindu segment. Other communities, though minuscule in number, made their presence felt in the city's economic, civic and cultural life.

The Hindus and the Muslims were the major communities and are discussed elsewhere in this work. This section concentrates on the minority communities of Parsis, Jews and Christians.

The Gujarati-speaking Parsis comprised a westernised and literate segment, which added verve and colour to Ahmedabad society. They enlivened the city's cultural scene, taking a keen interest in theatre, music and cinema. They also actively participated in the municipal activities of the city.

The Parsi population rose steadily from 440 in 1872 to 1,562 in 1921. In an earlier chapter, we have noted that the Parsi community had a *dokhma* or Tower of Silence and an *agiary* (a fire temple) built in 1842 and 1846 respectively. The *agiary* was built by Seth Kharshedji Behramji Nanavati in Bukhara Mohalla near the Khamasa Chowk, and the land surrounding it was donated by Seth Cawasji Mancherji Karanjwala who also built a *dharamshala* in 1849 at that place. The original *agiary* was damaged and the *dharamshala* destroyed in the great Sabarmati flood of 1875. Behramji Nanavati repaired the *agiary*, consecrated the *atash dadgah* and gave it to the Parsi Panchayat to manage.[5]

The Parsi Panchayat in Ahmedabad was founded in 1863 when Kharshedji Nusserwanji contributed Rs 2,000 towards its fund. Leading Parsi residents of the city such as Pestonji Vakil, Mancherji Karanjwala, Kharshedji Nanavati, Dinshaw Karaka and Shapurji Mughal were its trustees.[6]

As the Parsi community increased in number, it felt a great need for a proper religious establishment in the city. As a result, a new and more impressive *atash dadgah* was built on the site of the old one in Bukhara Mohalla in 1884. It was built at an expense of Rs 20,975 by Nowroji and Jehangirji Vakil, prominent Parsis of Ahmedabad, in memory of their parents. A residential building for the *mobeds* (priests) was built in the compound, which also housed the offices of the Parsi Panchayat. The establishment became a focal point for the Parsis of Ahmedabad and its environs.[7]

Later, in 1925, another *agiary* was built near the Kankaria Lake by Seth Ardeshir Dosabhai Wadia, Shapurshah Dhanjibhai Mistri and Bai Shirinbai Laher at an expense of Rs 30,000.[8]

Parsis were engaged in trading and in the mill industry. Many Parsis were engineers and technicians in the textile mills, among them were Dinshaw Karaka, Seth Ardeshir Dosabhai Wadia and Seth Shapurshah Dhanjibhai. It was a well-to-do community whose philanthropy benefited Ahmedabad. When the Sabarmati floods devastated the city in 1875, it was Cawasji Mancherji Karanjwala who extended personal and financial help to the victims of the flood.[9] He was active in public life, especially in municipal matters, and enjoyed the confidence of all sections of society.[10]

The Vakils of Ahmedabad were a prominent Parsi family. Pestonji Vakil was one of the city's early settlers. He came to Ahmedabad from Surat in 1814 and set up a shop selling European goods in 1826. He prospered in business to become a leading member of the Parsi community in Ahmedabad and contributed generously to the fund for the Provincial College in 1856. His two sons Nowroji and Jehangirji became prominent businessmen and citizens of the city. Nowroji started his business career when still very young. He undertook contracts to build roads, railway lines and storehouses. His business company was given the agency for salt for Gujarat in 1873 by the government, which later also granted him an opium agency. His younger brother Jehangirji was his business associate. Jehangirji's adopted son Rustamji promoted a textile mill in 1905. Nowroji was a member of the managing committee of the Gujarat Vernacular Society (GVS) and a trustee and president of the Parsi Panchayat. Jehangirji was on the Board of the Gujarat College and the president of the Ahmedabad municipality. He was the honorary secretary of the Parsi Panchayat of Ahmedabad from 1887 to 1901. Both brothers donated a generous amount to rebuild the *agiary* mentioned earlier. In 1893, Nowroji built a *dharamshala* for Parsis on the Salpore road in memory of his wife, Bachubai. It was on this same site that Sorabji Jamsetjee Jeejeebhoy had built a *dharmshala* in 1866 in memory of his daughter Gulmaiji. When the original *dharmshala* was destroyed in the floods, Nowroji built his new *dharamshala* on the same spot. He also built an ophthalmic ward in the compound of the Civil Hospital and instituted various scholarships for all communities.[11] The British government recognised the brothers' services by granting them several awards. In 1917, Nowroji was knighted in recognition of his meritorious services. His nephew Rustamji Vakil, too, was knighted later.

The Parsis were actively associated with the city's municipal affairs. Among the 33 municipal commissioners in 1899–1900, there were five Parsis. This is a telling measure of the involvement of this microscopic community in the city's affairs. Their interest in sports and games led them to start a Parsi Gymkhana in 1895 at the Gaikwad Haveli. Later, in 1905, a special building was built for the Gymkhana at Khanpur.[12]

Parsi women, too, actively participated in the activities of the Gujarat Ladies' Club. Being fashionable, they set the trends in fashion in the city. They attended evening parties and mixed functions. They also staged various entertainment shows and dramas in order to raise funds for various charities.[13]

Another microscopic community was that of the Marathi-speaking Bene Israel Jews. In 1872, there were only 40 Jews, which number rose to 258 in 1911. This small community played an active role in the public life of the city. The Bene Israelis recognised the value of western education and took to the professions of medicine and technology. Many Jews came to Ahmedabad to work in the railway workshop. Some of the city's prominent doctors were Jews. Dr Abraham Erulkar, a doctor in the Civil Hospital, induced Jews from outside Ahmedabad to settle in the city. Dr Joseph Solomon Dandekar, a doctor at the Lunatic Asylum, came to Ahmedabad in 1866. In 1876, he donated a piece of land outside the Delhi Gate on the way to Dudheshwar Temple to build a cemetery for the Jews. Dr Solomon Abraham Erulkar was a very popular doctor in the city. He was the municipal commissioner and member of the managing committee of the GVS. Yet another important Jew of the city was Dr Joseph Benjamin who was the honorary secretary of the Gujarat Sabha and was a champion of temperance. He, too, became municipal commissioner.[14]

Until 1934, there had been no synagogue in the city. To begin with, Dr Abraham Erulkar conducted congregational prayers at his own place. Later, a large place was rented by the Jews for prayers, and in 1934, a synagogue was built, aptly named Magen Abraham after Abraham Erulkar.[15]

The Christian missionaries did not make any distinct mark in Ahmedabad until 1861. They did not succeed in converting many natives. When Rev. Moor began his missionary work in 1863, he found only one Christian convert in the city.[16]

The Irish Presbyterian Church (IPC) began its mission operations in the city and its neighbourhood in 1861. A plot of 300 acres was acquired at Shahwadi. In 1862, nine families travelled 60 miles from Borsad to their new home in a long string of bullock carts and soon settled in their new homes.[17] The colony was popularly known as 'Taylor Para' among the people of Ahmedabad because Rev. TS Taylor of Borsad was instrumental in establishing it. The Christians, who were nicknamed *vishwasis* (believers) by the people of Ahmedabad, caused a flutter when they first arrived in the city. Various false rumours of forced conversions by the Christians spread, creating fear among orthodox people.[18]

36. Dr Motiben Kapadia

37. Sulochanaben Desai

38. Ansuyaben Sarabhai

39. Hargovindas Kantawala

40. Lalshankar Umiashankar

41. Ambalal Sakarlal

42. Ramanbhai Nilkanth

43. Dr Joseph Benjamin

44. Pestonji Vakil

45. Nowroji Pestonji Vakil

46. Bachubai Nowroji Vakil

47. Rustamji Jehangirji Vakil

48. Krishnarao Bholanath

49. Ambalal and
Saraladevi Sarabhai
in London, 1911

50. Ambalal Sarabhai in the first car in
Ahmedabad, near his Shantisadan bungalow, 1910

But the Christian colony at Shahwadi flourished. In 1877, there were 316 native Christians in and around the city. Except for a few boys who attended the city school and the Evangelists in the mission services, all Christians lived in Shahwadi. The number of families had grown from nine in 1861 to 64 in 1877. They had belonged to the Vania, Rajput, Kanbi, Koli, Lohana, Bhil castes before becoming Christians. Among them, the feeling of caste was repressed as far as possible. People originally of different class and castes intermarried. Early marriages were forbidden. Nearly all could read and write. Women were expert in plain and fancy needlework. However, their other social customs hardly underwent any change. They dressed in the same fashion, ate the same food and in most cases retained their Indian names. Most of them were cultivators and used English ploughs for farming.[19]

Shahwadi and its Christian inhabitants remained aloof from the mainstream of the city's life for a long time. Soon, however, their educational activities and their participation in the GVS brought the missionaries into closer contact with the people of Ahmedabad. Rev. JVS Taylor and Rev. R Gillespie participated actively in the literary and educational activities of the GVS. Rev. Taylor studied linguistics under the guidance of poet Dalpatram, Mahipatram, Shastri Vrajlal and some other Sanskrit and Persian scholars. He made a pioneering effort to compile a Gujarati grammar.

The Irish Presbyterian (IP) Mission opened vernacular schools in the city from 1865 onwards. In 1882, they ran six vernacular schools, of which two were for girls and one a mixed school for Dheds, which latter had 60 pupils on its rolls in 1882.[20] In 1866, the IP Mission also started the English school, which became a higher school in 1870 and erected an independent building in 1874.[21] In 1914, the IP Mission was running an English high school and five primary schools for boys and six for girls. It had also opened normal classes for male and female teachers.[22]

The Salvation Army started its missionary work in Ahmedabad in the late 1880s. Its activities and the pomp and show of the visit of its leader General Booth in December 1891 aroused a lot of criticism in the local press.[23] The Salvation Army started a primary school for boys and an industrial school for girls in the city.

The great famine of 1899–1900, popularly known as *chhapanio* (referring to the year 1956 of the Hindu calendar), was an important landmark in the history of Christianity in Gujarat. All over Gujarat, orphanages were being opened by Christian missionaries to deal with the problem of starving children. As a result, there was a substantial increase in the number of Christian converts during this period. In the district of Ahmedabad, there was a rise in the number of converts from 1,592 in 1891 to 3,450 in 1901.[24] The Christian missionaries of Ahmedabad and the Sabarmati baptized about 2,000 famine-stricken children for which they were subsequently criticised by the orthodox Gujarati press.[25]

In Ahmedabad, as elsewhere in Gujarat, the Christian missionaries' efforts in the field of education for women and the downtrodden were commendable. Where the social reformers of the city showed apathy towards the cause of the untouchables, the missionaries educated and reformed them. However, Christianity could not penetrate the bulwark of the orthodox society of Ahmedabad.

II

Increasing prosperity, growth of Western education, contact with the outside world and introduction of technological innovations brought changes in the lifestyle of the rich and middle classes in particular and the people Ahmedabad in general. The cultural interests of the people broadened. Photographs and advertisements in contemporary newspapers and periodicals clearly reveal the changing pattern of recreation and leisure activities, food habits, dress, fashions and cultural interests.

In the last quarter of the 19th century, the educated people of Ahmedabad started taking an interest in new modes of recreation and leisure activities. The theatre, for instance, gained great popularity. Until 1893, there was no regular theatre in the city. However, visiting theatre groups such as the Morbi and Vankaner Natak Mandalis from Saurashtra performed plays which drew large crowds. These plays were performed in Maganbhai Karamchand's *Vadi*, where the audience sat on mattresses or on *durries* on the ground. The repertoire of these plays was drawn from the epics and *puranas*. *Sulochana* and *Bhartruhari* were popular plays. Occasionally, adaptations of Shakespearean plays were performed. *The Merchant of Venice* was very popular. Soon, the city's first theatre group, Shri Deshi Natak Mandali, was established by Dahyabhai Dholsha in the last decade of the 19th century. In 1893, Seth Sarabhai built the first theatre in the city, Anand Bhuvan, at Ghee Kantha in the Shahpur ward. In 1898, Dahyabhai Dholsha also built a theatre called Shantibhuvan near the Civil Hospital at the Ghee Kantha.[26] Dahyabhai was a man of learning who knew Sanskrit, Gujarati and English, having attended college for a couple of years. He composed poems and introduced songs in his plays, which became very popular. His Deshi Natak Mandali staged some very good plays such as *Kanta*, *Ashrumati* and *Harishchandra*.[27]

The amateur theatre groups of the Gujarat Ladies Club, the Zoroastrian Stree Mandal and the Students' Brotherhood staged plays for charity shows. An unusual aspect of these productions was the presence of women on the stage. Theatre-going was gaining popularity. As a result, local newspapers regularly featured advertisement of the plays.

Alexandra, the first cinema hall, was opened in 1912 and showed motion pictures only on Sundays at 9 p.m.[28] Later, Cinema d'France was opened right opposite Ahmedabad railway station.[29] The Gaiety Theatre was converted into a cinema hall. By 1921, there were six theatres in the city.[30] Only English films were available, and an interpreter gave a running commentary in Gujarati so that the audience would understand the film.[31]

Various clubs emerged on the sociocultural scene from the 1880s onwards. The club was a western institution which was fast gaining popularity all over India. The oldest club of Ahmedabad was the Gujarat Club founded in March 1886. Mahipatram played a significant role in starting this club. To begin with, there were only 24 members, but the number increased rapidly to 675 in 1920–21. It was an elite club in which members were native princes, *sethias* and professionals. It was open to all castes and creeds. It had a reading room and facilities for card games, chess, table tennis, billiards, cricket, badminton and lawn tennis. The club began in rented premises and was housed in its own building near Bhadra from 1905.[32]

In 1895, the Ahmedabad Gymkhana Club was founded in the cantonment area mainly for the benefit of European residents. Its members enjoyed the facilities for playing tennis, billiards, badminton and golf. In 1896, the Industrial Club was established for mill owners, managers and technicians associated with the mill industry. In 1919, the Merchants' Club was established to encourage cooperation and friendship among the merchants of the city. Both these clubs provided facilities for outdoor and indoor games.[33]

The activities of the Gujarat Ladies' Club, founded in 1887 and where women of different castes and creeds participated, have been described earlier. The Parsi Gymkhana and the Medical Gymkhana also encouraged sports and other leisure activities.

A strong new interest in western sports and games such as tennis, cricket and football grew in the people of Ahmedabad, cricket becoming the city's most popular game. Cricket news was given coverage in the local newspapers. Various local inter-club and inter-school cricket matches were held, providing great excitement to the people. When Prince Ranjitsingh, the famous cricketer, visited Ahmedabad in 1905, some schools declared a holiday to enable students to watch him play.[34] Tennis, too, was gaining popularity in the city. Inter-club tennis tournaments between the Gujarat Club, Parsi Gymkhana and Ahmedabad Gymkhana were held regularly, providing excitement and entertainment to the elite who went to watch these games.[35] Advertisements of sports goods and stores were a regular feature in the local newspapers.

Evening parties became a common mode of entertainment for the city's elite. They were given and attended by the elite European and rich Parsi, Muslim and Hindu men and women of the city. Jehangirji Vakil, Nowroji Vakil, Ambalal Sarabhai, Shambhuprasad Lashkari, barrister Wadia and Sir Chinubhai threw frequent parties in the sprawling gardens of their stately villas. Gramophone music, band music, magic shows and games such as tennis and badminton were provided for the guests. Refreshments were served, including alcohol and aerated drinks, the latter being a novel item at that time. Separate arrangements for refreshment were made where only milk products and fruits were served for the orthodox Hindu guests. Many caste Hindus, however, did not mind eating at the same table with other communities. Local newspapers made a point of covering these evening parties.[36]

For the common man, there was still the traditional mode of recreation such as *bhajans* (religious group songs), *kathas* by the *manbhattas* (story recitation), *melas* and *urs* (fairs), religious festivals and *garba* and *raas* (folk dances). The Navratri festival was celebrated with great enthusiasm by the *pol* groups as well as by the Ladies' Club and the Mahila Mandal. The *manbhattas* recited *kathas* from the epics and the *puranas* at night in the *chaklas* (crossroads) and in the *pols*. Vidhyben Nilkanth remembered that when she was a child, she had heard tales from the Mahabharata recited by the *manbhatts*.[37]

Western education and wider contact with the outside world brought about changes in the dress and fashion of the people of Ahmedabad. The fashions of Bombay influenced the fashions of Ahmedabad. The Parsis of the city set the trend in fashions. Contemporary photographs show changes in dress and fashions. Shoes and sandals became common. *Dhotis*, *angarkhas* and *paherans* of the earlier period yielded place to trousers, shirts and coats after the European fashion. *Pagdhi* (head dress) gave place to skull caps, pheta or even hats. Many young men wore their hair short and did not wear any headdress. Barrister Krishnarao Bholanath, a son of Bholanath Sarabhai, was completely westernised in his dress. His photograph shows him wearing his hair short, no headdress and a three-piece suit with a bow tie.[38] Ambalal Sarabhai dressed totally in the European style.[39] However, the common thing for men was to blend Indian and western dress. Photographs of Ambalal Sakarlal, Umiashankar Lalshankar and Ramanbhai Nilkanth show them dressed in a long coat with *dhoti* or trousers and *pagdhi* or *pheta* as headdress, with shoes and socks. The fashionable women of Ahmedabad emulated Parsi women, leaving the *saree pallav* (end) hanging loose, clasped on the right shoulder by a fancy safety pin or a brooch. Their blouses had puffed short or long sleeves and laced frills. Women wore their hair in a loose bun at the nape of the neck with a side parting.[40] In spite of the taboo against women wearing footwear, many upper-class women wore sandals. Saraladevi Sarabhai wore high-heeled shoes.[41] However, many women still walked barefoot on the road. As a result, even the municipal authorities decided to water the road only once in winter lest these women caught a cold.[42] The imported Chinese, English, Japanese and French silks were popular. Women preferred imported cloth to indigenous textiles.[43] Later, Gandhi's simplicity changed the tastes of the people. Khadi and coarse, hand-spun textiles soon replaced imported textiles. The dress of men as well as women became simple.

Food habits, too, changed during the latter half of the 19th century. Earlier, tea-drinking was not common, but gradually, it became popular.[44] Advertisements for various brands of tea and coffee appeared in local newspapers and periodicals, which featured articles on how to make good tea. In the first decade of the 20th century, teahouses proliferated opposite the railway station. They became the most popular and profitable institution in the city. The municipal authorities were, however, worried about their filthy and insanitary condition.[45] An interesting aspect of the tea drinking habit is that the municipality soon proposed an octroi on tea as one-third of the city's population consumed tea worth Rs 45,000 per annum. Coffee, however, was not included in the proposed octroi list because its consumption was limited.[46] Other new tastes the palate acquired were for biscuits, ice cream and aerated waters. Advertisements for biscuits made for Hindus and for ice cream appeared in contemporary local newspapers from the beginning of the 20th century.

The lifestyle of the people of Ahmedabad was altered considerably by the introduction of various technological innovations. The Bombay Telephone Company inaugurated its services in Ahmedabad in July 1897 with 34 subscribers.[47] Photography was introduced in the 1880s. Photographers advertised regularly in the local newspapers from the last decade of the 19th century. The first automobile came to Ahmedabad in 1901. Ambalal Sarabhai was one of the first owners of a motor car.[48] Sir Chinubhai and other rich mill owners, too, possessed motor cars. The number of hired cars also increased and with it the need for revising the vehicle tax in Ahmedabad. As a result, a special general meeting of the municipality was called in August 1907 to include taxes on motor vehicles and cycles in the new schedule.[49]

Electric supply to the public was commenced in February 1915 and by September of that year, 261 consumers had been given main connections and 268 street lamps put into commission.[50] Consumption of electricity for lights and fans, both by the public and the municipality, increased steadily in the 1920s.[51] It is interesting to note here that before electricity was introduced, kerosene lamps were used at home and on the streets. Vidhyaben Nilkanth observed in her reminiscences that in her childhood in the early 1880s, only clay lamps or candles were used at home.[52]

There was no bus service in the city until about 1921. A hackney carriage service had started since the 1870s.[53] The rich kept *shigrams* driven by bullocks or used horse-driven victorias. Some young men drove gigs and dog-carts themselves.[54]

As the city's population increased, so did its business activities. Ahmedabad soon became congested, but despite this congestion, people preferred to stay in the overcrowded *pols* amidst their kin and caste. When Richey Road, the main thoroughfare, was built in the early 1880s, the municipality had bought up many of the houses in order to obtain open space for the road. The dwellers of these houses accommodated themselves in the already overcrowded *pols*, aggravating the congestion.[55] British rule ensured security, law and order to the people so that there was no longer a need for the security of the *pol*. In addition, the municipality looked after cleaning and lighting the streets, water supply, and other amenities. In spite of this, very few people left the walled city. Since Ahmedabad's corporate character continued, the *pol* retained its importance as a social institution of the neighbourhood. The *pol panch* adapted its functions to suit industrialisation and modernity. It undertook social welfare activities both for *pol* residents and for the public in general. In 1903, Dhanasutharni *pol* donated Rs 1,000 to the GVS for the promotion of female education.[56] *Pol* residents volunteered to pay one-eighth share of the expenses to improve *pol* roads in Totadeji's *pol* and in Raja Mehta's *pol*.[57] Festivals such as Navratri and Holi were collectively celebrated by the *pol* which helped to maintain and strengthen their neighbourhood bonds.

A few rich mill owners and well-to-do professionals built their bungalows and sprawling villas in the open spaces in Jamalpura and Shahpur areas on the Oliphant and Astodia roads of the walled city and in the Shahibag area, and later in the Ellis Bridge *pura*. Sir Chinubhai, chairman of the committee of the management of the Ahmedabad municipality, wrote a letter dated April 11, 1911, to the collector of Ahmedabad saying: "There is a marked tendency among the well-to-do people to build residential bungalows in the open area outside the city walls and the new buildings which have been constructed in the Shahibag and Dhulia Kot suburbs during the last decade indicate that the spirit of urban life is developing."[58]

During the plague epidemic and the First World War, many well-to-do professionals moved to the suburbs. Cooperative housing societies mushroomed outside the walled city.

Many mill owners spent ostentatiously on their residential houses. Seth Sarabhai built a sprawling mansion in Mirzapur called

Shantisadan while his son Ambalalbhai built a huge mansion in the Shahibag area. Other *sethias* and mill owners, such as Jehangirji Vakil, Nowroji Vakil, Shambhuprasad Lashkari, Mansukhbhai Bhagubhai, also built magnificent villas. Sir Chinubhai built a palatial villa named Shantikunj in a mixed architectural style, a blend of Indian and European styles. It had a well-laid garden embellished by statues and fountains.

The bungalows of the professionals and the well-to-do were not as pretentious as those of the mill owners. A typical bungalow was square or oblong in design and usually had an open portico. It was utilitarian in design and possessed no distinctive architectural style.

The interiors also changed. They had western furniture and European and Chinese curios and clocks. From the 1890s onwards, Ahmedabad residents enjoyed the facilities of tap water at home. To begin with, however, at least among the higher castes, a superstition existed against the use of tap water, but as its convenience was felt, this soon died away.[59]

III

The proliferation of textile mills, the consequent prosperity and growth of population, together with the various improvement schemes of the Ahmedabad city municipality changed the urban environment and the face of the city. Ahmedabad rapidly expanded beyond the city walls.

In 1879, the eastern wards of the walled city—Khadia, Kalupur and Dariapur—were thickly populated while the western wards—Shahpur, Raikhad, Jamalpur—were not so crowded and still had vast open spaces where earlier farming had been carried out.[60] It is not surprising that the first two textile mills of Ahmedabad were situated within the walled city in Shahpur and Raikhad areas. However, with the growth in population, the western wards were soon occupied by churches, schools, *agiarys*, clubs, public buildings, hospital and bungalows.

In spite of the increasing congestion, people did not want to move outside the city, being reluctant to move out of their *pols*. As a result, there were encroachments on roads and open spaces in *pols*, which made them even more narrow and crooked than before. Some of the *pols* were so narrow that carts could not enter them.[61] One pressing problem faced by Ahmedabad municipality was the removal of squatters' huts found wherever there were open spaces in the city.

The density of population in the walled city increased even more rapidly towards the end of the century. In 1872, the population per square mile was 58,436.50 in the city.[62] In the report on the survey of the suburbs of Ahmedabad, it was remarked that some parts of the main city of Ahmedabad were scandalous examples of how a *mofussil* town could become congested if left to itself. Some parts of the city were as crowded as the worst parts of Bombay.[63]

In 1902, the density in the walled city increased to 60,000 persons to a square mile and in the Kalupur area, it reached as high as 1,20,000 per square mile. However, the western parts of the city were still not very crowded. In Raikhad, the population per square mile was 34,000. Suburbs within the municipal limits were sparsely populated. There, the density was 7,000 per square mile.[64] There were very few small open spaces within the city in 1921.

In 1901, the municipality passed several resolutions to alleviate the overcrowding in the city. To encourage people to build on open sites, the municipality requested the government to allow agricultural and other government lands to be used for residential purposes on easy terms. The municipality also passed some stringent rules to prevent encroachment on the road. Balcony projections were not allowed. The municipality tried to open up *pols* to improve ventilation and to facilitate traffic.[65]

The municipality also considered building *chawls* for the poorer section of the society to solve the problem of squatters, but various constraints prevented it from doing so. To encourage people to build houses in the suburbs and reduce the congestion in the walled city, the government reduced the rate of assessment. It also undertook a survey of the suburbs, which was completed in 1901. In the survey report, it was suggested that the suburbs be developed in a planned manner with provision for open spaces and wide tree-lined avenues.[66] Later, from 1916 onwards, town planning schemes were prepared for the areas outside Jamalpur Gate, Kankaria and Ellis Bridge *pura*.

Serious thought was given to the removal of the city walls to alleviate congestion and improve ventilation and light in the city in the second decade of the 20th century. Even earlier, several suggestions had been made by sanitary officials regarding the removal of the city walls to improve ventilation,[67] but the sentiments of the citizens had turned these down. Ahmedabad's inhabitants looked on the walls as security. The rapid expansion of the city rendered the walls an impediment to traffic as well as to any future expansion of the city and town-planning schemes. A special committee was appointed in 1914 to consider the question of the feasibility of a few forward-planning schemes with a view to improvement[68] and asked to submit its report within six months. The committee was in favour of the demolition of the walls to allow easy movement between the city and the suburbs, allowing more air and light into the city and giving better traffic facilities to the city by the creation of a wide circular road or 'ringstrasse' round the city and tree-lined avenues.[69]

While this special committee was preparing this report, Professor Patrick Geddes, a noted town planning expert, visited Ahmedabad in November 1914 and again in April 1915. Professor Geddes being a romantic and a traditionalist opposed the scheme for the demolition of the walls on the ground that it was characteristic of an old city and therefore of historical and aesthetic value.[70] Soon, the question of the demolition of the walls raised a heated controversy among the people of Ahmedabad. A dispute arose between the traditionalists and modernists. In spite of the approval of the scheme by the municipality, the demolition was delayed. As a result, the walls were still standing until the late 1930s.

As mentioned earlier, the city's spatial expansion was linked to the growth of the mill industry and the population increase. Until 1875, the area of the city was confined to the area within the city walls and the walled suburbs of Saraspur about half a mile east of Ahmedabad city. In 1875, the railway suburb was included, which was outside the walled city and between the town walls in line from the Kalupur and the Saraspur gates on one side and the Bombay Baroda and Central India Railway fence on the other.[71] The location of the railway station on the eastern side of the city determined the spatial expansion of the city towards the east. The textile mills were set up near the railway sidings and the station. The cityscape of the eastern, north-eastern and southern sides was formed by the mills with their tall chimneys surrounded by the huts and *chawls* of the mill workers. The expansion of the city also followed this pattern, so that it spilled over beyond the walls.

In 1880, at the suggestion of Erskine, the commissioner of the northern division, the smaller suburbs of Madhavpura, Borradailpura, Phoolpura, Hathipura, Fatehpura and the rest of the railway *pura* were included within the municipal limits to keep the surroundings of the city clean and to improve their sanitary conditions. These *puras* were actually trading centres with marketplaces and warehouses established to avoid the octroi duty after the British took over the city.[72]

In 1882, some more suburbs were included within the municipal limits. The tract of land known as Shehr Kotda was included, which was between the city and Saraspur, which included the rest of the railway *pura*, the railway station, and the mills and ginning factories to the east of the station. On the south-eastern side, Ragunathpura, Kangalpuri, Kankaria, Bhavanipura were added, together with the brick kilns outside the Sarangpur Gate and a strip of land to the south of and adjoining the city. The suburbs of Kazipur and Kagdipith on the northern side were also added.[73] In 1894, the municipal limits were extended from the Delhi Gate to Dudheshwar where the waterworks stood.[74] As the mill industry expanded, there was a greater need for sanitary control and regulatory building activities. In 1899, a huge area was further included within the Municipal limits. These were the Asarwa village in the northeast corner of the city and part of Dariapur–Kazipur to the north of the city.[75] The importance of the village of Asarwa was increased because it was connected by the Prantij Railway and was an important station for freight trains.[76]

The Ahmedabad municipal boundaries extended in three principal directions in 1911—the Ellis Bridge *pura* to the west, the Shahibag area to the north and the Gomatipur area to the southwest.[77]

The inclusion of Ellis Bridge *pura* was significant because for the first time, municipal limits were extended towards the western side across the river Sabarmati. The dearth of bridges across the Sabarmati had hampered westward expansion. As a result, until the second Ellis Bridge was opened to traffic in September 1892, industrial and residential growth remained confined to the eastern side of the river. The first Ellis Bridge was built in 1870 but was swept away by severe floods in September 1875.[78] The Ellis Bridge opened up the western side of the river for residential expansion. However, urban development on the western side was slow and marginal until the close of the 19th century. *Prajabandhu*, the popular local newspaper, made a plea to the people of Ahmedabad in December 1899 to expand the city towards the west to relieve congestion in the city.[79] The Gujarat College buildings were established in this area in 1897. Some Christian missionary buildings, too, were situated there. When an epidemic of plague broke out during the First World War, some lawyers built bungalows there to distance themselves from the congested town. To induce the middle class gentry to settle in this suburb, one of the healthiest suburbs in Ahmedabad and within a few minutes of the city, the municipality wanted to extend the facility of piped water. Its importance further increased as the station on the Ahmedabad Dholka line was built there. In spite of that, the Ellis bridge area had a population of only 2,044 in 1921.[80]

The Shahibag area was sandwiched between the walled city and the cantonment, military headquarters of the northern division. The cantonment was situated three-and-a-half miles north-east of the city and was connected to the city by a well-made tree-lined road running through Shahibag suburb. Here, in Shahibag there were several bungalows and villas belonging to rich businessmen, and to provide this suburb with water and conservancy, it was included in the municipal limits of the city in 1911.[81]

Gomatipur was the industrial area situated to the south-east of the city. It was traversed by the main line of the BB & CI Railway and had a large goods station. This area was developing very fast and crowded with squalid huts and *chawls* forming an eyesore and a sanitary danger to the neighbourhood. To regulate building activity in the area and to provide it with water supply, Gomatipur was also included in the city.[82] In 1914, a small area on the southern side was added to the city near the Astodia Gate.[83]

By 1915, Ahmedabad covered the area of the walled city and the *puras* on its four sides. Thus, with the expansion of the textile industry, the city spilled beyond the walls. The walled city became the centre around which the city expanded in a concentric manner, resulting in its characteristic circular form. Humming with socioeconomic activities, it tended to remain congested, while the *puras* or suburbs, the modern extensions of the city, remained sparsely populated.

IV

The municipality of Ahmedabad played a significant role in bringing about changes in the urban environment. In addition to easing the problem of congestion, it undertook various urban improvement plans. Chapter 2 mentioned how the Town Wall Fund Committee began to informally perform the functions of a municipality, being replaced in 1858 by the municipal commission with a well-defined constitution by virtue of the Act XXXVI of 1850. In 1874, it became a city municipality by a government notification dated November 7, 1874, in the general department.[84] As early as 1874, the people of Ahmedabad were keen on having the democratic institution of a municipality, so they sent a petition to the government dated June 21, 1874, requesting it to introduce the elective principle for the city municipality of Ahmedabad. This was signed by Dahyabhai Anoopchand, the *nagarseth*, and a large number of citizens.[85] However, the request was turned down and they had to wait until January 1, 1885, when the principle of local self-government was introduced by Lord Ripon.

The Ahmedabad municipality was reconstituted on January 1, 1895, under the Bombay District Municipality Amendment Act II of 1884. The new municipality consisted of partly elected and partly nominated members. It had 30 members of all creeds and communities. Ranchhodlal Chhotalal was the first nominated president who remained in that position from 1885 until his death in 1898.

Originally, the members nominated by the government were in a majority and enjoyed great influence over the working of the municipality. However, the number of elected members gradually increased to equal the number of nominated members by 1901. The total number of members increased from 30 to 33 in 1892–93 and to 36 in 1901. In May 1910, the municipality was superseded by the government on the grounds of inefficiency and incompetence on many counts.[86] A committee of management was appointed by the government, with 21 members who were the leading citizens of Ahmedabad and under the presidentship of Sir Chinubhai Madhavlal, who carried out the work for five years. In 1915, the municipality was reinstated with an elected majority. Out of the total 40 members, 27 were elected, while 13 were nominated by the government, of whom not more than six could be government officers. The president was elected by the members.

Ahmedabad was fortunate in having a very able and devoted leader like Ranchhodlal Chhotalal, who contributed to the high level of urban development of Ahmedabad. Ranchhodlal, the founder of the first textile mill of Ahmedabad introduced a modern water supply and underground drainage system to improve sanitary conditions in the city. With his progressive zeal, he was truly the father of modern Ahmedabad.

In 1875, Dr TG Hewlett, sanitary commissioner of the Bombay government, drew the government's attention to the deplorable sanitary conditions of Ahmedabad. He pointed out that the mortality rate in Ahmedabad was the highest in Bombay presidency and that this could be attributed to the want of proper drainage and clean water supply.[87]

Prior to 1891, the water supply of Ahmedabad depended on wells, cement-lined household cisterns, the river Sabarmati, and the pump service from the river Sabarmati which was constructed in 1849 and improved in 1865. This pump service was situated at the southwest corner of the city, where water was pumped up from the river during the night into a 52 feet high tower, filtered through vegetable charcoal and gravel and then conveyed through pipes to the distributing hydrants in different parts of the city. This source was insufficient as it yielded not more than one gallon of water per day per person. The water remained impure even after filtration since the river flowed through the cantonment and the thickly populated parts of the city. The wells in the city were not usable because the water in them was impure, brackish and unfit for drinking. Well water was polluted by the water from the cesspools, which passed into the wells through the porous soil of Ahmedabad.

A great number of inhabitants depended on cement-lined cisterns built in their houses in which rain water was collected during the monsoon through cement channels from the roofs.[88]

The mode of conservancy was unhygienic and the city certainly needed an efficient system of drainage. This mode of conservancy in Ahmedabad was not very different from that of most contemporary cities in India. Before 1880, there were brick *khalkuvas* or cesspools in most houses. These cesspools were usually 25 to 30 feet deep, into which the sullage from the houses and sewage from the privies flowed. The dirty water seeped into the subsoil and was carried out of the city. This dirty water fouled the well water and even the river water. The surface appeared clean, but the subsoil was dirtied. As a result, such cesspools were ordered to be closed by the municipality in 1879–80. In the houses where there had been no cesspools earlier, people threw dirty water into the streets or poured it into large iron pans placed in the streets from which it was removed daily. The night soil from the surface privies was removed in covered carts and baskets to the depots outside the Jamalpur gate to the southeast of the city, where it was converted into manure. In the rainy season, when the *khalkuvas* were closed, the dirty water flowed in the streets, fouling the air and water. As many *pols* did not have surface drains, they remained muddy and damp and a foul smell pervaded the air all the time. Such streets naturally became a breeding place for mosquitoes. Cholera and malaria epidemics were regular features of the city. By modern or indeed by any standard it was an unhealthy city.[89] Overcrowding, and the presence of dangerous and offensive trades within the residential areas of the walled city also contributed to the increasing mortality rate and unhealthy environment in the city.

The credit for introducing modern water supply and sewage and bringing about awareness among the people regarding unhealthy conditions in the city goes to Ranchhodlal Chhotalal. He started his municipal career in 1868 as a nominee of the Bombay government on the municipal committee. In 1883–84, he was appointed the president of Ahmedabad municipality. He remained president of the municipality until his death in 1898. He was greatly concerned about the unhealthy conditions and high mortality rate of the city. He studied the best contemporary works on sanitary science and hygiene and made himself fully acquainted with the details of the municipal machine. In 1883, he drafted a memorandum on public health in which he drew the attention of the people to the insanitary conditions in the city and listed some primary needs. He was praised by government authorities for this memorandum. The sanitary commissioner for Bombay government described it on May 1, 1884, as "a remarkable document for a native gentleman to have written, as it exhibits a breath of view and a masterly appreciation of some of the main questions that affect the public health in the city". In his memorandum, Chhotalal offered some suggestions to improve the sanitary conditions. One of them was to introduce new schemes of water supply and underground drainage.[90]

It was not an easy task to persuade his colleagues on the municipal commission to accept these new and progressive schemes. Even western educated social reformers such as Mahipatram Rupram, Bechardas Lashkari and Mancherji Karanjwala showed a strong conservative attitude towards new ideas and vehemently opposed these schemes. Mahipatram wrote: "No system of underground drainage will remove these evils, on the contrary, it is likely to prove more destructive."[91] The press, too, was very hostile to the schemes. All the local newspapers, such as *Ahmedabad Times*, *Rajabhakta*, *Hitechhu, Prajamat* and *Samsher Bahadur*, were unanimous in their opposition to the scheme.[92] They feared that these schemes would entail heavy expenses and taxation.

In 1885, at the request of Ranchhodlal, the Bombay government agreed to lend the services of Col. Walter Ducat, consulting sanitary engineer to the Ahmedabad municipality for one month to prepare plans of water supply and drainage schemes.[93]

As soon as Col. Ducat's plans were submitted for approval to the municipal commissioners, considerable hostility was manifested towards the scheme by both the municipal commissioners and the general public. They found the proposals very costly and impractical. Mahipatram Rupram wrote to Sir TC Hope, the former collector of Ahmedabad who at that time was a member of the viceroy's council, requesting his opinion on the schemes proposed by Col. Ducat. Sir TC Hope condemned Ducat's scheme in the strongest terms. He recommended the removal of night soil by hand and recommended its removal to a sufficient distance from the city.[94] Sir TC Hope's opinion, though wrong, was a powerful weapon in the hands of Ranchhodlal's opponents.

Mass meetings were held daily against the scheme. The local press supported the opposition. One mammoth meeting was held at Tankshal, which was attended by Ranchhodlal. The crowd shouted at him and refused to give him a hearing, even pelting him with garbage and stones. The police had to escort him to safety.[95]

Many meetings of the municipality were convened to discuss these new schemes. There were 54 such meetings in 1887 and 64 in 1888. Some of these were quite riotous. However, in the end, through sheer perseverance, resolutions were passed in favour of these schemes.[96]

One incident clearly shows the hostility and apathy of the municipal commissioners. When Hewlett visited the city in 1887, Ranchhodlal, as the president, invited him and Col. Ducat to attend a meeting of the municipal commissioners convened to consider the report of the sub-committee on water supply. He thought it was a good opportunity for the municipal commissioners to hear what Col. Ducat had to say regarding the criticism of his schemes made by Sir TC Hope. But there was no quorum, and the meeting could not be held.[97]

A special sub-committee was appointed by the municipal commission to submit its proposals on the new schemes. The sub-committee accepted Col. Ducat's scheme of water supply with minor modifications but did not approve of the new drainage scheme. The committee recommended the adoption of a system in which sullage should be removed by pail. However, this plan was not approved by the government, and the municipal commissioners were asked to reconsider the matter.[98]

The people of Ahmedabad were so hostile to the drainage scheme that they sent a memorandum in 1888 to the governor general of India, signed by 7,000 citizens under the leadership of Keshavlal Khushalchand, expressing their opposition to the scheme. However, the memorandum had no effect on the government.[99]

On March 3, 1887, after a long discussion and a full enquiry, the majority in the municipal commission sanctioned a modified version of Col. Ducat's scheme for water supply. The government approved and sanctioned the scheme.[100] However, the work actually started in March 1889 and was completed in 1891. The new waterworks was situated in Dudheshwar on the left bank of the Sabarmati in the northwest of the city. By 1898, it consisted of supply wells, a pumping plant and a high-level reservoir. The water was pumped from the wells by steam power. Later, the number of supply wells and steam engines were increased to meet the needs of the enlarged area and the increased population of the city. Almost every street and house in the walled city was supplied with piped water by 1893 bringing great comfort and health to the city.[101]

In the matter of the new drainage system, there was more resistance. Ranchhodlal advocated a drainage system similar to that adopted in other parts of the civilised world. He was in favour of underground drainage, but the majority of the municipal commissioners preferred the hand removal system.[102]

To ensure better conservancy, Ranchhodlal got a light tramway constructed in 1885 to transport night soil to a distance of 2.5 miles from the city in the southeast direction from which the wind hardly blew.[103] This measure led to the fall of the death rate to 12 per 1000 population.

As desired by the government, the matter of drainage was reconsidered. It was thought advisable to try the system of underground drainage in one part of the town and observe the result before making further extension.[104] The drainage project was carried out in Khadia, a thickly populated area in which opposition to drainage was intense. The design was furnished by Baldwin Latham. The work was completed in 1893.[105] It was also resolved that the drainage system should be extended to the entire city as designed by Latham.

Soon, people realised what a boon a good drainage system was. The mortality statistics of the drained area of Khadia were much lower than the rest of the city.[106] In the rest of the city, night soil and sullage water were removed by means of carts from iron-pans and were dumped into tramway carts and thence removed to a depot, to be manufactured into manure and sold to cultivators.

Following the success of the drainage scheme in Khadia, Baldwin Latham was instructed to prepare plans for sewerage in the rest of the city. A comprehensive plan for the whole city was prepared by him in 1896, but it was not until 1903 that the sewage works were actually undertaken. Some 15,000 to 16,000 houses were connected to a drainage system in 1905.

The sanitary conditions in those portions of the city which enjoyed sewage facilities were vastly improved. People realised there were benefits to underground drainage and now clamoured for the extension of the scheme to the whole city.

By 1920, the whole of Khadia, half of Jamalpur, a part of Raikhad, two-thirds of Kalupur, half of Dariapur and a very small portion of Shahpur within the walled city were drained and only a part of the railway *pura* was drained.[107] Later, in the 1920s, when Vallabhbhai Patel became president of the municipality, the scheme of drainage for the whole walled city was undertaken. Thus, these two schemes—underground drainage and modern water supply—provided the two prime needs of modern urban life.

The other major functions of the municipality were the building and maintaining of roads and gardens in the city. In order to relieve traffic congestion and connect the city with the railway station, the municipality built some new roads. Earlier, the main roads ran north to south. To facilitate movement to the railway station on the east, the need arose for thoroughfares running west to east. Building new roads through the complex network of *pols* was not an easy task. *Pols* had encroached on the old thoroughfares during the turbulent times of the 18th century. Again, the making of thoroughfares and the widening of roads in congested areas aroused a lot of opposition because it disrupted the formation of *pols* in the city. Muslims were opposed to the opening of the *pols* because it interfered seriously with the seclusion of their women.

In 1863, Jardin Road, which ran from Delhi Gate in the north to Kalupur Gate in the east, was opened for traffic. It was named after the popular British officer Jardin, who had worked in Ahmedabad for more than 30 years.[108] Oliphant Road, named after a popular collector, was built during 1864–67 and ran from Maneck Gate in the west to Astodia Gate in the southeast of the city. It was 40 feet broad and had footpaths and drains. It passed through the sparsely populated part of the city. However, new buildings, colleges, schools, clubs and institutes were soon constructed on both the sides of the road. The Premchand Raichand College and its hostel buildings were built in 1868 to train teachers for primary schools in Gujarat. On the opposite side of the road, was the Mahalaxmi Training College built in 1875. A little distance from the Mahalaxmi College and across the street was the Bholanath Literary Institute for Women built in 1890. It housed the Gujarat Ladies Club with facilities for sports in its compound.

The architecture of these new buildings showed a blend of western and Indian traditions. Another interesting building was a Prarthana Mandir, a prayer hall of the Prarthana Samaj, which was built in 1876. It was built in a hybrid architectural style. It had a *shikhara* (tower) in the north Indian temple style but with a clock in its face. The inside of the tower had a room which housed the library. On each side of this room, there was a small room through which a staircase led to two side galleries on the upper floor where ladies sat for prayer meetings. The ground plan of the building was more like a Christian church, being rectangular in shape. On each side of the hall were covered verandas.[109] The hybrid architectural style with its tower from the Hindu temple and its ground plan of a church was in consonance with the hybrid character of a religion which had combined the elements of Hindu and Christian religions. Ratnamanirao Bhimrao, a chronicler of Ahmedabad, compared the Prarthana Mandir to a man wearing pants, coat and tie with a Bhavnagari *pagdi* (headdress).[110]

A road branching from Oliphant Road led to the municipal buildings and the telegraph office, which were built in 1872. Another street branched out from Oliphant road and lead to the

Parsi *agiary* at the Khamasa Chakla. Thus, Olipant Road with its various new buildings became an epitome of modern Ahmedabad. It became the centre of educational and reform activities in the 19th century.

The Richey Road (today known as Gandhi Road) was the first thoroughfare of Ahmedabad running east-west. It was opened for traffic in 1884. It ran from Teen Durwaja in the west to Panchkuva Gate in the east. This arterial road passed through one of the most thickly populated areas of the city, opening up several badly ventilated *pols*. Prior to 1884, there was only one road, Kalupur Road, which joined the congested eastern parts with the station. During the rainy season, people had to wade through two or three feet of water through the greater part of Kalupur. This inconvenience was removed by Richey Road, which became the principal road leading to the railway station.[111] It became the main artery which divided the city into two well-marked divisions, northern and southern Ahmedabad. On both sides of the road, shops and other commercial buildings were built. The traffic on this road increased with the rising population and the increasing number of vehicles in the city. To relieve the traffic, the municipality, during the presidentship of Vallabhbhai Patel, resolved to construct another thoroughfare, a Kalupur relief road, which was completed in the 1930s. Until then, Richey Road remained the principal road of the city.

The municipality watered the roads of the city twice a day. Until 1889, while the main roads were cleaned daily, the *pols* were cleaned only once in three days. As a result, the *pols* remained dirty. Many *pols* did not have surface drains, resulting in the flooding of *pol*s during the monsoon. It was horrible to enter the *pols* in the monsoon for they remained muddy and damp throughout the season.

The municipality lighted the streets with ornamental kerosene lamps. After 1915, these kerosene lamps were gradually replaced by electric lamps. In 1918–19, there were 427 electric lights, and additional lights were installed in Khadia, Kalupur, Kandoiol and Sakar Bazar.[112]

Ahmedabad had tree-lined streets and gardens under Muslim rule. However, the city became desolate under the Marathas and could not boast of any garden until 1877. A small municipal garden was laid facing the Bhadra Fort in Karanj in 1876–77.[113] At the beginning of the 20th century, a public garden was laid out by the municipality just outside Bhadra Fort near Ellis Bridge, on the site of the old jail garden. This garden was named Victoria Garden in memory of Queen Victoria. A statue of the Queen was installed in the garden and a bandstand was built where a band played once a week for a few years from 1906.[114] This garden was within easy reach of the city.

In 1912, Madhavbag, an excellent recreational ground was opened just outside Sarangpur Gate. It was built by Sir Chinubhai Ranchhodlal to commemorate his father Madhavbhai. A statue of Ranchhodlal Chhotalal was installed there. A separate corner was allotted for women, providing a boon to high caste women. The people of the Khadia ward and the railway *pura* took full advantage of it. The labourers working in the nearby mills also made use of this garden.[115]

Naginawadi, a beautiful garden, was laid at the Kankaria lake outside the city walls in the early 1880s.[116] A neat triangular garden was laid outside Delhi Gate.[117]

British rulers did not make any attempt to beautify this *mofussil* city by building impressive monuments. The new buildings of colleges, schools, hospitals, clubs and libraries were built from the subscriptions of the rich and the municipality of Ahmedabad. Only in a few cases did British rulers extend financial help. Some buildings on Oliphant Road have been described. Other important buildings were those of the Gujarat College built in 1897 in the Ellis Bridge *pura* and the Ranchhodlal Chhotalal High School in Mirzapur built in 1906. Both these buildings had a vernacular or mixed architectural style that combined Indian and western elements. The city had only one public hall, Premabhai Hemabhai Hall located near Bhadra, which was opened in 1899. None of these buildings were pretentious or monumental.

51. Gujarat College

52. Bungalow of Sir Chinubhai Madhavlal

53. Nowroji Hall—Vakil's bungalow

54. Kochrab Ashram

55. Sabarmati Ashram

From the last decade of the 19th century onwards, the textile mills proliferated on the eastern, southern and north-eastern sides of the walled city, and the city expanded much beyond its walls. Mills with their tall chimneys drastically changed the city's skyline. By 1915, the city looked a truly industrial city and nothing like it had in 1817 when the British took over.

Notes

1. *Census of India – 1911*, Vol. VII, Bombay, Part I, *Report*, Bombay 1912, p. 11.
2. *Census of India* – 1931, Vol. IX, *The Cities of the Bombay Presidency*, Part I & II, Bombay 1933. The details of the population of Ahmedabad are not included because the people of Ahmedabad did not cooperate with the census officials. The number 3,10,000 is an estimated figure of population and not an accurate one.
3. *Census of India* – 1921, Vol. IX, *Cities of the Bombay Presidency*, Part I, *Report,* Poona, 1922.
4. *Ibid.*, pp. 67–68.
5. Hariprasad Shastri and Bharati Shelat, 'Amdavadni Agiariona Shilalekh' (in Gujarati), *Buddhi Prakash*, December 1980, pp. 485–486.
6. Amdavad Parsi Panchayat, *Parsi Zoroastrian Rahevasio Vishe Mojni Prakashan Directory* (in Gujarati), Ahmedabad 1975, p. 3.
7. Noshir Khursed Dabu (ed.), *Vakil Anjuman Adran Golden Jubilee Granth* (in Gujarati), Ahmedabad, 1983, pp. 14–16 and 20–21.
8. Hariprasad Shastri and Bharati Shelat, 'Amdavad Agiariona Shilalekh', *op. cit.*, pp. 487–488.
9. *Buddhi Prakash*, November 1875, pp. 256–257.
10. Behramji Malbari, *Gujarat and the Gujaratis* (reprint of the third edition, 1889) Delhi, 1983, pp. 101–102.
11. FC Davar, *Sir Nowroji P Vakil: A Biographical Sketch*, Ahmedabad, 1955, passim.
12. *Prajabandhu*, October 22, 1905, p. 14.
13. *Ibid*, September, 29, 1907, p. 11.
14. Shankarrai Amritrai (ed.), *Amdavadno Jivan Vikas* (in Gujarati), Ahmedabad, 1921, p. 119,
15. M Ezekiel, *History and Culture of the Bene Israel in India*, Nadiad, 1948 passim; Dr Bharati Shelat, Amdavadno Tribashi, Yahoodi Shilalekh

and Tnyanu Kabrastan (in Gujarati), *Vidhyapith*, March-April 1981, pp. 3–8; Dr Hariprasad Shastri and Bharati Shelat, 'Gujaratna Yahoodio' (in Gujarati), *Pathik*, April 1981, pp. 13–15; Chandrakant Patel, 'Amdavadna Yahoodiono Purva Itihas ane Sanskritik Jivan' (in Gujarati), *Vidhyapith*, May-June 1972, pp. 162–168.

16. Robin Boyd, *Church History of Gujarat*, Madras, 1981, p. 48.
17. Bombay Government, *Gazetteer of the Bombay Presidency*, Vol. 4, *Ahmedabad*, 1879, p. 42. Henceforth cited as *Ahmedabad Gazetteer.*
18. *Buddhi Prakash*, November 1862, pp. 245–246.
19. *Ahmedabad Gazetteer*, pp. 42–43; Mary Carpenter, *Six Months in India*, Vol. I, pp. 78–81.
20. Education Commission of Bombay, *Evidence Taken Before the Bombay Provincial Committee and Memorials Addressed to the Education Commission*, Vol. II, Calcutta, 1884, in the section titled Memorials) pp. 8–9.
21. *Ibid.*
22. Government of Bombay, *Supplement to the Director of Public Instruction's Annual Report for 1913-14,* Bombay, 1914, pp. 36, 47 and 52.
23. Bombay Government, *Reports on Native Papers* for the week ending August 24, 1889, p. 12; January 16, 1892, p. 14. Henceforth cited as *RNP* and date.
24. *Census of India* – 1901, Vol. IX, *Bombay*, Part I, *Report*, Bombay, 1902, pp. 70 and 77.
25. *RNP*, for the week ending March 1, 1901, p. 22.
26. *Prajabandhu*, October 2, 1898, p. 7.
27. Krishnarao Divetia, 'Natak ane Rangbhoomi', *Buddhi Prakash*, April 1906, p. 107.
28. *Prajabandhu*, December 12, 1912, an advertisement.
29. Shankarrai Amritrai, *op. cit.*, pp. 65–66; *Prajabandhu*, August 22, 1913, an advertisement.
30. Shankarrai Amritrai, *op. cit.*, pp. 65–66.
31. Vinodhini Nilkanth, 'Mane Sambhre Chhe – Pachashek Varsh Pahelanu Amdavad' (in Gujarati), *Gujarat Dipotsvi*, Ahmedabad, 1977, pp. 65–66.
32. Shankarrai Amritrai, op. cit., pp. 60–61.
33. *Ibid.*, pp. 62–63.
34. *Prajabandhu*, September 24, 1905, p. 13.
35. *Ibid.*, November 2, 1913, p. 2.
36. *Prajabandhu*, April 23, 1899, p. 6.
37. Vidhyaben Nilkanth, *Phorum* (in Gujarati), Ahmedabad, 1955, p. 5; Shankarrai Amritrai, *op. cit.*, p. 71.

38. Hiralal Parekh (ed.), *Lady Vidhyaben Mani Mahotsava Granth*, Ahmedabad, 1930, p. 193.
39. Leena Mangaldas, *Akhand Divo* (in Gujarati), Ahmedabad, 1970, p. 17.
40. Narsinharao Divetia, *Smaranmukur* (in Gujarati), Ahmedabad, 1928, pp. 65–68.
41. Leena Mangaldas, *op. cit.*, p. 17.
42. *Annual Report of the Municipality for the Year 1886–87*, p. 12, in General Department, 8/1888.
43. Hemchandra Narayan, *Hun Pote* (in Gujarati), Bombay, 1900, pp. 246–249.
44. *Buddhi Prakash*, March 1861, p. 72.
45. *Administration Report of the Ahmedabad Municipality for the Year 1916–1917*, p. 52.
46. General Department, 93/1908, p. 145.
47. The Rotary Club of Ahmedabad, *Ahmedabad*, Ahmedabad, 1940, p. 77.
48. Leena Mangaldas, *op. cit.*, p. 18.
49. General Department, 80/1909, pp. 133–161.
50. The Rotary Club of Ahmedabad, *op. cit.*, p. 85.
51. *Ibid.*, p. 89.
52. Vidhyaben Nilkanth, *Phorum*, p. 5.
53. *Prajabandhu*, July 1906, pp. 2–3.
54. Vidhyaben Nilkanth, *Phorum*, p. 5.
55. *The Annual Report of the Ahmedabad City Municipality for the Year 1885-86*, p. 22, in General Department, 66/1886.
56. *Prajabandhu*, March 1, 1903, p. 9.
57. *Annual Report of the Ahmedabad City Municipality for the Year 1886-87*, p. 14, in General Department, 8/1888.
58. General Department, 13/1911, p. 353.
59. *Administration Report of the Working of the Municipality of Ahmedabad for the Official year 1892-93*, p. 43, in General Department, 8/1894.
60. *Ahmedabad Gazetteer*, pp. 320–325.
61. Hemchandra Narayan, *op. cit.*, p. 247.
62. Government of Bombay, *Census of the Ahmedabad Collectorate*, Bombay, 1873, p. 11.
63. General Department, 72/1901, p. 79.
64. General Department, 66/1903, p. 77.
65. *Administration Report of the Ahmedabad Municipality for the Official Year of 1901-02*, pp. 6–7.

66. General Department, 72/1901, p. 79.
67. General Department, 101/1887, p. 69.
68. General Department, Comp. file 896/1915, p. 31.
69. *Ibid.*
70. *Ibid.*
71. *Ahmedabad Gazetteer*, p. 330, General Department, 62/1881, p. 71.
72. General Department, 48/1880, pp. 53-167; 63/1880a map; 38/1879, pp. 434–435.
73. General Department, 13/1884, p. 2.
74. General Department, 90/1895, pp. 91–92.
75. General Department, 71/1899, pp. 17–74.
76. General Department, 72/1901, p. 86.
77. General Department, 132/1911, pp. 335–351.
78. *Report of the Ellis Bridge Over the Sabarmati*, Bombay, 1893, in General Department, 90/1894.
79. *Prajabandhu*, December 17, 1899, p. 2.
80. General Department, 132/1911, p. 337; *Census of India*, Vol. IX, *Cities of the Bombay Presidency,* Part II, *Tables*, Bombay 1922, p. 1 xxxiii.
81. General Department, 132/1911, p. 337.
82. *Ibid.*, p. 339.
83. General Department, Comp. file 1090/1914.
84. *The Annual Report of the City Municipality of Ahmedabad for the Year 1882–83*, p. 1, in General Department 13/1884.
85. General Department, 37/1874, pp. 107–108.
86. General Department, 103/1910, pp. 91–93; Comp. file 945/1915, pp. 3–11.
87. Dr Hewlett's Report in General Department, 97/1876.
88. *Ahmedabad Gazetteer*, p. 314; *The Annual Report of the Ahmedabad Municipality for the Year 1882–83*, pp. 13–14 in General Department 13/1884.
89. *Ahmedabad Gazetteer*, pp. 314–315; *The Annual Report of the Ahmedabad Municipality for the Year 1882–83*, p. 14 in General Department, 13/1884; *The Annual Report of the Ahmedabad Municipality for the Year 1883–84,* pp. 22-23, in General Department, 26/1884.
90. General Department, 104/1884, pp. 89–92; p. 83.
91. *The Annual Report of the Ahmedabad Municipality for the Year 1885–86*, p. 24, in General Department 60/1886.
92. *RNP* for the week ending February 18, 1888, p. 15; May 5, 1888, pp. 4–8.

93. *The Annual Report of the Ahmedabad Municipality for the Year 1885–86,* p. 20, in General Department 60/1886.
94. General Department, 101/1887, p. 15.
95. Edwards SM, *Memoirs of Rao Bahadur Ranchhodlal Chhotalal, C.I.E.*, Exeter, 1920, p. 34.
96. *Administration Report of the Municipalities in the Northern Division, for 1887–88,* Bombay 1888, p. 1, in General Department, 13/1889.
97. General Department, 101/1887, pp. 78–80.
98. General Department, 103/1889, p. 104.
99. *Ibid.*, pp. 91–141.
100. *Annual Report of the Municipality for the Year 1886–87*, p. 12 in General Department 8/1888.
101. *Administration Report of the Working of the Municipality of Ahmedabad for the Official Year of 1892–93,* p. 25.
102. General Department, 82/A/1888, pp. 33–53.
103. *The Annual Report of the Ahmedabad Municipality for the Year 1885–86,* p. 21 in General Department 60/1886.
104. *The Administration Report of the Working of Ahmedabad Municipality for the Official Year 1887–88,* p. 3 in General Department 13/1889.
105. General Department, 45/1893, p. 108.
106. General Department, 66/1903, p. 11.
107. General Department, 92/1907, pp. 47–48.
108. *Buddhi Prakash*, January 1864, p. 8.
109. *Ahmedabad Gazetteer*, pp. 325–36.
110. Ratnamanirao Jote B, *Gujaratnu Patnagar Amdavad* (in Gujarati), Ahmedabad, 1929, p. 668.
111. *The Annual Report of the Ahmedabad Municipality for the Year 1882–83*, p. 21, in General Department 13/1884. *Ibid.*, for the Year 1884–85, p. 19, General Department, 60/1886.
112. *The Administration Report of the Ahmedabad Municipality for the Year 1918–19,* p. 28.
113. *Ahmedabad Gazetteer*, p. 273.
114. General Department, 72/1901, pp. 69–73; *Prajabandhu*, July 1, 1906, p. 3.
115. Shankarrai Amritrai, *op. cit.,* p. 67; General Department, Comp. file 945/1915, p. 10. *Prajabandhu*, February 17, 1912, pp. 15–16.
116. *The Annual Report of the Ahmedabad Municipality for the Year 1882–83*, pp. 17–18 in General Department 13/1884.
117. The General Department, Comp. file 1945/1915, p. 10.

Epilogue

A new phase in the history of Ahmedabad began with the advent of Mohandas Karamchand Gandhi in the city in 1915. Ahmedabad was his home for 15 years until he left in 1930. These 15 years were very eventful for the city. Gandhi accelerated the process of social change which was started after the foundation of British rule in the city and gave it a new direction. His influence was all pervasive.

Although Gandhi, by his innovative genius, provided a unique leadership to Ahmedabad and changed the sociocultural and political ethos of the city, he also drew his strength from its culture and traditions that had developed from the time of its foundation. He knew how the city had changed in the course of time and yet had continued its traditions. In his autobiography, he has specifically mentioned:

> I had a predilection for Ahmedabad. Being a Gujarati I thought I should be able to render greatest services to the country through the Gujarati language. And then, as Ahmedabad was an ancient centre of handloom weaving, it was likely to be the most favourable field for revival of the cottage industry of hand-spinning. There was also the hope that, the city being the capital of Gujarat, monetary help from its wealthy citizens would be more available here, than elsewhere.

Nurtured in the Vaishnav-Jain traditions of Gujarat and being a product of the commercial ethos of Gujarat, Gandhi found Ahmedabad a congenial place for his mission. He could easily establish rapport and harmony with its people, who shared similar traditions and ethos. Soon, he occupied a central place in the political and social life of Ahmedabad.

Gandhi thoroughly identified himself with the city and its people and organisations in the formative years of his career in India. He became a life member of the Gujarat Vernacular Society in 1916 and thereby identified himself not only with the language but with the organisation that had been the nucleus of the literary, cultural and social regeneration of Gujarat.

Gandhi also associated himself with city politics. He brought about a qualitative change in the political culture of Ahmedabad. He established his hold over the Gujarat Sabha and through it, entered the political scene in Gujarat and started grassroots activities. He radicalised the Sabha and changed its moderate stance. He integrated all sections of society and activated apolitical Ahmedabad. Gandhi, with his irresistible charm, enticed a band of young public workers and leaders such as Vallabhbhai Patel, Ansuyaben Sarabhai, Mahadev Desai, Shankarlal Banker, Indulal Yagnik, Sharadaben Mehta and Narhari Parikh, who were trained in his ideology. Most of them had been active in public life before meeting Gandhi. Within 15 years, he politically mobilised all sections and communities—mill owners, traders, workers, students, the educated middle class, women, Hindus and Muslims. He skilfully linked the city's politics with national politics and directed the emerging local leaders towards the national movement in both urban and rural areas.

Vallabhbhai, inspired by Gandhi, instilled the spirit of nationalism in the civic affairs of the city and launched a vigorous improvement programme for it. Underground drainage, started by Ranchhodlal Chhotalal, was extended to the entire walled city. Water supply was made adequate for the expanding city. Primary education was made free and compulsory. Electrical lights were introduced in every nook and corner of the walled city. The municipality initiated the Kankaria and Ellis Bridge town planning schemes. The Kalupur Relief Road and the removal of the city wall were the two schemes that were initiated then but were completed many years later in the late 1930s.

Gandhi influenced the tone of the press of the city by his bold editorship of *Navjivan* and *Young India.*

Ahmedabad had already emerged as the Manchester of India before Gandhi settled there. Gandhi's arrival in the city coincided with the First World War. The shortage of shipping facilities during the war cut off textile imports from England and Europe, which helped the Indian textile industry to strengthen its base in the domestic market. This gave a tremendous boost to the textile industry of Ahmedabad.

Gandhi's presence in Ahmedabad, too, contributed directly and indirectly to the growth of the textile industry. He intensified the nationwide *swadeshi* drive that gave a fillip to the textile industry. Even though he revived the spinning wheel and launched the *khadi* movement from Ahmedabad, he declared that he had nothing against machine industries. To him, *khadi* and machine-made Indian textiles were complementary to each other and were an integral part of the *swadeshi* movement to combat the colonial policy of the British.

The most positive contribution of Gandhi was to the establishment of harmonious and peaceful relations between labour and capital, which ensured the industrial peace so necessary for industrial growth. He got directly involved in the labour movement in the city in 1918, and since then, the labour movement of Ahmedabad took a new turn under his guidance. He introduced the mechanism of conciliation, consensus and arbitration for resolving labour–capital disputes. These principles were the continuation of the pre-British traditions used for settling disputes of the city, which Gandhi adapted to the new industrial situation. After the successful strike of 1918, workers formed the Ahmedabad Textile Labour Association, or the Majoor Mahajan, in 1920 on Gandhian principles under the leadership of Ansuyaben Sarabhai. This was the first labour union of Ahmedabad. Gandhi guided it for many years. His ideas of peaceful industrial relations, class cooperation, trusteeship, conciliation and arbitration reduced the intensity of class conflict in the industrial society of Ahmedabad and contributed to healthy industrial growth in the city.

Unlike previous social reformers of the city, Gandhi showed sympathy towards the depressed castes. He attacked the most unjust and inhuman institution of untouchability, which according to him was a blot on Hinduism. He included a vow against untouchability as one of the vows to be taken by the inmates of his *ashram*. Though Gandhi attacked the very core of the caste system by combating the evil of untouchability, he was not opposed to the caste system itself. He agreed with the earlier reformers of the city who believed in carrying out social reforms through the agency of the caste system.

Being a profound humanist and crusader against social injustice, Gandhi denounced the social customs of child marriage, enforced widowhood, dowry, *purdah* and *sati*. He believed that women should be equal partners in winning *swaraj* as men. He legitimised women's role in politics and public life. He channelised the work of women leaders of the city for the national cause. He encouraged women to participate in programmes initiated by him. Sharadaben Mehta, Vidhyaben Nilkanth, Sulochanaben Desai and Ansuyaben Sarabhai assumed leadership of various regional and national organisations. He also brought out the ordinary women of the *pols* of the city from the seclusion of their homes to participate in the picketing of shops selling liquor and foreign goods. Women joined spinning classes and sold *khadi.* They organised and attended meetings and participated in political processions. Women of the city experienced a new feeling of courage and patriotism. Many new women leaders appeared on the scene who led women's movements.

Gandhi dominated the political, social and cultural life of Ahmedabad. He left Ahmedabad in 1930 but left his imprint in the forms of the Sabarmati Ashram, Majoor Mahajan, Gujarat Vidhyapith, Harijan Seva Sangh, Jyoti Sangh and other organisations, which carried on his legacy, and the city breathed the Gandhian ethos for a long time after he left it.

When Gandhi left Ahmedabad in 1930, it was no longer a small provincial town in western India but had emerged as a centre of the national movement. It also became the focus of international attention, especially after the Dandi march and the salt *satyagraha*.

Bibliography

Archival Sources:

Maharashtra State Archives, Mumbai.

Revenue Department.

Year	Diaries
1817	303
1818	125, 126, 127, 129, 130, 131, 132, 134
1819	137, 139, 143
1820	149, 152, 159

	Volumes
1821	17/17, 23
1823	24/76
1825	7/117
1826	5/137, 6/138, 19/151, 21/153
1827	23/177
1828	206, 1/206
1829	14/261
1830	12/293
1831	28/356, 34/361
1832	27/420
1833	30/497, 121/1488
1834	29/573
1835	3/625, 75/637
1836	18/705, 43/730
1837	11/769
1838	24/1884, 93/953
1839	6/969, 74/1037, 106/1069
1840	84/1168
1841	25/1254
1842	5/1338, 5/1339, 26/1359, 33/1366
1844	6/1563, 32/689, 76/1633
1845	139, 148, 196, 202, 262

1846	00/8, 8/1846, 182
1847	36, 119, 120, 144
1848	180, 450
1849	184
1851	19, 76
1852	58
1853	30, 1916
1854	37, 162, 163
1855	44, 211
1856	147
1857	138, 194
1858	13, 123
1859	12, 53
1860	08, 31, 40, 85
1861	3
1864	120
1862-1864	75

General Department

Year	Volumes
1874	37
1876	97
1879	38
1880	48, 63, 75
1881	62, 62A, 63
1882	8
1884	13, 26, 104
1886	6C
1887	101
1888	8, 82, 82A
1889	6, 13, 101, 103
1891	10
1892	7
1893	45, 48
1894	8, 90
1895	41A, 87, 88, 90

1897	71, 79
1898	103
1900	69
1901	72
1902	68
1903	66
1905	60
1907	92
1908	93
1909	80
1910	14, 103
1911	13, 132
1913	48, 114, 191

<u>Compilation files</u>

1914	896, 1090, 360
1915	896, 945
1917	219
1918	219
1919	219, 462
1920	219
1921	342, 385, 742, 1354A
1922	1427-I, 2511-1

<u>Judicial Department</u>

Year	Diaries
1818	90, 102, 103, 105
1819	109, 1110, 115, 116
1820	120
1821-22	3/3
1824	3/59
1895	222

<u>Political Department.</u>

1816	Diary No: 431

Reports on Native Newspapers Published in the Bombay Presidency, weekly reports from 1868 to 1920.

Museum Section, BJ Institute of Research and Learning, Ashram Road, Ahmedabad.

A large number of *khatpatras*, or legal documents, pertaining to the purchase, sale and mortgage of houses, shops and land belonging to Ahmedabad and its environs are preserved at the BJ Institute, Ahmedabad. Most of them are in Gujarati and in manuscript form and are given accession numbers. The following *khatpatras* are referred to in the present work: Accession Nos: 15, 23, 24, 30, 31, 84, 128, 212, 8836, 8837, 8840, 8852, 8874, 8893, 8896, 8907, 8911, 8912, 8914, 8916. An important *khatpatra*, *Kapasia Bajarnu Khatpatra* of 1892, is an agreement among cotton merchants. It throws light on the arbitration system of the *mahajan*. It is in Gujarati and no accession number has been given to it.

Government Publications

Ahmedabad Municipality, *Administration Report of the Working of the Municipality of Ahmedabad*, annually 1882–1920, Ahmedabad. Prior to the year 1886–1887, it was titled *Annual Report of the Ahmedabad City Municipality*.

Bombay Government,

- *Census of the Ahmedabad Collectorate – 1872*, Bombay 1873.
- *Census of Bombay Presidency, 1872, General Report and Tables of the Population, Houses Enumerated in the Bombay Presidency on the 21st February, 1872*, Part I & II, Bombay, 1875.
- *Directory of Vernacular Teachers Holding Certificates of Qualifications Recognized by the Education Department Employed in Local Board and Municipal Schools and in Native States in Northern Division*, annually 1900–1914, Ahmedabad, 1900 to 1915.
- *Gazetteer of the Bombay Presidency*, Vol. IV, *Ahmedabad*, Bombay, 1879.
- *Gazetteer of the Bombay Presidency*, Vol. IX: Part I, *Gujarat Population: Hindus*, Bombay, 1901.
- *Gazetteer of the Bombay Presidency*, Vol. IX: Part II, *Gujarat Population: Musalmans and Parsis*, Bombay, 1899.
- *General Report of the Administration of the Bombay Presidency*, annually 1864–1921. Bombay, 1865–1922.
- Labour Office, *Report on an Enquiry into Working Class Family Budgets in Ahmedabad*, Bombay, 1926.

- *Provincial Report on the Working of the Indian Factories Act*, annually 1888–1901; later listed as *Annually Factory Reports*, 1902–1923, Bombay.
- "Report on the Collectorate of Ahmedabad" by EG Fawcett, *Selections from the Records of the Bombay Government*, Vol. V, New Series, Bombay, 1854.
- *Report of the Commissioners Appointed by the Governor of Bombay in Council to Inquire into the Condition of the Operatives in the Bombay Factories and the Necessity or Otherwise for the Passing of a Factories Act*, Bombay, 1875.
- *Report and Proceedings of the Commission Appointed to Consider the Working of the Factories in the Bombay Presidency*, Bombay, 1885.
- *Report of the Board of Education*, annually 1849–50 to 1854–55, Bombay.
- *Report of the Director of Public Instruction*, annually 1855–56 to 1913–19.
- *Reports of Civil Cases Determined in the Court of Sudder Dewanee Adalat of Bombay, 1840–48*, Bombay, 1850.
- *Reports of Selected Cases Decided by the Sudder Dewanee Adalat, 1820–40*, Bombay, 1862.
- *Royal Commission on Indian Labour Memorandum from the Government of Bombay*, Bombay, 1929.
- *Royal Commission on Indian Labour, Memorandum of Written Evidence of Government Witnessed*, Bombay Presidency, Bombay, 1929.
- *Source Material for a History of the Freedom Movement in India, 1885–1920*, Vol. II, Bombay, 1958.
- *Statement showing Statistics of Cotton Mills in the Bombay Presidency for the Years 1890, 1894, 1905, 1908, 1914.*

East India (Factories Act), *Return to an Address of the Hon. House of Commons, dated 15 April 1889 for a Copy of Reports on the Working of the Indian Factories Act Made to the Government of India in Reply to Inquiries Recently Directed by the Secretary of State for India*, Ordered and Printed by the House of Commons, 16th April 1889.

Education Commission, *Evidence Taken before the Bombay Provincial Committee and Memorials Addressed to the Education Commission, Appendix to the Education Commission Report,* Vol. II, Calcutta, 1884.

Government of India, Census Commissioner.

- *Census of India: 1891*, Vol. VIII, *Bombay and Its Feudatories*, Part I & II, Bombay, 1892.
- *Census of India: 1901*, Vol. IX, *Bombay,* Part I & II, Bombay, 1902.
- *Census of India:* 1911, Vol. VII, Bombay, Part I & II, Bombay, 1912.
- *Census of India: 1921*, Vol. VIII, *Bombay Presidency*, Part I & II, Bombay, 1922.
- *Census of India: 1921*, Vol. IX, *The Cities of the Bombay Presidency*, Part I & II, Poona, 1922.
- *Census of India: 19*31, Vol. IX, *The Cities of the Bombay Presidency*, Part I *Report*, Bombay, 1933.

Government of India, Publications Division, *The Collected Works of Mahatma Gandhi*, Vol. XIII to XLIV, Ahmedabad, 1964–1971.

Government of Maharashtra, *Source Material for a History of the Freedom Movement in India,* Vol. III, *Mahatma Gandhi*, Part I, 1915–1922, Bombay, 1965.

Imperial Census of 1881, Operations and Results in the Presidency of Bombay including Sind, Vols. I & II, Bombay, 1882.

India, Factory Commission – 1890, *Report of the Indian Factory Commission, Appointed in September 1890, under the Orders of His Excellency, the Governor General in Council, with Proceedings and Appendices,* Calcutta, 1890.

India, Factory Labour Commission, 1908, *Report of the Indian Factory Labour Commission*, 1908, 2 Volumes, Simla, 1908.

Indian Industrial Commission, *Report of the Indian Industrial Commission, 1916–18, with Minutes of Evidence,* 5 Vols., Calcutta, 1918.

India, Textile Factories Labour Committee, *Report of Textile Factories Labour Committee Appointed by the Government of India on the 17th of December 1906 to Enquire into the Conditions of Factory Labour in India with Appendices*, Bombay, 1907.

Royal Commission on Labour, *Foreign Reports*, Vol. II, *The Colonies and the Indian Empire with an Appendix on the Migration of Labour, Parliamentary Papers*, 1892, XXXVI, Part V.

Royal Commission on Labour in India, *Report of the Royal Commission on Labour in India*, Calcutta, 1931.

Secretary of State for India in Council, *The Imperial Gazetteer of India*, Vol. V, New ed., Oxford, 1908.

Contemporary Newspapers, Periodicals and Caste Journals

Audichya Hitechhu Patra, a monthly caste journal published from Ahmedabad, 1884–1920. In Gujarati.

Brahmakshatriya Trimasik Patrika, a quarterly caste journal published from Ahmedabad 1907–1922. In Gujarati.

Buddhi Prakash, a monthly published from Ahmedabad, 1854–1920. In Gujarati.

Gujarat Shalapatra, a monthly published from Ahmedabad and for a short period from Rajkot, 1863–1920. In Gujarati.

Jain Hitechhu, a monthly caste journal published from Ahmedabad, 1899–1910. In Gujarati.

Kadva Vijay, a monthly caste journal published from Viramgam. In Gujarati.

Navjivan, a weekly published from Ahmedabad, 1919–1922. In Gujarati.

Prajabandhu, an Anglo-Gujarati weekly published from Ahmedabad, 1898–1920.

Shri Nagar Vijay, a monthly caste journal, published from Ahmedabad, 1911–12. In Gujarati.

Sundri Subodh, a monthly women's journal published from Ahmedabad, 1903–1920. In Gujarati.

Tolak Shubhechhak Patrika, a monthly caste journal published from Ahmedabad, 1880–88. In Gujarati.

Vaishya Patrika, a monthly journal of Meshri Vanias published from Ahmedabad, 1904–1915. In Gujarati.

Vasant, a monthly published from Ahmedabad 1903–1920. In Gujarati.

Other Primary Sources

Ahmedabad Mill-Owners' Association, *Report of the Ahmedabad Mill-Owners' Association*, Annually 1920–1930.

Annual Report of the Principal of the Gujarat College, Ahmedabad, annually 1891–1910, Bombay, 1892–1911.

Annual Report of the Gujarat Vernacular Society, 1880–1920, Ahmedabad.

'Revenue System in Ahmedabad and Karia' a collection of documents in manuscript form in the library of Bombay University (Fort) under the call number 352 and accession number 27630.

Interviews

The following interviews were conducted in January and February 1987.

Gandhi, Chandrakant Chhotalal (b. 1903), a lawyer and active in political and public life of Ahmedabad.

Joshi, Girijashankar (b. 1888), a Sanskrit scholar and a friend of M. Gandhi and a teacher in M. Gandhi's Ashram School.

Lalbhai, Lilavatiben (b. 1899), sister of industrialist Kasturbhai Lalbhai.

Lashkari, Kantaben Shambhuprasad (b. 1893), granddaughter of Bechardas Lashkari.

Mehta, Saudaminiben (b. 1903), daughter of Vidhyaben Nilkanth.

Munshi, Haji Muhammad Husain Haji Ranjitbhai (b. 1896), a tobacco merchant.

Patel, Shambhuprasad (b. 1904), a cotton merchant.

Pathak, Ramanbhai Gandabhai (b. 1896), a lawyer.

Shah, Champaklal (b. 1909), a textile merchant.

Sutaria, Atmaram Bhogilal (b. 1912), a textile merchant and president of the Maskati Market.

Thakar, Narmadashankar Ganpatram (b. 1890) taught at the Ashram School Kochrab and journalist.

Vanikar, Vinayak Sakharam (b. 1907) a Marathi-speaking resident of Ahmedabad, a college professor.

Contemporary Works, Autobiographies, Travelogues, Memoirs etc.

(These are valuable as primary sources.)

English

Briggs, HG, *The Cities of Gujarashtra*, London: Times Press, 1849.

Carpenter, Mary, *Six Months in India*, 2 Vols. London: Longmans Green & Co., 1868.

Edalji, Dosabhai, *A History of Gujarat: From Earliest Period to the Present Times*, Ahmedabad: United Printing and General Agency Company's Press, 1894.

Forbes, James, *Oriental Memoirs*, 4 Vols. London: White Cocharane & Co., 1813.

Forrest, GW, *Cities of India: Past and Present*, London: Archibald Constable & Co., 1905.

Gandhi, MK *An Autobiography or the Study of My Experiments with Truth*, trans. into English from Gujarati by Mahadev Desai, Ahmedabad: Navjivan Publishing House, 1989. (First published in 1927).

Hopkins, EW, "Ancient and Modern Hindu Guilds", *India: Old and New*, New York: Charles Scribner's Sons, 1901.

Houston, John, *Representative Men of the Bombay Presidency* (2nd ed.), Bombay, 1900.

Malbari, BM, *Gujarat and the Gujaratis*, reprint of the 3rd ed. (1889), Delhi: Mittal Publication, 1983.

Rea, GT, *A Broken Journey*, London: 1894.

Robertson, James (ed.), *Western India Reports Addressed to the Chambers of Commerce of Manchester, Liverpool and Glasgow by Their Commissioner the Late Alexander Mackay Esq.*, London: Nathaniel Cook, 1853.

Sherring, MA, *The History of Protestant Missions in India (1806–1881*), London: The Religious Tract Society, 1884.

Thorton, Edward, *A Gazetteer of the Territories Under the Government of the East India Company and the Native States on the Continent of India*, reprint of the 1858 ed., Delhi: DK Publishers, 1984.

Todd, James, *Travels in Western India*, Reprint, Delhi: Oriental Publishers, 1971. (First published in 1839).

Gujarati

Anonymous, *Hindustan ane Chin Vachhena Afinna Veparni Tawarikh*, Bombay, 1854.

Anonymous, *Mahipatram Vilayat Java Vishe*, Ahmedabad: Gujarat Vernacular Society, 1860.

Badshah, Bhagwanlal R., *The Life of Rao Bahadur Ranchorelal Chhotalal, C.I.E.*, Bombay: Times of India Steam Press, 1899. In English and Gujarati.

Dalpatram Dahyabhai, *Bhut Nibandh*, Ahmedabad: Gujarat Vernacular Society, 1849.

– *Gnyati Nibandh*, Ahmedabad: Gujarat Vernacular Society, 1851.

– *Punarvivah Prabandh*, Ahmedabad: Gujarat Vernacular Society, 1853.

– *Garbavali*, Ahmedabad: Gujarat Vernacular Society, 1854.

– *Balvivah Nibandh*, Ahmedabad: Gujarat Vernacular society, 1854.

– *Sheher Sudhara Vishe Nibandh*, Ahmedabad: Gujarat Vernacular Society, 1858.

– *Gujaratna Hinduoni Sthiti*, Bombay: Buddhivardhak Sabha, 1865.

– *Dalpat Kavya*, 2 parts (4th ed.), Ahmedabad: Gujarat Vernacular Society, 1924.

Dave, Narmadashankar Lalshankar (ed.) *Gujarat Sarva Sangraha*, Bombay: Education Department of Bombay Presidency, 1867.

– *Dharmavichar* (2nd ed.), Bombay: Jayshankar Narmadashankar, 1900.

Derasari, Dahyabhai, *Sathina Sahityanu Digdarshan*, reprint, Ahmedabad: Gujarat Vidhyasabha, 1969. (First published in 1911).

Dhanjibhai Vithaldas, *Gujaratna Bhikhario*, Ahmedabad: Gujarat Vernacular Society, 1901.

Divetia, Narsimhrao Bholanath, *Smaran Mukur*, Ahmedabad: Sahitya Prakashak Co., 1926.

– *Rojnishi*, Ahmedabad: Gujarat Vidhyasabha, 1953. (It is the author's diary from 1892 to 1935).

Edalji, Dosabhai, *Gujarat no Itihas*, Ahmedabad: Gujarat Vernacular Society, 1850.

Kadva Kanbini Natma Dikriona Samrakshan Saru Niyam, Ahmedabad: Darbarshri Jorawarsanghiji of Patdi, 1869.

Kantawala, Hargovinddas D, *Deshi Karigarine Uttejan*, Part I & II, Ahmedabad: 1876.

– *Nat Sudharo*, Ahmedabad: published by the author, 1886.

– *Sansar Sudharo* (3rd ed.), Vadodra: Thakkar Vithalbhai Ashram, 1923.

Krishnarao Bholanath, *Bholanath Sarabhainu Jivan Charit*, Bombay: Nirnay Sagar Press, 1888. (It also contains notes from Bholanath's diary).

Maganlal Vakhatchand, *Amdavadno Itihas*, reprint, Ahmedabad: Gujarat Vidhyasabha, 1977, (First published by the Gujarat Vernacular Society in 1851).

Mahipatram Rupram, *Sasu Vahuni Ladai* (2nd ed.), Ahmedabad, 1873.

– *Englandni Musafarinu Varnan*, Ahmedabad, 1864.

– *Parvatikunvar Akhyan*, Ahmedabad, 1881.

Mehta, Sharadaben S., *Jivan Sambharna*, Baroda; Published by the author, 1938.

Mehta, Sumant, *Atmakatha*, Ahmedabad: Prabhudas Patwari, 1971.

Motilal Keshawlal, *Bhojan Vyahavar Tyan Kanya Vyahvhar*, Ahmedabad: Gujarat Vernacular Society, 1893.

Narayan Hemchandra, *Hun Pote*, Bombay: N. Hemchandra, 1900.

Nilkanth, Vidhyaben R, *Phorum,* Ahmedabad: Gujarat Vidhyasabha, 1955. (It contains reminiscences of the author).

Patel, Maganlal Narottam, *Mahajan Mandal*, 2 Vols., Ahmedabad, 1896.

Sansar Vyavaharni Chopdi, Ahmedabad: Pustak Vriddhi Karnar Mandali, 1847 (The first book to be printed in Ahmedabad. It is a textbook).

Shankarrai Amritrai (Ed.), *Amdavadno Jivan Vikas*, Ahmedabad: Published by the author, 1921.

Thakor, Vaikunthlal S (Ed.), *Sw. Ambalal Sakarlal Desaina Bhasano ane Lekho*, (3rd ed.), Ahmedabad: Published by the author, 1942.

Tripathi, Mansukhram, *Forbes Jivan Charitra*, Bombay: Forbes Gujarati Sabha, 1869.

Uttamram, *Amdavadnu Varnan*, Ahmedabad, 1853.

Vallabhji Sundarji Punjabhai, *Rajnagarna Ratno*, Rajkot: Shri Saraswati Chandroday Office, 1918.

Yagnik, Indulal, *Atmakatha,* Part I & II, Ahmedabad: 1955.

Persian

Ali Muhammad Khan, *Mirat-i-Ahmadi: A Persian History of Gujarat Circa 1751*, trans. into English by Lokhandwala, MF, Baroda: Oriental Institute, 1965.

Ali Muhammad Khan, *The Supplement to the Mirat-i-Ahmadi*, trans. by Syed, Nawab Ali and Seddon, Charles, Baroda: Syed N A, 1924.

Firastha, *Tawarikhe Firastha*, trans. into Gujarati by Diwanji Atmaram Motiram as *Firastha Krut Gujaratno Itihas*, Poona: Gujarati Sahitya Parishad Bhandol Committee, 1917.

Sikandar, *Mirat-I-Sikandari*, 1611, trans. into Gujarati by Diwanji, Atmaram Motiram, Ahmedabad: Gujarat Vernacular Society, 1914.

Folklore

Various folk songs in the form of *garba*, *rasada*, *lavani* and folk stories and oral traditions are preserved in manuscript form in the Gujarati Forbes Sabha, Bombay.

Bibliography

In the present work the following are referred to:

- Amdavadni Shehrni Lavni
- Chadiani Lavni
- Chadiani Varta
- Shelulkarno Garbo
- Shri Satibai no Garbo

Books

English

Advance Mills, *A Short History of the Ahmedabad Advance Mills Ltd., 1903–1953*, Bombay, 1953.

Agnew, Vijaya, *Elite Women in Indian Politics*, New Delhi: Vikas Publishing House, 1979.

Asthana, Pratima, *Women's Movement in India*, Delhi: Vikas Publishing House, 1974.

Ballhatchet, Kenneth, *Social Policy and Social Change in Western India, 1817–30*, London: Oxford University Press, 1957.

Ballhatchet, K and Harrison, J (Ed.), *The City in South Asia: Pre-Modern and Modern,* London: Curzon Press, 1980.

Bayly, CA, *Rulers, Townsmen and Bazars: North Indian Society in the Age of British Expansion, 1880–1870,* Cambridge: Cambridge University Press, 1983.

Boman Behram, BK (Ed.), *The Rise of Municipal Government in the City of Ahmedabad*, Bombay: Taraporevala Sons & Co., 1937.

Boyd, Robin, *The Church History of Gujarat*, Madras: The Christian Literary Society, 1981.

Chandra, Bipin, *The Rise and Growth of Economic Nationalism in India*, New Delhi: People's Publishing House, 1982.

Chavda, Vijaysingh, *Modern Gujarat*, Ahmedabad: New Order Book Depot, n.d.

Choksey, RD, *Economic Life in the Bombay Presidency – 1880–1939,* Mumbai: Asia Publishing House, 1968.

Commissariat, MS, *Mandelslo's Travels in Western India*, London: Oxford University Press, 1931.

– *Studies in the History of Gujarat*, Bombay: Longman's Green & Co. Ltd., 1935.

– *A History of Gujarat, 1297–1573*, Vol. I, Bombay: Longman & Green Co., 1938.

– *A History of Gujarat, 1573–1758*, Vol. II, Bombay: Orient Longmans, 1957.

– *A History of Gujarat: The Maratha Period 1758–1818*, Vol. III, Ahmedabad: Gujarat Vidhya Sabha, 1980.

Davar, FC, *Sir Nowroji P Vakil: A Biographical Sketch*, Ahmedabad: Behramji S Lalkaka,1955.

Desai, AR, *Social Background of Indian Nationalism*, Bombay: Popular Prakashan, 1984.

Desai, Govindbhai and Clarke, AB, *Gazetteer of the Baroda State*, Vol. I, *General Information*, Bombay, 1923.

Desai, Mahadev H, *A Righteous Struggle (A Chronicle of the Ahmedabad Textile Labourer's Fight for Justice)*, Ahmedabad: Navjivan Publishing House, 1951.

Desai, Natwarlal N, *Directory of Ahmedabad Mill Industry*, Ahmedabad: Stock Holders' Association, 1951.

Desai, Neera, *Women in India*, Bombay: Vora & Co., 1957.

– *Social Change in Gujarat: Study of Nineteenth Century Gujarat Society*, Bombay: Vora & Co., 1978.

Derasari, Dahyabhai (ed.), *Society for Prevention of Cruelty to Animals, Ahmedabad 1881–1931.*

– *A Jubilee Number*, Ahmedabad, 1931.

Dharaiya, RK, *Gujarat in 1857*, Ahmedabad: Gujarat University, 1970.

Dobbin, Christine, *Urban Leadership in Western India: Politics and Communities in Bombay 1840–1885*, London: Oxford University Press, 1972.

Doshi, Harish, *Traditional Neighbourhood in a Modern City*, New Delhi: Ahbhinav Publications, 1974.

Edwardes, SM, *Memoir of Rao Bahadur Ranchhodlal Chhotalal, C.I.E., Late Member of the Legislative Council, Bombay and Founder of the Mill Industry of Gujarat*, Exeter: William Pollard, 1920.

Eisenstadt, SN, *Modernization: Protest and Change*, Englewood Cliffs, New Jersey: Prentice Hall, 1966.

– *Tradition, Change and Modernity*, New York: John Wiley & Sons, 1973.

Enthoven, RE, *The Tribes and Castes of Bombay*, 3 Vols. Reprint, Delhi: Cosmo Publications, 1975. (First published in 1920-22.)

Erikson, Erik H, *Gandhi's Truth*, London: Faber & Faber Ltd., 1970.

Everett, Jana M, *Women and Social Change in India*, New Delhi: Heritage Publications, 1979.

Ezekiel, Moses, *History and Culture of the Bene Israel in India*, Nadiad: JJ College of Science, 1948.

Forbes, Alexander K, *Rasmala or Hindu Annals of the Province of Goozerat in Western India*, reprint of the 1878 edition, New Delhi: Heritage Publishers, 1973.

Gandhi, MK, *Constructive Programme: Its Meaning and Place*, Ahmedabad: Navjivan Publishing House, 1941.

Ghurye, GS, *Caste and Class in India*, Bombay: Popular Book Depot, 1957.

Gillion, Kenneth, *Ahmedabad: A Study in Indian Urban History*, Berkeley: University of California Press, 1968.

Gopal, Surendra, *Commerce & Crafts in Gujarat*, Delhi: People's Publishing House, 1976.

Jones, Emry, *Towns & Cities*, London: Oxford University Press, 1966.

Jones, Gareth Stedman, *Languages of Class: Studies in English Working Class History 1832–1982,* Cambridge: Cambridge University Press, 1983.

Kulke, Echchad, *The Parsees in India*, Delhi: Vikas Publications, 1974.

Kumar, Lal Sheo, *The Urban Elite*, Delhi: Thompson Press (India) Publication, 1974.

Kumar, Ravinder, *Western India in the Nineteenth Century: A Study in the Social History in Maharashtra*, London: Routledge & Kegan Paul Ltd., 1968.

Essays in the Social History of Modern India, New Delhi: Oxford University Press, 1983.

Leach, E and Mukherjee S (Eds.), *Elites in South Asia*, Cambridge: Cambridge University Press, 1970.

Majumdar, MR, *Cultural History of Gujarat from Early Times to Pre-British Period*, Bombay: Popular Prakashan, 1965.

Maskati Cloth Market Association of Ahmedabad, *Articles of Amrut Mahotsava: Souvenir with Photos 1906–1982*, Ahmedabad, 1982.

Mehta, Kapilrai (Ed.), *Ahmedabad: 1918*, Ahmedabad: Gujarat Publishers, 1959.

Mehta, Makrand J, *The Ahmedabad Cotton Textile Industry: Genesis and Growth,* Ahmedabad: New Order Book Co., 1982.

Mehta, SD, *The Cotton Mills in India, 1854–1954*, Bombay: The Textile Association of India, Bombay, 1954.

Mishra, SC, *Muslim Communities in Gujarat: Preliminary Studies in the History and Social Organization*, Bombay: Asia Publishing House, 1964.

Mishra, BB, *The India Middle Classes: Their Growth in Modern Times*, Delhi: Oxford University Press, 1983.

Morris, David Morris, *The Emergence of an Industrial Labour Force in India: A Study of the Bombay Cotton Mills, 1854–1947*, Berkley: University of California, 1965.

Oddie, GA, *Social Protest in India: British Protestant Missionaries and Social Reforms 1850–1900,* New Delhi: Manohar Publications, 1979.

O'Malley, LS (ed.), *Modern India and the West*, London: Oxford University Press, 1941.

Parikh, Narhari D, *Sardar Vallabhbhai Patel,* 2 Vols. Trans. from Gujarati into English by the author, Ahmedabad: Navjivan Publishing House, 1953, 1956.

Parulekar, RV (Ed.), *Survey of Indigenous Education in the Province of Bombay (1820–1830)*, reprint, Bombay: Asia Publishing House, 1951.

– (Ed.) *Selections from the Record of the Government of Bombay Education*, Part I, 1819–1852, Bombay: Asia Publishing House, 1953.

Parulekar, RV and Bakshi, CL, *Selections from Educational Records (Bombay), Part II, 1815–1840,* Bombay: Asia Publishing House, 1955.

– *Selections from Educational Records (Bombay)*, Part III, *1826–1840*, Bombay: Asia Publishing House, 1957.

Patel, Sujata, *The Making of Industrial Relations: The Ahmedabad Textile Industry 1918–1939*, Delhi: Oxford University Press, 1987.

Priyolkar, AK, *The Printing Press in India: Its Beginning and Early Development*, Bombay: Marathi Samshodhan Mandal, 1958.

Rotary Club of Ahmedabad, *Ahmedabad*, Ahmedabad: Rotary Club of Ahmedabad, 1940.

Rudolph, Lloyd and Rudolph, Suzanne, *The Modernity of Traditions: Political Development of India,* Chicago: The University of Chicago Press, 1967.

Rutnagar, Jal S (ed.), *The Indian Textile Journal Special Souvenir Number of Mark the Centenary of the Cotton Textile Industry of India—1854–1954*, Bombay, 1954.

Rutnagar, SN, *Bombay Industries: The Cotton Mills*, Mumbai: The Indian Textile Journal Ltd., 1927.

Sen, S, *Working Class of India: History of its Emergence and Movement 1830–1970*, Kolkata: KP Bagchi & Co., 1977.

Sharma, RS and Jha, V (Eds.), *Indian Society: Historical Probings: In Memory of DD Kosambi*, New Delhi: People's Publishing House, 1974.

Sharma, RS (Ed.), *Survey of Research in Economics and Social History of India*, Delhi: Ajanta Publications, 1986.

Singh, Yogendra, *Modernization of Indian Tradition: A Systematic Study of Social Change*, (2nd ed.), Delhi: Thomson Press (India) Ltd. Publication, 1973.

Sinha, Pradip, *Calcutta in Urban History*, Kolkata: Firma KLM Pvt. Ltd., 1978.

Sjoberg, Gideon, *The Pre-industrial City: Past and Present*, Giencoe Illinois: The Free Press, 1960.

Spodek, Howard, *Ahmedabad: Shock City of Twentieth Century India,* Bloomington: Indiana University Press, 2011.

Srinivas, MN, *Social Change in Modern India*, Delhi: Orient Longmans, 1979.

Thompson, EP, *The Making of the English Working Class*, London: Penguin Books, 1968.

Thoothi, NA, *The Vaishnavas of Gujarat*, Kolkata: Longmans Green & Co., 1935.

Tripathi, Dwijendra, *The Dynamics of a Tradition: Kasturbhai Lalbhai and His Entrepreneurship*, New Delhi: Manohar Publications, 1981.

Yagnik Achyut and Sheth Suchitra. *Ahmedabad: From Royal City to Megacity*. New Delhi: Penguin Books, 2011.

Gujarati

Banker, Shankarlal G, *Gandhiji ane Majoor Pravrutti: Sansmarano ane Anubhavo*, Ahmedabad: Navjivan Publication House, 1965.

Bhatt, Diwaliben and Budha, Shridevi, *Apna Nariratno*, Bhavnagar: Gurjar Sahitya Bhandar, 1944.

Bhatt, Usha G, *Amdavad Shaherni Stree Netrutva Shakti, 1920-1947*, Ahmedabad: Gujarat University, 1982.

Brahmakshatriya, Kashinath, *Brahmakshatriya no Ujjval Itihas,* Panchora, 1927.

Dabu Noshir K (ed.), *Vakil Anjuman Adran: Golden Jubilee Granth*, Ahmedabad: Vakil Anjuman Adran Golden Jubilee Committee, 1983.

Dave, Kashisankar, *Dalpatram*, Baroda: MC Kothari, 1925.

Desai, Pranlal K and Parekh, MT, *Amdavad Municipality Shatabdi Smarak Granth*, Ahmedabad: Ahmedabad Municipality, 1935.

Dhruv, Anandshankar, *Apno Dharma*, Ahmedabad, 1942.

Dhruv, Gatubhai, *Prarthana Samaj*, Bombay: Parichay Trust, 1967.

Dwivedi, Narmadashankar V, *Gujaratna Ayitihasik Sadhano*, Bombay: Gujarati Forbes Sabha, 1928.

Ek Jankar Tabib, *Amdavadna Janita Banu Doctor (Miss) Motibai Rustomji Kapadia L.R.C.P. L.R.C.S.L. M.F.R.C.S. (Ireland) ni Jindagino Aheval*, Ahmedabad, 1938.

Gandhi, Bhogilala, *Gujarat Darshan*, Vadodra: Chetan Prakashan Griha, 1960.

Jani, Ambalal Bulakhiram, *Shri Forbes Gujarati Sabhana Hastalikhit Pustakoni Savistar Namavali*, 2 vols., Bombay: Forbes Gujarati Sabha, 1923.

Jhaveri, Bipinchandra, *Ramanbhai Nilkanth*, Ahmedabad: Gujarat Vidhyasabha, 1953.

Joshi, Umashankar, *Akho: Ek Adhyagyan*, (2nd ed.), Ahmedabad: Gujarat Vidhyasabha, 1973.

- Jote, Ratnamanirao Bhimrao, Gujaratnu Patnagar Amdavad, Ahmedabad: Gujarat Sahitya Sabha, 1929.
- *Gujaratno Sanskrutik Itihas: Islam Yug*, 4 Vols., 2nd ed., Ahmedabad: Gujarat Vidhyasabha, 1964.

Amdavadno Parichay, Ahmedabad: Gujarat Sahitya Sammelan, 1936.

Jyoti Sangh, *Jyoti Vikas Yatra*, Ahmedabad: Urmilaben Girdharlal, 1971.

Mangaldas Leena, *Akhand Divo*, Ahmedabad: Shreyas Publications, 1970.

Mashruvala, Kishorelal D, *Swaminarayan Sampraday Athva Sahajanand Swami*, Ahmedabad: Navjivan Prakashan Mandir, 1940.

Marshal, Ratan, *Gujaratna Patrakaritvano Itihas*, Surat: Gandiv Sahitya Mandir, 1950.

Mavlankar, Ganesh V, *Sansamarano*, Ahmedabad: Gujarat Vidhya Sabha, 1954.

Med, Susmita, *Vaitalik*, Ahmedabad: Jyotisangh, 1987.

Mehta, Kapilrai, *Amdavad Sarvasanghna*, Ahmedabad: Gujarat Publishers, 1948.

Mehta, Bhanushankar N, *Mahipatram Charitra*, Baroda: Saiyaji Sahitya Mala, 1930.

Mehta, Yashodhar, *Ranchhodlal ane Bija Natako*, Ahmedabad: Gujarat Sahitya Sabha, 1948.

Navi Markit Udghatan Smaranika, Ahmedabad: Amdavad Maskati Kapad Markit Mahajan, 1962.

Nilkanth, Ramanbhai, *Dharma ane Samaj*, Vol. II, Ahmedabad: Gujarat Vernacular Society, 1935.

Nilkanth, Vidhyaben, *Narikunj*, Ahmedabad: Gujarat Vidhyasabha, 1956.

Nilkanth, Vibodini, *Vidhya Gauri Nilkanth*, Bombay: Parichay Trust, 1976.

Oza, Dhanwant, *Anandshankar Dhruv*, Ahmedabad: Ravani Prakashan, 1963.

Parekh, Bansidhar G, *Sheth Mangaldas Girdhardas: Jivan ane Karya*, Ahmedabad: Sheth Mathuradas Mangaldas, Ahmedabad, 1955.

Parekh, Girdhardas Uttamram, *Rao Bahadur Bhogilal Pranvallabhdasnu Jivan Charitra*, Ahmedabad, 1925.

Parekh, Hiralal T., *Arvachin Gujaratnu Rekhadarshan*, (2nd ed.), Ahmedabad: Gujarat Vidhya Sabha, 1976. (First published in 2 vols. in 1935–36.)

– *Gujarat Vernacular Society no Itihas*, 3 vols. Ahmedabad: Gujarat Vernacular Society, 1932–34.

Parekh, Hiralal T (ed.), *Lady Vidhyaben Manimahotsava Granth*, Ahmedabad: Gujarat Vernacular Society, 1936.

Parekh, Madhusudan, *Dalpatram*, Ahmedabad: Kumkum Prakashan, 1980.

Parikh, Purushottam, *Kanbi Kshatriya Utpatti ane Itihas*, Ahmedabad, 1912.

Parsi Zoroastrian Rahevasio Vishe Mojni Prakashan Directory, Ahmedabad: Ahmedabad Parsi Panchayat, 1975.

Prabhakar, Alishabhai, *Suvartanu Parodh Yane Paratparnu Parakram*, Mehsana: Published by the author, 1982.

Shukla, Shivshankar, *Ansuyaben Sarabhaini Jivankatha*, Ahmedabad: Majoor Mahajan Sangh, 1975.

Sutaria, Atmaram Bhogilal, *Atmaram Bhogilal Sutarianu Nivedan*, Ahmedabad: Amdavad Maskati Kapad Mahajan, 1962.

Tejpal Rajras, *Gujaratna Khristhi Mandaliono Itihas*, Ahmedabad, 1920.

Thakar Dhirubhai, *Parampara ane Pragati: Swa Kasturbhai Lalchainu Jivaneharitra*, Bombay: AD Shroff Memorial Trust, 1980.

Thakkar, Pravina, *Gujaratno Stree Shikshanno Itihas*, Ahmedabad: Anada Book Depot, 1979.

Tolat, Shantilal G, *Bhogindrarao Divetia*, Ahmedabad: Divetia & Sons, 1934.

Trivedi, Navalram, *Samaj Subharanu Rekhadarshan*, reprint, Ahmedabad: Gujarat Vidhya Sabha, 1974 (First published in 1934).

Articles:

English

Abbot, JE, "Inscription on the 'Three Gateways' Ahmedabad", *The Journal of the Bombay Branch of the Royal Asiatic Society*, Vol. XIX, 1895–97, 348–56.

Acharya, Hemlata, "Creative Response in Indian Economy: A Comment", *Economic Weekly*, Vol. IX, April 27, 1957, 547–549.

Bhattacharya, S, "Social History of Modern India: A Trend Report" in Sharma, RS (Ed.), *Survey of Research in Economic and Social History of India,* Delhi: Ajanta Publication, 1986, pp. 169–247.

Chakraborty, Dipesh, "Class Consciousness and the Indian Working Class: Dilemmas of Marxist Historiography", *Journal of Asian and African Studies*, Vol. XIII, No. 1–2, 1988, 21–31.

Chandavarkar, R, "Industrialization in India before 1947: Conventional Approaches and Alternative Perspectives", *Modern Asian Studies*, Vol. 19, 3 (1985), 623–669.

Dixit, Yatindra, "Khatpatras: An Important Historical Source Material on 18th Century Ahmedabad", *Quarterly*, Bhartiya Itihas Sanshodhan Mandal, Pune, Vol. 61, July 1982, pp. 34–48.

Gokhale, BG, "Ahmedabad in the XVII Century", *Journal of the Economic and Social History of the Orient*, Vol. XII, April 1969, 187–197.

Gupta, PS, "Notes on the Origin and Structuring of the Industrial Labour Force in India 1880–1920" in Sharma, RS and Jha, V (ed.), *Indian Society: Historical Probings*, New Delhi: People's Publishing House, 1974, pp. 421–41.

Kamerkar, MP "History: Where are the Women?" in Krishnaraj, M (ed.) *Women's Studies in India: Some Perspectives*, Bombay: Popular Prakashan, 1986, pp. 86–94.

Mehta, Makrand, "A Study of the Practice of Female Infanticide among the Kanbis of Gujarat", *Journal of the Gujarat Research Society*, Vol. XXVIII, 1966, 57–65.

Mehta, Makrand, "Educational Changes in Gujarat in the First Half of the Nineteenth Century", *Quarterly Review of Historical Studies*, Vol. VIII, No. 4, 1968–69, 253–261.

– "From Sahajanand to Gandhiji: Role Perceptions and Methods", in Sen, SP (ed.), *Social and Religious Reform Movements in the Nineteenth and the Twentieth Centuries,* Kolkata: Institute of Historical Studies, 1979, pp. 229–248.

– "Business Environment, Urbanization and Economic Change in India: A Case Study of Ahmedabad in the 19th Century", *Vidya* Vol. XXIV, No. 1, January 1981, 5–18.

– "Khatpatras as a Source of Urban History" *Indian Archives*, Vol. XXX, No. 1, January–June, 1981, 21–29.

– "Indigenous Paper Industry and Muslim Entrepreneurship: Case Study of Paper Technology and Trade of Ahmedabad with Special Reference to the 19th Century", *Indian Journal of History of Science*, Vol. XVII, No.1, May 1982, 46–62.

– "Continuing Tradition and Change in 19th Century Gujarat: The Role of Dalpatram (1818–1898)" *Quarterly*, the Bharat Itihas Samshodhan Mandal, Pune, Vol. 63, No. 2, October 1984, 57–68.

– "The Leader and His Milieu, Gandhi and Ahmedabad, 1915-1920", *The Indian Historical Review*, Vol. XII, Nos. 1–2, July 1985, January 1986, 173–187.

Mehta, Makrand and Dixit, Yatindra, "The Mahajans of Gujarat – Some Questions Relating to the Problems of Transition from Ancient to Medieval Period", *India Past and Present*, Vol. II, No. 2, 1985, 229–240.

Mehta, Makrand and Mehta, Shirin, "The Caste System and Social Reform Movement in Gujarat in Nineteenth Century", *Journal of the Gujarat Research Society*, Vol. 1 xxvii, October 1965, 315–320.

Mehta, Shirin M, "Social Background of the Swadeshi Movement in Gujarat", *Vidya,* XXIV, No. 1, January 1981, 31–46.

Pandit, DP, "Creative Response in Indian Economy: A Regional Analysis", *Economic Weekly*, February 23, 1957, 283–285 and March 2, 1957, 315–317.

Raval, RL, "Tradition and Modernity in the Context of Social Reform Movement in Gujarat During the Nineteenth Century", *Vidya*, Vol. XIX, No. 2, August 1976, 88–102.

Sarkar, Sumit, "Social History: Predicaments and Possibilities", Presidential Address, *Indian History Congress Proceedings*, 45th Session, Annamalai University, 1984, 479–502.

Siddiqi, Asiya, "The Business World of Jamsetjee Jeejeebhoy", *The Indian Economic and Social History Review,* Vol. XIX, Nos. 3 & 4, 1982, 301–324.

Spodek, Howard, "The Manchesterization of Ahmedabad", *Economic Weekly*, Vol. XVII, March 13, 1965, 483–490.

– "Traditional Culture and Entrepreneurship", *Economic and Political Weekly*, Vol. IV, February 22, 1969, M27–M31.

– "Studying the History of Urbanization in India", *Journal of Urban History*, Vol. IV, No. 3, May 1980, 251—295.

Tripathi, D and Mehta, ML, "The Nagarsheths of Ahmedabad: The History of Urban Institute in a Gujarat City", *The Indian History Congress Proceedings, 39th Session*, Hyderabad, 1978, 481–495.

Gujarati

Bhatt, Vibhuti V, "Gujarat Vidhyasabha ane BJ Vidhyabhavanma Sangrahit Britishkalin Khatpatronu Avlokan", *Samipya*, April–June 1985, 34–40.

Jamindar, Rasesh, "Azadini Rashtriya Ladatman Amdavadnu Vidhayak Pradan", *Vidhyapith*, Vol. 16, No. 2, March–April, 1978, 1–11.

Mehta, Makrand, "Samajik Parivartan ane Gujaratna Ashprushyo: Ognismo Saiko", *Arthat,* Vol. I, No. 1, October 1981, 29–54.

Mehta, Makrand and Mehta, Shirin, "Dalpatram ane Forbes: Gat Shatakni Mantri Upar Ek Drashtipat", *Shri Forbes Gujarati Sabha Traimasik*, Vol. 33, No. 4, October-December, 1968, 8–22.

Mehta, Shirin, "Amdavad Shaherna Mahajan ane Panchhoni Utpatti and Vikas", *Arthat*, Vol. IV, No. 3, July–September 1985, 34–47.

Nilkanth Vindoni, "Mane Sambhre Chhe Pachhasek Varsh Pahelanu Amdavad", *Gujarat Dipotsvi Ank*, 1977, 65–66.

Patel, Chandrakant, "Amdavadna Yahoodiono Poorvaitihas ane Sanskritik Jivan", *Vidhyapith,* Vol. X, No. 3, May–June 1972, 162–168.

Sandesra, Bhogilal, "Amdavadni Pol Aithihasik Drashtie", *Sandesh Dipotsvi Ank*, 1951–52, 103–105.

Shastri, Hariprasad and Shelat, Bharati, "Amdavadni Agiariona Shilalekh", *Buddhi Prakash,* Vol. 127, No. 12, December 1986, 485–489.

Shastri, Hariprasad and Shelat, Bharati, "Amdavadni Parsi Dharmashalana Shilalekho", *Pathik,* Vol. XX, No. 3, 1980, 18–20.

Shastri, Hariprasad and Shelat, Bharati, "Gujaratna Yahoodio", *Pathik*, Vol. XX, No. 7, April, 1981, 13–15.

Shelat, Bharati, "Amdavadno Traibhasi Yahoodi Shilalekh ane Tnyanu Kabrastan", *Vidhyapith*, Vol. XIX, No. 2, April, 1981, 3–8.

Unpublished Works

Thesis

Mehta, Makrand, "Ranchhodlal Chhotalal and the Ahmedabad Cotton Textile Industry: A Study in Entrepreneurial History" Ph. D Thesis, Gujarat University, Ahmedabad, 1979.

Raval, RL, "Socio-Religious Reform Movements in Gujarat during the 19th Century" Ph.D Thesis, Gujarat University, Ahmedabad, 1983.

Papers

Bajpai, Geeta, "Some Aspects of Urban Growth in Colonial India: A Case Study of Surat City in the Second Half of the Nineteenth Century", paper presented at the Seminar on Urban Development and Urban Institution in Western India at the Gujarat University, Ahmedabad, November 1984.

Mehta, RN, "Urban Development and Urban Institutions in Western India: Ahmedabad a Case Study", paper presented at the Seminar on Urban Development and Urban Institutions in Western India at the Gujarat University, Ahmedabad, November 1984.

Mehta, Shirin, "The Continuity and Change in the Urban Institutions: A Case Study of Maskati Cloth Mahajan of Ahmedabad 1906–1947", paper presented at the Seminar on Urban Development and Urban Institutions in Western India at the Gujarat University, Ahmedabad, November 1984.

****

Glossary

adalat	:	law court
agiary	:	Parsi fire temple
ahimsa	:	non-violence
bhajan	:	religious group song
Bhangi	:	sweepers, the caste placed lowest in hierarchy of untouchable castes
bhavai	:	folk drama
chadia	:	informer
chakla	:	place where four roads meet, crossroads
chawl	:	block of tenements consisting of one- or two-room homes
Dhed	:	untouchable caste of weavers
dewan	:	minister, head of revenue department
dharamshala	:	rest house provided as charity
dokhma	:	Parsi Tower of Silence
durry	:	mat
faujdar	:	police officer of high rank
farman	:	ordinance
gnyati panchayat	:	caste council
garba	:	folk dance of Gujarat performed to a folk song
gumasta	:	clerk
haveli	:	large residential house
hundi	:	bill of exchange
jamatbandhi	:	Muslim guild system
kacheri	:	office
kagdi	:	artisan who made paper
Kanbi	:	Hindu agriculturist community
kazi	:	Muslim judge
karkhanas	:	factories or workshops manufacturing handicrafts
khadi	:	hand spun, hand woven cloth
khalkuva	:	cesspool
khatpatra	:	legal document pertaining to purchase, sale or mortgage of a house, shop or land
kinkhab	:	brocade, silk cloth woven with gold and silver thread
madrasa	:	school attached to a mosque, which imparts knowledge of Islamic theology

majoor	:	labourer
man		measure of weight, equivalent to 40 Indian *shers* or approximately 18 kilos
mandali	:	association
masjid	:	mosque
maharaj	:	spiritual head of the Vallabhacharya Vaishnav sect
mashru	:	cloth woven with silk warp and cotton weft
mofussil	:	interior or remote areas of the country
mukadam	:	jobber or supervisor in a mill
nagarseth	:	leading merchant of the city
natra	:	divorce
octroi	:	tax levied on imports
panch	:	artisans' guild
panjrapol	:	shelter for sick and old animals
pallu	:	money given by the bridegroom or father-in-law to the bride
patel	:	chief of artisans' guild
parwadi	:	bird house, bird feeder
phatanas	:	obscene songs sung on the occasion of wedding
pedhi	:	family or partnership firm
peshkash	:	gift or offering
pir	:	Sufi saint
pol	:	residential quarter found in the walled city of Ahmedabad, consisting of a street with one or two gateways
pura	:	suburban settlement
retia	:	spinning wheel
rasada	:	folk dance accompanied by a folk song
sabha	:	association
sadhu	:	holy man or Hindu saint
sahib	:	European officer
sahukar	:	financier
satsang	:	religious gathering
seth	:	big businessman or merchant
shravakas	:	Jains
swadeshi	:	indigenous, a movement to buy indigenous goods
vadi	:	caste lodge
vadas	:	residential quarters for lower castes in the walled city
vania	:	businessman by caste
vero	:	tax
urs	:	Muslim religious fair

Index